The Trials of Allegiance

The Trials of Allegiance

Treason, Juries, and the American Revolution

CARLTON F.W. LARSON

OXFORD
UNIVERSITY PRESS

OXFORD
UNIVERSITY PRESS

Oxford University Press is a department of the University of Oxford. It furthers the University's objective of excellence in research, scholarship, and education by publishing worldwide. Oxford is a registered trade mark of Oxford University Press in the UK and certain other countries.

Published in the United States of America by Oxford University Press
198 Madison Avenue, New York, NY 10016, United States of America.

CIP data is on file at the Library of Congress
ISBN 978-0-19-093274-9

1 3 5 7 9 8 6 4 2

Printed by Sheridan Books, Inc., United States of America

To my parents, Carl and Esther Larson

Contents

Acknowledgments

THIS PROJECT ORIGINATED in the mid-1990s, as my undergraduate thesis at Harvard College. I have accumulated numerous debts along the way, which I am grateful finally to acknowledge.

At Harvard, David J. Hancock, now of the University of Michigan, introduced me to the intellectual dimensions of the American Revolution and helped craft my initial thesis proposal. Mark Peterson, now of Yale University, graciously took me on as an orphan advisee when Professor Hancock departed for Michigan, and carefully guided my writing over the course of a year. A research grant from the Charles Warren Center for Studies in American History supported my visits to archives and courthouses throughout Pennsylvania. Bernard Bailyn provided valuable encouragement along the way. Paul Mapp and the late Mark Kishlansky were incisive readers. I am also grateful to Charles Donahue for a splendid introduction to the field of English legal history.

At Yale Law School, Akhil Reed Amar encouraged my research into treason, juries, and the remarkable career of James Wilson. The late Morris Cohen provided me with a solid grounding in research methods in American legal history, and John Langbein taught me the intricacies of eighteenth-century criminal procedure.

At UC Davis, I have benefitted from the assistance of talented and diligent research assistants, including Amber Dodge, Rachel Thyre Anderson, and Jasmine Tzeng. Mark Ramzy applied his quantitative skills to a statistical analysis of the Philadelphia tax records. Faculty support assistants Jennifer Angeles, Linda Cooper, and Liliana Moore helped with numerous administrative tasks. Neil Willits of the UC Davis Statistical Laboratory helped me make sense of the juror records. The staff of the Mabie Law Library at the UC Davis School of Law, especially Peg Durkin, have tracked down endless requests for obscure sources. In the dean's office, the late Rex Perschbacher, Kevin Johnson, Vikram Amar, Madhavi Sunder, and Afra Afsharipour have supported this project with summer research funding and have been patient when my overly optimistic estimates of its completion date failed to materialize. I am also indebted to the Office of Research at UC Davis, which provided funding for many of my archival visits, access to databases, and permissions for the book's illustrations.

The archival staffs at the Historical Society of Pennsylvania, the Pennsylvania State Archives, the American Philosophical Society, the Philadelphia City Archives, and the Friends Historical Library at Swarthmore College were especially helpful for this project. Stephen Corson and Bradley Kerr provided significant information relating to their ancestors, who participated in the treason trials.

Several of the chapters were initially presented at faculty workshops at the Dedman School of Law at Southern Methodist University, at William & Mary Law School, and at the annual meetings of the American Society for Legal History in Ottawa and Miami and the Law & Society Association in Montreal and Honolulu.

An early version of Chapters 6 and 7 was published as "The Revolutionary American Jury: A Case Study of the 1778–1779 Philadelphia Treason Trials," *SMU L. Rev.* 61 (2008): 1441–1524. Occasional paragraphs are drawn from "The Forgotten Constitutional Law of Treason and the Enemy Combatant Problem," *U. Penn. L. Rev.* 154 (2006): 863–926. Fragments of Chapters 5 and 7 also appeared in "The 1778–1779 Chester and Philadelphia Treason Trials: The Supreme Court as Trial Court," in *The Supreme Court of Pennsylvania: Life and Law in the Commonwealth, 1684–2017*, ed. John J. Hare (University Park: Penn. St. Univ. Press, 2018), 315–324.

I am especially grateful to Gordon Wood, who encouraged me to turn the material in the *SMU Law Review* article into a book.

Mark Box, the late Floyd Feeney, Sally Hadden, Margaret Johns, David Konig, Peter Lee, Donna Shestowsky, Robert Spoo, Bruce Smith, and William Wiecek provided helpful comments on drafts of individual chapters. Gerard Magliocca, Carl Larson, Esther Larson, and Elaine Lau read the entire manuscript and saved me from numerous errors. Amanda Tyler and Daniel Sharfstein provided insights into the publishing world. Judge Michael Daly Hawkins of the United States Court of Appeals for the Ninth Circuit, for whom I had the honor to serve as a law clerk, has been a consistent source of encouragement. We share an admiration of James Wilson, whose footprints can be found throughout this book.

At the Strothman Agency, Wendy Strothman helped me sharpen my arguments and found a good home for the manuscript with Oxford University Press. Lauren MacLeod assisted with numerous details. I am also deeply grateful to my Oxford University Press editor, David McBride, editorial assistant Holly Mitchell, the Press's anonymous reviewers, and copyeditor Leslie Safford.

My wife, Elaine Lau, in addition to providing helpful insights on the manuscript, has been an endless source of inspiration and encouragement. My children,

Carina and Elliot, although too young to understand the issues in this book, have taught me much about loyalty and allegiance. Their happy shouts of "Daddy!" when I come home from the office are the greatest joys of my life.

Finally, I am grateful to my parents, Carl and Esther Larson, who have fostered my love of history from an early age. Our house in western North Dakota was filled with thousands of books of history, ranging from the ancient world to the history of the automobile. When I was six years old, our family spent the summer in Massachusetts. Seeing landmarks such as Faneuil Hall, the Freedom Trail, and the Concord Bridge left an indelible impression and a fascination with the American Revolution that has endured to this day. Through their own work, my parents demonstrated the importance of doing "hard research" and getting the story exactly right. This book is dedicated to them, with affection and love.

The Trials of Allegiance

Introduction

WHEN DAWN BROKE on the morning of October 4, 1779, in the fifth year of the American War for Independence, James Wilson of Philadelphia was not expecting to face combat. If he had stood on ceremony, he could have called himself Colonel Wilson (he was formally a colonel in the Cumberland County militia), but his countrymen would probably have rolled their eyes. A scholarly, bespectacled lawyer with no obvious martial abilities, Wilson had yet to draw his sword in battle (Figure I.1).

But he had contributed notably to the cause of American independence with an even more powerful weapon—his pen. After emigrating from his native Scotland in his twenties, Wilson had become a leader of the Pennsylvania bar and the author of an influential pamphlet advocating the cause of the American colonies.[1] Elected as a delegate to the Second Continental Congress, Wilson had proudly signed the Declaration of Independence at the Pennsylvania State House, the building that future generations would enshrine as Independence Hall.

Wilson's conduct had thus made him one of the most prominent American traitors to Great Britain and a rich prize for any British military unit that managed to capture him. When Wilson heard the beat of the drums on October 4, 1779, he suspected that the armed men marching through the streets of Philadelphia might be on his trail. Hunkered down in his elegant brick mansion at the corner of Third and Walnut Streets, just a few blocks from where he had signed the Declaration of Independence, Wilson and a group of wealthy friends were prepared to resist, to the death if necessary.

Soon the armed men reached Wilson's house, and the battle, one of the war's rare instances of urban combat, erupted in full. The attackers began shooting at the windows of the house and attempting to force open the front door. From the second floor, Wilson and his friends returned fire. The battle might have continued much longer, but a Pennsylvania cavalry force arrived and quickly ended

FIGURE I.1 Attorney James Wilson, one of only six men who signed both the Declaration of Independence and the United States Constitution.
Credit: Shutterstock.

the fighting. The battle of "Fort Wilson," as it later came to be called, claimed at least six lives and injured many more. Wilson proved to be one of the lucky ones; he survived and later became a primary architect of the United States Constitution and one of President George Washington's first appointees to the United States Supreme Court.

The armed and bitterly angry men attacking the house detested James Wilson for his political beliefs and for his actions at the Pennsylvania State House. But despite what one might expect, they were not British soldiers. Quite the opposite—the attackers were Wilson's fellow Americans, Pennsylvania militiamen who were convinced that Wilson was insufficiently committed to the American cause. Wilson's primary offense was the deployment of his legal talents in a cause that the militiamen found inexplicable—he had represented men accused of treason against the state of Pennsylvania for aiding the British army during the detested British occupation of Philadelphia. Just two days before the attack, in the grand courtroom at the State House, Wilson had won another acquittal for a man accused of treason. But many of Wilson's fellow citizens were utterly perplexed. Why was a signer of the Declaration of Independence representing men accused of undermining the very Revolution to which he had pledged his life, his fortune, and his sacred honor? When the militiamen later sought to justify their conduct, they pointed to the "exceeding lenity which has been shown to persons notoriously disaffected to the Independence of the United States" as one of the reasons for the attack on Wilson's house.[2]

As the Fort Wilson incident vividly demonstrated, the American Revolution ripped the fabric of American society in half. Although sometimes portrayed as a genteel, intellectual rebellion, it was in fact a violent and bloody civil war, in which brothers fought against brothers and fathers fought against sons.[3] An astute Frenchman living in America noted the changes with disbelief: "The rage of civil discord hath advanced among us with astonishing rapidity. Every opinion is changed, every prejudice subverted, every ancient principle annihilated, every mode of organization which linked us before as men and citizens is now altered."[4] It was, in the words of a popular seventeenth-century song, a "world turned upside down."

The most serious—and frightening—implications of the new upside-down quality of American life related to the law of treason. When the troubles with England began, colonial Americans repeatedly denounced acts of Parliament, but stoutly insisted on their devotion to their English king. Betraying the king was not just a matter of political disloyalty—it was high treason, the most significant offense known to English law.

By the time the War for Independence erupted, the duty of allegiance had been fundamentally transformed. Loyalty to the king was no longer a duty, but a crime—high treason against the nascent American nation. As the British and American armies rampaged across the continent, the duty of allegiance imposed by law shifted with them. In Philadelphia, for example, this duty shifted from George III to the United States, then back to George III during the British occupation of Philadelphia, and finally back to the United States when the British army departed. As the late Robert Ferguson put it, "Nothing conveys the utter fluidity in Revolutionary American Culture more dramatically than the concept of treason."[5]

Although Benedict Arnold remains the Revolution's most famous traitor, the charge of treason could potentially be leveled against every American. Loyalty to the United States was treason against Great Britain, and loyalty to Great Britain was treason against the United States. Even those who tried to remain neutral were criticized on the ground that anyone who was not an active supporter was an enemy. The "Trials of Allegiance" referred to in this book's title are thus not only court trials, but also the broader trials that the war and societal disruption posed to everyone living in British North America.

This book is an invitation to view the American Revolution from a new perspective—that of the law of treason. We have numerous accounts of the Revolution rooted in military, diplomatic, social, economic, political, and constitutional history. By contrast, the Revolution's interaction with the law of treason has remained largely unwritten. But in at least six key areas, treason played a fundamental role in the Revolution and in the lives of ordinary Americans.

First, in the years before the war broke out, American resistance leaders sought to justify the actions they were taking against British measures. These writers repeatedly distinguished legitimate resistance to tyranny, which was permissible, from outright treason, which was criminal. Although the arguments grew more and more distant from British law as the resistance activities increased, they provided much of the intellectual justification for the open defiance of British policies. Similarly, when British leaders threatened to try Americans for treason in England, American leaders responded with vigorous defenses of their right to a trial by a jury of their peers.

Second, although American resistance leaders insisted that they were innocent of treason, they did not hesitate to accuse others of the same offense. Prior to the Declaration of Independence, accusations of treason multiplied, generating rhetoric that was increasingly nationalistic in scope. Opponents of resistance activities were denounced as traitors against America and traitors against liberty. This rhetoric was soon converted into action and individuals accused of treason against America were tried before committees of safety and the military. These trials, scarcely noticed in much of the literature of the Revolution, demonstrated that American sovereignty was a functional reality well before independence was declared. As a practical matter, Americans no longer owed allegiance to the king of Great Britain, but to the individual colonies, to the nascent American state, or even to broad abstractions such as liberty itself.

Third, the Declaration of Independence was itself partially motivated by concerns over treason law. So long as the American colonies remained technically united with Great Britain, the adherents of the king could be indefinitely detained by extra-legal entities, but they could not formally be tried by a jury in a court of law or executed. The Declaration of Independence permitted the full force of the criminal law to be brought upon the Loyalists, and many proponents of the Declaration justified it for precisely that reason.

Fourth, the law of treason loomed large over the daily lives of ordinary people. Allegiances shifted with changes in military occupation, and that allegiance was now enforced through criminal penalties. Thousands of Americans played a role in the criminal justice system, whether as defendants, as witnesses, as bondsmen, or as jurors. Through the jury system, ordinary Americans would be forced to confront the reality that other ordinary Americans may well have sided with the enemy. But the juries did something extraordinary—they consistently refused to send the defendants to the gallows. In case after case in Pennsylvania, the subject of this study, grand juries refused to indict and trial juries refused to convict. Even in the few cases in which they convicted, juries sought clemency for the defendant. The jury system would prove far more lenient to accused traitors than the two primary alternatives, military trials and trials by committees of safety.

Fifth, confiscation of Loyalists' property became a major issue during the Paris peace negotiations. Although the states contended that the confiscations were justified under state treason laws, British officials viewed them as illegal and sought compensation. Ultimately, the reintegration of former Loyalists into American society would produce heated denunciations, yet most Loyalists who returned found the path relatively smooth. Reconciliation, not vengeance, would be the order of the day.

Finally, the issue of treason became an early issue testing the strength of the new national government under the Constitution. Two rebellions in Pennsylvania, the Whiskey Rebellion and Fries's Rebellion, raised difficult questions about the application of English treason law in the new American republic. Should the law apply in the same manner, or had the Revolution limited its bounds, permitting even forceful resistance to particular laws, so long as the participants retained their underlying loyalty to the United States?

This book explores these issues in the course of answering a fundamental question: How did revolutionary Americans apply the law of treason, forged over many centuries in an island monarchy three thousand miles away, to instances of criminal disloyalty in their new republic? This question raises several subsidiary questions. How was the seeming tension between liberty and security resolved? To what extent did the law deviate from English patterns? To which legal entities was allegiance owed? How did patterns of prosecution change during the Revolution itself? And, perhaps most importantly, did institutions make a difference? What can one learn from the differing experiences of the military, committees of safety, and courts?

To be clear, my subject is not the general phenomenon of Loyalism or the motivations that drove people to one side or the other. It is not concerned with the details of treasonable plots or the frequency with which treasonable acts might have been committed. These topics, although fascinating, are beyond the scope of this work and have been well examined by other scholars.[6] My purpose is different—to understand how the law of treason was understood and applied in the context of a convulsive, divisive civil war in which few people were free of the imprecation of treason.[7] Many of the legal questions that American leaders confronted during the war were not easy, and they continue to be debated even to this day—whether to suspend the writ of habeas corpus, whether to detain suspected traitors without trial, whether to exercise military jurisdiction over American civilians suspected of aiding the enemy, and whether to permit judicial review of executive detentions.

The book tells the story through the experience of Pennsylvania, as it was here that the issues raised by treason took on their greatest national significance. Pennsylvania was central to the Revolution from the very beginning. Its capital, Philadelphia, was the seat of the Continental Congress and the effective national capital, as well as America's largest city and busiest port.[8] Philadelphia was the "political, economic, and cultural center of the colonies and the new nation."[9] What happened there had nationwide implications. The cast of characters includes some of the most significant figures of the revolutionary era. A series of treason trials in Philadelphia, for example, were presided over by one signer of the Declaration of Independence, defended by two other signers, and involved participants who played a major role in the creation of the United States Constitution. In the early trials, both the presiding judge, Thomas McKean, and the principal prosecuting attorney, Joseph Reed, were simultaneously serving as members of the Continental Congress. Pennsylvania also generated the war's most intense controversy over treason trials, resulting in extensive newspaper discussions about the proper role of juries and, ultimately, in the violent confrontation and bloodshed of the Fort Wilson incident.

One should not necessarily extrapolate the experience of Pennsylvania without qualification to the other American states. Although I have been researching this issue in Pennsylvania off and on for over twenty years, I have not devoted similar efforts to other jurisdictions, and therefore can offer only a limited comparative perspective.[10] Certain factors rendered the Pennsylvania experience distinctive. The patterns of war were different from those in any other state. Although the British occupied New York from 1776 to 1783, they occupied Philadelphia for only nine months in 1778 and 1779. Pennsylvania escaped the early years of the war, which focused on New England, as well as the later years, which focused on the South. Moreover, the large population of Quakers, religiously opposed to bearing arms, presented peculiar problems that were less salient in other states. Pennsylvania's unusual and controversial 1776 constitution, with its unicameral legislature and plural executive, further rendered Pennsylvania distinctive among the states. Nonetheless, certain broad themes were consistent across jurisdictions, including the pre-Revolution debate about the nature of treason, the role of committees of safety, and the general question of the harshness to be meted out to Loyalists, even though the details may have differed from state to state.

The subsidiary theme of this book is the role of juries. The colonists' insistence on their right to a jury of their peers was a primary grievance in the years prior to the outbreak of the war. Yet when the fighting started, and internal enemies needed to be detected and subdued, colonial Americans did not resort to juries. Instead, investigatory and detention powers rested in committees of safety or the military, both of which acted without juries, a pattern that continued after independence. When jury trial was finally operational for treason trials, Pennsylvania juries proved exceptionally lenient and this leniency persisted through the rebellions of the 1790s.

The subject of jury service in eighteenth-century America has not been well explored by scholars. In 1975, historians Harold Hyman and Catherine Tarrant lamented the "very thin body of American legal history concerning juries," and argued that "[f]ew areas of legal history need attention more."[11] In 1984, John Murrin observed that the history of the American jury "has almost completely eluded sustained scholarly attention."[12] Jury trials have received some attention in the intervening years, but it is safe to say that we still know very little about how criminal juries actually functioned in late eighteenth-century America.[13] It has been relatively straightforward to document what learned contemporaries *said* about juries, but it is much harder to determine what juries actually *did*. This lack of information is regrettable, because as historian J.R. Pole pointed out in 1993, trial by jury "is of the highest importance for understanding the character of American history in its colonial period and beyond."[14]

Chapters 6 and 7, the heart of this book, consider twenty-three jury trials prosecuted in Philadelphia in the fall of 1778 and the spring of 1779. These trials were aggressively prosecuted by the state in an atmosphere of widespread popular hostility to opponents of the American Revolution. The juries, however, convicted only four of these men, a low conviction rate even in an age of widespread jury lenity; moreover, in three of these four cases, the juries petitioned Pennsylvania's executive authority for clemency. What explains this lenity?

To answer this question we need to know more about the jurors themselves. Although the jury is often described as a black box, it can be illuminated, even after the passage of several hundred years. This book provides the most thorough analysis yet undertaken of a group of eighteenth-century American jurors. On the basis of extensive research in demographic records, I have reconstructed the Philadelphia jury box and identified not only the social status of the jurors, but also the intricate network of connections linking the grand jurors, the trial jurors, and the defendants. This study reveals, for the first time, how eighteenth-century American defense counsel creatively used peremptory challenges, deployed on the bases of religion, age, ethnicity, wealth, occupation, and political beliefs, to create juries more favorable to the defense. Jurors were also heavily influenced by the death penalty, effectively nullifying Pennsylvania's treason laws rather than risk exposing accused persons to the hangman's noose.

But the jury verdicts did not go unchallenged. Significant popular opposition to the jurors' decisions led in 1779 to widespread condemnation in newspapers, to direct interference with a jury trial, and eventually to the armed attack on James Wilson's house. After Fort Wilson, attacks on juries diminished dramatically, and the jury recaptured its central role as a bulwark of popular liberty.

Recovering the world of treason and the American Revolution requires immersion in a much broader array of sources than the few accounts of American treason law have traditionally employed. Prior work has tended to emphasize statutes and the tiny handful of reported cases. Statutes are an important part of the story, but as legal historian Bruce Mann has emphasized, "The best evidence for the presence or absence of legal change lies not in what people said but in what they did. For that, one must consult court records in tedious, preferably quantitative, detail."[15] The court records of Pennsylvania are not located in one place, and I have had to piece together information on court proceedings from a variety of archival and other sources. This material is presented in quantitative, although I hope not especially tedious, detail.

Many years ago, James Willard Hurst argued that

> even a brief canvass of the variety of historical sources of potential help in explaining the policy background of the Constitution's treason clause suggests the complex wealth of material which such an approach may add to the case-trained lawyer's familiar tools of decision and opinion. But, likewise, it suggests that since the historical approach seeks nothing less than to comprehend the whole pattern of causes which shape a given policy, it requires of the advocate an imaginative readiness to forego the abstract logic of doctrine for the living logic of events.[16]

To fulfill Hurst's vision, I have also examined what Steven Wilf calls "extraofficial legal actions—what might be called law out-of-doors, vernacular legal storytelling, the bric-a-brac of criminal trials, and, above all, the explosion of law talk with a volatile mix of law and politics."[17] These materials are supplemented with newspaper sources, pamphlets, and manuscript collections of letters and diaries, all of which provide a rich description of law on the ground, as it actually played out in the lives of ordinary and not-so-ordinary Pennsylvanians.

For the convenience of other researchers, I have cited published versions of eighteenth-century sources when possible, although in many cases I have examined the originals myself. Obviously, some editions are more reliable than others, and there are particular problems with the *Colonial Records* and

Pennsylvania Archives series, including the bowdlerization typical of nineteenth-century editors.[18]

In some cases, I have modernized punctuation and capitalization for the ease of the reader, although I have tried to do so with a light touch. I have tried to retain the terminology of the eighteenth-century sources as much as possible, although this task presents occasional difficulties. There is no perfect term for the opponents of the Revolution. They were described as "Tories" by the Revolution's supporters, but this wasn't a term they embraced themselves. The term "Loyalist" wasn't coined until later in the conflict. Some historians have used the term "disaffected" to describe persons alienated from the revolutionary governments for a wide variety of reasons, many of which had nothing to do with loyalty to Great Britain, but this doesn't always capture the spirit of the contemporary sources.[19] I have tried to use terms that are appropriate in context, but there is no perfect solution to this problem.

Another troublesome term is "prisoner." In the late eighteenth century, before the introduction of the modern American prison, the term was used to describe any person held in captivity, including persons awaiting trial. Modern usage tends to define "prisoner" as a person sentenced to a term of imprisonment in prison after a trial. Using "prisoner" in its eighteenth-century sense is therefore more likely to be confusing than helpful to a modern reader. Accordingly, I use the admittedly anachronistic term "detainee" to describe persons who have been detained, but not formally sentenced in a court of law. Although the term was not used in the eighteenth century in this context, I can think of no other way of precisely describing the legal situation of these individuals to a modern reader.

A brief overview by way of orientation: Chapter 1 explores the background of treason in colonial Pennsylvania, including the adoption of British treason law and the legal complexities that led to a general failure of the state to prosecute individuals for treason. Chapter 2 turns to the bitter debates between 1765 and 1775, when Americans defended themselves against charges of treason, while simultaneously hurling the same charge at British officials, and even at the king himself. Chapter 3 addresses the period between the outbreak of the war and the adoption of the Declaration of Independence, focusing primarily on the treason trials conducted by committees of safety. The tumultuous period between formal independence and the reopening of the courts is the subject of Chapter 4, including the controversial suspension of habeas corpus in the wake of the British invasion. The difficulties of reopening the courts, the issuance of attainder proclamations, and the wave of cases generated by the British invasion are considered in Chapter 5. Chapters 6 and 7 provide an extensive analysis of the Philadelphia treason trials of 1778 and 1779, the most significant treason trials of the American Revolution. Chapter 8 evaluates the aftermath of the trials, including the turbulent year of 1779, the repercussions of Benedict Arnold's treason in 1780, and disputes over the scope of executive detention powers. Chapter 9 deals with the aftermath of the war, the adoption of the Treason Clause of the United States Constitution, and the first federal treason trials, those arising out of the Whiskey Rebellion of 1794 and Fries's Rebellion of 1799.

1

Treason in Colonial Pennsylvania

ON OCTOBER 22, 1682, the English ship *Welcome* sailed up the Delaware River, after a horrific fifty-three-day trans-Atlantic voyage in which nearly a third of the ship's passengers died from an outbreak of smallpox. The weary survivors who straggled onto the shore included a group of Quakers and their formidable leader William Penn, to whom King Charles II had granted vast land holdings in the new colony of Pennsylvania. The *Welcome* was packed to the brim with supplies for life in the New World, including nails, window glass, horse collars, saddles, candles, shoes, and glue.[1] But the ship also carried baggage of a more metaphorical sort: a long, complicated relationship with English criminal procedure.

As a persecuted minority in England, the Quakers had repeatedly found themselves on the wrong side of English law. In numerous cases, English judges had browbeaten juries, which were often sympathetic to Quaker defendants. William Penn himself had been prosecuted for his religious publications and preaching, and one of his cases led to a significant precedent on the scope of jury independence (Figure 1.1). When the presiding judge sought to punish the jurors for acquitting Penn on a charge of unlawful preaching, the Court of Common Pleas ruled in *Bushel's Case* in 1670 that judges could not punish jurors for verdicts with which the judges disagreed.[2] Transplanted to the New World, Penn now found himself exercising the same governmental authority his fellow Quakers had so stoutly resisted in England. His new colony of Pennsylvania would need to fulfill the basic function of protecting itself and its residents from external and internal threats, while at the same time recognizing the role of jury trials in protecting persons accused of dissenting views.[3]

Within the criminal law, the law of treason was a key tool for addressing basic security threats. Yet in Pennsylvania's earliest years, it was unclear whether there was any applicable treason law at all. The 1681 charter granted to William Penn provided that certain English laws, including the law of "felonies," would be in

THE

Peoples {Ancient and Juſt} Liberties

ASSERTED,

IN THE

TRYAL

OF

William Penn, and *William Mead*,

At the Seſſions held at the *Old-Baily* in *London*, the firſt, third, fourth and fifth of *Sept*. 70. againſt the moſt Arbitrary procedure of that Court.

Iſa. 10. 1, 2. *Wo unto them that Decree Unrighteous Decrees, and write grievouſneſs, which they have preſcribed; to turn away the Needy from Judgment, and to take away the right from the Poor, &c.*

Pſal. 94. 20. *Shall the Throne of Iniquity have fellowſhip with thee, which frameth miſchief by a Law.*

Sic volo, ſic jubeo, ſtat pro ratione voluntas.

Old-Baily, 1ſt. 3d. 4th, 5th of *Sept*. 1670.

Printed in the Year, 1670.

FIGURE 1.1 William Penn's legal struggles helped vindicate the rights of jurors.
Credit: Document describing the trial of William Penn in London for preaching the Quaker religion, 1670 (print), English School (17th century)/Private Collection/Peter Newark American Pictures/Bridgeman Images.

effect until altered by Penn and the freemen of the province. Although this provision might be read to include treason, seventeenth-century usage routinely distinguished "felonies" from "treason." Another provision of the charter granted Penn the power to grant pardons for "all crimes and offences. . . . Treason and willful and malicious murder only excepted," language that implies that treason prosecutions were at least theoretically possible. Moreover, various early judiciary statutes explicitly reserved prosecutions for treason to the colony's highest court.[4]

Although Pennsylvania's colonial assembly passed legislation identifying numerous offenses as crimes, it never enacted a treason law. It came very close in 1684, with a statute that prohibited compassing the death of the proprietor and the governor, levying hostility against them, or moving with force to invade the province.[5] The statute did not formally use the term "treason," but much of its language came directly from English treason law. This statute, however, was abrogated in 1693. A similar statute enacted in 1700 was rejected by British officials several years later, a fate that also befell a companion statute that prohibited speaking and writing that tended "to sedition or disaffection to this government."[6]

The question of whether English parliamentary criminal statutes, the primary source of English treason law, directly applied in the colonies was fiercely contested.[7] Arguably, treason could be prosecuted under England's unwritten common law, but such prosecutions had been effectively prohibited since the mid-fourteenth century, and Governor William Penn had little enthusiasm for recognizing common-law crimes.[8] In 1685, David Lewis was arrested "upon suspicion of treason" in one of the counties that later became part of Delaware for allegedly declaring his involvement with the Duke of Monmouth's Rebellion in England. However, no trial appears to have occurred.[9] The legal authority to try cases of treason in the early decades of the Pennsylvania colony was therefore highly uncertain.

The Adoption of English Treason Law

In 1718, the Pennsylvania Assembly enacted a comprehensive criminal statute that put any such doubts to rest. The colony's full-throated embrace of English law is apparent in the statute's opening lines:

> And whereas it is a settled point that as the common law is the birthright of English subjects, so it ought to be their rule in British dominions. But acts of parliament have been adjudged not to extend to these plantations, unless they are particularly named in such acts.

The statute then provided the following:

> [A]ll inquests and trials of high treason shall be according to the due order and course of the common law, observing the directions of the statute laws of Great Britain, relating to the trials, proceedings, and judgments in such cases.[10]

With this statute, English treason law became fully applicable in Pennsylvania. By 1718, this law was reasonably well developed, explicated by numerous commentators and reports of notable treason cases.

The foundation of English treason law was a centuries-old statute that most Pennsylvanians probably could not even read. The Statute of Treasons of 1351 (25 Edward III), written in Law French (the language of Norman governance), limited the crime of treason to seven basic categories. Roughly translated, they are (1) compassing or imagining the death of the king, the queen, or their eldest son and heir; (2) violating the wife of the king, the king's eldest unmarried daughter, or the wife of the king's eldest son; (3) levying war against the king in his realm; (4) adhering to the king's enemies in his realm, giving them aid and comfort in the realm, or elsewhere; (5) counterfeiting; (6) killing the chancellor, the treasurer, or the king's justices; and (7) the murder of a master by a servant, a husband by a wife, or a prelate by a cleric. The last category would come to be called "petty treason" to distinguish it from the other categories, which constituted "high treason." The statute further provided that "if any other case, supposed treason, which is not above specified, doth happen before any justices," the case should be delayed until the king and Parliament could declare whether the offense constituted treason. This provision would be later used to justify parliamentary acts of attainder (which declared persons guilty of treason without a trial), as well as additional statutes expanding the crime of treason.[11]

Although English lawyers occasionally argued that the Statute of Treasons did not entirely supplant the common law of treason, the more typical professional view was that treason offenses must meet the statutory definition. Indeed, limiting the offenses that constituted treason was one of primary purposes of the statute. In the early seventeenth century, Sir Edward Coke wrote that the Parliament that enacted the statute "was called Benedictum Parliamentum, as it well deserved." As Coke explained, "For except it be Magna Charta, no other Act of Parliament hath had more honor given unto it by the King, Lords Spiritual and Temporal and the Commons of the Realm . . . , then this Act concerning treason hath had."[12] During the Tudor, Stuart, and Commonwealth periods, a number of additional treason statutes were passed, many of which were aimed at disloyal forms of speech.[13] By 1718, however, these statutes were no longer in effect, and treason indictments were required to be based on the statute of 25 Edward III.

Under this statute, the primary focus of treason law was the betrayal of the king. Yet by 1718, a strand of legal thinking had developed that viewed treason not as a betrayal of personal loyalty to a monarch, but as an offense against an impersonal state.[14] As early as 1607, an English civil lawyer defined treason as "an offense committed against the amplitude and majesty of the commonwealth."[15] This view culminated in the most spectacular trial in English history, when King

Charles I was tried and convicted of high treason. In January 1649, the House of Commons declared that by the "fundamental laws of this kingdom, it is treason in the King of England, for the time being, to levy war against the Parliament and Kingdom of England."[16] The Kingdom of England was thus completely abstracted from the person of the king.[17] From this perspective, treason was not limited to monarchical governments and could be readily adapted to republican regimes. When Charles II was restored to the throne, however, the regicides themselves were prosecuted as traitors for having compassed the death of the king.[18]

The offense of levying war against the king was explicitly limited to offenses within the king's realm, and the offense of adhering to the king's enemies was somewhat awkwardly expressed, leaving some doubt as to whether adherence outside the realm could be prosecuted. In 1544, near the end of Henry VIII's reign, Parliament enacted a statute designed to address "doubts and questions" about treasons committed outside the realm of England. The statute provided that all treasons committed outside the realm could be tried in the Court of King's Bench, before a Westminster jury. Alternatively, the king could appoint special commissioners in any English county, who would hear the case with a jury drawn from that county. In some ways, the statute was beneficial to the accused. If the offense happened in France, or some other country where English law could not impose a local jury, the accused traitor at least received an English jury trial, as opposed to a summary or military proceeding. Prior to 1718, this statute might readily have been used to try treasons committed in America in England. But Pennsylvania's adoption of English treason law complicated matters. Under one view, the statute's explicit adoption of English treason law included the Henrician statute about offenses committed outside the realm. A suspected traitor could be tried either in Pennsylvania, before a local jury, or could be sent to England for trial there. Alternatively, the adoption of English treason law in Pennsylvania obviated the need for removal to England, because a local jury could always be obtained in Pennsylvania, and the subject's right to a jury trial guaranteed. It appears that no one in 1718 gave this matter any particular degree of thought, thus leaving unanswered a question that would become highly critical in the years prior to American independence.

By 1718, the consensus of professional opinion was that words alone could not constitute treason, although there was debate over the precise scope of this doctrine. The core principle dated back to *Pine's Case* of 1627, in which the twelve common-law judges concluded that treason required proof of some overt act. Speaking in derogation of the monarch was not in itself treason; words could be used only as evidence of "the corrupt heart of him that spake them" with respect to some other overt act.[19] Subsequent treatise writers, such as William Hawkins, Michael Foster, and William Blackstone, echoed this point.[20]

The offense of treason was not limited to the king's subjects. A treason prosecution required a breach of allegiance, but, in certain circumstances, aliens owed allegiance to the British crown.[21] Aliens lawfully present within the king's realms owed him what was termed "temporary", or "local", obedience. A breach of this obedience subjected the alien to culpability for treason. This aspect of treason law is regularly misunderstood, but the English sources are clear. As Sir Edward Coke put it, "all Aliens that are within the Realm of England, and whose Sovereigns are in amity with the King of England, are within the protection of the King, and do owe a local obedience to the King . . . and if they commit High Treason against the King, they shall be punished as Traitors."[22] Writing in the early eighteenth century, William Hawkins contended in his *Treatise of the Pleas of the Crown*, "Also it seems clear, that the subject of a foreign prince coming into England and living under the protection of our King, may, in respect of that local allegiance which they owe to him, be guilty of high treason." By contrast, when "aliens" invaded the kingdom in a "hostile manner," they "cannot be punished as traitors, but shall be dealt with by martial law."[23] English law thus made a sharp distinction, rooted in allegiance, between persons subject to the criminal law of treason and persons subject to military authority. This distinction was repeatedly recognized in American law until World War II.[24]

After a series of notoriously biased treason trials under Stuart judges, Parliament passed the Treason Trials Act of 1696, which provided significant new procedural protections to persons accused of treason. Under English felony procedure, the accused was denied both the assistance of counsel at trial and compulsory process for securing witnesses, and defense witnesses were not sworn. The Treason Trials Act permitted the assistance of defense counsel both in pretrial proceedings and at the trial itself, and granted compulsory process for defense witnesses, who were now allowed to be sworn. The act also required that the accused receive a copy of the indictment at least five days before trial and a list of the jury panel at least two days before trial. The act did not extend these new protections beyond cases of treason, but it increased procedural fairness in precisely those trials that had been viewed as most heavily weighted against the accused.[25]

Pennsylvania's 1718 legislation adopting English treason law explicitly extended many of these protections to all persons accused of capital crimes. Under the Pennsylvania statute, all capital defendants could have the assistance of "learned counsel," compulsory process, and the privilege of sworn defense witnesses.[26] These innovations dated back to William Penn's Charter of Privileges of 1701, which stated that "all Criminals shall have the same Privileges of Witnesses and Council as their Prosecutors."[27]

The punishment for treason was the most horrific that English law had ever devised. As Blackstone described it:

> 1. That the offender be drawn to the gallows, and not be carried or walk . . . 2. That he be hanged by the neck, and then cut down alive. 3. That his entrails be taken out, and burned, while he is yet alive. 4. That his head be cut off. 5. That his body be divided into four parts. 6. That his head and his quarters be at the king's disposal.[28]

Formally, this punishment was fully applicable in British America. But who would perform it? As John Bellamy has noted, even Tudor England "was not well provided with proficient executioners." Hanging a man was relatively straightforward, "but the more demanding arts of decollation and disemboweling, which were peculiar to the crime of treason, were rarely practiced with great competence."[29] A death sentence for high treason in colonial America would have most likely placed the convict in the hands of a complete novice, greatly increasing the likelihood of a bungled execution even more hideous than the one contemplated by law.

Although colonial courts occasionally ordered this grisly punishment, it was never actually carried out. In 1691, Jacob Leisler and his associates were sentenced to death for high treason in New York. Although the presiding judge ordered the traditional English punishment, Leisler and his son-in-law were hanged and then beheaded, without the intervention of disembowelment.[30] In 1766, a New Yorker convicted of high treason was given the traditional sentence, but he was subsequently pardoned.[31] Similarly, in 1771, several men were convicted of high treason in North Carolina for their role in the Regulators' Rebellion. The presiding judge's imposition of the English sentence was so noteworthy that newspapers throughout the colonies reported it verbatim.[32] The defendants, however, were simply hanged.[33]

Lawyers in colonial Pennsylvania had ready access to the main sources of English treason law. When the colony adopted the English statutory law, Edward Coke's *Institutes* were widely available. Subsequent decades saw the publication of major works by Matthew Hale, William Hawkins, Michael Foster, and William Blackstone, all of which carefully analyzed English treason law. These treatises were supplemented by a wide variety of statutory compilations and case reports.[34] Major Jacobite rebellions in England in 1715 and 1745 had made treason a subject of considerable interest and had produced a number of reported decisions.[35] Aspiring colonial attorneys used all of these sources to transcribe and annotate English treason law in their commonplace books.[36]

Pennsylvania's Earliest Treason Cases

Pennsylvania's first treason case was heard in 1720, just two years after the formal adoption of English law. Edward Hunt was convicted of high treason for counterfeiting Spanish silver coins.[37] The prosecution seems not to have rested on the statute of 25 Edward III, which prohibited counterfeiting only English currency. Under a statute of Queen Mary, however, Parliament had declared it high treason to counterfeit foreign coins in current use in the realm. Since Parliament had recognized Spanish coinage as legal tender in the American colonies, Spanish coin was thus protected from counterfeiting under the later statute of Mary.[38] Hunt himself nonetheless complained bitterly that he "was judged and condemned to die for the breach of a law of man that was not duly published, which for that reason I transgressed it ignorantly."[39]

Hunt's plight triggered some sympathy with members of Pennsylvania's Provincial Council, several of whom felt that since this was the first offense of that nature in the colony, "it therefore seemed to claim some compassion." Other members acidly pointed out the "very little or no service at all that a reprieve to so miserable a life could be to him." The Council was equally divided and left Hunt's fate in the hands of the governor, who allowed the execution to proceed.[40] Hunt's only bit of good fortune was that English law had traditionally imposed hanging as the punishment for counterfeiting, rather than the more elaborate procedure of decollation and disembowelment.[41]

Pennsylvania convicted and executed several other individuals for counterfeiting in the early 1770s, but none seem to have been specifically charged with high treason.[42] By this point, the colony had adopted more specific anti-counterfeiting legislation, and the offenders were most likely prosecuted under these statutes, rather than as traitors under 25 Edward III.[43] In 1793, Justice William Bradford of the Pennsylvania Supreme Court noted that "the monstrous folly of considering [counterfeiting] as an usurpation of sovereignty, and, therefore as a species of high treason, is past; and it may now be safely ranked with other base frauds against individuals."[44]

In 1731, Catherine Bevan was convicted of petty treason in one of the Delaware counties for murdering her husband, with the assistance of a servant. Under 25 Edward III, petty treason was defined as the murder of a husband by a wife, or the murder of a master by a servant. Men convicted of this crime were drawn and hanged; women were drawn and burnt. Benjamin Franklin's *Pennsylvania Gazette* described Bevan's execution: "[The rope] was designed to strangle her dead before the Fire should touch her; but its first breaking out was in a stream which pointed directly upon the Rope that went round her Neck, and burnt it off instantly, so that she fell into the Flames, and was seen to struggle."[45]

The Outbreak of War

High treason, of course, is a crime most associated with war and rebellion. The relative tranquility of Pennsylvania's first fifty years was finally shattered with the outbreak of the Seven Years' War and the subsequent conflict known as Pontiac's Rebellion. For the first time, Pennsylvania's leaders had to confront difficult issues of war and peace and address potentially treasonous behavior.[46]

The troubles, and eventually the Seven Years' War itself, began in the Pennsylvania backcountry, where colonial troops under George Washington came into conflict with French forces in 1754. The Delaware and Shawnee tribes soon sided with the French and unleashed a series of devastating attacks on the Pennsylvania frontier.[47] In response, Pennsylvania, for the first time in its history, declared war. On April 14, 1756, Lieutenant Governor Robert Hunter Morris declared that the Delaware Indians were "enemies, rebels, and traitors to His Most Sacred Majesty." By attacking Pennsylvanians, these Indians had acted "contrary to their most solemn treaties." Accordingly, Pennsylvanians were invited to "embrace all opportunities of pursuing, taking, killing, and destroying the said Delaware Indians."[48] As an incentive, the colony offered bounties for Delaware scalps, a controversial and relatively ineffective policy.[49] Pennsylvania's declaration of war against the Indians preceded the larger imperial war with France. Great Britain did not declare war against France until May 17, 1756, and it took several months for news of this declaration to reach Pennsylvania.[50]

Despite the official declaration of the Delaware Indians as traitors, no Indian was ever tried for treason in a Pennsylvania courtroom. Such a prosecution would have raised legal issues of considerable complexity. Most fundamentally, did the Indians owe allegiance to either the British king or to the government of Pennsylvania, the breach of which could constitute treason?[51] In William Penn's 1701 treaty with various Pennsylvania tribes, the Indians had acknowledged "the authority of the Crown of England and Government of this Province."[52] Moreover, under the treaty, Penn's government provided protection and friendship to the Indian tribes.[53] Arguably, this provision was sufficient to bring the Indians within the compass of English and provincial treason law. Since the Indians received the protection of the crown of Great Britain, they owed a corresponding duty of allegiance. There was even a possible precedent. In 1676, in the aftermath of King Philip's War, the colony of Rhode Island had tried various Indians before a court-martial on the charge of "disloyalty to his majesty" by "trayterously" and "rebelliously" murdering his majesty's inhabitants.[54]

But the matter was far from straightforward. The Rhode Island prosecutions were not technically for treason. Treason was not cognizable before a court-martial and the punishment imposed, death by firing squad, was not an accepted punishment for treason.[55] Indeed, British officials in the mid-1760s were concerned about the legal implications of recognizing the Indians as subjects of the British crown. As Sir William Johnson pointed out, if Indians were British subjects, they might be "liable to the punishments for high treason," an "impossible" outcome, in Johnson's view.[56] Moreover, viewing the Indians as subjects would have been inconsistent with the practice of making treaties with them, since treaties are agreements between governments, not between a sovereign and his subjects. No precedent supported treating a breach of a treaty as a form of treason against the other contracting party. The scalp bounty itself illustrates the distinctive status of the Indians. Pennsylvania officials would never have considered such a bounty to contain a rebellion of white subjects. Even after American independence, members of Indian tribes were not treated as citizens, but as members of domestic dependent nations capable of entering into government-to-government relations with the United States. Despite numerous military conflicts, no nineteenth-century American Indian was ever tried for the crime of levying war against the United States.[57] Pennsylvania's declaration notwithstanding, it is hardly surprising that no eighteenth-century Indian was tried for treason, either.

The Seven Years' War eventually concluded with these questions entirely avoided. No individual, either European or Indian, was prosecuted by Pennsylvania for treason.[58] The only evidence hinting at treason prosecutions is a November 1756 report from the colony's chief justice to the Provincial Council on evidence "given against some Roman Catholicks of this City, for disaffected and Treasonable."[59] The surviving records break off at this point, and although the Council may have issued arrest warrants in response, no actual trials appear to have ensued.[60]

An important consequence of the war was the early resignation of a number of Quaker members of the Pennsylvania Assembly, who concluded that enacting defense legislation was inconsistent with the Quaker peace testimony. As historian Jack Marietta has pointed out, "Perhaps nothing in the lives of this generation of [Quakers] staggered them as much" as the proclamations against the Delaware Indians.[61] Foreshadowing many of the problems that Quakers would experience during the Revolution, the Quaker withdrawal from politics ensured that future Pennsylvania governments would be unencumbered by doubts about the propriety of military action.[62]

Pennsylvania's problems with internal violence, however, were just beginning. Soon a bloody epilogue to the Seven Years' War would bring Pennsylvania to the brink of serious rebellion, and expose deep fissures between the colony's Quakers and Presbyterians and between western settlers and residents of the more developed eastern counties.

In 1763, Pontiac's Rebellion, as it came to be called, erupted with a series of Indian attacks throughout the American Northwest, including numerous frontier areas of Pennsylvania. Western settlers, concerned that the government in Philadelphia was insufficiently attentive to frontier security, aimed to take matters into their own hands. The most controversial incident was the attack of the so-called Paxton Boys on a peaceful Indian village on December 14, 1763. A group of men marched forty-five miles from the small community of Paxton on the Susquehanna River to the Indian village of Conestoga Indiantown, where they brutally murdered six Indians. Colonial officials quickly moved the surviving fourteen Conestoga Indians to presumed safety in Lancaster. But the Paxton Boys struck again, marching to Lancaster on December 27, 1763 and killing the remaining Indians.[63]

These savage attacks on seemingly peaceful Indians were intensely controversial, and were especially unpopular in Pennsylvania's eastern counties, which were heavily populated by Quakers. The Paxton Boys were denounced as murderers who must be brought to justice. Word quickly spread that the Paxton Boys were not finished with their attacks; the next victims would be a group of Moravian Indians living at Province Island, near Philadelphia. Lieutenant Governor John Penn issued a proclamation denouncing the "riotous and tumultuous" behavior of the Paxton Boys and offering rewards for their apprehension.[64]

As hundreds of Paxton Boys began marching toward Philadelphia, the Assembly passed a "Riot Act." Modeled on an English statute enacted in 1714 at the beginning of George I's reign, Pennsylvania's new Riot Act authorized colonial and local officials to order the dispersal of any group of twelve or more people "unlawfully, riotously and tumultuously assembled together to the disturbance of the public peace." Any person who failed to disperse within one hour would be subject to capital punishment if convicted of the offense. The act also authorized the use of force against any persons who failed to disperse. The Assembly viewed the act as a temporary measure to deal with the Paxton crises; by its own terms the act expired one year after publication.[65]

The march of the Paxton Boys filled Philadelphia with alarm. A volunteer militia was quickly formed, headed by Benjamin Franklin, to defend the city. When the Paxton Boys finally arrived, crossing a bridge that had erroneously been left unguarded, the potential for violence was high. But calmer heads eventually prevailed. A delegation of leading colonial officials, under the leadership of Benjamin Franklin, met with the Paxton Boys, and after extensive negotiations, the marchers agreed to disperse and to submit their grievances in writing.[66]

By engaging in an armed march on their provincial capital, the Paxton Boys came very close to outright rebellion and treason. Could Pennsylvania officials have launched a treason prosecution? Technically, such a prosecution might have been viable. The offense of levying war against the king had been defined under English law to include "insurrections . . . for redressing national grievances, or for the expulsion of foreigners in general, or indeed of any single nation living here under the protection of the king."[67] An armed insurrection to attack Indians living under the protection of the Pennsylvania government could easily fall within this broad definition of levying war. Critics of the Paxton Boys hinted at this idea by frequently using the language of treason and rebellion to denounce their conduct. The march on Philadelphia was described as "downright rebellion,"[68] the "late insurrection,"[69] the "late rebellion,"[70] and "treasonable conduct,"[71] and the Paxton Boys themselves were denounced as "insurgents."[72] Quaker pamphleteers prided themselves on not "promoting or countenancing any plots or insurrections against the government" and on abhorring any "traitorous proceedings."[73] Another pamphlet directly linked the Presbyterian faith of the Paxton Boys to treason, noting "Presbyterianism and Rebellion, were twin-Sisters, sprung from Faction. . . . What King has ever reigned in Great Britain, whose Government has not been disturbed by Presbyterian Rebellions?"[74] The Paxton Boys themselves, in their *Declaration and Remonstrance*, sought to clear themselves of the taint of treason by insistently claiming to be "loyal Subjects to the best of Kings, our rightful Sovereign George the Third, firmly attached to his Royal Person, Interest and Government."[75]

One of the paradoxes of internal rebellions, however, as the English government well knew, is that the larger the rebellion, the less likely it is that any particular participant will be executed for treason. Although thousands of rebels participated in the 1715 Jacobite rebellion, only 40 people were executed for treason; another 638 were transported to various English colonies.[76] Similarly, in the 1745 Jacobite rebellion, the government captured thousands of rebels, but ultimately executed a little over a hundred, while transporting hundreds more to the colonies.[77] It is plausible to execute every member of a five-person rebellion; it is nearly impossible to devote the resources necessary for the trial and execution of thousands of people. Indeed, after the 1745 rebellion, British authorities resorted to a lottery to determine which prisoners would stand trial for treason; only one out of every twenty prisoners would be tried.[78] The pattern would recur during the American Civil War. Most members of the Confederate army were guilty of treason against the United States of America, but none was ever successfully prosecuted.[79]

Moreover, once a rebellion has been quelled, the government has a strong interest in maintaining the hard-earned peace. This is almost always far more likely to be accomplished through leniency than by executing every last defeated rebel. Such considerations governed the treatment of the Paxton Boys. Treason trials and executions would have inflamed backcountry resentments and potentially jeopardized the internal security of the colony. Moreover, the Pennsylvania government ultimately agreed to one of the Paxton Boys' demands, issuing a declaration of war against several Indian tribes, denouncing them as "enemies, rebels, and traitors to his most sacred majesty." As in 1756, the colony again offered bounties for Indian scalps.[80]

A potentially more clear-cut case of treason arose in April 1764, when a man named Gershom Hicks appeared at Fort Pitt. Hicks had lived for years among the Indians, and General Thomas Gage suspected Hicks of espionage and of participating in Indian warfare against the British. Although initially intending to try Hicks under military authority as a spy, Gage changed his mind.[81] Instead, Gage recommended that both Hicks and his brother be tried as "Traitors to their Country." Under long-standing principles of treason law, however, such a trial had to be in a civilian court. As Gage explained, "these Trials must be in the Country below by the Civil Magistrates, to whom they should be given up. The Military may hang a spy in Time of War, but Rebels in Arms are tried by the Civil Courts." This practice, Gage noted, had been followed in Scotland in the aftermath of the 1745 rebellion.[82] The Hicks brothers were accordingly ordered to be transferred to the custody of the Sheriff of Carlisle County to await trial for high treason.[83] There are no surviving records that shed any light on the brothers' subsequent fate; Gershom was clearly not executed, however, since he re-emerged during the Revolution to serve as a spy, sometimes dressed in Indian attire, for George Washington.[84]

The summer of 1765 presented another potential treason case, but it, too, fizzled out. General Gage reported to John Penn that the Cumberland County inhabitants "daily appear in arms, and seem to be in a state of rebellion." The "King's troops are fired upon, and his forts threatened with assaults by men in arms, headed by magistrates, who refuse the ordinary course of justice demanded of them by the officers."[85] Penn promptly traveled to Cumberland County and gathered evidence. These actions, if true, might have constituted treason by levying war against the king. The grand jury that heard the witnesses' testimony, however, concluded that "there was not sufficient testimony to convict a single person charged" and refused to issue any indictments.[86]

The Disputes with Virginia and Connecticut

In the early 1770s, in addition to the growing resistance to parliamentary policies, Pennsylvania confronted a problem that was perhaps unique among the American colonies: it was engaged in what amounted to low-level open warfare with two other colonies, Virginia and Connecticut.[87] In both cases, the disputes turned on land claims.

The Virginia dispute was the less serious of the two, although it was nonetheless highly troubling to Pennsylvania's leaders. In 1772, the British army had evacuated Fort Pitt and Pennsylvania officials declined to fortify it. The result was a jurisdictional vacuum in the area surrounding Pittsburgh, an area claimed by both Pennsylvania and Virginia.[88] The newly appointed governor of Virginia, John Murray, the Earl of Dunmore, was eager to assert Virginia's authority over the region, and many prominent Virginians, including George Washington, supported him.[89] In a curious twist, Dunmore had a deep personal history with respect to armed disputes over governmental legitimacy—his own father had been convicted of treason for supporting the 1745 Jacobite rebellion and he himself had served as a "page of honor" to Bonnie Prince Charlie.[90] Dunmore's primary agent in the region was a former surgeon in the British army named John Connolly, who did everything he could to undermine Pennsylvania authority. On New Year's Day 1774, Connolly issued a proclamation announcing that the Pittsburgh region was now incorporated into Virginia's Augusta County.[91] Arthur St. Clair, the leading official of Pennsylvania's competing Westmoreland County, responded by arresting Connolly, only to eventually release him on bail.[92] Connolly responded by arresting a Westmoreland County sheriff's officer and three Pennsylvania magistrates, whom he sent to Virginia for trial, an outrage for which Penn firmly blamed Lord Dunmore.[93] Penn was especially worried that Connolly's aggressive conduct would provoke a war with the Indians, who were engaged in a series of revenge killings against the Virginia settlers.[94] Penn's fears were confirmed when what became known as Dunmore's War broke out between the Virginia forces and the Shawnee and Mingo tribes later that year.[95] In February 1775, Connolly's forces openly attacked the Westmoreland County jail and continued their pattern of harassing Pennsylvania officials.[96] In June 1775, however, St. Clair managed to arrest Connolly on a charge of raising a body of men against the liberties of America. Connolly's forces retaliated by capturing three Pennsylvania officials, who were then exchanged for Connolly as part of a prisoner swap.[97] The outbreak of the War for Independence did little to resolve these tensions, and the region persisted in a state of jurisdictional confusion until 1780, when Pennsylvania and Virginia finally resolved the dispute.[98] Connolly, as we shall see in Chapter 3, would become one of the first Pennsylvanians charged with treason during the Revolution.

The Connecticut dispute had deeper roots and proved even more intractable. In 1753, a group of prominent Connecticut men formed The Susquehannah Company, with the intention of settling on land allegedly within Connecticut's jurisdiction. The land, located in modern northeastern Pennsylvania, however, also fell within the grants to the Penn family, Pennsylvania's proprietors. As early as 1754, the Pennsylvania Provincial Council was concerned that the

Connecticut claim risked a "civil war."[99] Pennsylvania's Attorney General warned, "To enter and seize the Lands of the Proprietaries or Others without their Permission, are Acts against the Laws, and manifest Breaches of the Public Peace. Such offense, by a multitude, are of dangerous Example, and highly penal, as they tend to Sedition, and are likely to terminate in Capital Crimes."[100] Delayed by the outbreak of the French and Indian War, Connecticut settlers did not arrive in the Wyoming Valley until 1760. In 1761, Pennsylvania Lieutenant Governor James Hamilton issued two proclamations demanding the departure of the Connecticut settlers and stating that they would be "prosecuted with the utmost Rigour of the Law."[101] Hamilton seemed to have the law on his side. The English Solicitor General in 1761 had found no validity to Connecticut's claims, and the settlements were denounced by both the Connecticut governor and George III, who ordered that the Connecticut settlements be stopped. But ultimately Indians accomplished what official proclamations could not.[102] In late 1763, they attacked and killed most of the Connecticut settlers, temporarily ending the intrusion into Pennsylvania.[103]

The Susquehannah Company eventually regrouped and more Connecticut settlers arrived in the late 1760s. Not surprisingly, Pennsylvania officials remained unwilling to tolerate settlements that did not recognize Pennsylvania's jurisdiction and they responded with repeated attempts at force, coupled with invocation of the criminal law. In early 1769, Northampton County authorities arrested three Connecticut settlers for riot.[104] A settler tartly responded that they would "mind our own business & affairs Cultivate our own lands Manufacture our own Necessaries eat our own Cheese & drink our own Beer and Carefully Avoid Superfluities all which taken together I hope will not be Constructive Treason even in England."[105] A Northampton County grand jury later indicted 31 Connecticut settlers for riotous and unlawful assembly.[106] By May 1769, Pennsylvania Lieutenant Governor John Penn had concluded that the Connecticut settlers were so numerous that they could be removed only by a military force, but he continued to try to resolve the problem through the criminal courts.[107] He issued yet another proclamation demanding the settlers' immediate removal.[108] When the hapless sheriff of Northampton County read the proclamation to the Connecticut settlers, they treated the proclamation "with Great Contempt & as Soon as the Sheriff was finished one of them fired a Gun over his Head."[109] In June 1769, a Northampton grand jury indicted an additional 120 Connecticut settlers for riot and forcible entry.[110] Although the Northampton County sheriff managed to arrest some of the settlers, many escaped from the Easton jail, and only 16 were ultimately convicted.[111] For their part, the Connecticut settlers expressed willingness to have the title issue resolved through civil litigation in a Pennsylvania court, but they deeply resented Pennsylvania's attempt to resolve the dispute through the use of the criminal law.[112]

By late 1769, the tide had seemingly turned in Pennsylvania's favor. In November, Pennsylvania forces ejected numerous Connecticut settlers from the Wyoming valley.[113] A large number of additional indictments of Connecticut settlers followed.[114] But just when things looked bleakest, the settlers formed a providential alliance with the Paxton Boys, essentially guaranteeing a dramatic escalation in violence.

Fortified by the Paxton Boys, the Connecticut settlers went on the offensive, driving out rival Pennsylvania settlers and destroying their houses.[115] A few months later, John Penn concluded that it was "impossible for the civil power to serve any process against them."[116] But Penn soldiered on, issuing yet another proclamation against the Connecticut settlers and securing indictments against the leaders of the Paxton Boys.[117] Indeed, the tide seemed to again turn in Pennsylvania's favor in September 1770, when Pennsylvania forces captured a prominent fort as well as a number of Connecticut settlers, who were sent to Easton and Philadelphia.[118]

This victory was short lived. The leading Paxton Boy, Lazarus Stewart, managed to escape from custody while under indictment for arson.[119] The Pennsylvania Assembly, reviewing Stewart's activities on behalf of the Connecticut settlers, complained about the "daring insult he has committed on the authority of government," and darkly warned "there is cause to suspect the said Stewart hath been guilty of a crime of a more atrocious nature."[120] Several months later, Stewart shot and killed a Pennsylvania deputy sheriff.[121] This violent attack prompted the Pennsylvania Assembly to quickly pass a new Riot Act.[122]

As the Connecticut settlers saw it, Pennsylvania was essentially treating them as traitors. One group of Connecticut men complained, "Why is the Riot Act against rebellious and traitorous Rioters become necessary to be introduced against a Number of Inhabitants on those Lands, who claim an Absolute Title to them, and stand ready to maintain their Rights, and are willing to have it decided by Either Law or Equity."[123] Others worried about the threat of treason prosecutions.[124]

In May 1771, the conflict with the Connecticut settlers took on a far more dangerous tone. Previously, the dispute was between Pennsylvania and The Susquehannah Company; now, the Connecticut legislature formally asserted its claim to the lands in question.[125] And violence continued to erupt. Pennsylvania officials issued another proclamation against the Connecticut settlers and sent in forces to enforce the Riot Act.[126] Lazarus Stewart, who had escaped to Connecticut, returned and led an attack on Fort Wyoming. A Pennsylvanian complained that summer, "A Kind of internal War is carried on within the Bounds of this Province, which, if not speedily check'd, will have serious consequences to us, and prove as dangerous as the Regulators of North Carolina."[127] This complaint provoked an indignant response from a supporter of the Connecticut claim, who argued that the Connecticut settlers were peaceful and wished to have the title dispute settled in a court of law. Moreover, he pointed out, Pennsylvania's Riot Act was an "implicit declaration of war against the colony of Connecticut." Using the criminal law to enforce disputed titles was pernicious. "If Mr. Penn can extend his claim at pleasure, and in consequence thereof make riot acts, and punish those with death who venture to dispute the strength of his title, (for this is the whole of the Connecticut people's crime; let them call it a riot, rebellion, or by what name they please) if he is vested with such an absolute, and unlimited power, the parliament of Great Britain, or the inhabitants of any other world, as far as I know, might be guilty of high treason in disputing his claim to the universe."[128]

In August 1771, Connecticut forces captured a significant Pennsylvania fort, leaving Connecticut in control of virtually the entire disputed region.[129] The President of the Pennsylvania Council denounced the attack, claiming Connecticut settlers had obtained their possession "by open War" in a manner analogous to the Regulator's Revolt in North Carolina. The Connecticut settlers, the President claimed, will soon "take upon themselves, in a little time, to give laws to government itself; and in the end bring on us all the evils which have lately been experienced by a neighboring colony to the southward."[130] There was little Pennsylvania could do, other than renew the Riot Act for another six months and issue more proclamations.[131] A glimmer of hope came in June 1773, when 100 Northumberland County men, encouraged to take action against the "lawless intrusions of these insurgents," lined up against 140 Connecticut men, who eventually dispersed.[132]

In January 1774, Connecticut upped the ante significantly. Bolstered by new English legal opinions supporting Connecticut jurisdiction, the colony formally organized the disputed area as the new Connecticut town of Westmoreland.[133] John Penn responded with a proclamation forbidding obedience to Zebulon Butler, whom Connecticut had appointed as a justice of the peace for Westmoreland.[134] In addition, the Assembly passed a new extension of the Riot Act.[135]

By 1775, with the colonies now at open war with Great Britain, the Continental Congress desperately sought to end the conflict, urging peace on both sides and discouraging all new settlements.[136] Shortly thereafter, however, another violent conflict broke out between Pennsylvania and Connecticut forces, resulting in the death of one Connecticut man, and the capture of seventy-two more.[137] Pennsylvania settlers continued to complain bitterly about the "hostile invasions of the Connecticut intruders" and they began to arm and organize a large private army.[138] For their part, Connecticut settlers claimed to "despise" the laws of Pennsylvania and said they "never would submit to them unless compelled by force."[139] A rumor circulated that the private army was composed of Tories preparing for the invasion of royal troops.[140] Although the Continental Congress continued to urge maintenance of the status quo, open combat again erupted on December 21, 1775, in a battle between approximately four hundred Connecticut men and five hundred Pennsylvania men.[141]

Throughout the controversy, Pennsylvania officials believed the Connecticut settlers were criminals, and they routinely sought their indictment for riot and unlawful entry. They did not, however, bring treason prosecutions. In some ways, this omission is surprising. The Connecticut settlers, like many of the Virginia settlers, did not recognize the Pennsylvania government and they engaged in open warfare against Pennsylvania officials. In England, individuals who engaged in such conduct would have been readily prosecuted for the crime of treason of levying war against the king.[142] Why didn't this happen in Pennsylvania?

The problem, from a legal perspective, was that the Connecticut settlers (and the Virginia settlers as well) were actively disloyal to Pennsylvania authority, but not to British government in general. Indeed, the Connecticut settlers repeatedly professed their "True and Sincere Allegiance to his Majesty King George the Third."[143] In May 1771, British officials had declared that the dispute was an internal Pennsylvania problem, which could be best addressed by Pennsylvania authorities. Since the king's interests were not at stake, royal interference "would be both unnecessary and improper."[144] In the absence of any open assault on royal authority, it would have been extremely difficult to conclude that the Connecticut settlers had committed treason against the king.

Their actions, at most, constituted treason against the colony of Pennsylvania—if such a crime existed. But did it? Although Pennsylvania officials often invoked the rhetoric of treason, they never officially recognized a distinct offense of treason against Pennsylvania. The 1718 legislation was quite vague, essentially adopting English treason law, but not specifying whether treason could be committed against the colony of Pennsylvania in the absence of treason against the king. In a 1762 grand-jury charge, Pennsylvania [Chief] Justice Edward Shippen asserted that the only form of high treason "that can be committed in this country . . . is the counterfeiting [of] the King's coin."[145] If Shippen's view was not idiosyncratic, Pennsylvania could prosecute the Connecticut and Virginia settlers only for other crimes, such as riot and unlawful entry. Despite the

Connecticut and Virginia settlers' open warfare against Pennsylvania's authority, the criminal law of treason would be unavailing.

* * *

By the beginning of the dispute with Great Britain, Pennsylvania had a fifty-year history of formally embracing the English law of treason. With a few halting exceptions, however, that law, although formally available, was essentially a dead letter. It had little relevance to the day-to-day concerns of the colony, and even in situations in which it might have been most helpful—the crisis of the Paxton Boys and the intrusions of the Connecticut settlers—it remained silent and unused. The increasingly contentious nature of colonial resistance activities, however, moved the issue of treason to the forefront. The nature of treason—and who constituted the real traitors—would become a central theme of legal and political discourse.

2

Resistance and Treason, 1765–1775

IN 1818, JOHN ADAMS observed that the American Revolution was "effected before the war commenced. The Revolution was in the minds and hearts of the people.... This radical change in the principles, opinions, sentiments and affection of the people, was the real American Revolution."[1] This conceptual revolution was most vividly demonstrated by American perceptions of treason. Over the course of a decade, colonial Americans moved from insisting on their loyalty to their king to denouncing such loyalty as the blackest form of treason.

This difficult, tumultuous decade began with the enactment of the Stamp Act of 1765, which triggered widespread protests and riots throughout Britain's American colonies. In Philadelphia, a large mob prevented the stamp collector from enforcing the Act.[2] Although Parliament quickly repealed the Stamp Act, subsequent legislation proved equally unpopular, and colonial Americans organized boycotts of British goods, published vehement denunciations of British policies, and occasionally undertook more forceful measures.

In this combustible atmosphere, it was perhaps inevitable that accusations of treason would be hurled across the Atlantic. As early as 1767, rumors were spreading in America that Lord Mansfield favored trying colonial leaders for treason in England.[3] By the early 1770s, British officials concluded that certain resistance activities amounted to treason and that American defendants could be legally tried before an English jury.

Colonial Americans were stung by the accusation of treason and, not surprisingly, vigorously argued that their actions were not criminal. In formulating their defense, many Americans turned the accusation of treason on its head. The real traitors, they insisted, were not American resistance leaders, but the British officials themselves. Virginians who burned a stamp collector in effigy in 1765 accused him of "traitorously aiding and assisting in the destruction of his country's liberties."[4] A 1771 diatribe in a Connecticut newspaper argued, "To say that subjects in general are not proper judges, when their governors oppress them and play the tyrant . . . is as great *treason* as ever man uttered; 'tis *treason*—not against one single man, but against the state—against the whole body politic—'Tis *treason* against mankind—'Tis *treason* against common sense—'Tis *treason* against God!"[5]

Between 1765 and the outbreak of war in 1775, these twin themes permeated American thought with respect to treason. On the one hand, Americans argued defensively, fiercely rejecting the notion that resistance activities amounted to treason. American leaders were not traitors, but loyal subjects who simply sought to restore prior British policy with respect to the colonies. Broad accusations of treason were inappropriate and risked bringing legitimate political activity under the purview of the criminal law. On the other hand, many Americans showed no hesitation in making precisely those same broad accusations against others. Treason was real, pervasive, and dangerous, but the real traitors were the British ministers who were conspiring against American liberty. The carriers of the *Pennsylvania Journal*, in a January 1775 handbill, went so far as to name names: "North, and Wedderburne, and Bute" were "traitors who glory in their crimes."[6] British actions, whether supported by the monarch or not, amounted to treason against something larger—against the British state, against the constitution, or against liberty itself.

The potential application of English treason law to colonial resistance activities raised two distinct issues. First, did any of the resistance activities constitute treason under the statutory definitions of 25 Edward III? Second, if resistance activities did constitute treason, could the perpetrators be tried outside of the colonies? English and American answers to these questions diverged dramatically.

Justifying Resistance

English legal experts initially hesitated before labeling American resistance activities as treason.[7] Expansive treason statutes from the Tudor and Stuart reigns were widely viewed as a regrettable departure from the more limited definition set forth in 25 Edward III. William Blackstone stated conventional eighteenth-century English thought by warning against "forced and arbitrary constructions" of treason. Citing Montesquieu, Blackstone argued that if "the crime of high treason be indeterminate, this alone . . . is sufficient to make any government degenerate into arbitrary power."[8] As late as February 1775, members of the House of Lords warned, "We are the more cautious of pronouncing any part of his Majesty's dominions to be in actual rebellion, because the cases of constructive treason under that branch of 25th of Edward the Third, which describes the crime of rebellion, have been already so far extended by the Judges, and the distinctions thereupon so nice and subtle, that no prudent man ought to declare any single person in that situation, without the clearest evidence of uncontrovertable overt acts to warrant such a declaration."[9]

By 1772, however, English legal experts concluded that at least some resistance measures had crossed the line into outright treason. That year, a group of Rhode Islanders, with connections to some of the most prominent people in the colony, attacked the British royal ship *Gaspée*, which was patrolling for smugglers on the Providence River. Shortly after midnight, the raiders boarded the ship, seized the crew, and set the ship on fire, completely destroying it.[10] Attorney General Edward Thurlow and Solicitor General Alexander Wedderburn determined that the attack "was an act of high treason . . . of levying war against his majesty."[11] The crown lawyers offered no analysis to buttress this conclusion, which was at least debatable. Although attacking the crew of the ship was likely treasonous, an early-eighteenth-century treatise had stated that "Setting Fire to one of the King's Ships is not Treason within the Statute 25 Edw. III."[12] To ensure there was no room for dispute, Parliament enacted legislation explicitly making it a felony (but not treason) to burn or destroy the king's dockyards, magazines, ships, ammunition, and stores.[13] The Privy Council appointed a commission of inquiry to investigate the *Gaspée* incident, but the case quickly fizzled out. Despite extensive investigation, the commission was unable to develop sufficient evidence against any individual to justify an indictment and trial.[14]

The Boston Tea Party of 1773 prompted a similar legal conclusion. In February 1774, Thurlow and Wedderburn advised the Earl of Dartmouth that various actions undertaken to thwart the Tea Act amounted "to the crime of high treason, namely . . . levying of war against His Majesty." The proceedings were an "attempt . . . made with open force . . . to obstruct the execution of an Act of the Parliament . . . and to put a general restraint upon the exercise of a lawful trade as if it were a public grievance." Moreover, on the basis of the facts represented to them, they identified specific individuals, including Samuel Adams and John Hancock, who appeared to be culpable.[15] The Chief Justice of the Court of King's Bench, Lord Mansfield, in a speech in the House of the Lords, agreed that the Tea Party "was the last overt act of high treason, proceeding from over-lenity and want of foresight."[16]

The final British legal analysis before the outbreak of hostilities turned on the Massachusetts Provincial Congress of 1774, which had appropriated money for the formation of a colonial militia. In February 1775, Thurlow and Wedderburn concluded that "seizing public money and new-officering and disciplining militia for the purpose avowed in Provincial Congress of Massachusetts" amounted to "high treason." Moreover, "being present at meetings where resolutions were taken is *prima facie* evidence of treason."[17]

The prospect of treason trials enraged colonial resistance leaders, who responded with a vigorous defense of their actions. Much of the vast pamphlet literature generated by the American colonists was implicitly devoted to the distinction between legitimate resistance and treason. Legitimate resistance to arbitrary government was the right, even the duty, of every free people. In an address to the Pennsylvania Convention in January 1775, James Wilson attacked the seeming British view that "all resistance to forces commissioned by his majesty, is a resistance of his majesty's authority and government, contrary to the duty of allegiance and treasonable." Wilson argued that this view rested on "chicanery and sophistry" and twisted quotations from legal authorities. Labeling resistance as treason had "not even the remotest alliance with the principles of reason or of law."[18] A New Yorker stoutly maintained during the Stamp Act crisis that it was not "treason in any subject or body of subjects to declare what they apprehend the rights of Englishmen to be."[19] A member of the Sons of Liberty warned, "Our Denial of the Parliament's Power to tax us, has been called Treason" by "miscreants" who are prepared to "try our Patriots at Westminster, and quarter them at Tyburn."[20]

American propagandists placed special emphasis on the statute of 25 Edward III and the danger of introducing new treasons by construction. William Bollan, the former London agent for Massachusetts, insisted on the "utility and necessity of strictly observing" the medieval statute; it was "dangerous . . . to depart from the letter of that statute" and make treasons "by construction and analogy."[21] Virginia's instructions to its delegates to the First Continental Congress noted,

> We would remind [the king], that the statute 25 of Edward III, has expressed and desired all treasonable offences, and that the legislature of Great Britain hath declared, that no offense shall be construed to be treason, but such as is pointed out by that statute: And that this was done to take out of the hands of tyrannical Kings, and of weak and wicked Ministers, that deadly weapon, which constructive treason had furnished them with, and which had drawn the blood of the best and honestest men in the kingdom.[22]

In the *Pennsylvania Gazette*, "Britannicus" complained,

> So great is the lawyer's art, that he would wiredraw treason from the most sacred truth, and make a libel of the Lord's Prayer; As for instance in these words, "For thine is the Kingdom;" oh, says Mr. Attorney, that is a treasonable expression; for by innuendo, it is saying the king hath no right to

> the crown. There are indeed, no words which lawyers cannot, by forced constructions, torture into treason.[23]

A Maryland writer worried that "statutes of treason are to be extended, by construction, contrary to the known maxims of law and justice" and that "we may soon expect to see that treated, as treason, in an American, which is not even a misdemeanor in an inhabitant of Great Britain."[24]

Some English critics of the ministry echoed similar ideas. The eighteenth edition of *The Crisis*, an anonymous series published in 1775 and 1776, used verse to criticize expansive definitions of treason:

> *Since ev'ry act brings forth some grievance new,*
> *Enlarge the narrow bounds of treason too.*
> *Like Mary' Minion in her tyrant reign,*
> *Enlarge old Edward's act amend, explain,*
> *Shew Edward's sages they mistook the case;*
> *Declare new treasons—'tis an act of grace.*
> *Declare it treason but to wish success*
> *To freedom's arms, or supplicate redress.*[25]

A Jury of One's Peers

Adding further fuel to the fire was the potential elimination of the fundamental right to a trial by a jury of one's peers. In late 1768 and early 1769, Parliament had encouraged the king to employ the statute of 35 Henry VIII, which permitted the trial in England of treasons committed outside the realm. The *Gaspée* commissioners were directed to proceed under the same provision; Thurlow and Wedderburn had concluded that the offenders could be tried either in England or in Rhode Island. American resistance leaders thus faced the prospect of trial in England for the crime of high treason. If convicted, they would face the traditional punishment of beheading and disembowelment.[26]

This specter of English treason trials provoked a vehement reaction in the American colonies and played an important role in the colonial dialogue about resistance and, ultimately, about independence. If Americans could be dragged to England for trial, what would become of their cherished right to trial by a jury of their peers? A member of Parliament presciently argued in 1769 that invocation of 35 Henry VIII "was more calculated to promote than prevent rebellion."[27] The "American Whig" warned in 1769 that there was "much uncertainty in the construction of the statute of treasons," which made the jury's role in factual determinations all the more important. "If an American can be seized in his bed by a band of soldiers, be loaded with irons, and sent home to New-gate, be thence dragg'd to a trial at the Old Baily, and in two or three days after, hang'd and quarterd at Tyburn, who can be safe? This is a door undoubtedly wide enough to let in the most absolute despotism that can be conceived by the heart of man."[28] In September 1774, John Adams proposed that any English use of 35 Henry VIII be regarded as a "Declaration of War and a Commencement of Hostilities against all the Colonies."[29] A few months later, he warned that treason trials in England would "produce resistance and reprisals, and a flame through all America, such as eye hath not seen nor ear heard."[30] "Lucius Verus" complained that "obsolete Statutes have been revived for the punishment of offenders, and the bloody axe of Henry VIII has been scoured up and whetted for the necks of poor Americans."[31]

The Virginia Resolves of 1769 argued that treason trials must be held in the colony where the alleged acts occurred and that sending defendants "beyond the Sea to be tried, is highly derogatory of the Rights of British Subjects."[32] The North Carolina Assembly agreed, denouncing the potential application of the act as "unconstitutional and illegal."[33] In neighboring South Carolina, a convention concluded that it would be "oppressive and illegal, and highly derogatory to the rights of British subjects."[34] As a writer in the *Pennsylvania Gazette* explained, Parliament had "extended the obsolete and arbitrary act of 35 Henry VIII for trial of treason and misprision of treason . . . depriving the subject of a fair trial in the proper county, and exposing him to the most grievous exertions of tyranny and injustice."[35] Philadelphia druggist Christopher Marshall sarcastically noted that all those who had sent aid to Boston should be arrested, "secured in irons, put on board his Majesty's ships and sent to France . . . to take their trial (this would be consistent with the late act of Henry the 8th sent here)."[36] In a similar vein, in his "Rules By Which a Great Empire May be Reduced to a Small One," Benjamin Franklin mockingly advised the British government, "If the injured and exasperated Farmers, unable to procure other Justice, should attack the Aggressors, drub them and burn their Boats, you are to call this *High Treason* and *Rebellion*, order Fleets and Armies into their Country, and threaten to carry all the Offenders three thousand Miles to be hang'd, drawn and quartered. *O! this will work admirably!*"[37] In Parliament, Edmund Burke noted that "the Vote for sending such Persons as may have been guilty of Treasons, or Misprision of Treason, upon the Act of Henry VIII was justly alarming to the Americans, and an unconstitutional Measure."[38]

The British invocation 35 Henry VIII was not entirely implausible. America, after all, was not part of the realm of England, and the statute thus literally seemed to apply. Matthew Hale's treatise, for example, had emphasized that the phrase "in his realm" in the levying war offense applied to England, but not to Ireland or the Channel Islands.[39] Lord Beauchamp argued in Parliament, "I can't conceive it is any unnatural construction of the Act to make it extend to America. It is a maxim of legislation that whatever is within the letter of Acts of Parliament should not be construed to be without the meaning."[40] The attorney general mockingly asked, "[The Americans] carried with them the 25 Edward III, and shall they not carry with them the 35 Henry VIII?"[41] Lord North claimed, "To people who have been so near committing treason, it is not a cruelty, it is a warning. It is proper to give them notice that they are not to depend upon impunity from an American jury, but to depend upon an English jury."[42]

On the other hand, the statute was enacted long before the American colonies were even established and arguably had no application where courts of justice were operating under the king's name.[43] William Dowdeswell, a member of Parliament from Worcestershire, made precisely this point in the 1769 parliamentary debates. He doubted that "in law . . . there is any man whatever, who thinks that Act ought to be applied to the colonies. We had no colonies at that time." A subject of Great Britain was "entitled to the laws of his country, which say that crimes are local, and shall be tried where they are committed."[44] Another member claimed that the statute "was passed in the worst time of the worst reign that ever disgraced our annals."[45] Another argued, "If I were an American, rather than have that Act of Henry VIII, I would undergo any suffering. It is giving a horrid impression of the government of this country to be raking into the acts of arbitrary times."[46]

The legal points of the parliamentary dissenters were echoed throughout America. The Virginia Resolves contended that 35 Henry VIII could be applied in America only through an "arbitrary and cruel Construction," given that the American colonies were perfectly capable of conducting treason trials themselves. The "American Whig" pointed out that the statute applied only to actions taken "in a foreign dominion, where our Sovereign had no authority to punish the criminal." It made no sense to apply the statute within the king's "dominions, where the administration of justice is established, and regularly dispensed."[47] A South Carolina convention insisted that the act could not apply "where there is sufficient provision, by the law of the land, for the impartial trial of all such persons."[48] The prominent treason treatise by Michael Foster implicitly agreed with this position, arguing that the statute was beneficial to the subject because it deprived him of no advantage "to which he was before entitled"; rather, it guaranteed him a trial at common law "instead of a trial according to the course and order of the civil law."[49]

British officials themselves expressed pragmatic concerns about transporting accused traitors to England for trial. Thurlow and Wedderburn, for example, preferred that the principal culprits in the Boston Tea Party be tried in America.[50] The Earl of Dartmouth's instructions to General Thomas Gage concluded that "there seemed to be no other method of proceeding against them but in the ordinary courts of justice within the colony." Although he encouraged Gage to gather evidence and secure treason indictments against colonial resistance leaders, he recognized that such measures might ultimately fail, warning that "the prejudices of the people" might "prevent a conviction, however clear and full the evidence might be." In such a case, "it would be better to desist from prosecution, seeing that an ineffectual attempt would only be triumph to the faction and disgraceful to the government."[51] As it turned out, no Massachusetts citizen was ever charged with treason for complicity in the Boston Tea Party.[52]

The issue of treason trials in England was nonetheless identified in the great state papers of the Revolution as a significant cause of complaint. Legal historian John Philip Reid notes that the proposed use of the statute of Henry VIII was "a serious grievance helping to drive Americans to rebellion."[53] A New York writer in 1776 cited "the revival of an arbitrary act, made in the tyrannical reign of Henry VIII, to remove persons accused of crimes committed in the Colonies, to England for trial, and thereby depriving them of the assistance of their friends, the evidence they might procure in their favour, and the right of being tried by a jury of the vicinage" as one of the causes of the outbreak of the war.[54] The Declaration and Resolves of the First Continental Congress condemned the application of the statute of 35 Henry VIII and asserted that the colonies were entitled to "the great and inestimable privilege of being tried by their peers of the vicinage." The Articles of Association complained that Parliament had directed "a new and illegal trial beyond the seas."[55] The Declaration of the Causes and Necessity of Taking up Arms complained that it had "been resolved in Parliament, that colonists charged with certain offences, shall be transported to England to be tried."[56] The Declaration of Independence denounced the king "for transporting us beyond Seas to be tried for pretended offenses." As Pauline Maier has pointed out, however, "[e]ven the most assiduous efforts have . . . identified no colonists of the revolutionaries' generation who were actually transported 'beyond seas to be tried for pretended offenses.' "[57] British leaders discussed the possibility repeatedly, but the dreaded event never actually occurred. The threatened treason trials succeeded only in alienating colonial Americans and making them even more suspicious of British intentions.

Identifying the Real Traitors

In a curious paradox, while colonial leaders were faulting the British ministry's expansive view of treason, Americans were themselves expanding the notion of treason in potentially new directions. As many Americans saw it, the real traitors were those Americans and Britons who supported imperial policies. They—not the resistance leaders—were the secret enemies who threatened the security of their country. Governor Thomas Hutchinson of Massachusetts, for example, was denounced as an "arch Hypocrite and Traitor" and as an "infamous old traitor," one "detested by all true friends to liberty."[58] In Connecticut, attorneys concluded that a man who worked for General Gage was a "Traitor to his Country" and refused to represent him.[59] In the summer of 1774, Virginians conducted a mock trial of Lord North for "high treason."[60]

These people were traitors. But traitors against what? They could not be easily described as traitors against their king. Instead, colonial Americans denounced them as traitors against liberty, traitors against the constitution, and traitors against their country. This rhetorical trope was not entirely novel. John Peter Zenger's *New York Weekly Journal* had argued in 1737 that whoever attempted to suppress the freedom of speech or the liberty of the press "ought to be regarded as an enemy to liberty and the constitution."[61] The vehemence of these claims, however, increased dramatically during the years prior to independence.

The concept of liberty played a particularly powerful role. As Bernard Bailyn has argued, colonial political ideology posited a sharp dichotomy between the spheres of liberty and power. Unchecked, power would always encroach upon liberty, which required zealous measures for its preservation.[62] As early as the Stamp Act crisis, people unwilling to offer resistance were denounced in a Philadelphia newspaper as "cowards and traitors to liberty."[63] Virginians burned a stamp collector in effigy for the crime of "traitorously aiding and assisting in the destruction of his country's liberty."[64] Intimately tied to the concept of liberty was the concept of rights. It would be "treason in us tamely to give up" our rights, South Carolinians concluded, lest we be rendered "infamous to future generations."[65] As one writer put it, "The man who refuses to assert his right to liberty, property, and life is guilty of the worst kind of rebellion. He commits high treason against God."[66]

The betrayal of liberty was cast in constitutional terms. As John Philip Reid has carefully demonstrated, constitutional arguments played a major role in the American path to revolution.[67] Many Americans concluded that the unconstitutional actions of Parliament were the true acts of treason. During the Stamp Act crisis, a New Yorker pointed out that it was "not Treason in any Legislature to pronounce, declare, and resolve that those are Enemies to their Country who assert and maintain Doctrines diametrically opposed to the fundamental principles of the Constitution." Moreover, "to attempt the Subversion of the most happy Constitution upon Earth, is Treason" and "to maintain that the King and Parliament may enact Laws contrary to the Fundamentals of the Constitution, is Treason."[68] Boston minister John Allen argued after the *Gaspée* affair "that the King's Ministry and Parliament must be Rebels, to God and mankind, in attempting to overthrow (by guns, swords, by the power of war) the laws, and government of Rhode Island."[69] Another writer warned that persons who undermined the rights of the colonies engaged in a "treasonable conspiracy against the constitution."[70] John Dickinson claimed, "We should be guilty of treason against our sovereign and the majesty of the people of England, if we did not oppose [ministerial policies.] England must be saved in America."[71] James Wilson made the point powerfully in a January 1775 speech. "Are we deficient in loyalty to his majesty?" Wilson asked. "Our loyalty has always appeared in the true form of loyalty—in obeying our sovereign according to law: Let those who would require it in any other form know that we call the persons who execute his commands, when contrary to the law, disloyal and traitors."[72] A month later, a Massachusetts writer concluded that "submission" had become "treason against the constitution."[73] Even Thomas Coombe, the minister of Philadelphia's Christ Church who would later side with the British and flee to England, preached a sermon at the opening of the Second Continental Congress, arguing "We asked but for peace, liberty, and safety; privileges derived from heaven and the constitution. . . . privileges, which, had we been so tame as to have surrendered without a struggle, we should have been guilty of treason against posterity."[74]

Treason against one's "country" was an especially powerful charge, particularly when coupled with personal denunciation as an "enemy to his country." The Sons of Liberty in Norfolk County, Virginia, resolved in April 1766 to treat every person employing "the detestable papers called the Stamps . . . to all intents and purposes [as] an enemy to his country."[75] A writer in the *Pennsylvania Journal* concluded that any "friend to the stamp-act is an enemy to his country, and deserves, justly deserves, the curse of God, and the detestable abhorrence of his countrymen."[76] John Hughes, the Philadelphia stamp distributor, complained to British officials that the primary response to his office was "YOU ARE AN ENEMY TO AMERICA, AND OUGHT TO HAVE YOUR BRAINS BEAT OUT."[77] A few years later, a Philadelphia Committee of Merchants resolved that any person violating the non-importation agreements "shall be considered as a Person who has not a just Sense of Liberty, and as an Enemy to his Country."[78] A Lancaster County committee agreed, denouncing any person who violated the non-importation agreements as "Traitors to the true Interests of this Country."[79]

These repeated references to "country" suggest a common reference point, but it is not entirely clear precisely what that "country" was. The term may refer to the empire of Great Britain, to the American colonies as a whole, or to an individual colony itself. Under any interpretation, however, they suggest an increasing perception that treason was a breach of allegiance to an impersonal state or to the community at large, rather than a breach of allegiance to a personal monarch.[80]

The tea controversy of 1773 provided particularly fertile ground for allegations of treason and betrayal. A group of Philadelphians resolved that any person who unloaded the tea of the East India Company was an "Enemy to his Country."[81] A Philadelphia "Committee for Tarring and Feathering" published a broadside entitled "To the Delaware Pilots." It warned that any pilot who guided a ship containing English tea would "be marked for his Treason, and will never after meet with the least encouragement in his business. Like Cain, he will be hung out as a spectacle to all nations, and be forever recorded as the damned traitorous pilot who brought up the tea ship."[82] Another Pennsylvania writer warned that all persons who assisted with the unloading of British tea were "base traitors to this country, without exception [and] should be immediately and resolutely dragged from Concealment; they should be transported, or forced from every place in America, loaded with the most striking Badges of Disgrace."[83] A pamphlet published in Lancaster, Pennsylvania, argued, "Continuing to purchase tea, under present circumstances, is high treason against three millions of Americans."[84] New Yorkers similarly concluded that any person unloading tea should be "deemed an enemy to the liberties of America."[85]

The idea that some Americans amounted to enemies was explicitly sanctioned by the First Continental Congress. Meeting in Philadelphia in 1774, the Congress adopted Articles of Association to govern the proposed boycott of British goods. The Eleventh Article required local committees to publish the names of persons who violated the boycott, "so that all such foes to the rights of British-America may be publicly known, and universally condemned as the enemies of American liberty; and thenceforth we respectively will break off all dealings with him or her."[86]

Local committees across the country enthusiastically embraced their role as enforcers of congressional policy. The consequences of social ostracism could be quite severe. A Pennsylvanian explained it this way in January 1775:

> If a man renders himself obnoxious to his countrymen, let him be driven from us, by a total declension of dealing with him; neither buy from him, nor sell to him, neither work for him, speak to him, nor serve him; put him (as the military phrase is) into perpetual coventry. If we have the virtue unanimously to persist in this course, we shall soon drive from the continent every enemy to our liberty.[87]

With these techniques, the notion of "enemies" to their country took firm root. In an anonymous pamphlet, John Drinker, a Philadelphia Quaker, lamented that "enemy to your country, ministerial minion, detestable traitor and what not, have been the opprobrious epithets successfully bandied among us."[88]

The underlying question could not have been of more consequence. A Massachusetts writer summed it up well in February 1775: "What is treason in relation to the present contention, and who are the traitors, those who oppose or those who endeavor to support and enforce the new-fangled laws?"[89]

* * *

When the War for Independence erupted on April 19, 1775, colonial resistance ripened into full-fledged, indisputable treason. Americans were now openly levying war against their king. On June 15, General Gage, the British commander in Boston, proclaimed that all people in arms were "rebels and traitors, and as such to be treated."[90] King George III followed up on August 23, proclaiming that many of his American subjects were in open rebellion, "traitorously preparing, ordering, and levying war against us." He urged all of his subjects "to bring the traitors to justice" and to disclose all "treasons and traitorous conspiracies."[91]

As the American colonies were engaged in a continental war, treason now became a matter of immediate practical concern. What was to be done with those people who opposed the Revolution, or worse, who actively aided the British? The answer was readily at hand; for ten years, individuals who opposed resistance measures had been rhetorically singled out as "traitors" and "enemies to their country." Once the war had begun, it was easy to conclude that these individuals were no longer traitors in a rhetorical sense, but real traitors who directly threatened the American cause. In the coming months, Pennsylvanians would take firm measures against those people who remained loyal to their king. They were traitors—traitors to America and traitors to liberty. And despite all the previous heated rhetoric about the importance of jury trial in treason cases, these men would not be tried by juries.

3

Treason against America, 1775–1776

THE CANNONS OF the Revolution had been firing for almost a year when Benjamin Chew, the seventeenth chief justice of Pennsylvania, entered the large courtroom on the first floor of the State House in Philadelphia (now known as Independence Hall) to open the Court of Oyer and Terminer for Philadelphia County on April 10, 1776. This room (Figure 3.1), with its high ceiling and large painting of the coat of arms of George III, was the grandest courtroom in eighteenth-century America, and it radiated the authority of the English common law. Chief Justice Chew, appointed by Pennsylvania's proprietary government two years earlier, had studied at Middle Temple in London and he presided over a court steeped in English tradition and precedent. The opening of the court of oyer and terminer for the trial of felonies provided a highly public and visible display of the scope of English law, beginning with the presiding judge's description of the crimes subject to the grand jury's jurisdiction. Chew began his charge to the grand jury, as tradition required, with the highest crime—the offense of high treason. Yet as Chew spoke, the grand jury grew increasingly uncomfortable. Perhaps some of the members looked at that day's *Pennsylvania Gazette*, which noted that recently "a party of about 150 of our troops landed on Bedlow's-Island [the later home of the Statute of Liberty] . . . and destroyed some works that had been erected there by the crew of his Majesty's ship the *Asia*, and burnt down a house that was supposed to be possessed by some tories."[1] Finally, a grand juror interrupted, "What then is to become of us who are now opposing the arbitrary power attempted to be exercised by the British Ministry?" Chew's response would not likely have pleased the monarch under whose royal emblem he sat: "An opposition of force of arms to the lawful authority of the King or his ministers . . . is High Treason; but in the moment when the King or his ministers shall exceed the constitutional authority vested in them by the constitution, submission to their mandates becomes Treason."[2]

FIGURE 3.1 The Pennsylvania Supreme Court chamber in Independence Hall.
Credit: Shutterstock

This distinction was tenuous, both legally and practically, as it obscured the essential question of who may determine when the king has exceeded his authority. Nonetheless, it demonstrates the perilous intellectual tightrope that the law of treason presented prior to independence. The American colonies had raised an army and were engaged in open warfare against the forces of their king, while at the same time insisting that they remained the king's loyal subjects. In the early months of the conflict, some American soldiers even claimed to be the true forces of the king, whereas General Gage's men were merely the "Parliament Troops."[3] The awkwardness of the American position was resolved by invoking themes developed in previous years—that it was the king's ministers, and perhaps even the king himself, who were the real traitors. Americans were simply exercising their lawful right to resist illegal authority.

But it was not just the king and his ministers who were perceived as traitors. Thousands of Americans opposed the resistance movement, and many of them took active steps to support the king. These people were viewed as perhaps the most dangerous traitors of all, secretly lurking among other Americans, just waiting for the right moment to spring their nefarious plots. These enemies to American liberty would need to be rooted out and controlled. Prosecution in a colonial court, however, was not a viable option until independence was declared. American resistance leaders thus necessarily had to develop techniques that were formally extra-legal, but that nonetheless did not depart too radically from existing legal norms.

In Pennsylvania, responsibility for investigating persons suspected of being enemies to America fell to the committees of safety. These committees proliferated after the outbreak of hostilities and assumed a wide array of governmental functions. The foremost committee was the Pennsylvania Committee of Safety, created by the Pennsylvania Assembly in June 1775 to defend the "Lives, Liberty and Property" of the people. As the institutions of Pennsylvania's proprietary government atrophied, the Pennsylvania Committee quickly came to assume de facto executive powers for the colony. It would govern the state until July 22, 1776, when it was replaced with a provisional Council of Safety. Affiliated with the Pennsylvania Committee were local committees of safety, organized in the counties and in the city of Philadelphia. Many of these committees had been formed in late 1774 and early 1775 as mechanisms to enforce the policies of the Continental Congress.[4]

Although there was occasional friction, the Pennsylvania Committee and the county committees seem to have worked out a rough division of authority with respect to opponents of the resistance measures. The Pennsylvania Committee largely addressed overt acts of disloyalty, cases that seriously threatened the safety of the colony. In these cases, the committee did not hesitate to order imprisonment.[5] By contrast, the county committees largely handled verbal offenses, which were punished primarily through social sanctions. This division of authority would be reflected in the state's later distinction between high treason, an offense prosecuted at the court of oyer and terminer, and misprision of treason, a lesser offense subject to the jurisdiction of the county courts.

In an influential 1964 monograph, Bradley Chapin argued, "The origins of the American law of treason were national, developing from the experience of the Continental Army between June, 1775 and June, 1776."[6] Although the army experience was certainly significant, Chapin greatly overstated its importance in the year prior to independence. The military cases, which rested on various army rules and regulations, were not technically cases of treason, as they were all brought before courts-martial. Treason, as the leading contemporary treatise on courts-martial made clear, was not cognizable in military courts.[7] Moreover, the experience of the Continental Army had little effect on the day-to-day handling of disloyalty in colonies outside the theater of military operations. In Pennsylvania, civilian authorities, acting through committees of safety, investigated and punished "treason against America" without any assistance from the military.

The War's First Treason Charges

Pennsylvania's first revolutionary "treason" trial was triggered by a series of bizarre incidents that unfolded in Philadelphia in the fall of 1775. The initial protagonist was Isaac Hunt, a Philadelphia lawyer and pamphleteer who had been a prominent opponent of the Paxton Boys.[8] Benjamin Franklin had encouraged Hunt's early career, because of their shared antipathy to Pennsylvania's proprietary government.[9] By 1775, however, their politics had diverged dramatically, and Hunt published a pamphlet strongly defending American ties to Britain.[10] On behalf of a client named William Conn, Hunt filed a lawsuit against George Schlosser, a member of the Philadelphia Committee of Safety. The lawsuit alleged that Schlosser had unlawfully detained linen belonging to Conn, who was suspected of violating the non-importation agreements.[11] Hunt was ordered to appear before the committee to justify his conduct, and he claimed that he was unaware that Schlosser was a committee member at the time he filed his suit. An affidavit later obtained from Conn, however, suggested that Hunt had been fully aware of Schlosser's status.[12] Hunt's apparent perjury before the committee, and his related refusal to withdraw the suit, enraged the members of Philadelphia's Sons of Liberty. As they later explained, since Hunt had "for a long time done everything in his power to hurt the cause of American liberty," the "laws of nature and the customs of nations [justified] the severest punishment."[13] Although initially planning to tar and feather Hunt, they instead seized him on the morning of September 6, placed him in a dung cart, paraded him through the town, and, as a Quaker observer drily noted, "at every corner compelled him voluntarily to renounce his former heretical Tory principles."[14] Hunt later recalled that "every moment" he had "expected to be torn to pieces by a multitude, spirited up to a frenzy."[15]

This noisy procession soon approached the home of John Kearsley, a Philadelphia physician. Hearing the drums, Kearsley became convinced that the mob was coming for him. He had good reason to be frightened. Since the spring of 1775, Kearsley had been holding secret meetings to encourage all Englishmen to join the British forces, should they arrive in Pennsylvania.[16] Kearsley's response to the procession accorded with his reputation as a "pre-eminently ardent and rash" member of the disaffected.[17] Leaning out of his window, Kearsley swore violently at the crowd and brandished his pistol.[18] He was immediately seized and in the ensuing scuffle injured his hand.[19] The crowd then released the hapless Hunt and placed Kearsley in the cart in his stead.[20] Alexander Graydon later recalled that Kearsley, "foaming with rage and indignation, without his hat, his wig dishevelled and bloody from his wounded hand, stood up in the cart and called for a bowl of punch."[21] Although Kearsley was threatened with "a bucket of tar before his eyes," he was finally returned to his home after "many hours" of carting.[22] The Sons of Liberty subsequently defended their conduct in the *Pennsylvania Journal*, noting that both Hunt and Kearsley were "well known enemies to their country" and "traitors to their country."[23]

The carting incident suggested that Kearsley was an unreliable character who needed to be closely watched. On the evening of October 5, 1775, two young men, including the son of Philadelphia's sheriff, entered the back parlor of Kearsley's home and discovered "sundry persons in conversation and sundry letters packed in different packages which were to be conveyed to London."[24] One of these men alerted the Philadelphia Committee of Safety, which sent a group of men to track one of the suspects, an apothecary named Christopher Carter, who had emigrated from London several years earlier.[25] Apprehended on a ship in Chester, Carter initially denied any knowledge of suspicious letters. After threats to bring him before the Philadelphia Committee of Safety, Carter confessed and revealed the letters' location in the petticoats of a female passenger.[26]

The letters were promptly forwarded to the Philadelphia Committee of Safety, which found the letters to be "base and cruel invectives against the liberty of America, and calculated by wicked men to inflame the minds of the people in England against the colonies in general."[27]

One of the letters was addressed to Charles Jenkinson, a member of the Privy Council who was regarded with deep suspicion in America. The letter warned of the "menaces of rebellious faction" and asserted that it was the duty of every Englishman "to eradicate and destroy such unnatural attempts in the embryo."[28] Another letter contained a proposal for sending five thousand royal troops to Philadelphia, to be joined by five thousand American troops raised by Kearsley and his associates.[29]

That same day, the Continental Congress, sitting in Philadelphia, resolved that the colonial assemblies and committees of safety should "arrest and secure every person in their respective colonies, whose going at large, may, in their opinion, endanger the safety of the colony, or the liberties of America."[30] Although this resolution may have been motivated in part by the discovery of Kearsley's letters, John Adams's notes of congressional debates suggest that the primary purpose was to authorize the capture of the Earl of Dunmore, the royal governor of Virginia.[31] The resolution was nonetheless highly significant. By authorizing seemingly indefinite detentions, the Congress was taking the revolutionary movement into new and uncharted territory. The disputes of the seventeenth century had placed personal liberty at the forefront of English constitutional thought. As Blackstone's *Commentaries* had noted, "the glory of the English law consists in clearly defining the times, the causes, and the extent, when, wherefore, and to what degree, the imprisonment of the subject may be lawful."[32] Yet the Congress seemed to be authorizing indefinite detentions at the pleasure of the extra-legal committees of safety. Although perhaps justified by the peculiar circumstances then existing, such detentions risked becoming a form of unchecked tyranny themselves. To their credit, in Pennsylvania the committees did not exercise this power to the utmost and generally provided at least rudimentary trials for persons suspected of endangering the liberties of America.

With respect to the Kearsley matter, the Pennsylvania Committee acted swiftly on the Congress's recommendation, issuing arrest warrants for the reputed authors of the letters: John Kearsley, James Brooks, and Leonard Snowden, a Quaker brewer.[33] The warrants stated the accused were charged with "practices inimical to the liberties of America, and dangerous to the peace and safety of this province."[34] The three men were quickly arrested and confined in the State House.[35] Christopher Carter was arrested shortly thereafter on similar charges.[36] The Pennsylvania Committee interpreted Congress's resolution as vesting jurisdiction over such cases exclusively with itself, and not with the local committees. After a lengthy and "warm" discussion, a divided Philadelphia Committee agreed and surrendered the cases to the Pennsylvania Committee.[37]

On October 9, before a "multitude of spectators," the four men were tried, convicted, and sentenced by the Pennsylvania Committee.[38] The men were led to their trial by a guard of over fifty militiamen, with "drums, fifes, etc." The trial lasted from noon until dusk, a substantial length by eighteenth-century standards. The Pennsylvania Committee of Safety presided, "assisted" by fifteen members of the Philadelphia Committee.[39] Christopher Marshall described the trial as "fair and impartial," but we have no formal record of the actual proceeding.[40] In papers later filed with the British government, Christopher Carter stated that he had been "examined by the Committee of Safety," which suggests that he was interrogated directly by the committee.[41] The committee's final resolution stated that it had heard live witnesses and that the defendants were allowed to cross-examine the witnesses and to "state what [they] thought proper to allege" in their defense.[42] By contrast, Kearsley's widow later claimed that the committee had "not suffered him to go into . . . a defense of his conduct."[43] The defendants do not appear to have had the assistance of counsel or the ability to call their own witnesses.

The four men's sentences varied significantly. John Kearsley was sentenced to imprisonment "without bail or manprize in York jail without pen, ink, or paper, or liberty to converse with any person except in the presence of the jailer during the pleasure of Congress and the Committee." James Brooks received an identical sentence to the Lancaster jail.[44] At least one Philadelphian felt that the imprisonment of Brooks and Kearsley was actually for their own benefit, "as the only expedient that could save their lives from the exasperated people."[45] Leonard

Snowden, who "did not appear to be deep in the plot,"[46] was sentenced to one month in the Philadelphia jail with a five-hundred-pound bond for good behavior due at the time of his release. Christopher Carter received the lightest sentence, being obligated to provide a five-hundred-pound good-behavior bond and not to depart Philadelphia without leave from the Congress and the Committee.[47]

Everything about their trial and sentence suggested that the men had committed a serious offense. Newspapers across America reported that the men had been sentenced for "high crimes against this country."[48] The only surviving documents that precisely describe their offense concern James Brooks. He was charged with "practicing and endeavouring to procure this province to be invaded in a hostile manner by British forces."[49] After the trial, the Pennsylvania Committee of Safety entrusted Brooks to the Lancaster committee, stating that Brooks had "been convicted of holding a traiterous correspondence with some of the British ministry, and of having communicated intelligence that has a tendency to exasperate them against the Americans and provoke them to an invasion of this colony."[50] The notice described Kearsley as convicted of "similar offenses."[51] Kearsley and Brooks, in short, were traitors. For the first time, a governmental entity in Pennsylvania had labeled correspondence with the British as a form of treason. When Brooks escaped from prison in 1777, Pennsylvania officials stated that he had been convicted of "high treason."[52]

The invocation of "treason" in an official context marks a significant turning point. These men had not betrayed their king; if anything, they were behaving as loyal subjects should. That same month, John Adams had argued for the establishment of new governments in America, since "it could not well be considered as a crime to communicate intelligence, or to act as spies or guides to the enemy, without assuming all the powers of government."[53] Yet that was precisely what Pennsylvania had done. To imprison these men for treason—a breach of allegiance—suggests that the locus of allegiance had fundamentally shifted, well before the adoption of the Declaration of Independence. Kearsley and Brooks had betrayed the "liberties of America," "this province," "the Americans," and "their country." The Pennsylvania Assembly confirmed this idea, adopting militia regulations stating that any person who refused to march would be "held to the public as a coward and a betrayer of his country."[54]

The shift in allegiance was exemplified by the actions of two Philadelphia fraternal societies. Christopher Carter was a member of the Society of Englishmen and Sons of Englishmen, established "for the Advice and Assistance of Englishmen in Distress."[55] Yet the Society did not come to Carter's assistance when he appeared before the Pennsylvania Committee. Instead, the Society "unanimously expelled" Carter for being "inimical to the Liberties of America."[56] Similarly, Dr. Kearsley was unanimously expelled from the St. George's Society for having "shewn himself inimical to the liberties of this country, and thereby rendered himself unworthy of being a member of this Society."[57]

Pennsylvania delegate John Dickinson subsequently presented the cases of Kearsley and Brooks to the Continental Congress. The Congress "declined making any particular order respecting them" and referred Dickinson to their prior resolution concerning the detention of dangerous persons. The Pennsylvania Committee of Safety accordingly concluded that it was the sense of the Congress that Kearsley and Brooks "should be closely confined."[58] Later that year, George Washington expressed his approval of such detentions, asking, "Would it not be prudence to seize on those Tories who have been, are, and that are known will be active against us? Why should persons who are preying upon the vitals of their country be suffered to stalk at large, whilst we know they will do us every mischief in their power?"[59]

The Second Round of Treason Charges

Pennsylvania's second major treason case prior to the Declaration of Independence involved John Connolly, who had made himself deeply unpopular in Pennsylvania while serving as Lord Dunmore's agent in the western border dispute with Virginia.[60] In July 1775, Connolly began serving as a courtier between Lord Dunmore and General Thomas Gage, the British commander. Connolly presented Gage with proposals for raising a colonial army in the backcountry and in Canada to support the British, and he accepted a commission as commandant of this proposed regiment.[61] By October 1775, the Continental Congress had learned many of the details of Connolly's plot and it warned the state committees of safety to be on the alert.[62] Connolly was eventually captured by a committee of safety in Frederick, Maryland, in November 1775 along with two associates, Alan Cameron and John Smyth. The committee, with future Supreme Court Justice Samuel Chase presiding, discovered Connolly's proposals and other letters of the same tenor, detained the three men, and notified the Continental Congress.[63]

The Continental Congress ordered the men brought to Philadelphia, "to be confined in prison in Philadelphia until the further order of Congress, at the continental expence."[64] In early 1776, the Congress recommended that the Pennsylvania Committee of Safety "carry into execution the resolution of Congress for confining said Connolly, and his associates, in the gaol of Philadelphia, and that they take their examinations."[65] The Pennsylvania Committee viewed the men as "persons inimical to the liberties of America" and in their commitment order stated that Connolly and Cameron were charged "with treasonable practices against America."[66] A few weeks later, Connolly's third associate, John Smyth, who had managed to escape from captivity in Frederick, was similarly detained by the Pennsylvania Committee for "practices inimical to the liberties of America."[67]

Perhaps motivated by Connolly's arrest, the Continental Congress expressed its concern about "unworthy Americans" who "regardless of their duty to . . . their country and their posterity, have taken part with our oppressors" and opposed "the friends of American liberty." The Congress recommended that the various conventions and committees of safety in the "United Colonies" disarm such men and, reiterating its earlier resolution, that the more dangerous be either "kept in safe custody, or bound with sufficient sureties to their good behavior."[68]

Several weeks later, Connolly, Cameron, and Smyth appeared before the Pennsylvania Committee. Surviving records reveal little about the format of these proceedings, so it is difficult to know the extent to which they approximated a criminal trial. Given that the committee conducted a large amount of other business on the days of the examinations, it is likely that the hearings were fairly cursory. Smyth appeared first and confessed to "acting an unfriendly part in the present dispute between Great Britain and these colonies."[69] The committee found that Connolly was a "person inimical to the Liberties and dangerous to the safety of these Colonies"[70] and that Cameron "had acted an inimical part in the present dispute between Great Britain and these colonies."[71] The committee ordered all three men detained "until discharged by this Board or the orders of the Continental Congress."[72] Whether the men were prisoners of the Continental Congress or of Pennsylvania would become a divisive issue in subsequent years.[73]

In the end, all three men managed to return to the British side. Smyth escaped from captivity in Baltimore in 1778 and joined the Queen's Rangers. In 1784, he published a two-volume description of the United States of America, in which he complained of the "barbarous treatment practiced by [the Americans] upon those unhappy persons who have had the misfortune of falling into their hands."[74] Cameron, suffering from bad health, was released in the winter of 1778 as part of a prisoner exchange and made his way to England.[75] Connolly made repeated attempts to be treated as a prisoner of war. In November 1778, the Congress forcefully rejected this claim, concluding that Connolly "cannot of right claim to be considered and treated as a prisoner of war, but that he was, at the time he was apprehended, and still is, amenable to law martial as a spy and emissary from the British army."[76] Connolly found this conclusion preposterous, arguing, "I was the King's commissioned officer, taken in the execution of my duty, to a sovereign, at that time, acknowledged by themselves. America was not a separate state; no independency was declared; no penal laws promulgated. Neither was there anything to spy."[77] Smyth, too, complained to Congress, noting the blatant inconsistency of treating Cameron, but not Connolly, as a prisoner of war.[78] Finally, in 1780, Congress relented and Connolly was sent to New York as part of a prisoner exchange. He rejoined the king's army and was captured again at Yorktown. Released on parole, he made his way to Philadelphia, where he was imprisoned for over two months, but the state government eventually permitted him to go to New York, where he sailed to England.[79]

What is perhaps most remarkable, however, is the labeling of Connolly and Cameron as traitors against America. The implicit assumption is that these men, like Kearsley and his associates, owed allegiance, not to Great Britain or to the king, or even to Pennsylvania, but to something larger. They owed allegiance to America. The concepts of American citizenship and of American nationhood were not simply byproducts of the Declaration of Independence; they existed well before that document was ever signed. As the Pennsylvania Assembly concluded in late 1775, "All national distinctions in dress or name" should be avoided in the militia, since "we should now be united . . . under the sole Denomination of *Americans*."[80] Conceptually, the locus of allegiance had shifted long before the formal mechanisms of the law could catch up. Imprisoning individuals for treason is one of the defining hallmarks of a sovereign government. By taking these significant steps, Pennsylvania recognized its functional independence from the British crown.[81]

County Committees of Safety

County committees of safety, for their part, also investigated cases of suspected disloyalty. Most of these cases involved utterances hostile to resistance activity and did not generally result in imprisonment. Rather, the committees either demanded recantation or imposed various forms of social ostracism. Few counties went as far as the Northampton County Committee, which resolved in May 1775 that any townships that refused to participate in the militia shall be considered as "Enemies to the County and all dealing and commerce whatsoever be forborn with them."[82] Denouncing a township as an "enemy to the county" was unusual, to say the least. Nonetheless, the committee's resolution captures the importance of social ostracism to the resistance movement. In many ways, the committees' actions paralleled the earlier efforts to label violators of the non-importation agreements as "enemies to their country." This labeling, however, took on increased significance before the committees of safety, which held a quasi-official status, and which did not hesitate to issue rudimentary search warrants when necessary. The county committee records prior to mid-1776 are incomplete and somewhat cursory, so we do not know as much about the conduct of these cases as we would like. Although the accused did not enjoy the full protection the law traditionally offered in a criminal court, it does seem that there was at least some attempt at fairness.[83] The Cumberland County Committee, for example, examined "sundry witnesses . . . upon oath" before concluding that John Clark, a miller, was "an enemy to the rights and liberties of the United Colonies."[84] Similarly, the Lancaster County Committee heard the evidence of six witnesses on a charge of "Toryism" against James Sullivan.[85] A committee in Hamilton Bann Township in York County found "on solemn oath" based on "two sufficient evidences," that Alexander McMillen had made expressions "inimicable to the cause of American Liberty."[86]

County cases were initiated much earlier than cases before the state committee. The war was only a few months old when William Moore, a prominent citizen of Chester County, was brought before the county committee of safety in June 1775 on the charge of expressing "himself in terms inimical to the liberties of America, and derogatory to the Continental Congress."[87] Three witnesses had given depositions of Moore's alleged remarks, and someone arranged for these depositions to be printed and distributed as a handbill. The depositions themselves acknowledged the king's authority, as they began, "Personally appeared before me Isaac Davis, one of his Majesty's Justices." According to the witnesses, Moore had said that members of the Continental Congress were "fools and damned rascals," that the people of Boston were a "vile set of rebels," and that everyone who mustered as part of the militia should be committed to prison.[88] A few weeks later, Moore apologized to the committee "for any unguarded expression . . . that may have dropped from me." Moore prayed that American "liberties may be preserved to the latest times" and noted that he was an "old man" who "could not possibly entertain a thought but what is friendly to America."[89]

Similar cases arose in Bucks County. In July 1775, Benjamin Hare reported to the Bucks County Committee that John Hoff "had uttered expressions derogatory and injurious to the American Cause" and that Thomas Meredith had "uttered expressions inimical to the Cause and Liberties of America in general and especially of the inhabitants of the town of Boston."[90] Both Hoff and Meredith quickly retracted their statements. The case of Thomas Smith, also brought before the committee that day, was more troublesome. According to "incontestable evidence," it had been proved that Smith had uttered the following:

> That the measures of Congress had already enslaved America and done more damage than all the acts the Parliament ever intended to lay upon us, that the whole thing was nothing but a scheme of a parcel of hot-headed Presbyterians and that he believed the devil was at the bottom of the whole; that the taking up arms was the most scandalous thing a man could be guilty of, and more heinous than an hundred of the grossest offenses against the moral law.[91]

On August 21, the committee resolved that Smith's "virulent and indecent invectives" should be punished by declaring him an "Enemy to the Rights of British America, and that all persons break off every kind of dealing with him until he shall make proper satisfaction to this committee for his misconduct." While this order was being prepared for publication, Smith expressed his remorse, and the order of publication was canceled.[92]

The bitterness and divisiveness engendered by the resistance movement were vividly displayed in two cases from Northampton County. In the first case, Michael Ohl, a former committee member himself, was charged in January 1776 with "uttering disrespectful words against the Honorable Congress and Assembly." Jacob Grenewalt testified that Ohl had a militia book and had claimed that anyone could have it, "for he was sure that nobody would sign it—and that he would shit in such a book." Grenewalt and other witnesses alleged that Ohl's words had dramatically reduced militia membership in his township. After "hearing the evidences on both sides," the committee determined that Ohl was "highly culpable and blamable in opposing himself to the utmost of his power against the salutary measures of the honorable House of Assembly for associating ourselves together in defence of the sacred liberties of America." The committee ordered Ohl to sign a recantation, or he would be "published in the public newspapers," both English and German, "as an enemy to the common cause of America." Ohl promptly signed the recantation.[93] The second case, that of Joseph and John Romig, was initially even more difficult. The two brothers had disobeyed a summons to appear before the committee, remarking that they "shit upon it" and would come when they pleased; if not, they would stay at home. The committee sent a group of men to the Romig home to force them to appear. Although the brothers initially greeted the men with arms, they were eventually persuaded to appear before the committee, where their case was resolved in the same manner as Ohl's.[94]

In the months prior to independence, verbal offenses continued to attract the most attention at the county level. In Chester County, Abel Green apologized for expressing "himself in terms inimical to America, and against the measures adopted for the protection of the liberties of these Colonies."[95] In Berks County, Nicholas Hermany apologized for discouraging taking up arms against Great Britain and promised to "support the present opposition . . . against all the enemies of America."[96] But the committees also began imposing the more significant sanction of imprisonment, albeit with some reservations. The Cumberland Committee imprisoned several men in April 1776 as "enemies to the American Cause." The committee had acted on a warning from the Continental Congress about the men, but remained unsure what do with them and requested advice from the Pennsylvania Committee as to whether the men should remain in custody.[97]

Similarly, a Berks County man was imprisoned by his county committee in June 1776 for abusing the persons collecting arms from non-associators.[98]

No formal record survives of a county committee imposing the punishment of tarring and feathering, but claims later filed before the Loyalist Claims Commission alleged that this punishment did occur. William Caldwell, for example, testified that he was tried before a committee at Reading on June 14, 1775 for declaring "his sentiments in favor of the British government at several town meetings in Union Township." The committee then imposed a sentence of tarring and feathering, which was promptly carried out.[99] Although this event could certainly have happened, I have found no independent confirmation of it. Since the claim was submitted after the war to secure benefits from the British government, Caldwell had strong incentives to exaggerate his mistreatment.

The committees demanded the loyalty of all Pennsylvanians to the cause of American liberty. Charles Willson Peale confidently predicted in August 1775 that very few Tories would be left in Philadelphia, since "it is almost a settled point that those who do not enter the fight with us is against us."[100] Committee charges came in a variety of heads, but they all revolved around the theme of being "inimical to the Liberties of America." It is a striking phrase. Nowhere in the records do we hear anything about enmity to the state of Pennsylvania, or to the government of Pennsylvania. Rather, as we shall see throughout the revolutionary period in Pennsylvania, the ideological expression was almost entirely national. Thomas Meredith had spoken ill of Bostonians; accordingly, he was inimical to the "cause and liberties of America." At times, the demands of loyalty were taken to extremes. In October 1775, for example, a Philadelphia newspaper denounced British general Thomas Gage as a "grand rebel to his god, his country, and his king." It similarly described former Massachusetts governor Thomas Hutchinson as the "arch American traitor."[101]

The opponents of revolutionary activities complained, almost entirely in private, about aggressive committee actions. After the carting of Dr. Kearsley, Miers Fisher observed, "The Sons of Liberty have by such means eradicated almost every Tory principle, the boldest of them not now daring to speak their sentiments publicly, so that there is apparently the greatest unanimity in America that was ever known in any country."[102] In a letter to his brother, Quaker historian Robert Proud noted,

> Things being arrived to such a state here, that if a person is suspected even to think different from the common belief and popular cry, he is in danger, threatened, abused and looked upon as an enemy to his country . . . If [they do not recant], they are grossly abused and put in great danger of their lives, condemned in the public papers as enemies to their country, with

> their names at length, in a form like that of a popish excommunication, forbidding thenceforward all people trading, dealing or bartering with them, this is done by sets of men called Committeemen in every district, generally composed of the hottest and most zealous that can be found, and what is more the populace, in order to put these conclusions in the most rigid execution, are worked up almost everywhere into an amazing degree of madness![103]

Proud complained that phrases such as the "liberties of the people" and "inimical to the rights of mankind" were some of the "cant, or trite terms and phrases of these times," fine language used to "cover the foulest deeds."[104] A group of Bucks County men complained in December 1775 that Kearsley and his associates were "imprisoned contrary to the known laws of this province" and threatened to break them from prison by armed force.[105]

Denunciation of Enemies

In the months prior to independence, the term "enemy to his country" increasingly took on a wider meaning, as more and more people found themselves denounced as enemies. The Pennsylvania Committee of Safety resolved in September 1775 that any pilot aiding British ships would be "deemed an enemy to American Liberty, a Traitor to his Country and as such published & held forth to the public."[106] Later that fall, the Pennsylvania Assembly adopted a militia rule stating that any member who refused "to appear and march with his arms, ammunition and accoutrements . . . shall be held up to the public as a coward and a betrayer of his country."[107] In January 1776, the Continental Congress authorized local committees to try persons who refused to accept the continental currency. A convicted person was to be "deemed, published and treated as an enemy to this country, and precluded from all trade or intercourse with the inhabitants of these colonies."[108] The Philadelphia committee, for example, held up "to the world . . . BENJAMIN SHARPLESS as an ENEMY to his country."[109] The Pennsylvania Committee went even further with respect to three Quaker merchants, placing their stores and warehouses under lock and key.[110] Public ostracism of this sort had a considerable effect. Joseph Shippen, for example, warned of the "danger of having the least dealing with those persons who have been publicly advertized as enemies to America."[111] The Berks County Committee went so far as to imprison a man in January 1776 for speaking disrespectfully of the Continental Congress and attempting to depreciate the currency. After apologizing, however, he was released.[112]

"Enemies" were also subject to disarmament. Expanding on an earlier resolution, the Continental Congress recommended on March 14, 1776 that the "several assemblies, conventions, and councils or committees of safety of the United Colonies" immediately disarm all persons "who are notoriously disaffected to the cause of America, or who have not associated, and shall refuse to defend, by arms, these United Colonies, against the hostile attempts of the British fleets and armies."[113] The Pennsylvania Assembly issued implementing orders a few weeks later.[114]

The final blow against the persons advertised as enemies came when Pennsylvania deprived them of the right to vote. On May 10, 1776, the Continental Congress approved John Adams's resolution calling for the formation of new state governments. In June 1776, a provincial conference of committees met in Philadelphia and called for elections to a state constitutional convention. Although this meeting arguably had "no legal foundation nor any basis at law," it successfully organized Pennsylvania's constitutional convention.[115] The conference imposed two significant restrictions on the right to vote for delegates to the convention. First, every voter was required to take an oath renouncing allegiance to George III. Second, no person who had been "published by any committee of inspection, or the committee of safety, in this province, as an enemy to the liberties of America, and has not been restored to the favor of his country" would be permitted to vote.[116]

The Continental Congress took some steps to limit hostile actions against persons suspected of being enemies, resolving on June 18, 1776 that "no man in these colonies, charged with being a tory, or unfriendly to the cause of American liberty, be injured in his person or property, or in any manner whatever disturbed, unless the proceeding against him be founded on an order of this Congress, or the Assembly, convention, council or committee of safety of the colony, or committee of inspection and observation, of the district wherein he resides."[117]

At the same time, thoughtful Pennsylvanians worried about the legal justifications for many of the committee actions. As one man pointed out, the "habeas corpus act and trial by jury . . . were sometime since expelled the country in all cases which respect our opposition to British tyranny."[118] The improvisatory committee structures, however, allowed "the enemies to this country [to] escape the punishment they deserve" and "a man to be a traitor without punishing him for treason."[119] Another writer pointed out one of the benefits of a declaration of independence: it would deliver the colonies from "the disorders which arise from the unlimited, undescribed, and sometimes arbitrary powers of conventions, committees of safety, and committees of inspection."[120] In a later edition of *Common Sense*, Thomas Paine complained, "Nothing is criminal; there is no such thing as treason." A "line of distinction," Paine argued, "should be drawn between English soldiers taken in battle, and inhabitants of America taken in arms. The first are prisoners, but the latter traitors. The one forfeits his liberty, the other his head."[121]

It appears that no person filed a writ a habeas corpus in a Pennsylvania court to challenge the legality of his detention by a committee of safety.[122] Several reasons may explain this failure. In some places, the courts may not have been open. In August 1775, Lancaster attorney Jasper Yeates noted, "The general opinion is that the Courts will be shut up by the middle of next month. Indeed they are nearly such already."[123] Moreover, the legality of the detentions in the unusual legal climate presented an exceptionally difficult question. Opponents of the war could not be legally tried for treason, but permitting them to operate with impunity was not plausible either. A court might therefore conclude that preventive detentions authorized by the Continental Congress were legal. But even judges inclined to issue a writ may have hesitated, since the committees of safety may have simply ignored any writ from a court.

The British Legal Response to the Rebels

For their part, the British were confronted with the problem of the treatment of American prisoners. Americans captured in arms were subject to prosecution for the crime of treason by levying war against their king.[124] British officers in North America took this approach in late 1775 with Ethan Allen, captured in a failed raid on Montreal. After being detained as a common criminal, Allen was sent to England for trial. His arrival was not especially welcome, as it forced British officials to squarely address the legality of his detention.[125] Under the British view, the Habeas Corpus Act (which authorized legal challenges to detentions) did not apply in the colonies, meaning Allen could be indefinitely detained there with no resolution of his status. But the Act applied fully in England. If Allen brought a habeas corpus petition, the government would be forced either to release him or charge him with treason.[126]

Trying and executing Allen as a traitor, although legally unexceptionable, presented intractable practical problems for the British war effort. If the British were to execute American soldiers as traitors, the Americans would almost certainly retaliate by executing British prisoners held in American custody. In an August 1775 letter to General Gage, George Washington had emphasized that he would treat British prisoners in exactly the same way that American prisoners were treated.[127] In a series of high-level meetings in late 1775 and early 1776, British officials recognized the inevitable: execution of Allen would provoke tit-for-tat retaliation by American forces against British prisoners, a policy explicitly confirmed by the Continental Congress in its December 6, 1775 response to the king's declaration of rebellion.[128] Accordingly, Allen was returned to North America to be treated as a de facto prisoner of war, as would all subsequent American prisoners captured by the British.[129]

This policy was confirmed by a 1777 act of Parliament that eliminated bail, habeas corpus, and trials for any person who committed high treason in the American colonies or on the high seas. The statute required such persons to be imprisoned and released only with the approval of the Privy Council. Originally set to expire on January 1, 1778, the statute was renewed annually until 1783. Although the act was criticized by ministerial critics such as Edmund Burke, the practical effect of the act was to treat American prisoners essentially as prisoners of war. Nothing in the act, however, prevented the subsequent trial of American prisoners for treason in the event that Britain prevailed, and Americans detained in Britain, most notably Henry Laurens, were committed on warrants under the charge of high treason. But American victory ensured that none of those cases would ever go to trial. In the end, no American was ever tried for treason against Britain during the American Revolution. The only treason trials were those of Americans charged with betraying America.[130]

Independence

By May 1776, the movement for independence was gathering strength. A writer in a Philadelphia newspaper argued for "proclaiming [George III] a traitor and dissolving our allegiance to him." Indeed, failure to do so might itself be treason: "Is it not treason to the British constitution to maintain any longer the least shadow of his power amongst us?"[131] Another Pennsylvanian noted that the British ministry had committed "treason against the Constitution, which we Americans look upon as the first and most dangerous species of rebellion."[132] John Adams worried about a "chain of Toryism" extending from Canada to Pennsylvania that might "have for its object, treasons and conspiracies of the deeper die."[133]

Surprisingly, the fundamental shift in the definition of allegiance did not occur on July 4, 1776, with the adoption of the Declaration of Independence. Rather, it occurred ten days earlier on June 24, 1776, when the Continental Congress issued a major resolution with respect to treason. The Congress began by effectively abolishing allegiance to the British crown and transferring it to the colonies: "all persons abiding within any of the United Colonies, and deriving protection from the same, owe allegiance to the said laws, and are members of such colony." The English doctrine of temporary allegiance was explicitly retained: "all persons passing through, visiting, or making a temporary stay in any of the said colonies, being entitled to the protection of the laws during the time of such passage, visitation or temporary stay, owe during the same time, allegiance thereto." Congress then concluded that any such person owing allegiance "to any of the United Colonies . . . who shall levy war against any of the said colonies within the same, or be adherent to the King of Great Britain, or others the enemies of the said colonies or any of them, within the same, giving to him or them aid and comfort, are guilty of treason against such colony." In so doing, Congress recognized two strands of English treason law: the offense of levying war and the offense of adhering to enemies, the two offenses that would ultimately be included in the Treason Clause of the United States Constitution. Finally, Congress recommended that "the legislatures of the several United Colonies . . . pass laws for punishing such persons before described, as shall be proveably attainted of open deed, by people of their own condition, of any of the treasons before described." With this recommendation, Congress suggested two more elements of English treason law—the requirement of proof by an overt act and the requirement of a trial by a jury of one's peers, the issue that had triggered so much consternation with respect to the statute of 35 Henry VIII.[134]

That same day, the Pennsylvania Provincial Conference of Committees, the body that had called for the constitutional convention, formally declared that the "obligations of allegiance (being reciprocal between the King and his subjects) are now dissolved on the side of the colonists by the despotism and declaration of the said King, insomuch that it now appears that loyalty to him is treason against the good people of this country." The Conference accordingly declared its willingness "to concur in a vote of the Congress declaring the United Colonies Free and Independent States."[135]

A significant benefit of a Declaration of Independence was the legitimization of treason prosecutions. So long as the colonies were formally loyal to the British crown, active adherents to Britain might be detained, but they could not suffer capital punishment for treason. As a Massachusetts man put it, "No one thing made the Declaration of Independence indispensably necessary more than cutting off traitors. It is amazingly wonderful that, having no capital punishment for our intestine enemies, we have not been utterly ruined before now. . . . Our Tories . . . knew very well the absurdity of punishing as high treason any acts or deeds in favor of the government of the King of Great Britain, so long as we all allowed him to be King of the Colonies."[136] In April 1776, a Pennsylvanian had justified "a declaration of the independence of the American Colonies" by noting that "a criminal correspondence with the enemies of this country will be prevented, or punished under the article of high treason."[137] John Adams predicted that new treason laws would "make Whigs by the thousands."[138] "Republicus" put it more bluntly: "Upon the whole, we may be benefited by independence, but we cannot be hurt by it, and every man that is against it is a traitor."[139]

The formal announcement of American independence on July 4, 1776 was in some sense a formality—a declaration of preexisting fact.[140] By the time of the Declaration, committees of safety had been examining and jailing people for treason, the ultimate act of a sovereign government, for over eight months. As resistance matured into revolution, the notion of treason against America and against the liberties of America matured along with it. A few blocks away from the State House, where the Continental Congress approved the Declaration of Independence, was the Philadelphia jail, filled with people imprisoned for being inimical to the rights and liberties of America or for committing treason against America.[141] The idea that treason could be committed against America did not originate with the Declaration. Rather, the Declaration permitted Americans to punish treason in a legally proper manner: through statutory definition and jury trial. Moreover, traitors to America now risked not only indefinite detention, but also the very real risk of execution. As Thomas Paine put it, "The transition from Toryism to treason is nearly effected, and the rude custom of tarring and feathering will soon give way to the severer punishment of the gibbet."[142] A civil war already drenched in blood had the potential to become even bloodier.

4

From Independence to Invasion, 1776–1778

WHEN CHIEF JUSTICE Benjamin Chew responded to the grand juror's query about treason and resistance in April 1776, he knew that the war might eventually come to Pennsylvania. He could not have imagined, however, just how close that war would come. On October 4, 1777, the Battle of Germantown erupted on the grounds of Chew's country estate, bringing the war to his own doorstep and even into his own bedroom. Chew was justly proud of his mansion house, which he called Cliveden; its ornate interiors and large law library made it one of the most elegant private homes in North America (Figure 4.1). But Cliveden was no longer a peaceful retreat from the larger world. The house now resounded with the stomps of soldiers' boots—British soldiers, from occupied Philadelphia, who would tenaciously hold the house against a ferocious attack by George Washington's troops.

Everything, it seemed, had turned upside down. The State House where Chew had presided over his courtroom and where the Continental Congress had declared independence was now in enemy hands and serving as a detention center for American prisoners of war.[1] Pennsylvania was invaded, the capital city had fallen, and the state and continental governments had fled. Across the state, courtroom doors remained closed. Chew himself never heard the guns of Germantown; he had been hustled off to detention in New Jersey without any form of a trial. Dozens of other Pennsylvanians were similarly detained, and fears of secret Tory conspiracies were rampant.

The Battle of Germantown was the capstone of a long chaotic interregnum in which government, for many purposes, ceased to exist. James Allen noted that since the courts had closed, "we have continued without justice, in a state of nature."[2] Another Pennsylvanian warned James Wilson that in York, "there are no Justices—no Law—every one seems to do what he listeth."[3] The functions

FIGURE 4.1 Cliveden, home of former Pennsylvania Chief Justice Benjamin Chew and site of the 1777 Battle of Germantown.
Credit: Shutterstock.

of courts were variously assumed by county committees, by mob action, by the military, and by the Council of Safety, the successor to the Committee of Safety. This disarray coincided with a pervasive and heightened fear of potential treason, creating a situation in which Pennsylvania's leaders knew that disloyalty must be addressed, but the mechanisms for prevention, detection, and punishment were woefully underdeveloped. A regularly constituted court with jurisdiction over treason cases would not sit until April 1778. In the tumultuous months between independence and the reopening of the courts, Pennsylvania adopted a new constitution, enacted legislation against treason, continued to use the committee system for preventative detentions, exiled prominent Philadelphians without a trial, and suspended the writ of habeas corpus.

The Pennsylvania Constitutional Convention and the Treason Ordinance

Pennsylvania's leaders moved promptly to replace the old proprietary government. Elections for the constitutional convention were held on July 8, 1776, and proceedings began one week later at the State House. The convention unanimously selected Benjamin Franklin as its president, but he had little active involvement in its affairs.[4] Although arguably limited to drafting a constitution, the convention, urged on by the Continental Congress, quickly assumed various legislative tasks. On July 23, the convention created a "Council of Safety," which would exercise the state's executive authority until a new government was formed. This Council of Safety essentially continued the functions of the old Committee of Safety.

A key legislative task was the drafting of a treason ordinance, which the convention approved on September 5, 1776.[5] This ordinance drew heavily on the congressional resolution of June 24, 1776. It began by defining the scope of allegiance, asserting that all persons residing in Pennsylvania (other than prisoners of war), and all persons voluntarily coming into the state hereafter, owed allegiance to the state. The exclusion of prisoners of war from the scope of allegiance was consistent with the longstanding English legal principle that enemy soldiers were not subject to domestic treason law. What was slightly less clear was the status of British soldiers who were not prisoners of war. Presumably such persons did not "reside" in Pennsylvania for legal purposes, even if part of a long-standing enemy camp. In other respects, however, the ordinance deviated significantly from English law. A person born into allegiance to the British monarch owed a lifelong duty of allegiance to the crown, wherever he might go.[6] The Pennsylvania ordinance, by contrast, did not impose permanent allegiance based on birth; a person born in Pennsylvania could seemingly renounce his allegiance by simply leaving the state permanently.

With respect to the substance of treason, the ordinance borrowed language from 25 Edward III. Any person owing allegiance to Pennsylvania who should "levy war against this State, or be adherent to the King of Great Britain, or others the enemies of this State, or to the enemies of the United States of America, by giving him or them aid or assistance within the limits of this State, or elsewhere" would be guilty of high treason. Trials were required to be held in courts of oyer and terminer "hereafter to be erected," thus implicitly requiring a jury trial. An initial draft of the ordinance published in the *Pennsylvania Gazette* imposed the death penalty on a convicted traitor and the forfeiture of one-half of his estates.[7] The final version, however, eliminated the death penalty and instead required that a convicted traitor would be imprisoned for "any term not exceeding the duration of the present war with Great Britain, at the discretion of the Judge or Judges." The forfeiture, on the other hand, was increased to the traitor's entire estate, with the proviso that the judge could make "provision for the wife or children" of the traitor from the estate.

The separate offense of misprision of treason was defined as concealing a treasonous act or as receiving or assisting a traitor. Those found guilty would be imprisoned for no longer than the present war and would forfeit one-third of their estates. The ordinance did not specify what courts would have jurisdiction of this offense. The final version of the ordinance also added a sunset clause, stating that the ordinance would expire at the end of the first session of the first assembly under the new constitution.

Although a forceful statement of treason law, the ordinance was ultimately a dead letter. The convention's legal authority over statutory matters was doubtful. By its own terms, the convention "ordained and declared"; it did not "enact." These concerns almost certainly explain the reluctance to impose capital punishment. No indictments were ever brought under the treason ordinance and it was superseded by statute in February 1777.

A week after enacting the treason ordinance, the convention adopted another provision aimed at disloyalty. Entitled an ordinance for "punishing persons guilty of certain offenses therein mentioned against the United States of America," it provided for the punishment of any person who spoke or wrote against "the measures carrying on by the United States of America for the defense and support of the freedom and independence of said states." Justices of the peace were empowered to order such persons to provide good behavior bonds, but if a justice found the offender "too dangerous, unfriendly, or inimical to the American cause," he, with the assent of two other justices, could order the person imprisoned "for such time as they shall deem proper not exceeding the duration of the present war with Great Britain." An aggrieved person could file an appeal with the council of safety, which was directed to resolve such appeals "without delay."[8] This ordinance provoked a swift denunciation from a surprising quarter—the moribund Pennsylvania Assembly. On the last day that it sat, the Assembly resolved that the ordinance empowering justices of the peace "to imprison, for an indefinite Time, at their Discretion, all Persons whom they shall judge to be guilty" is a "dangerous Attack on the Liberties of the good People of Pennsylvania, and . . . a Violation of their most sacred Rights." Accordingly, the ordinance "ought not to be considered as obligatory."[9]

In late September 1776, the convention completed its primary task, promulgating the Revolution's most radical and democratic state constitution, a controversial document that would generate conflict and turmoil for the next fourteen years. The constitution created a unicameral legislature, eliminated property qualifications for voting and office holding, and vested the state's executive authority in a multi-member Supreme Executive Council, headed by a President. Assembly elections were held in November 1776, but because of quorum problems, the body passed no legislation until January 21, 1777. The Supreme Executive Council did not convene until March 4, 1777.

The Council of Safety and the County Committees

During this period, the investigation and detention of potentially disloyal persons continued largely as it had since the outbreak of the war. The provisional Council of Safety heard cases at the state level, as did the county committees at the local level. There were also occasional ad hoc private actions taken by groups of varying levels of organization and legitimacy. In none of these proceedings did the accused enjoy the privilege of a jury trial.

The Council of Safety, like its predecessor the Committee of Safety, focused on cases of overt disloyalty and regularly sentenced defendants to imprisonment. In August 1776, for example, the Council issued an arrest warrant for John Hatton and his son, accused of "Treasonable Practices against the states of America." Since the Hattons were in New Jersey, the Council wrote to a New Jersey committee of safety to request its assistance "in securing two Men who are enemies to our Country."[10] The elder Hatton was quickly arrested and brought to Philadelphia, where the Council ordered him imprisoned for "practices inimical to the States of America."[11] Similarly, in late 1776, the Council jailed Alexander Maurice for "being inimical to the American states;"[12] William Sutton for "being an Enemy to the Rights and Liberties of America;"[13] John Biles for "Treason against the United States of America,"[14] and seven men for being "Enemies to the United States."[15] The Council also continued to monitor the imprisonment of persons detained prior to independence, such as John Kearsley, whom the Council viewed as a "dangerous Enemy to the American States."[16]

Although Pennsylvanians formally owed allegiance only to their state, the Council's rhetoric in these cases was sharply nationalistic. Treason necessarily implies a breach of allegiance, yet no one was singled out for offenses solely against Pennsylvania; in every case, the offense was described as against America, the United States of America, the American states, or "our country." In a very real sense, ideas of national citizenship and national loyalty were driving the Council's actions. Individuals took oaths before the Council that they "would not take up arms against the United States of America."[17] County cases displayed the same pattern. In Northumberland County, suspected opponents of the revolution swore oaths of loyalty, not to the state of Pennsylvania, but to the "United States of America."[18]

The Council played an active role in encouraging both the nascent federal government and the local committees to be attentive to the risks posed by disloyalty. In December 1776, the Council warned that persons who refused to provide assistance "at this time of eminent public danger, may justly be suspected of designs Inimical to the Freedom of America." Where such designs were "very apparent, . . . such persons ought to be confined during the absence of the militia."[19] The Council urged local committees to follow suit, asking the Chester Committee, for example, to deal with "a very extraordinary instance of Toryism."[20] The Council suggested that General Washington "seize and treat as enemies" all persons who obstructed the summoning of the militia in Bucks and Northampton Counties as well as "every person in those Counties who are known or suspected to be enemies to the United States."[21] It also resolved that Berks County militia members who refused to join General Washington's army should be seized and "sent under guard to Philadelphia."[22] Similarly, the Council warned the Continental Congress of plots developing outside of the state and urged the Congress to make "severe examples . . . of such traitors."[23]

Disputes over currency led to an increase in the Council's investigative and punitive duties. The Continental Congress had introduced a new currency, continental bills of credit, in 1775. The Council easily concluded that persons who refused to accept these bills were enemies to their country. On October 31, 1776, the Council heard the case of a cordwainer named John Baldwin, who told the Council that he refused to accept the currency. Baldwin was ordered imprisoned at the Council's pleasure and was publicly advertised as an "Enemy to his Country."[24] The Continental Congress, however, believed that more needed to be done. It requested that the Council of Safety take "vigorous and speedy measures" to deal with the widespread refusal of the currency. The Council responded with a sweeping resolution against the "disaffected and enemies to the United States of America." Any person who refused the currency would be deemed a "dangerous Member of Society" and would forfeit the goods or debt at issue. Hearings would be held in front of any three members of a county committee or any three field officers of the militia, subject to an appeal to the Council. For a second offense, the punishment was banishment from Pennsylvania, "to such place and in such manner, as this Council shall direct."[25] Banishment and forfeiture were significant punishments, especially in the absence of a jury trial, but accused persons may have found these punishments less burdensome than indefinite detention at the Council's pleasure.

Ad hoc meetings of private citizens also played a role in bringing cases to the attention of the Council. In November 1776, a group of seventy-three Philadelphians met at the Indian Queen Tavern to deal directly with persons suspected of disloyal behavior. The meeting was chaired by attorney Thomas McKean, a signer of the Declaration of Independence and the future chief justice of Pennsylvania. After concluding that there was insufficient evidence to accuse William Imlay before the Council as being an "Enemy to the liberties of America," the meeting turned to the case of Joseph Stansbury, suspected of having sung "God Save the King" with a number of other men at his house. The participants resolved to collect "the names of such persons who are suspected as Tories & unfriendly to the cause of America." At a later meeting at the Philosophical Society's Hall, the participants heard the cases of James Prescott, "suspected of being a Tory and an enemy to the United States of America," and Joel Arping, accused of drinking toasts and singing songs "to the injury of America." Isaac Atwood, Dr. Kearsley's old associate, appeared and provided testimony against his former comrades. Both Prescott and Arping were brought directly to the Council of Safety.[26]

Although the meeting notes do not reflect this, the participants somehow arranged for the imprisonment of Joseph Stansbury, who bitterly complained that the "God Save the King" allegations had been previously investigated by the Council and dismissed.[27] Stansbury petitioned the Council for his release, arguing that his detention was "in violation & defiance of the Bill of Rights" and urging them to "give a timely check to such arbitrary, unlawful, & unprecedented Proceedings."[28]

The Council responded by appointing six men to examine Stansbury's detention as well as several other cases. If it appeared to the six that the detainees were "guilty of any practices tending to alienate the minds of the people from the present Government of this State, or anything treasonable against the same," they were to confirm the commitments; otherwise, the detainees were to be released upon taking an oath of allegiance to the state.[29] This review was extended more generally a month later, when the Council appointed three of its members to "Visit the State Prisoners in the New Jail, enquire & understand the cause of their Commitment, how long they have been confined, & to release such as in their discretion they shall judge ought to be released."[30]

The Council also took a stand against mob actions, warning one county committee that "acts of violence have been offered to persons in your district upon very slender foundations of their being inimical to us & that even tender women have not been spared." "Every outrageous proceeding by Mobs," the Council admonished, "is disreputable and tends to destroy all order & good government."[31]

The county committees continued to hear cases similar to those prior to independence. But with some committees there was an increased sense of formality and legitimacy. The Northampton County Committee, for example, resolved to take upon itself "to keep the peace and call offenders to justice in the name of the State of Pennsylvania until it shall be otherwise ordered by the Convention or any other Superior Authority of this State."[32] The committee minutes bear striking resemblance to the form in which indictments were entered in criminal docket books, suggesting that the committee saw itself more and more as a regular court. For example, in February 1777, the committee heard the case of "The State of Pennsylvania vs. William Thomas & others," who were charged with "treasonable practices." The committee concluded that all eleven defendants were "guilty" and ordered them to pay their jail fees, sign a parole, and provide bail to secure their future good behavior.[33] In carrying out its work, the committee issued summonses to witnesses and took oral testimony.[34] It was not, however, especially receptive to criticism. The committee jailed Thomas Wigdon for "uttering false and opprobrious words against this Committee in general as being Tories and disaffected to the common cause of American liberty." Upon examination, Wigdon not only "justified the said indecent language but openly and publicly called the chairman a Scotch bugger." Wigdon was eventually released after asking pardon of the committee and paying jail fees.[35]

Imprisonment orders by county committees and officials increased significantly after the Declaration. Matthew McHugh, for example, was examined by a Lebanon justice of the peace on suspicion "of being inimical to the freedom of America." McHugh declared himself firmly against independence, and the justice ordered him imprisoned until "discharged by the Council of Safety or a Committee thereof."[36] Similarly, the Northampton Committee ordered the indefinite imprisonment of three men for "damning the Congress, Convention, & Committee, saying that they were all a parcel of Damned Rascals & were Selling the People's Liberties."[37] After the men acknowledged that they "were heartily sorry" for their conduct and promised "to behave better for the future," they were released upon payment of a bond.[38] Because of the proximity of the British army to Northampton County, the committee sent its prisoners to Reading, the seat of neighboring Berks County, where an official complained that the jail was beginning to overflow with "all the Tories that Northampton can find."[39] Some orders may have backfired. After being imprisoned and published as an "enemy to the liberties of America" by a county committee in November 1776, John Wilson found himself "rendered so obnoxious" that he fled to the British, where he became a lieutenant in the British army.[40]

The surviving county records provide little information about procedure. The fullest record comes from a December 1776 case in Northumberland County. The defendant, Robert Robb, was accused of discouraging participation in the militia and speaking against the Congress, against Benjamin Franklin, and against the constitutional convention. The committee appears not to have taken live evidence, instead reviewing the depositions of seven individuals, several of whom offered testimony favorable to Robb. Concluding that there were "just grounds . . . to suspect [Robb] of being not only unfriendly, but even inimical to our common cause," the committee ordered Robb to either "take his gun and march immediately with the militia of this county into actual service for the defence of the United States" or be confined "until released by further authority." Robb requested an appeal to the Council of Safety, which the committee permitted. Several days later, however, Robb attacked another man and accused the committee members of "horse-stealing, robbery, and murder." The committee sent Robb under guard to Philadelphia to the Council of Safety.[41] In a similar case a few months later, the committee concluded that Nicholas Pickard was "an enemy to the States," but it did not order imprisonment; rather, the committee sent Pickard to the Supreme Executive Council, "to be dealt with as their superior judgments shall direct them."[42]

Enactment of a Treason Statute

As the British army began moving closer to Philadelphia in late 1776, revolutionary leaders became convinced that the state was the target of secret enemies, of treasonous plots being hatched by sinister conspirators. No one fulminated more against potential traitors than Thomas Paine. In his *American Crisis* papers, which first appeared in December 1776, Paine asked, "Why is it that the enemy have left the New England provinces, and made these middle ones the seat of war? The answer is easy: New England is not infested with Tories, and we are."[43] The approach of Lord Howe's armies was actually a benefit, for "bringing forth traitors we were unwilling to suspect." Although convinced that a "traitor is the foulest fiend on earth," Paine also felt that "it is time to have done with tarring, feathering, carting, and taking securities for their future good behavior; every sensible man must feel a conscious shame at seeing a poor fellow hawked for a show about the streets, when it is known that he is only the tool of some principal villain."[44]

For some revolutionary leaders, Pennsylvania's seeming impotence demanded a decisive response. In January 1777, General John Cadwalader, a wealthy Philadelphian who had played a prominent role a few weeks earlier in Washington's crossing of the Delaware, prepared a blunt warning to the Council of Safety. Members of the army, Cadwalader claimed, "find cowards, disaffected men, and open enemies to the liberties of America are suffered to go abroad sowing sedition and dispersing their poison in every department without punishment or notice. If these evils are not remedied, instantly, we tremble for the consequences to the state of Pennsylvania and to all America." Cadwalader warned, "We wish to see the civil authority regulate and direct all our public measures and should greatly lament the necessity, which may compel the military power to take the direction into their hands, in order to save this country from absolute ruin—but you may depend that the military will exert its authority whenever the weakness, languor, or timidity of your councils shall render it their duty so to do, and all the world will justify them in it." Cadwalader recommended that militia members who did not immediately join Washington's army should be banished from the country and their estates seized.[45] Cadwalader's letter was signed by eight other militia officers.[46] That same month, Colonel John Armstrong became convinced that deputies from Lord Howe or "a secret junto of Tories" operating on his behalf in Philadelphia were laying the foundations for a Tory army and he recommended to the Council of Safety that ex post facto laws might be necessary to deal with such cases.[47]

The absence of both a treason statute and functioning courts was deeply felt. George Stevenson of Carlisle warned James Wilson that people who had not joined the militia were "undoubtedly secret enemies to the United States, they use every indirect means to injure the common cause, but are too cunning to say or do anything that will subject them to the censure of a committee; such men ought not to go unpunished." Stevenson recommended a "law to ascertain the various degrees of Tory crimes" and the erection of courts of justice "to try and convict them."[48]

The new Pennsylvania Assembly finally began legislating in early 1777. One of its first acts was to establish continuity of the laws. On January 28, 1777, the Assembly enacted legislation stating that all Pennsylvania laws in effect on May 14, 1776 would be in effect as of February 10, 1777. Specifically excluded from this revival was "so much of the statute laws of England . . . relating . . . to treason or misprision of treason."[49]

The legislature filled this gap two weeks later by enacting a statute defining the offense of high treason. The statute began with a definition of allegiance; the Assembly largely copied the earlier ordinance of the constitutional convention, imposing the duty of allegiance on all persons, other than prisoners of war, "inhabiting, residing or sojourning within the limits of the State of Pennsylvania."

With respect to the substance of high treason, however, the Assembly broke new ground. Whereas the ordinance had prohibited levying war against Pennsylvania or adhering to the king of Great Britain, the Assembly's statute was more specific. Seven acts would constitute high treason: (1) receiving a commission from the King of Great Britain or from other enemies of Pennsylvania or of the United States of America; (2) levying war against the state or its government; (3) aiding or assisting enemies at open war with the state by joining their armies, or persuading others to join their armies; (4) furnishing enemies with arms, ammunition, or other provisions for their aid or comfort; (5) carrying on a traitorous correspondence with the enemy; (6) forming any "combination, plot, or conspiracy" to betray the state or the United States of America to a foreign enemy; and (7) sending intelligence to the enemy.[50]

This statute deviated significantly from the statute of 25 Edward III. Only the "levying war" provision used the distinctive terminology of English law. There was no open-ended prohibition of "adhering to the enemy, giving them aid and comfort"; rather, specific acts of aiding the enemy were identified. Pennsylvanians thus arguably had greater notice of what acts constituted treason than they did under English law. The failure to clarify the phrase "levying war," however, left open the question of how closely that provision should track English law, a question that would arise repeatedly in the years ahead.

More importantly, the statute (as had the earlier ordinance) eliminated any provision analogous to the heart of 25 Edward III—the prohibition on "compassing or imagining the death of the king." Of course, there was no longer a king in Pennsylvania, or even a governor. But the Assembly might have considered an analogous provision, making it treason, for example, to kill a member of the Supreme Executive Council or the commander of the Continental Army. The Assembly's refusal to do so suggests the explicit "republicanization" of treason law. Although English treason law had shifted during the seventeenth century from the medieval conception of betrayal of a personal sovereign to betrayal of an impersonal state, Pennsylvania's statute, like those of other American states, made this distinction explicit. Treason thus no longer looked upward to a king, but in a sense looked downward, to the people who were the nominal foundation of republican government in Pennsylvania. Treason was not about betraying a particular individual, but about violating the ties that connected one to every other member of the political community.

The statute also displayed strong nationalistic tendencies. Although it is a state statute punishing violation of allegiance to the state of Pennsylvania, the statute deliberately invoked the interests of other states. Thus it repeatedly singled out assistance to the enemies of the state of Pennsylvania *or* "the United States of America." Helping the British raid New Jersey towns, for example, was treason, and a defendant could not escape culpability by arguing that he was only aiding the enemies of New Jersey. Pennsylvania citizens, although owing allegiance to Pennsylvania, also had a broader, national allegiance, one that prevented them from assisting the enemies of any of the other states. As Thomas Paine noted a few months later, "Every attempt, now, to support the authority of the king and Parliament of Great Britain over America, is treason against *every* State."[51] Only the levying-war provision, traditionally directed at internal uprisings, was limited to Pennsylvania.

The statute followed English law in requiring the testimony of two witnesses for conviction, but there was no explicit overt-act requirement.[52] Trials were to be held in courts of oyer and terminer, and the punishment was death, but the statute did not specify any particular mode of execution. As in English law, convicted traitors would forfeit their estate to the commonwealth, with a significant exception: judges could order a portion of the estate set aside for the benefit of the traitors' wives and children. These innocent victims would not suffer because of the misdeeds of a family member. Moreover, there was no provision mandating corruption of blood, the English doctrine that prevented a line of inheritance from passing through a convicted traitor.

With respect to conspiracy, the statute may have narrowed the law more than the Assembly actually intended. Under English law, conspiracy to commit treason was not treason, but a separate crime subject to lesser penalties, although courts had recognized conspiracy to levy war as a form of compassing the death of the king.[53] By eliminating the compassing clause and not specifically punishing conspiracy to levy war, Pennsylvania had arguably eliminated these conspiracies from the scope of the state's criminal law. Moreover, by specifying only conspiracies to betray the state into the hands of a foreign enemy, all other conspiracies were potentially excluded, both under the *expressio unius est exclusio alterius* maxim (the expression of one thing is the exclusion of the other) and the doctrine that criminal statutes should be narrowly construed. On the other hand, as legal historian Willard Hurst pointed out, "In view of the obviously inexpert character of much state legislation in this period, one may doubt the extent to which this result would actually be in the minds of local legislators."[54]

The statute also defined the lesser offense of misprision of treason. Under English law this offense consisted of "bare knowledge and concealment of treason, without any degree of assent thereto."[55] Pennsylvania's statute redefined the offense dramatically. Misprision now consisted of (1) attempting to convey intelligence to the enemies of Pennsylvania or of the United States; (2) publicly and deliberately speaking or writing against the public defense; (3) maliciously and advisedly endeavouring to excite the people to resist the government of Pennsylvania or to persuade them to return to the government of Great Britain; (4) maliciously and advisedly terrifying or discouraging the people from enlisting into the service of the commonwealth; (5) stirring up, exciting or raising tumults, disorders or insurrections, or disposing the people to favor the enemy; and (6) opposing and endeavouring to prevent the measures "carrying on in support of the freedom and independence of the said United States."[56]

Much of the misprision statute was directed at verbal offenses, the types of cases that had been routinely heard by county committees for nearly two years. And there was some attempt at limitation. Only publicly speaking against the public defense, for example, was punishable; private grumblings in one's house were not. Raising up tumults and disorders, which was sometimes punished as high treason in England, was distinguished as misprision. But there was no careful distinction between "raising" an "insurrection," which was misprision, and levying war against the state, which was high treason.

As with high treason, a misprision conviction would require the testimony of two witnesses. Trials would be held before justices of the peace in the courts of quarter sessions. Unlike trials for high treason, jurisdiction for misprision was specified; trials could be held in any county where the "offense was committed, or where the offender can be found." A person convicted of misprision would be imprisoned for the present war and forfeit one-half of his estate to the commonwealth, with no provision for the defendant's spouse or children.

The Case of James Molesworth and the Scope of Military Jurisdiction

The passage of the treason statute prompted a warning from the Council to Bucks County officials: "The House of Assembly having enacted a Law for the punishment of treason and misprision of treason, this Council are of opinion that no steps ought to be taken against any offender, (except in extraordinary cases) but in a legal manner under the Laws of the commonwealth."[57] But this was wishful thinking—the laws of the commonwealth could not function until the courts reopened, and events were not going to wait for the courts. In late March 1777, a month after the enactment of the treason statute, authorities uncovered an alarming plot. James Molesworth, who had previously served as a clerk to several of the mayors of Philadelphia, was apprehended after attempting to recruit pilots for Lord Howe to bring the British up the Delaware River.[58] Molesworth had undoubtedly committed a serious offense and his conduct could not go unpunished. But his case raised difficult questions about the line between civilian and military jurisdiction. If Molesworth was a Pennsylvania civilian, he would be subject to the state's treason law for aiding the enemy. The problem, however, was the absence of functioning courts in Pennsylvania; courts with jurisdiction over capital cases would not convene for another year. But if Molesworth was a British soldier (he allegedly had a lieutenant's commission from General Howe[59]), he could be subject to military jurisdiction as a spy, as John André would be after the Benedict Arnold affair. In August 1776, the Continental Congress had resolved that "all persons, not members of, nor owing allegiance to, any of the United States of America . . . who shall be found lurking as spies in or about the fortifications or encampments of the armies of the United States . . . shall suffer death, according to the law and usage of nations, by sentence of a court martial."[60] Whether Molesworth fit this description turned on the date of his departure from Pennsylvania. If it was before the passage of the February 11, 1777 treason statute, Molesworth arguably owed no allegiance to Pennsylvania or to any other state. He remained a British subject and could be treated as an alien enemy, not as a citizen. Further complicating the matter was the fact that Molesworth was not "lurking" around an army camp. As James Wilkinson later recalled, "several circumstances occurred to produce embarrassments; the law martial could alone apply to the offence charged against the culprit, but it had not been committed within the precincts of a military camp or garrison, nor was the attempt made on a military character."[61]

The final decision was made by the military and the Continental Congress. General Horatio Gates convened a court-martial to try Molesworth as a spy. The court-martial found Molesworth guilty, although by a non-unanimous verdict, and sentenced him to death.[62] The Continental Congress reviewed the proceedings and approved the order of execution.[63] On March 31, 1777, Molesworth was executed before "an immense Crowd of Spectators" in Philadelphia.[64] It was later claimed that Molesworth had made a gallows speech in which he "exhorted the spectators to return to their duty and allegiance to their royal sovereign and to defend the rights of the British government."[65] James Wilkinson recalled that Congress had insisted on the execution to punish a dangerous example and to "deter evil doers from the repetition of it."[66]

Yet doubts remained in some quarters as to the legality of Molesworth's conviction. Roger Sherman, Connecticut delegate to the Continental Congress, learned of a similar execution in New Haven after sentence by a court-martial. Sherman argued, "If he was an Inhabitant of the State & not of the Army, I think he ought to have been tried before the Superior Court. The resolution of Congress for the punishment of Spies respects only persons who are not inhabitants of any of the United States, or under the protection of their laws. We can't be too careful of Military encroachments." The case of Molesworth, Sherman noted, "was approved by Congress, but it was from necessity, because there was no Civil Courts established in this State."[67] George Washington expressed similar views about military trials of civilians. In an exasperated letter to a French adventurer who was serving in the Continental Army, Washington condemned the execution of a Tory by military authority. As Washington pointed out, "it was a matter that did not come within the jurisdiction of martial law, and therefore the whole proceeding was irregular and illegal. . . . The temper of the Americans and the principles on which the present contest turns will not countenance proceedings of this nature."[68]

If Molesworth was legally a Pennsylvania civilian, the only justification for military jurisdiction was Sherman's argument of necessity. A variant of this argument would eventually be embraced by the United States Supreme Court in the 1866 case of *Ex parte Milligan*. The Court held, "If, in foreign invasion or civil war, the courts are actually closed, and it is impossible to administer criminal justice according to law, then, on the theatre of active military operations, where war really prevails, there is a necessity to furnish a substitute for the civil authority, thus overthrown, to preserve the safety of the army and society; and as no power is left but the military, it is allowed to govern by martial rule until the laws can have their free course."[69] But Sherman's argument in 1777 had even broader implications, since it wasn't limited to the theater of active military operations. In theory, any civilian act of treason could be subject to military authority anywhere in the state. This possibility made it all the more important to open the courts in a timely fashion.

Shortly after Molesworth's execution, a "gang of conspirators" was detected, and seven or eight men were committed to jail for "carrying on a traitorous Correspondence with our Enemies, or conniving at it."[70] One of these men, John Brown, was tried before a court-martial and convicted of various acts of aiding the enemy. Although death was the prescribed punishment, the court nonetheless recommended Brown as "an object of mercy." General Philip Schuyler presented these findings to the Continental Congress, which referred them to the Board of War.[71] After conducting an inquiry into Brown, "now under Sentence of Death as a Spy and a Traitor," the Board determined that the recommendation for mercy "was founded only on the Criminal's apparent Ignorance and Illiteracy." The Congress postponed consideration of Brown's case, at which point he disappears from the record.[72] Another Molesworth associate, Thomas Wharton Collins, was tried by a court-martial for "treasonable practices against the United States."[73] Major General Benedict Arnold announced Collins's acquittal in the *Pennsylvania Gazette*, stating that no proof had appeared to substantiate the charges.[74]

Two women implicated in Molesworth's plot were deemed to fall outside of military jurisdiction. The Continental War Office committed Sarah O'Brien and Abigail McKay to the state prison as Molesworth's accomplices. The Board concluded that the women "were not so immediately the objects of military Power" and turned them over to Pennsylvania's Supreme Executive Council "for their trial by the civil Authority" so that if convicted they may "receive such punishment as crimes of so black a Dye entitle them to."[75] The Council ordered the women examined by James Young, who concluded that McKay's "full confession . . . comes under the Treason Act," and that O'Brien, although there was not "sufficient & legal testimony" against her, was nonetheless "a very Dangerous Person, and ought to remain in Custody from the present situation of our Publick Affairs."[76] McKay was freed several months later upon payment of a bond to appear at the next Court of Quarter Sessions.[77] There appears to be no further record of Sarah O'Brien.

The Test Act

In his third *American Crisis* paper, published in April 1777, Thomas Paine argued vigorously for legislation that would force every citizen to cast his lot with the American cause. Anyone who was not a supporter "of the independent states of

America" was, "in the American sense of the word, a Tory." It would be "unnatural and impolitic" to admit such men "to have any share in our legislation, either as electors or representatives. . . . All we want to know in America is simply this, who is for independence, and who is not? Those who are for it, will support it, and the remainder will undoubtedly see the reasonableness of paying the charges; while those who oppose or seek to betray it, must expect the more rigid fate of the jail and the gibbet."[78]

In June 1777, the Assembly responded to Paine's appeal with one of the most divisive pieces of legislation of the revolutionary period. Popularly known as the "Test Act," the law required all white male inhabitants of the state to take an oath renouncing allegiance to George III and proclaiming allegiance to Pennsylvania. Moreover, the oath included a promise to do nothing injurious to the freedom and independence of Pennsylvania and to disclose "all treasons or traitorous conspiracies . . . against this or any of the United States of America." The penalties for failure to take the oath were severe: exclusion from all public offices and jury service, exclusion from suffrage, disarmament, and, most dramatically, the inability to sue for debts or to buy and sell land. Any person who traveled outside of his home county without a certificate verifying the taking of the oath "may be suspected to be a spy and to hold principles inimical to the United States." Persons who refused to take the oath after being brought before justices of the peace would be imprisoned without bail until they did so. The Assembly justified the Act as a means to distinguish "the disaffected deriving undeserved service from the faithful and well affected." Those persons who would not commit to allegiance to Pennsylvania would receive no protection from it.[79]

The Test Act was difficult to enforce and profoundly alienated the very people it was ostensibly intended to conciliate.[80] A York County official reported several months later that the Act "instead of strengthening us, hath, in my opinion, weakened us very much; not one fourth part of the inhabitants hath, or will take it."[81] Robert Strettel Jones, a Philadelphia merchant who would be tried for treason in the fall of 1779, noted, "The Test Act has not in one Instance, that has come to my knowledge, been carried into Execution."[82] Nonetheless, individuals were routinely jailed as spies under its provisions, and at least once, the Council had to step in to discourage improper use of this power by local magistrates.[83]

Reopening the Courts

Reopening the courts was one of the most difficult challenges facing the fledgling Pennsylvania government and a critical test of its viability. A group of prominent Philadelphians, calling for a new state constitution, warned, "Weakness and languor are apparent in every part of the government. . . . There is no regular administration of justice, whereby the enemies of our country may be punished, and its friends protected."[84] A "Whig Society," chaired by artist Charles Willson Peale, defended the state government, noting "we have a law for the punishment and suppression of treason and disaffection." Nonetheless, the Society believed that the state had become a "rendezvous for disaffected persons" and that "until some method be determined upon, and executed, by which the friends to American independence can be distinguished from those who are its enemies, it signifies nothing what our form of government is."[85] Gouvernor Morris, in a letter to Alexander Hamilton, concluded that Pennsylvania "would experience many good effects from a vigorous manly executive." The Tories needed an "ocular demonstration . . . that we really do hang them."[86]

The delayed reopening of the courts was due in part to the refusal of many lawyers to accept office under what they deemed a deformed constitution.[87] The Supreme Executive Council offered the position of Chief Justice to Joseph Reed in March 1777, but Reed dithered, to the Council's great disgust, before finally declining the appointment in July.[88] The Council then offered the position to Thomas McKean, a well-known opponent of the new constitution.[89] McKean was serving as a delegate to the Continental Congress from the state of Delaware, and the Pennsylvania constitution prohibited state judges from serving as delegates to Congress.[90] McKean quickly accepted the office of chief justice, but nonetheless retained his Delaware congressional seat, on the theory that the constitution prohibited service only as a Pennsylvania delegate.[91] The two other justices of the Supreme Court, William Augustus Atlee and John Evans, were appointed in August.[92] All three justices were sworn in on September 1, but the Supreme Court would not officially meet until the following April.[93]

The county courts slowly began reopening in the latter half of 1777. The city court of Philadelphia opened first, on July 21, "before a great crowd of citizens."[94] The next month, the Lancaster County Court opened. Christopher Marshall attended and noted that the court business was "conducted decently" and that it closed "with great decorum."[95] Several weeks later the Chester court opened. By the end of 1777, most of the county courts had held sessions.[96]

Although the early reports were promising, many of the county courts encountered significant problems. Archibald McClean, serving as York County's prothonotary (the distinctive Pennsylvania term for "clerk-of-court"), reported in August 1777 that George Ross, a Pennsylvania delegate to the Continental Congress, had openly attacked the court's jurisdiction and successfully dampened enthusiasm for its opening.[97] By October 1777, the court had still not opened, and a desperate McLean sought advice from the Supreme Executive Council. Since experienced lawyers either were in the militia or refused to have anything to do with the new courts, there was no knowledgeable person in York County to whom he could turn.[98] A Northampton justice begged the Council for copies of the assembly acts and council resolutions, "for want of which in some instances, my Brethren the Justices & myself, are frequently at a loss how to act."[99] Another problem frustrating the county courts was the refusal of former prothonotaries to relinquish the court records to the new officials—records essential for the smooth continuation of lawsuits begun before independence. For example, it was reported in July 1777 that Michael Hoofnagle, former deputy prothonotary of Westmoreland County, had "in an unlawful and clandestine manner, removed and secreted" the Westmoreland records to Lancaster.[100] By February 28, 1778, the records had still not been turned over, and the Council issued a warrant for Hoofnagle's arrest.[101] Similar problems arose in a majority of Pennsylvania's eleven counties.[102]

These difficulties reflected the acute divisions that now permeated Pennsylvania society. In June 1777, James Allen noted in his diary that "America is more divided than ever & tories increase. There is no doubt but a vast majority of the people wish a reconciliation."[103] A delegate to the Continental Congress complained, "In this State, Toryism (or rather Treason) stalks triumphant."[104] Alexander Graydon, returning to Philadelphia that summer, discovered that "the better sort were disgusted and weary of the war," and that the spirit of Whiggism and liberty had been considerably dampened. The militia, however, was "still brimfull of patriotism, the prevailing feature of which was, to be no less ardent in their pursuit, than fervent in their hatred of Tories." As to the Whigs, Graydon observed, "the very cause for which they contended was essentially that of freedom, and yet all the freedom it granted, was, at the peril of tar and feathers, to think and act like themselves."[105]

The Exiles to Virginia

Fears of British invasion intensified over the summer of 1777, prompting the most extreme action yet taken by Pennsylvania's government against persons suspected of disloyalty. The initial prompting came from the Continental Congress, which recommended on July 31 that Pennsylvania "make prisoners, such of the late crown and proprietary officers, and other persons in and near this city, as are disaffected, or may be dangerous to the public liberty, and send them back into the country, there to be confined, or enlarged upon parole, as their characters & behavior may require." The Congress also recommended that Pennsylvania move the state prisoners out of Philadelphia and double their guard.[106]

The Council responded immediately, issuing arrest warrants for three dozen named individuals, including former governor John Penn, former chief justice Benjamin Chew, and many other prominent Philadelphians. It also authorized five men to "imprison, remove, confine, and enlarge on their Parole as you see fit, all . . . persons whatsoever whom you may know or suspect to be disaffected to, & inimically disposed against the United free States of North America or against this Commonwealth."[107] A warrant issued the next day authorized the five men to employ the militia to carry out the arrests.[108] Two days later the Council issued another warrant, with more names, this time with specific directions as to whether the men should be paroled or detained.[109]

The individuals subject to these arrest orders denounced them bitterly. James Tilghman wrote to the Council that "the proceeding against me is the most arbitrary that can be imagined, being imprisoned by a Precept which expresses no offence."[110] James Hamilton complained that he "does not find himself charged with any crime, or suspicion of crime against the present Government or the American cause in general."[111] Benjamin Chew argued that the detention order "was subversive not only of my rights as a freeman, but of the first principles of natural justice," since it deprived him of his liberty without the opportunity to be heard. The proceeding was "arbitrary and oppressive in the highest degree" and it "struck at the liberties of everyone in the community." Chew demanded the "benefit of the laws" and those "rights and privileges . . . which had never been denied or withheld to the most atrocious criminal or malefactor."[112] Benjamin Rush, writing to John Adams, noted, "The time is now at an end when danger is to be apprehended from the tories. If we are undone at all, it must be by the aristocratic, the mercenary, the persecuting, and the arbitrary spirit of our own people—I mean the people who are called whigs."[113]

The two most prominent detainees, John Penn and Benjamin Chew, refused to sign any parole, and Pennsylvania officials presented their case to the Continental Congress, which resolved to detain the two men in Fredericksburg, Virginia.[114] The threat of removal to Virginia had the desired effect, and a few days later, the men agreed to sign a parole, acknowledging that they were prisoners of the "United States of America" and promising to do nothing injurious to the American cause.[115] Congress then suspended the detention order.[116]

The long-feared British invasion finally commenced on August 25 as Lord Howe landed at Head of Elk in Maryland with 17,000 men and prepared to march north toward Philadelphia. The next day, the Continental Congress resolved that the "executive authorities of the states of Pennsylvania and Delaware, be requested to cause all persons within their respective states notoriously disaffected, forthwith to be apprehended, disarmed and secured, till such time as the respective states think they may be released without injury to the common cause." Congress concluded that this measure was necessary to prevent "all persons who may reasonably be suspected of aiding or abetting the cause of the enemy . . . from pursuing measures injurious to the general weal."[117] Two days later, Congress went further, launching a fierce attack on Quakers. A congressional committee reported that "the uniform tenor of the conduct, and conversation of a number of persons of considerable wealth, who profess themselves to belong to the society of people commonly called Quakers, render it certain and notorious, that those persons are, with much rancor and bitterness, disaffected to the American cause." Accordingly, Congress recommended that the Supreme Executive Council arrest thirteen named Quakers. In addition the Congress recommended that all of the states "apprehend and secure all persons . . . who have, in their general conduct and conversation, evidenced a disposition inimical to the cause of America." Finally, Congress recommended that the states secure and carefully examine the records of the Quaker Meetings of Sufferings, and transmit "such parts of them as may be of a political nature" to Congress.[118] In a letter to his wife, Abigail, John Adams claimed, "We have been obliged to attempt to humble the Pride of some Jesuits who call themselves Quakers, but who love Money and Land better than Liberty or Religion."[119] That same day, Congress again ordered the detentions of John Penn and Benjamin Chew, who were eventually sent to the Union Iron Works in New Jersey.[120]

The Supreme Executive Council complied with the congressional request, but only in part. The Council did nothing with respect to three persons named by Congress and agreed that nine others could be released upon signing a parole. Only one person named by Congress, Samuel Rowland Fisher, was ordered detained. The Council, however, supplemented Congress's list with thirty additional names, twenty of whom were permitted to be paroled and ten of whom were to be detained. The Council recommended the Free Masons' Lodge as a detention facility, and strongly discouraged commitments to the common jail or the state prison.[121] Three days later, twenty-four people had been detained at the Lodge; many men who had been offered a parole refused to sign.[122] The Council recommended to Congress that the detainees be sent to Virginia; Congress agreed and recommended Stanton, Virginia.[123] The Council then ordered that the men be moved to Stanton "agreeable to the Resolve of Congress."[124] The next day, the Congress consented to the release of any detainee who agreed to take the oath of allegiance to Pennsylvania.[125] The *Pennsylvania Evening Post* heartily approved these actions, arguing that "matters are become too serious to suffer bosom enemies, under pretence of conscience, to carry on traitorous practices to the common ruin."[126]

At this point, the Council and Congress began squabbling over who was ultimately in charge of the prisoners. Three detainees obtained the services of an attorney, who demanded that the Council allow them to speak in their own defense; theirs was a case, the attorney argued, "in which every Freeman in the State is interested."[127] Their written remonstrance argued that the detentions were "arbitrary, unjust, and illegal," since they had been given "no opportunity . . . to be heard."[128] The Council refused to hear them, claiming that the arrests had been made on the recommendation of Congress. The detainees then turned to Congress, which, after five hours of debate, recommended that the Council "hear what the said remonstrants can allege, to remove the suspicions of their being disaffected or dangerous to the United States."[129] This the Council pointedly refused to do, informing Congress that it had no "time to attend to that business, in the present alarming crisis, & that they were, agreeably to the recommendation of Congress, at the moment the said Resolve was brought into Council, disposing of everything for the departure of the Prisoners."[130] Two days later, the Council rebuffed another petition from the detained men, claiming the Council "had referred their case to Congress."[131] Shortly thereafter, Congress resolved that it "would be improper . . . to enter into any hearing of the [prisoners] . . . , they being inhabitants of Pennsylvania." Congress recommended that the Council order the immediate departure to Virginia of any detainee who had not taken the oath of allegiance.[132]

The Council then prepared a final order justifying the detentions and the banishment to Virginia. It described the men as "persons who have uniformly manifested by their general conduct & conversation a Disposition highly inimical to the cause of America." Their refusal to take the oath of allegiance meant that they had renounced "all the privileges of Citizenship" and considered themselves "subjects of the King of Great Britain." As such, they should be treated as enemies of the United States of America. The Council then noted, a touch defensively, that other states had undertaken similar actions, and that "such proceedings may be abundantly justified by the conduct of the freest Nations & the authority of the most judicious Civilians."[133]

The detainees, for their part, made repeated remonstrances to the Council and the Congress. They argued that their imprisonment violated "the fundamental rules of justice, . . . the laws of the land, and . . . the express provision of the present constitution. . . . No man can be lawfully deprived of his liberty without a warrant from some persons having competent authority, specifying an offense against the laws of the land, supported by oath or affirmation of the accusers, and limiting the time of his imprisonment, until he is heard, or legally discharged, unless the party be found in the actual perpetration of a crime." The detention order was a "more flagrant violation of every right which is dear to freemen, than any act which is to be found in the records of the English Constitution." It threatened to "establish a system of arbitrary power unknown but in the Inquisition, or the despotic courts of the east."[134] Moreover, by acting without authorization from the Assembly, the Council had usurped legislative powers for itself, thus overturning "the only security the constitution has given the people against absolute despotism."[135] As they argued more fully later, "[w]e were condemned and sentenced to banishment, before we even knew that we were accused; and that, not for any crime, but for the tenor of our conduct and conversation; such a mode of administering justice is sufficient to alarm every freeman in America, for no man can be safe while those in power will listen to the whispered accusation of a concealed enemy, resolve that the party is guilty, and refuse to hear his defence."[136] At least some revolutionary leaders seemed to agree. Benjamin Paschall, a Philadelphia justice of the peace, thought it a case of an "alarming nature" and a blow "fatal to the liberties of Pennsylvania."[137] James Allen learned that "many of the warmest Whigs think this an instance of unjustifiable oppression."[138]

When numerous remonstrances went unanswered, the detainees' attorneys filed petitions for a writ of habeas corpus with Chief Justice Thomas McKean, who issued the writ and set a return date for arguments before him. These actions prompted a speedy response from the Assembly, which resolved that it approved "of the Conduct of the supreme Executive Council . . . in apprehending and removing certain suspected Persons from this State" and appointed a committee to draft legislation empowering the President and Council "to arrest and detain suspected Persons, and to restrain for some limited Time the Operation of the Habeas Corpus Act."[139] The legislation, enacted two days later, authorized any two members of the Supreme Executive Council to "arrest any person or persons within this commonwealth who shall be suspected from any of his or her acts, writings, speeches, conversations, travels or other behavior, to be disaffected to the community of this or all or any of the United States of America." Similar detention powers applied to any persons who provided intelligence to the enemy, or who spread false news, or who did "any other thing to subvert the good order and regulations that are or may be made and pursued for the safety of the country." A separate section of the act indemnified state officials from any actions at law and suspended the writ of habeas corpus with respect to any actions taken under the act.[140] This act had been anticipated by the *Pennsylvania Evening Post*, which had argued a week earlier that the legislature "could authorize the executive power, for a short and limited time, to imprison suspected persons, who in that case lose their liberty only for a while, to preserve it forever."[141]

In a lengthy letter to John Adams, McKean defended his conduct in setting the initial return date to the prisoners' petitions for a writ of habeas corpus. He noted that the writs complied with the Habeas Corpus Act of 1679; this Act formed "part of the Code of the Pennsylvania laws, and has been always justly esteemed the palladium of liberty." Since he had been away from Philadelphia, he was unaware of developments in the case, and the only authority asserted for the confinement was a letter from the vice president of the Council. Under the 1679 Act, he was obligated to issue the writs or incur a five-hundred-pound fine.

In any event, issuing the writs resolved no issue on the merits; it simply permitted McKean to hear both sides: "No injury could arise by returning the writs & bringing the parties before me." McKean declared himself satisfied with the Assembly's suspension of habeas corpus, noting that "in almost every war since the making of the statute, the like had been done in England."[142] He echoed this view a year later, arguing that the "government was doing a necessary and usual act in like cases for its preservation; the restraining men whose going at large was thought dangerous to the community, and putting them for a time under gentle confinement."[143] At the time, however, McKean may have been more upset than he let on. A young Philadelphia diarist heard from a man who had visited McKean that the chief justice had "made many professions of his disapproval of the unprecedented measure, and would willingly, were it in his power, grant them a hearing."[144]

What McKean might have done with the case if the Assembly had not suspended the writ can obviously never be known. It is certainly possible that he might have granted the writs. In his letter to John Adams, McKean pointedly noted that the Latin maxim "fiat justitia, ruat caelum" (let justice be done though the heavens fall) "pleases me as a sentiment."[145] As later events would show, McKean took a dim view of claims that military necessity trumped the ordinary processes of the law. Nonetheless, McKean might still have hesitated. An order to free the prisoners would constitute a highly visible second-guessing of the state's legislative and executive authorities on a security matter in the middle of a foreign invasion. Indeed, state authorities may have simply ignored any writ issuing from his court. The suspension of habeas corpus allowed McKean to avoid the issue entirely and place responsibility for the detentions squarely in the hands of the legislature.

As the British occupation of Philadelphia continued through the winter, the continued exile of twenty Pennsylvanians in Virginia became an embarrassment, both to the Continental Congress and to the state of Pennsylvania, each of which held each other responsible for the men's fate.[146] Finally in March 1778, the Council requested that Congress transfer custody of the exiles to the state, since "the dangerous example which the longer continuance of the prisoners in banishment may afford on future occasions has already given uneasiness to some good friends of the independence of these States."[147] Moreover, Pennsylvania's courts were now established, and the men could be tried if necessary.[148] Congress quickly agreed, and the exiles returned to Pennsylvania, where they were released.[149] By this time, however, two of the men had died in captivity.[150] In a final indignity, the Council ordered that the "whole expence of arresting and confining the prisoners sent to Virginia . . . be paid by the said prisoners."[151] Benjamin Chew and John Penn were released several months later.[152]

The exile orders nonetheless continued to generate controversy, and modern historians have tended to reach disparate conclusions as well. Richard Bauman concluded that the entire affair was "conducted in a most arbitrary and unjust manner . . . prompted largely by hysteria and vindictiveness."[153] Leonard Levy argued that the exile orders represented "perhaps the grossest violation of a constitutional provision" by a state government during the war and that "nothing the British had done equaled the violation of privacy rights inflicted by Pennsylvania on its 'Virginia Exiles.'"[154] Numerous contemporaries reached the same conclusion. Edward Burd felt the men were detained "because of their general character and conversation." Such detentions were inconsistent with the rhetoric of liberty advanced by the revolutionary state government, which "declared that every man . . . ought to be allowed freedom of speech and that liberty cannot be in any state where it is denied."[155] For James Allen, the detentions bore "the mark of the most wanton Tyranny ever exercised in any Country"; it violated "the express laws" of the state government as well as "natural justice and humanity"[156] Robert Morton contended, "hadst thou given them even the form of a trial, then thou would have been less blameable, but thou hast denied them that in a manner more tyrannical and cruel than the Inquisition of Spain."[157] This view was echoed by detainee Owen Jones, who contended that "had I had an opportunity of defending myself before an impartial Jury of my Country I could have proved my innocence."[158] An unsigned memorial to the Council argued that the people of the state ought to "feel their Liberty and to be convinced from experience, that Freedom is more than a name."[159]

There is much to be said for these views, but it should also be noted that Pennsylvania's suspension of habeas corpus was not inconsistent with British practice under the Habeas Corpus Act.[160] Moreover, it would be permitted even under modern American law. The United States Constitution explicitly permits the suspension of habeas corpus when "in Cases of Rebellion or Invasion the public Safety may require it." At the time of the suspension, British troops had invaded and the state was in severe peril. The state government was understandably reluctant to conduct extensive individualized hearings on the loyalty of each suspected person when it was confronting so many other pressing demands. Indeed, Pennsylvania in September 1777 may represent the paradigmatic case for suspension. If these factual circumstances do not justify suspension, it is hard to imagine any that would.

The exiles were treated as gentlemen, in the same manner as eighteenth-century officers held as prisoners of war. The journey to Virginia was reasonably pleasant, including a stop to visit a cave and evenings spent dining at taverns. The sixth day of their journey included a "second breakfast" and a "good glass of Madeira wine."[161] In Winchester, Virginia, their final destination, the exiles took lodgings in multiple houses after concluding it was too cramped to stay in one house. They had the liberty to go on rides and walks in a six-mile radius; indeed, one exile simply got on his horse and returned to Philadelphia, an act that the other exiles viewed as dishonorable.[162] Although the absence from home, family, and friends was an undoubted hardship, the exiles were never subject to physical violence or restraint. When compared to the atrocities against civilians that have marred warfare throughout human history, the removal, without a trial, of a handful of wealthy gentlemen from their homes for six months hardly ranks among the most reprehensible.

In the context of Anglo-American liberty, however, the exile was significant, and was legitimately perceived to be so by the detainees. The taint of religious bigotry against Quakers permeated the entire proceeding. Moreover, although the initial denial of hearings was arguably justified by the chaotic circumstances of the British invasion, those circumstances had disappeared once the state government had resettled in Lancaster. Perhaps the most telling feature about this incident is how quickly everyone involved came to perceive that a significant mistake had been made. Neither the Continental Congress nor the Pennsylvania government wished to claim responsibility for the exiles. No one argued that the detentions had served any useful purpose; rather, the general view was that the whole regrettable incident should be forgotten as quickly as possible, and that it should never be repeated. Indeed, when the Pennsylvania Council of Censors met in 1784 to review violations of the state constitution, it concluded that the Council's actions with respect to the exiles "were very great stretches of power, and highly unconstitutional."[163] Many of the exiles easily regained their standing in the community, and in 1789, four of them were elected to the Philadelphia common council.[164]

The Fall of Philadelphia and Military Trials

The revolutionary cause suffered setback after setback throughout September 1777. On September 11, the British won a significant victory at Brandywine Creek south of Philadelphia, forcing Washington's army back to the capital. Five days later a conspiracy to burn the public storage facilities at Lancaster, York, and Carlisle was uncovered. One of the leaders, James Rankin, had previously served on the Committee of Safety for York County and as a member of the Pennsylvania Assembly.[165] The Supreme Executive Council was furious, denounced the plot as treason, and reluctantly agreed to pardon one of the conspirators, Daniel Shelley, if he would give evidence against his accomplices.[166] Shelley implicated, among others, two York County clergymen,[167] one of whom was also alleged to be "carrying on a correspondence with the enemies of this state, and of the United States of America."[168] The depth of the plot surprised many. Edward Burd knew that Shelley was a "great Tory" and "very imprudent in his confidence and expressions," but he found it difficult to believe that Shelley "could be guilty of so villainous a design."[169] The exposure of this plot appears to have led the Continental Congress to recommend that the state legislatures enact laws providing capital punishment for any person who willfully burned or destroyed magazines of provisions belonging to the United States.[170]

On September 26, 1777, the British Army finally marched into Philadelphia. The state and federal governments had already fled, along with 12,000 other Philadelphians. Approximately 23,000 Philadelphians, however, remained in the city and now faced difficult decisions of loyalty.[171]

The British occupation of Philadelphia prompted both the Continental Congress and the Pennsylvania Assembly to take additional measures against potentially disloyal individuals. The Congress resolved that any "inhabitant of these states" who acted as a guide for the enemy or who provided them with intelligence or provisions and was captured within thirty miles of enemy lines would be subject to trial by court-martial. Although the initial resolution expired on January 1, 1778, Congress later extended it until April 10, 1778.[172] For its part, the Assembly provided that any adult white male traveling out of the city of Philadelphia or his home county, and any adult white male "suspected of being unfriendly to the freedom and independence of the United States" would be imprisoned if he refused to take the oath of allegiance to the state.[173] The Assembly also created a new Council of Safety, consisting of the members of the Supreme Executive Council and twelve named individuals. The Council of Safety was empowered to "seize, detain, imprison, punish, either capitally or otherwise as the case may require, in a summary mode either by themselves or others by them to be appointed for that purpose, all persons who shall disobey . . . the laws of this state heretofore made for the purpose of restraining or punishing traitors or others, who from their general conduct and conversation may be deemed inimical to the common cause of liberty and the United States of North America." In an ambiguous caveat the statute also noted that "the exercise of the ordinary course of justice in the trial and punishment of offenders shall proceed and take its effects."[174]

On its first day in operation, the Council of Safety required that all persons refrain from furnishing the enemy with provisions, to "save us the irksome task of punishing them with immediate death, as their crimes deserve."[175] Four days later, the Council passed an ordinance directing the seizure of the estates of persons who had joined the British army or had provided the army with provisions.[176]

Although the Council of Safety was in theory given sweeping powers, including the nearly unheard-of power to impose summary execution, its bark was far more extensive than its bite. In practice, it did not differ significantly from the

Supreme Executive Council. It issued occasional arrest warrants for individuals suspected of treasonable behavior, but there were no summary executions.[177] The most well-known case involved that of John Brown, an associate of Robert Morris, who emerged from occupied Philadelphia with a message from General Howe. The Continental Congress, now sitting in York, concluded that Brown was a spy, ordered his arrest, and turned him over to the Council of Safety.[178] Brown was interrogated and detained "for aiding and assisting the Enemies of this Commonwealth, and forming Combinations with them for betraying the United States into their hands."[179] Only after forceful intervention by Robert Morris and George Washington did the Council agree to Brown's release.[180] There were also some limited seizures of property; for example, a Cumberland County official, pursuant to the Council's ordinance, arranged for the seizure of the personal estates of seven men.[181]

The great victory at Saratoga, which occurred just a few days after the Council's formation, did much to lift revolutionary spirits and lessened the perceived need for drastic measures. The Council's statutory authorization expired in December, and since the "progress of the Enemy hath been restrained" and the "ordinary powers of government are at full and free liberty to proceed in the usual course," the Council declared itself dissolved.[182] On a related note the Continental Congress resolved in December 1777 that any inhabitants "of these United States" serving in the British army would, upon capture, "be delivered up to the respective states, to which they belong, to be dealt with agreeably to the laws thereof."[183]

During the period in exile, the Continental Congress and the Pennsylvania government worked closely together with respect to potentially disloyal individuals. The Congress, for example, apprehended Robert Jones, a York County resident who "directly or indirectly" had "intercourse with the Enemy," and turned him over to Pennsylvania officials.[184] At the same time, Congress occasionally intervened to recommend leniency on the part of the state. Although attentive to the "delicacy of interfering" with internal matters, Congress recommended that one of the ministers implicated in the Shelley plot be released upon taking an oath of allegiance.[185]

As the British occupation continued into the early months of 1778, roving bands of Tories began emerging from Philadelphia to capture some of the more active Whigs, who were then turned over to British military authorities. American forces had captured several of these Tories and confined them at Washington's headquarters at Valley Forge. John Bayard wrote to Thomas McKean that they would "be delivered up to the civil authority as it is thought the martial law does not extend to this crime." Civilian acts of this sort constituted treason and would have to await trial in civilian courts. Bayard felt that holding a court was very important, as "there are great numbers in the several jails charged with the highest crimes which call for immediate and exemplary punishment." The people, he noted, seemed "very anxious" for the opening of the court.[186]

But the court had still not opened, and a frustrated Continental Congress decided to intervene. It resolved that any person involved in any way with the carrying of Americans to the enemy shall "suffer death by the judgment of a court-martial, as a traitor, assassin, or spy" if the offense was committed within seventy miles of the army headquarters.[187] The resolution was printed as a broadside with the heading "The deluded tools of the enemy, who are committing treason against America, would do well to peruse the following resolution of Congress with attention."[188]

Military jurisdiction had been authorized by earlier resolutions of the Continental Congress with respect to spies and to civilians who acted as pilots or guides to the British or who provided them with provisions. These resolutions, and possibly the more recent one, were the basis for a series of trials held in March 1778. That month, William Bradford had complained that "this state still teems with traitors who are continually attempting to supply the army with provisions."[189] General Washington convened a court-martial in Lancaster to try persons accused of "being spies, carrying on a traiterous correspondence, and supplying the enemy with horses."[190] Three men were convicted of spying and sentenced to death; one subsequently died in jail, and the other two, Henry Mansin and Wendal Myer, obtained a new trial.[191] The new trial "lasted some days" and resulted in a unanimous guilty verdict and death sentence for both defendants. The Prussian-born Mansin had lived briefly in Philadelphia prior to the Revolution, but had moved away and received a British officer's commission.[192] Military jurisdiction over Mansin was thus unexceptional. But Myer was a civilian, an inhabitant of Lancaster County.[193] As George Washington had noted in convening the court-martial, Myer was "not triable on the articles of war, but must be tried on a special resolution of Congress."[194] After acknowledging the "justice of their sentence," both men were hanged "amidst a very numerous concourse of spectators."[195] At the same court-martial, Wendal Bowman and George Campbell, most likely civilians, were convicted of holding correspondence with the enemy. Bowman was sentenced to imprisonment during the war; Campbell was sentenced to death but was subsequently pardoned. Another man was acquitted on charges of spying.[196] A separate court-martial convened in April resulted in seven people being imprisoned indefinitely for supplying provisions to the enemy.[197] Another court-martial imposed the death sentence on John Burk, an inhabitant of Philadelphia County, for "aiding, assisting, piloting, and giving intelligence to the enemy." General John Lacey reported to George

Washington that Burk was "universally hated by the inhabitants where he used to live" and that not "even one man" could be found "that speaks a good word of him." Lacey concluded that Burk would be a "very proper person to make an example of."[198] A week later, however, Burk evaded capital punishment by escaping from custody.[199]

The effectiveness of these trials was greatly debated. George Washington complained, "We have daily proof that a majority of the people in this quarter are only restrained from supplying the enemy with horses and every kind of necessary, thro' fear of punishment, and although I have made a number of severe examples, I cannot put a stop to the intercourse."[200]

Washington also read the congressional authorization narrowly, noting that it "was not so extensive as to include all cases," and concluded that two prisoners, whose offenses were "entirely of civil cognizance," must be sent to Lancaster for trial by civil authorities.[201] The Supreme Executive Council initially advised General Lacey that the state was ready to take on the trading with the enemy cases, "as the treason law of this state will reach the crime . . . if proper proof be exhibited."[202] A few weeks later, however, the Council backtracked, concluding that the "difficulty of procuring the evidence against such persons . . . and many other weighty reasons make it appear to be the best to try them in the usual military way at camp."[203] When the congressional resolution authorizing the trial of civilians by court-martial expired in mid-April, Washington did not seek an extension and noted that "it will therefore be needless to apprehend any more."[204]

Trial of civilians by court-martial emerged again as an important issue only briefly, in the wake of General Benedict Arnold's declaration of martial law in recently evacuated Philadelphia in June 1778.[205] A court-martial sentenced Frederick Verner, a civilian, to die as a spy. In a letter to the President of the Continental Congress, Arnold expressed doubts about this proceeding, noting that "the evidences do not appear to me sufficiently full and clear to touch the life of a citizen." He suspended the death sentence "until the pleasure of Congress is known."[206] The Congress referred the matter to Pennsylvania's Supreme Executive Council,[207] which, "not being lawyers," sought the opinion of Chief Justice McKean.[208] McKean advised "in favor of life," and recommended that Verner "be tried by the Laws of Pennsylvania for treason." The Council approved McKean's suggestion and forwarded the recommendation to Congress.[209] Four months later, Congress had taken no action and Verner, who remained in custody at the State Prison, wrote a petition to Congress, seeking to be released on bail. Congress referred the petition to the Board of War.[210] Finally in March 1779, Joseph Reed, President of the Supreme Executive Council, managed to obtain Verner's release from Congress as part of a prisoner exchange with the British.[211]

* * *

When Pennsylvania's civilian courts finally reopened, they emerged into a chaotic environment in which their success was far from assured. Philadelphia had fallen to the enemy, and fear of secret Tory plots was pervasive. Multiple institutions were dealing with the problem of disloyalty, but not in any systematic way. The Supreme Executive Council was accustomed to detaining individuals at will, and the state had suspended the writ of habeas corpus to permit the exile of some of the most powerful and prominent people in the state. County committees of safety continued to try and imprison individuals suspected of being enemies to their country. Even the military played a role, exercising jurisdiction over civilians in exceptional cases.

The courts faced exceptional challenges. Would they smoothly wrest jurisdiction over cases of disloyalty from the committees of safety and the military? How would the treason statute, to date a dead letter, be applied? How many people would be prosecuted? How would juries, the darling of William Penn, react to persons accused of treason? And most importantly, how many Pennsylvanians would march to the scaffold for aiding the king of Great Britain? In 1778, these questions began to be answered.

5

The Winding Path to the Courthouse, 1778

IN THE EARLY morning hours of September 7, 1778, a group of men crept into the Quaker Burying Ground in Philadelphia. They were there on a politically charged mission—to recover the body of James Molesworth, the spy who been executed under American military authority in early 1777. Molesworth was not a Quaker and had originally been buried in a different location. During the British occupation of Philadelphia, however, Molesworth's body was exhumed and taken to the Quaker burying ground, where it was reinterred in the presence of a number of people. This reburial caused considerable dissension, as it would inevitably be perceived as a highly public indication of Quaker support for the British. Quaker diarist Elizabeth Drinker, whose husband had been exiled to Virginia, thought that "putting [Molesworth] into our Ground was a ridiculous, foolish act."[1] Others felt that the Quaker officials who had approved the reburial should be removed from office.[2]

Several months after American forces reoccupied Philadelphia in June 1778, a notice appeared in the *Pennsylvania Packet* addressed to those "concerned in removing the body of that infamous traitor, James Molesworth." The notice demanded that those involved remove the body to its proper place within two weeks; otherwise "ample vengeance will undoubtedly fall on the heads of the delinquents."[3] Two subsequent notices by Samuel Richards and Thomas Harrison announced that the order had been obeyed, with Harrison claiming that the body had been initially moved "not from any party matter, nor particular respect to said Molesworth, but solely to gratify the earnest desire of a young woman nearly allied in kindred."[4] There was nonetheless considerable suspicion that the persons involved had merely "taken him out of one hole and put him into another in the same ground." It was also rumored that the second reburial had been the "greatest and largest yearly meeting for a long time past."[5]

James Molesworth's peripatetic corpse was an apt metaphor for the shifting allegiances and loyalties that confronted Pennsylvanians in the turbulent years after independence. Philadelphia, initially under British rule, had shifted to American rule, then British rule, and finally back to American rule. Each change in jurisdiction carried with it a change in allegiance, potentially enforced through the criminal law of treason. Much like the shifting state religions of Tudor England, the shifting political identities left considerable confusion in their wake. Thomas Paine observed some men "skulking in secret, many making a market of the times, and numbers who are changing to Whig or Tory with the circumstances of every day."[6]

In September 1778, Pennsylvania's first jury trial for high treason was held before the justices of the Supreme Court in Chester County. But the justices were relative latecomers to the judicial treatment of disloyalty. The initial cases were heard by the county courts, which had jurisdiction over low-level cases of disloyalty and were largely unaffected by the British invasion. For its part, the exiled Pennsylvania Assembly took a decisive new step by enacting legislation allowing for the attainder of traitors without a trial, an act that would ultimately ensnare nearly five hundred people, far more than were ever tried in a court of law.

Prosecutions in the County Courts

The county criminal courts, formally known as the courts of quarter sessions, played a significant role in the treatment of disloyalty, but their experiences varied widely. In some counties, lawyers simply refused to appear. In February 1778, Lancaster attorney Jasper Yeates stated, "I did not go near the Justices, nor do I think I shall until I cannot help it. In my idea there is little law amongst us."[7] A few months later, Attorney General Jonathan Dickinson Sergeant reported that the Berks County Court of Quarter Sessions was unable to proceed "for want of a man of character and abilities to act in the courts." "Not one lawyer here," he noted, "and the people anxious to have business done."[8] Similarly, in the fall of 1778, the Northumberland County justices complained that the "business of this County is much impeded for want of an Attorney to prosecute for the Commonwealth." Two court sessions had elapsed with no state attorney appearing.[9] The most significant outrage occurred in Northumberland County in August 1778. The justices of the peace were meeting at a house in Sunbury to examine some prisoners when a group of armed men led by George Moy, a lieutenant colonel of the Berks County militia, burst onto the scene. With "threats, menaces, and the most horrid oaths and imprecations (too prophane and vulgar to be repeated)," Moy sought to "bias or pervert" the judgment of the court. This action so intimidated the constable and the jail keeper that they did not dare leave the building. Finally, one of the justices volunteered to return a prisoner to the jail. He managed to do so, but was surrounded by "Moy's gang with threats and fixed bayonets," who offered "opprobrious epithets and vulgar expressions in the German language."[10] In sharp contrast, Bedford County prothonotary Robert Galbraith noted in May 1778 that the county courts "at Bedford, Carlisle, and York, are held with great propriety, and more business done in the sessions in a week, than used formerly to be done under the old constitution."[11]

Misprision of treason was the most serious offense subject to the jurisdiction of the quarter sessions courts, but several courts were not fully prepared to deal with it. In January 1778, William Montgomery was convicted of misprision by a York County jury, and his attorneys intended to move to arrest the judgment. Such a motion was routinely available in criminal cases,[12] but the court prothonotary, Robert Galbraith, intervened. "Rather than risk a motion of that kind with the Court, who were but young hands, and no precedent of a conviction of the kind yet established," he later explained, "I thought it most prudent to have the verdict of the jury recorded, and Montgomery sent back to prison, until the opinion of the Council was had in the matter."[13] What exactly happened next is unclear, but the attorneys' efforts were successful; Montgomery was discharged at the April sessions and was not retried.[14] The failure of the Montgomery prosecution may have induced caution on the part of the York County justices; a misprision of treason case initially brought in April 1778 was carried over without trial until the defendant, released on bail, finally died a year later.[15] The next misprision case would not be heard by a York County jury until April 1780. In January 1779, the Council learned that the Philadelphia City Court of Quarter Sessions "had adjourned so early that divers persons said to have been guilty of misprision of treason, remained without trial." The Council requested the court to reopen to afford time for the trial of the misprision cases, which were "of great importance to the Safety of the State."[16]

The strangest departures from prevailing legal norms occurred in Cumberland County, where the court in its first months functioned more like a committee of safety than a true court of law. At the January 1778 sessions, John Gibson was indicted for and pled guilty to the offense of "speaking inimical to the United States etc." He was fined three pounds and ordered to submit to a good-behavior bond. Edmond Kean was similarly fined after pleading guilty to the charge of "uttering words inimical to this state etc."[17] Hugh McNeal was charged with "being unfriendly to the American cause," but the grand jury refused to indict.[18] Seven people were entered into the docket book under the charge "being inimical and unfriendly to the rights and liberties of America."[19] These charges appear to have been later dropped and were not presented to a grand jury. At the April sessions, Henry Magee was indicted as "inimical to the United States."[20] None of these alleged offenses were specifically prohibited under Pennsylvania criminal law, and the fines imposed on Gibson and Kean were almost certainly unlawful. The appropriate charge for a subset of carefully described verbal offenses was misprision of treason, and the court adopted this practice in the summer of 1778. Paul Pierce, for example, was initially charged in January with "uttering words inimical to the United States," but this was changed to "misprision of treason" in July.[21]

The justices for Northampton County may have also overstepped their authority in a case involving Michael Ohl, the outspoken man who had previously clashed with the county's committee of safety. Two of the justices committed Ohl to jail without bail after finding him "guilty of entertaining two men in his house on the 12th January 1778 at night & not true to the State." Ohl alleged that the order had been issued without any examination of him, and the full court then bailed Ohl on the condition that he appear at the next Court of Quarter Sessions.[22]

Many of the cases were handled directly by state officials or by persons appointed on the state's behalf. The indictments of three men in Northampton County, for example, were drawn by Attorney General Jonathan Dickinson Sergeant in March 1778, December 1778, and June 1779.[23] In August 1777, the Council appointed John Morris to prosecute on behalf of the state at the Philadelphia County Court of Quarter Sessions,[24] and he was reappointed to serve in the York and Cumberland quarter sessions in October.[25] In May 1778, the Council urged the Assembly to provide additional funding to cover the expenses incurred by the attorney general at the oyer and terminer courts as well as "the prosecutions in the sessions of the peace."[26] The attorney general offered the Lancaster, Berks, and Northampton county prosecutions to Edward Burd in September 1778, but it is unclear whether Burd accepted.[27]

In other cases, private prosecutors were used. In July 1778, Joseph McCoy was "indorsed" by the court as prosecutor for the misprision trial of Thomas Kerr in Cumberland County.[28] In January 1779, Alexander McDonald was "indorsed" by the court as prosecutor for the misprision trial of Herman Stitger in York County.[29] "Endorsing" a prosecutor meant that the prosecutor was subject to costs if the prosecution failed, and courts routinely imposed bonds on prosecutors to guarantee their appearance.[30] This was not an unreasonable concern. William Downward, for example, was charged with misprision of treason in Westmoreland County, but was discharged when "no person [appeared] to prosecute against him."[31] Following the British evacuation of Philadelphia, justice of the peace Benjamin Paschall imposed bonds on private parties to prosecute seven different misprision cases in the county court, but only one of these cases was presented to a grand jury.[32]

Although little detail of trial procedure is recorded, defendants were frequently represented by attorneys and the courts enforced basic norms of fairness. At the April 1779 sessions in York County, defendant Herman Stitger informed the court that he had served a subpoena on three witnesses, but they had failed to appear. Without their testimony, Stitger argued, he could not "safely go on trial." The court ordered an attachment to issue against the recalcitrant witnesses for contempt of court and postponed Stitger's trial.[33]

The surviving court records seldom disclose the precise acts upon which the misprision charge was based, but it appears that most offenses were verbal, typically intemperate arguments against the war. The tumultuous Robert Robb, who had previously appeared as a defendant before the Northumberland Committee of Safety, was charged in Northumberland County with opposing the "Government of this Commonwealth" and injuring "the freedom and sovereignty of the United States" by exciting "tumults and disorders" and by persuading people to "return to a dependence on the Crown of Great Britain." Specifically, Robb had asserted that "public affairs in general were now governed by a tumultuous mob," the members of the Assembly "were all perjured," and the "United States were damned."[34] Daniel Lee was charged with speaking against the Continental currency, for using the "opprobrious names of Rebel and Yankee" and for asserting that the king's laws "would soon come in force and that the damned Congress money would be good for nothing."[35] James Molesworth was charged with "publicly and deliberately speaking against our public defense" for claiming, "I would see the Devil have all the States of America before I would go out with the militia two months."[36] Daniel Fields was charged with living with "such tribes of the Indian Nations as are in open and avowed enmity to this and the United States of America with design to comfort and cherish them in their savage efforts to reduce and impoverish the frontier settlements in the County of Northumberland."[37] In Northampton County, Philip Lumbach was charged with misprision for speaking against the public defense by claiming that large numbers of British troops would soon arrive, that Washington would be taken in his quarters, and that the Indians would begin to murder people on the frontier.[38] Another man was charged with damning the Congress and stating, "Hurra for King George the Third. God prosper him and his family."[39] Two men were charged with speaking against the public defense, speaking against the "just laws of this Commonwealth" and declaring "that the people of this state are rebels."[40] In Lancaster County, Abraham Hare was alleged to have damned the Congress, who were "a panel of blackguard villains every one of them," and to have wished the English were in Lancaster "for then we would have better times."[41] Unprosecuted cases that were initially presented in Philadelphia in 1778 included charges of "drinking damnation to General Washington and all his army," "being a Constable under the King of Great Britain," attempting to persuade someone "to return to his former allegiance to the Crown of Great Britain," calling the complainant a "rebel," and disarming the complainant while he was "making his escape from the enemy."[42] Some of the misprision cases may have been rooted in private quarrels. Herman Stitger was indicted in January 1779 in York County for misprision of treason, but he was also charged with assault and battery against Robeson York. At the April sessions, York was charged with assault and battery against Stitger.[43]

The Court of Quarter Sessions for Philadelphia County was one of the few to consider the charge of "going to the enemy," an offense criminalized by the Assembly in April 1778. At the September 1778 sessions, the court discharged five defendants after concluding that the offences had been committed before the act of the Assembly that criminalized them. The grand jury indicted one defendant and refused to indict another. The indicted defendant, Rosanna Jenkins, was convicted at the December sessions and fined fifty pounds.[44] In Bucks County, Joseph Green was convicted and fined for going into Philadelphia while it was in possession of the enemy. The Council remitted the fine.[45]

Table 5.1 provides summary data on misprision of treason cases in the county courts between 1777 and 1783 for which clear evidence survives.[46] A total of fifty-two cases were presented to grand juries, which found indictments in forty-five (86.5%) of the cases. Only twenty-one cases went to trial. Of those, twelve (57%) resulted in conviction and nine in acquittal. Only nine of the twelve convictions resulted in a judgment being entered against the defendant, and eight of those were later pardoned, at least in part.[47] Thus only one person suffered the full penalties of a conviction for misprision of treason in Pennsylvania during the Revolutionary War. Given the broad nature of the offense, and the high likelihood that it was committed quite frequently, these are staggeringly low numbers. County courts, with the protections of grand juries and jury trial, detained far fewer people between 1777 and 1783 than the county committees and the Supreme Executive Council detained between 1775 and 1777.

The Attainder Statute and Property Forfeitures

In March 1778, the Pennsylvania Assembly enacted a statute for the "attainder of divers traitors if they render not themselves by a certain day, and for the vesting their estates in this commonwealth."[48] The statute was the product of several months of work, and was probably drafted by Chief Justice McKean himself.[49] Even prior to his appointment as chief justice, McKean had weighed in on the prospect of attainder without trial. In June 1777, most likely at the request of the Supreme Executive Council, McKean had prepared an opinion addressing

Table 5.1 Misprision of Treason Cases: Pennsylvania County Courts of Quarter Sessions, 1777–1783

County	Ignoramus/ True Bill	Acquitted/ Convicted	Judgment Entered	Pardoned*
Bedford	1/1	0/0		
Berks	2/4	0/3	2	2
Bucks	0/2	0/0		
Chester	0/0			
Cumberland	0/4	2/2	1	0
Lancaster	1/4	1/0		
Northampton	0/7	2/0		
Northumberland	2/3	1/0		
Philadelphia	1/2	0/0		
Philadelphia (City)	0/7	2/3	3	3
Westmoreland	0/6	0/1	1	1
York	0/5	1/3	2	2
TOTAL	7/45	9/12	9	8

*Includes partial pardons and pardons on condition.

the hypothetical case of an inhabitant of Pennsylvania who had crossed the Delaware River, and had joined the enemy's armies in New York, where he was tried, convicted, and attainted of treason. The opinion addressed three legal questions arising from this conduct.[50]

The first was "[c]an he legally allege that he is not a subject of, nor owes allegiance to New York?" McKean concluded that he could not, arguing "even an alien, who comes there at first peaceably, has a right to protection of the laws of the said State, and in return he owes a local Allegiance to it." This conclusion was consistent with a long line of English precedent holding that visitors owed a temporary allegiance to the jurisdiction where they were present.

The second question was "[h]ow would such attainder affect his estate, in Pennsylvania?" McKean replied that there would be no effect, because "[t]reason may be a different thing and differently punished in New York." Moreover, "a traitor should be tried by a jury of the County, in which the overt act of treason was committed." Mere conviction in New York would not have extraterritorial effect in Pennsylvania.

The third question was the most difficult: "Is there any process that can issue by the laws of Pennsylvania, for outlawing a person who will not appear, or by what means can such a person's estate be forfeited?" Pennsylvania's treason statute did not contain a jurisdictional element. If the overt acts occurred in Pennsylvania, the statute obviously applied. But in the hypothetical presented to McKean, the overt acts occurred in New York; as McKean had already noted, traitors should be tried by the jury of the county where the overt act occurred. Thus a strict reading of the overt act requirement would suggest that Pennsylvania had no jurisdiction over this offense at all; only New York could punish the traitor.

McKean nonetheless concluded that Pennsylvania treason law applied. He noted that the statute "prohibits joining the armies of the enemies" of Pennsylvania, and that "the Enemies of the State of New York are the enemies of Pennsylvania." Accordingly, such an individual could be indicted "for it in the county where the fact was inchoate, or in which he resided." By limiting jurisdiction to those counties only, McKean narrowed English law, which permitted treasons committed outside the realm to be tried in any of England's counties.[51]

Yet trials were seemingly not the goal; many of the people who had fled to the British would not be coming back anytime soon. McKean turned to the 1718 colonial statute that had secured English common law in Pennsylvania. Since the colonial laws had been declared in force by the new Assembly, this statute still governed. It set forth a procedure for dealing with individuals who failed to appear to answer an indictment. The justices would issue a capias writ addressed to the sheriff of the county, who would then seek to find the indicted person and would "make proclamation in every court of quarter sessions, which shall be held for the said county." If the person did not appear within three months, he would be "pronounced outlawed, and attainted of the crime whereof he is so indicted" and would forfeit "all his lands and tenements, goods and chattels."[52] McKean concluded that this procedure could be used for persons suspected of treason.

Despite McKean's seal of approval, proclamation followed by attainder does not appear to have been used by any Pennsylvania court during the war.[53] Instead, the attainder process initiated in 1778 was simpler and more direct. The attainder act named thirteen prominent individuals who had "joined and adhered to" the British army and remained in occupied Philadelphia "where they daily commit divers treasonable acts without any sense of honor, virtue, liberty [*sic*] or fidelity to this state." The individuals included Joseph Galloway, former speaker of the Pennsylvania Assembly and former Pennsylvania delegate to the Continental Congress; Jacob Duché, the former chaplain to the Congress who had notoriously written to George Washington to encourage him to make a separate peace with the British; Samuel Shoemaker, former mayor of the city of Philadelphia; Nathaniel Vernon, former sheriff of Chester County; and John Biddle, former deputy quartermaster in the Continental Army. The act required each man to turn himself in for trial by April 20, 1778; failure to do so would result in being "convicted and attainted of high treason to all intents and purposes whatsoever."

The statute was a conditional bill of attainder. It declared individuals guilty of a crime, but it gave them a short window in which to appear and contest the charges in court. Once that window had closed, it operated as a traditional bill of attainder. It is doubtful that the Assembly seriously expected the act to lure the named men out of Philadelphia for trial, as they would have had little incentive to do so. Rather, the Assembly's primary motive was to permit the confiscation of the estates of those Pennsylvanians who had sided with the British. As attainted traitors, their estates would forfeit to the state, which could auction them off and use the revenue for the war effort. The bulk of the statute was thus devoted to intricate procedural and legal issues associated with the seizure of estates. To mitigate the potentially harmful consequences to innocent parties, the justices of the Supreme Court were authorized to award portions of the estate for the support of the attainted traitor's wife and children.[54]

In a highly significant provision, the act also authorized the Supreme Executive Council to issue additional proclamations of attainder for Pennsylvanians who joined the British army "within this state or elsewhere." This authority did not extend to cases of other forms of assistance to the British, even though such assistance would constitute treason under Pennsylvania law. Nonetheless, the authority was striking in its implications. Under English practice, bills of attainder required an act of Parliament; they could not be issued unilaterally by the king. By contrast, Pennsylvania was delegating this authority to its executive branch. The Council took full advantage of this new power. Between May 8, 1778 and June 15, 1778, it issued three separate proclamations, totaling 332 people.[55] By the time the last proclamation was issued on April 27, 1781, nearly 500 people had been named. Their numbers represented a broad cross section of Pennsylvania society, and included lawyers, bakers, farmers, laborers, hatters, millers, innkeepers, gentlemen, surgeons, peruke makers, dancing masters, Indian traders, and mariners, among others.[56]

Pennsylvania's attainder policy was in considerable tension with a congressional policy announced in April 1778. The Congress observed that "persuasion and influence, the example of the deluded and wicked, the fear of danger, or the calamities of war, may have induced some of the subjects of these states to join, aid or abet the British forces in America, and though now desirous of returning to their duty, and anxiously wishing to be received and re-united to their country, they may be deterred by the fear of punishment." The American people were more ready "to pardon than to punish offenders." Accordingly, the Congress recommended that the states offer pardons to "such of their inhabitants or subjects, who have levied war against any of these states, or who have adhered to, aided or abetted the enemy, and who shall surrender themselves to any civil or military officer of any of these states, and shall return to the State to which they may belong, before the 10th day of June next." Moreover, Congress recommended that "the good and faithful citizens of these states . . . receive such returning penitents with compassion and mercy, and to forgive and bury in oblivion their past failings and transgressions."[57] Henry Laurens stated that the Congress was "induced to this measure from well founded suggestions that great advantages would follow."[58] He forwarded two hundred copies of the measure to General Washington "to be dispersed at proper opportunities in the City of Philadelphia & wherever else good effects may be expected, Congress taking for granted that each State will enact a proper Law under the present recommendation."[59] Pennsylvania's Supreme Executive Council forwarded Congress's resolution without comment to the Pennsylvania Assembly.[60]

The Assembly ignored the congressional recommendation entirely. Indeed, it had moved in precisely the opposite direction by enacting an even more stringent version of the Test Act on April 1, 1778. The new legislation barred all adult white males who had not taken the oath of allegiance from prosecuting cases in court, serving as a guardian, executor, or administrator, making a will, and inheriting property. They were also excluded from the professions of law, medicine, and education, and were subjected to double property taxes. The justices of the peace were authorized to summon any person before them who had not taken the oath. If the person still refused, he would be sentenced to three months in jail; continued refusal would result in banishment from Pennsylvania and the forfeiture of all "his goods and chattels" to the state. A separate provision criminalized going into occupied Philadelphia without official approval.[61]

The tension between the state's expansion of punishment and the Congress's recommendation of mercy were well captured in the diary of a young woman shortly before the British evacuation of Philadelphia. A member of the Continental Army told Sarah Wister that he "would retaliate whenever he had an opportunity." Wister "strenuously opposed such a procedure, observing that it would be erring in the same way and tho they might deserve it, yet it would be much nobler to treat them with lenity." The soldier responded, "[Y]our sentiments are noble, but we must retaliate sometimes."[62]

Chief Justice Thomas McKean and the Reopening of the Pennsylvania Supreme Court

Pennsylvania's Chief Justice, Thomas McKean, although little remembered today, was one of the most visible and prominent men of the Revolution (Figure 5.1).

FIGURE 5.1 Thomas McKean, Chief Justice of Pennsylvania, with his son Thomas McKean, Jr.

Credit: Portrait of Chief Justice Thomas McKean and His Son, Thomas McKean Jr., by Charles Willson Peale/Philadelphia Museum of Art, Bequest of Phebe Warren McKean Downs, No. 1968-74-1.

He was born in 1734 to Scotch-Irish parents and began his early legal career in Delaware, where he served as a justice of the peace and as a delegate to the Stamp Act Congress. Nominally a member of London's Middle Temple, he had never made the journey to England. During the Revolution, he was a member of the Delaware constitutional convention and served simultaneously as a Delaware delegate to the Continental Congress and as Chief Justice of Pennsylvania. He served in the Congress longer than any other member and was its president at the time of Cornwallis's surrender. He was a prominent delegate to the Pennsylvania convention for the ratification of the United States Constitution, and later served as governor of Pennsylvania. One of McKean's biographers points out that none of his contemporaries could match his record for multiple office holding. McKean eventually "served in both executive and judicial posts in two states and in the federal government, and in a legislative capacity both in one state and in the federal government."[63]

McKean was a vigorous proponent of judicial independence and was convinced that the success of the new nation depended on the government remaining a "government of laws and not of men."[64] He was well positioned to put these ideas into practice. His service in the Continental Congress meant that he was both more prominent and more widely connected than the relatively obscure men who served on the state's Supreme Executive Council. Writing to John Adams, McKean noted that "difficulties, public and secret attacks, will eternally attend public characters and high stations. The man who discharges his trust with fidelity and according to the best of his abilities will always have the consolation of his own mind, a consolation the world cannot give."[65] As legal scholar William Loyd aptly described McKean, he was a "democrat in theory" but "an aristocrat in bearing."[66]

McKean's forceful assertion of judicial power was vividly illustrated in the Hooper incident of 1778. Robert Hooper, a colonel and deputy quarter master in the Continental Army and a resident of Pennsylvania, refused to take the oath of allegiance as required under Pennsylvania's Test Act. The Supreme Executive Council warned the Pennsylvania delegation to the Continental Congress that Hooper had also "used his influence to prevent others from taking it, which has doubtless been greatly injurious to the general cause of America."[67] Hooper was aware that Pennsylvania Attorney General Jonathan Dickinson Sergeant had played a role in developing evidence against him. Hooper found the diminutive attorney general at a meeting of the Court of Quarter Sessions for Berks County in Reading and violently assaulted him.[68] In a subsequent letter to Gouvernor Morris, Hooper bragged about having "horsewhipped the Attorney General" and he threatened to similarly assault the members of the Supreme Executive Council.[69]

Hooper's actions were a serious affront to the dignity of the Pennsylvania government and its judicial system. McKean issued a special warrant for Hooper's arrest for libeling the officers of the state government. Hooper's commanding officer, General Nathaniel Greene, wrote to McKean from Valley Forge, explaining that the army was about to march through Hooper's district and he "could not without great necessity consent to [Hooper's] being absent, as there is no other person that can give the necessary aid upon this occasion." Greene claimed that he did "not desire to interrupt the course of the law, or to secure [Hooper] from its proper operation" and he proposed that Hooper enter into a recognizance before a Northampton County magistrate.[70] McKean's reply was a powerful declaration of both judicial independence and civilian authority over the military:

> I do not think, Sir, that the absence, sickness, or even death of Mr. Hooper could be attended with such a consequence, that no other person could be found who could give the necessary aid upon this occasion, but what attracts my attention most is your observation that you cannot without great necessity consent to his being absent. As to that, Sir, I shall not ask your consent nor that of any person in or out of the army, whether my Precept shall be obeyed or not in Pennsylvania . . . I should be very sorry to find that the execution of criminal law should impede the operations of the army in any instance, but should be more so to find the latter to impede the former.[71]

McKean dismissed the recognizance proposal out of hand, insisting that he alone could issue a recognizance for a special warrant. Although it is unclear when Hooper finally appeared, Hooper later admitted that he had a "very great contempt" for Sergeant and that his letter to Gouverneur Morris contained expressions that "were generally ungentlemanly and indecent."[72]

Yet McKean's forceful, domineering personality led many people to fear the rule of law was coming perilously close to the rule of McKean. In late 1777, Edward Burd observed that the new Chief Justice "behaves in the most violent and imperious manner. He is principally governed by his passions, an excellent quality in a Chief Justice."[73] William Rawle, who would later prosecute participants in the Whiskey Rebellion, claimed "all epithet would fall short of his badness."[74] Jonathan Dickinson Sergeant wrote, "I have been forced to hear the long detail of all [McKean's] honors, and all his promotions, and all his exploits, and all his greatness, and all his marvelous doings above a thousand times over;—and so has everybody else that has had the happiness of keeping his company."[75] In 1789, McKean wrote to George Washington to seek a federal judicial appointment. The letter displayed McKean's characteristic immodesty. "I have lived in troublesome times in an unsettled and tumultuous government," McKean wrote. "A good judge cannot be very popular, but I believe my integrity has never been called into question. It is certain no judgment of the Supreme Court of Pennsylvania since the Revolution has been reversed, or altered a single iota."[76]

In April 1778, the justices of the Supreme Court finally convened in Lancaster to hear criminal cases. Technically, these cases did not fall under the jurisdiction of the Supreme Court itself, but, following English and colonial practice, they were assigned to the justices under what was known as a commission of oyer and terminer and general gaol delivery. These commissions authorized the justices to hold court in each county, as a three-judge trial court, to preside over cases of treason and felony. As eighteenth-century law did not permit appeals in criminal cases, the justices were the first and last word with respect to the law. A convicted defendant's only avenue for relief was to seek a pardon or a reprieve from the Supreme Executive Council.

McKean was joined on the bench by his two colleagues, John Evans and William Augustus Atlee, both of whom would be largely overshadowed by McKean. Evans was a fifty-year-old lawyer from Chester County who had previously served on the Supreme Executive Council. Atlee, a relative of William Pitt, was a lawyer from Lancaster County. He had served on the committee of safety for Lancaster County and as the state's commissary of prisoners.[77] Everything went smoothly. McKean wrote to his wife, "Matters have been conducted equal to my most sanguine hopes, indeed everything is as I would wish it."[78]

McKean's most public and visible task was the charge to the grand jury, routinely used by eighteenth-century judges to set forth broad statements about the role of law in civil society, as well as detailed descriptions of particular crimes. McKean undoubtedly put considerable effort into his charge, which he used as a template for subsequent charges at other courts.[79] A few weeks later, he delivered a similar charge to a York grand jury, which requested that the charge be published.[80] These charges provide valuable insight into McKean's thoughts on treason and the criminal law.

McKean began with a description of the British actions that had led to the revolution. These included deprivations of the right of trial by jury, and he particularly singled out Parliament's declaration that the act of 35 Henry VIII was fully applicable in America. Such a declaration, McKean argued, was clearly contrary to the Habeas Corpus Act. "By this vote any person in America, who might be obnoxious to a British minister . . . might be charged with treason . . . and sent to England for trial; and though ever so innocent, for want of testimony or an unbiased jury, might be convicted and executed; but at any rate reduced to beggary." Subsequent British actions had effectively declared America out of the king's protection. "Allegiance (which is reciprocal between a king and his subjects) being thus broken on his part absolved us from any farther obedience." Indeed, McKean argued, "to bear it longer was so far from a duty, it became criminal." McKean described the Declaration of Independence as an "ever memorable and glorious act, [by which] our internal enemies could be punished."[81]

The first subject of the grand jurors' inquiry, McKean announced, was the crime of treason. This offense, "of all the others in the black catalogue is of the most dangerous and fatal consequence to society, [and] is immediately against the State." Although other eighteenth-century charges sometimes discussed the English statute of Edward III or offered generalities about the offense, McKean turned directly to the 1777 Pennsylvania statute defining treason. In his view, the statute encompassed three broad forms of treason: (1) taking a commission from the king of Great Britain or from other enemies of Pennsylvania or of the United

States of America; (2) levying war against the State or government thereof; and (3) "knowingly and willingly aiding or assisting any enemies at open war against this State or the United States of America, by joining their armies, or by inlisting or procuring or persuading others to enlist for that purpose, or by furnishing such enemies with arms or ammunition, or any other article or articles for their aid and comfort or by carrying on a traitorous correspondence with them; or by forming, or being anywise concerned in forming any combination, plot, or conspiracy, for betraying this State, or the United States of America, into the hands or power of any foreign enemy, or by giving or sending any intelligence for that purpose."[82]

McKean then turned to the specifics of each offense, drawing large portions of his charge verbatim from Michael Foster's well-known treatise on treason law, published after the 1745 Jacobite uprising.[83] McKean provided no elaboration of the offense of taking a commission, but he offered substantial analyses of the other offenses. With respect to aiding the enemy, McKean noted that the "bare sending [of] money or provisions" to the enemy, even if they were intercepted and never reached the enemy, would constitute treason, since "the party in sending it did all he could; the treason was complete on his part." McKean also offered clarification on the nature of an "enemy," following traditional English principles. States in actual hostility with the United States were enemies within the meaning of the statute, regardless of whether there had been a formal declaration of war. Similarly, "if the subject of any foreign prince in amity with us invadeth any of the United States, without commission from his sovereign, he is an enemy." Aiding or assisting any such enemies would be treason under the Pennsylvania statute.[84]

McKean also spent considerable time parsing the phrase "levying war against the State or government thereof." As he told the jurors, this phrase may "require some explanation." Although McKean had signed the Declaration of Independence, he treated the phrase as a legal term of art, explicable only under English precedents. Levying war included not only the paradigm case of "those who directly rebel against the State, and take up arms with design totally to abolish it," but also "many other cases" where those "who in a violent and forcible manner withstand [the state's] lawful authority, or endeavor to reform the government thereof." Examples included persons who "held a fort against the forces of the State, or keep together numbers of armed men, without the authority of Congress and against the express command of the President of the Supreme Executive Council of the state."[85]

Moreover, those "who make an insurrection in order to redress a public grievance, whether it be a real or pretended one, and of their own authority attempt with force to redress it," are guilty of levying of war, even if they have no direct design to overthrow the state. Such persons "insolently invade [the state's] authority by attempting to do that by private authority, which the State by the laws and public justice ought to do." Examples included using force and a "warlike manner" to "lay violent hands upon the President, or a member of the Supreme Executive Council, or a magistrate of the State," to "bring down generally the price of victuals," to "reform the law or religion," to "pull down all brothels," to "remove all inclosures," or to "break all the prisons and to set all the prisoners at liberty." Such acts had a "tendency to dissolve all the bonds of society and to destroy all property" and were "a general defiance of public government."[86]

These examples were all based on English precedents. Most notoriously, a case in the late seventeenth century, decided by a meeting of all the common-law judges, had held that a "rising with intent to pull down bawdy-houses in general," and put into execution with force, was an act of levying war against the king under the statute of 25 Edward III.[87] One scholar notes that "it is hard to understand why this was treason, rather than riot, unless we let our knowledge of the licentious and profligate character of Charles II, then King of England, lead us to the conclusion that it was regarded as an attack upon a royal institution."[88] McKean's use of this example is particularly striking, since Sir Matthew Hale, a figure revered by American Whigs (and cited by McKean himself as an inspiration for accepting the chief justiceship),[89] had been the only judge to dissent from the decision, and Michael Foster deliberately omitted the case from his summary of the law and mentioned it only in passing.[90]

English law obviously did not refer to the "President of the Supreme Executive Council." McKean analogized to cases finding high treason to assemble with force to lay violent hands upon a magistrate.[91] In certain ways, the recognition of this offense might be seen as inconsistent with the abolition of treason by compassing the death of the king. The difference, however, rested in the nature of the attack. Under Pennsylvania law there would have to be some assembly of armed men for the purpose of attacking the President. By contrast, even a solitary individual could commit treason under the compassing clause by attacking the king.

McKean followed English law in emphasizing that conviction for levying war required actions undertaken to resolve public grievances: "where a number of men rise to remove a grievance to their private interest, as to pull down a particular house, or lay open a particular enclosure, and other acts of the like kind, they are only rioters."[92] Finally, McKean announced the traditional English rule that "there are no accessories in treason, all are principals."[93]

As a practical matter, of course, it was unlikely that the Pennsylvania courts would confront many instances of armed men seeking to tear down brothels or lay open enclosures. There were more than enough cases of aiding the enemy to keep the courts busy. Nonetheless, the nature of the levying war provision would prove deeply divisive in the federal treason prosecutions brought in Pennsylvania in the 1790s. McKean's reflexive application of English law would not be accepted then without challenge.

McKean concluded the charge with a note of restraint, advising the grand jurors in "all doubtful cases to incline rather to acquittal than crimination; for it is safer to err in acquitting than in punishing, on the side of mercy than on the side of justice."[94]

The Special Commission for Bedford County

There was one exception to the general pattern of the Supreme Court justices trying treason and felony cases. The situation in Bedford County posed special difficulties. In early May 1778, approximately thirty-five people "marched toward the Indian Country" in order to join the Indians and help attack frontier settlements. Five of these persons were captured and confessed "to their crime and intention of destroying both men and property." Since there was "great reason to believe them . . . in some dangerous confederacy with the common enemy," Colonel John Piper urged the Supreme Executive Council to order commissioners "for their immediate and speedy trials" to "give an immediate check to so openly avowed rebellion."[95] Chief Justice McKean doubted that the Supreme Court justices would be able to hear the cases promptly. Indians had recently scalped eleven women and children near the town, and the people were "all in arms." It would be difficult for the judges and the attorney general "to make so long a journey." Thus, despite the need "to make examples of some of the most wicked of the prisoners in Bedford as soon as possible," McKean advised that the trials be delayed.[96] By August 1778, no court had convened in Bedford and Robert Galbraith reported that the jail was filled with people said to "have been guilty of treasonable practices." The Supreme Court justices would be busy with the upcoming Philadelphia trials and there was a risk of the "traitors being rescued." Accordingly, the Council determined that "a speedy trial" of the offenders was "highly necessary," and appointed five men as a special commission of oyer and terminer to try the accused.[97] Although they would receive no salary, they were entitled to payment of their expenses.[98] When one of the appointees hesitated, the Council emphasized the importance of the trials of "the traitors who took the desperate course of joining the Indians against their Country."[99]

The commission convened on September 28, 1778 and heard cases until October 2, 1778. Although Robert Galbraith had specifically identified thirty-one men who had been "under arms to join the Enemy at the Kittaning against the United States," only fourteen treason cases were presented to the grand jury.[100] The grand jury indicted five of the accused, but rejected the charges against the nine others. Three of the indicted defendants went to trial, and all were acquitted. It is hard to know precisely why no convictions were obtained. Although the commission's report survives in the Pennsylvania State Archives, it does not include the names of the grand jurors, the trial jurors, or the witnesses.[101] The commission was reportedly "conducted well," primarily because of the "superior abilities and attention" of Archibald McLean of York County. One of the other appointees, Barnard Dougherty, admitted to being "totally ignorant of the law."[102]

The Return to Philadelphia

When the British army finally evacuated Philadelphia on June 18, 1778, approximately three thousand Americans fled with them, while many others who had aided the British remained behind, nervously awaiting the arrival of their countrymen.[103] British officials had done little to help the Philadelphia loyalists; indeed, Lord Howe simply told them to make as good a deal as they could with the rebels.[104] When the exiled Philadelphians returned, they were greeted by a devastated city. The streets were littered with filth and debris. Approximately six hundred houses had been completely destroyed. Most other houses had been stripped of their personal possessions. The stench from dead horses and human corpses was so strong at the State House that the Continental Congress was forced to hold its meetings at the College of Philadelphia. Stores had been vandalized and most boats in the harbor had been burned. Even churches suffered tens of thousands of pounds in damages.[105]

The initial mood appears to have been one of shock and resignation. Charles Willson Peale noted that people reunited with their former friends were now "fearful and distrustful lest they should take one by the hand who had played the traitor's part."[106] Yet there were no immediate acts of vengeance. Peale observed, "I have often heard those exiled say how they will use those who had been active on the enemy's taking possession of the city, and I have often feared what might be the effect of that resentment, but now to my surprise, I have not seen or heard of one rude encounter."[107] Timothy Matlack informed Attorney General Sergeant that the city's "inhabitants, in general, Whig & Tory throughout, appear to be fully reconciled to independency, and acknowledge their detestation of the conduct of their formerly reputed best friends the British troops."[108] The Supreme Executive Council even complained that "there is a great unwillingness in the People of the City to give the necessary information against the disaffected," which "subjects both the Council and the Chief Justice to very great difficulties."[109]

A group of Philadelphians submitted a petition to the Council proposing the appointment of persons to "seize suspected persons" and to take inventories of merchandise and furniture. The Council rejected this proposal, concluding that it would be "opposed by the best friends of liberty as a most arbitrary exercise of assumed authority" and "would establish a precedent which would have the most dangerous tendency to set up in the executive branch of government an arbitrary power destructive of the liberty and safety of the people."[110]

For their part, those Philadelphians who had remained in the city throughout the occupation began what Peale claimed was "the doleful tale of their sufferings, how the Tories had abused them."[111] Their laments were not without foundation. The presence of 20,000 British troops in Philadelphia had placed enormous burdens on the civilian population. The occupation was so poorly managed that historian Robert Oaks has concluded that it "alienated many people from the Tory cause, infuriated those like Galloway who remained loyal, and in the end may have helped prolong the war until the Americans could win."[112]

Any initial mood of reconciliation, however, quickly turned to anger and vengeance. Peter Deshong, one of the men named in the attainder proclamations, found "his house surrounded by a party of men, armed with clubs, who were in search of him for the avowed purpose of revenge." Deshong's attorney complained that "this is not the only instance by many taking revenge out of the course of regular proceedings."[113] A few days later, an anonymous submission to the *Pennsylvania Evening Post* warned,

> A Hint to the Traitors and those Tories who have taken an active part with the enemy, during their stay in this city. You are desired, before it is too late, to lower your heads, and not stare down your betters with angry faces. For you may be assured the day of trial is close at hand when you shall be called upon, to answer for your impertinence to the Whigs, and your treachery to this country.[114]

By late July, complaints were being made that persons "notoriously disaffected to the American cause, and others of suspicious characters, presuming upon the indulgence and lenity of their virtuous and forebearing countrymen, have lately manifested an unbecoming and insolent spirit." In particular, they had "endeavoured to suppress all evidence and discovery of the oppression of the friends of America, and other misdoings before and during the enemy's possession of this city, by intimidating and discouraging the good people of this State from appearing against them."[115] Nearly two hundred men formed a "Patriotic Association" and resolved to disclose all "facts within [their] knowledge tending to bring such offenders to proper trial."[116] Historian Steven Rosswurm notes, "Except for its few moderates and conservatives, the roll reads like a who's who of the Philadelphia radical leadership from 1775 to 1780."[117]

For his part, Chief Justice McKean was occupied with the problem of the people named in the attainder proclamations. The attainder statute specified the consequences if they failed to appear before a judicial officer, but was vague about the procedure that applied if they did appear, stating only that they would "abide their legal trial for . . . their treasons." McKean argued that the proclamation "amounts to no more than a charge of treason," and the judges were entitled to use reasonable discretion in admitting the proclaimed persons to bail: "If the evidence amounts to no more than common fame, or public notoriety, that the party named in the proclamation has left his usual place of abode and gone into the city of Philadelphia, without some proof of an overt-act, such as bearing arms, or annexing his person to the troops of the enemy as a pioneer, labourer, or soldier, or furnishing them with provisions, or intelligence . . . I think he ought to be bailed." The general rule, McKean stated, was "if it stands indifferent or doubtful in the opinion of the Judge, whether the party is innocent or guilty, he ought to be bailed; if the evidence of guilt preponderates it should be done with caution."[118] The Council echoed this conclusion, arguing that if the evidence was "full," bail should be granted only "with great caution," but "where the charge is doubtful, it is held to be his duty to take bail."[119]

Under this procedure, someone would need to come forward and present evidence at the initial appearance of the person who had been proclaimed. It is unclear whether the attorney general personally appeared at these proceedings; gathering evidence against the large numbers of people named in the proclamations would have been a Herculean task. In many cases, it appears that no evidence was ever brought forth on the part of the state. McKean informed his fellow justice William Atlee that "I sit daily in the courthouse from 9 to 11 o'clock, and sometimes to 12," dealing with persons named in the proclamations. Two justices of the peace served as assistants "to inform of the abilities of the persons who offer themselves as sureties, and to hear accusers, should any offer." But the "inhabitants appear to be either afraid of one another, or the Whigs cannot yet believe that their friends have the government of the city."[120]

Some of the accused took steps to ensure that no witnesses appeared. Surgeon Anthony Yeldall, named in the attainder proclamation of June 15, 1778, was charged with taking arms from Philadelphians during the British occupation.[121] In papers later filed with the British government, Yeldall admitted that he had "prevailed on the witnesses against him not to appear, by paying them very exorbitant prices for the arms he had taken."[122] Yeldall was discharged in December 1778, although he was attainted again after the Benedict Arnold affair, at which point he fled permanently to the British.[123]

In some cases, McKean may have taken extra measures to insure that evidence was presented. McKean believed that treason was widespread; earlier that summer he claimed that "as there was one Judas among the twelve apostles, there may very probably be a traitor to his country in most of the General Assemblies, or at least among their officers."[124] In one of the first cases of a proclaimed person, McKean complained that James Bracken "was brought before me yesterday without any testimony or evidence whatsoever against him." McKean examined Bracken at length, and formed an "unfavorable impression of [him], as I am told he has been uniformly inimical." Although he ordered Bracken imprisoned, McKean was concerned that denying bail on such minimal evidence would reflect poorly "on the justice of the State." Unless the Council could come forward with "some evidence against" Bracken or "know the names of some persons who may be witnesses against him," McKean would be obliged to release him on bail.[125] When no further evidence materialized, Bracken was bailed.[126]

One of the proclaimed persons who appeared before McKean was the young merchant Tench Coxe (Figure 5.2), who had fled Philadelphia for

FIGURE 5.2 Tench Coxe escaped trial for treason despite collaborating with the British.
Credit: Tench Coxe (1755–1824) (oil on canvas), by Jeremiah Paul (1761–1810)/Philadelphia History Museum at the Atwater Kent/Courtesy of Historical Society of Pennsylvania Collection/Bridgeman Images.

British-occupied New York in late 1776. He returned to Philadelphia in the company of Howe's troops when the British occupation began and his business affairs prospered.[127] One of Coxe's friends, Benjamin Yard, warned him that many people viewed his conduct as "rash and imprudent." Yard warned Coxe to "be very cautious how you engage in any public measure in opposition to the American cause" and advised him to do nothing "that may increase the resentment of your countrymen."[128] It was almost certainly too late. Coxe was proclaimed as a traitor on May 21, 1778. Two days later, he somehow left Philadelphia and swore the required oath of allegiance to the state of Pennsylvania.[129] In June, he wrote to his brother that if he could escape conviction he was likely to "become a perfect American." Nevertheless, he requested that his brother destroy his letters, so that he would not "suffer from their being seen by either side—both might perhaps blame me."[130] Coxe did not depart with the British and therefore appeared before McKean in July 1778. He found the chief justice to be "much more friendly than I could have expected and perfectly genteel." Coxe was admitted to bail and noted the "general opinion" that no "proofs would be laid against [him] before the grand jury."[131]

The failure to prosecute Coxe was somewhat surprising. Although the attainder proclamation was inaccurate (Coxe had never joined the British armies or held any position under their authority), he had entered into lucrative contracts with the British military.[132] Moreover, his abrupt flight to New York vividly demonstrated his intent to join the British side. These actions were clear acts of treason under Pennsylvania law by providing the enemy with provisions for their aid and comfort.

Coxe almost certainly benefited from an extended network of contacts on the American side. Joseph Reed, who would prosecute treason cases for the state later that fall, actively worked to restore Coxe's standing in the community while serving as President of the Supreme Executive Council. Reed expected that "magnanimity" would "overlook casual errors" and that Coxe would be "fully restore[d]" to his "friends and country."[133] Coxe had been a groomsman at the 1776 wedding of Benjamin Rush, who signed the Declaration of Independence, and his cousin Tench Tilghman was a close aide to General Washington. Even Thomas McKean was a friend of the Coxe family.[134] These connections in themselves might not have saved Coxe from trial (the equally well-connected William Hamilton was nonetheless tried for treason that fall), but they made it less likely that full evidence would be presented against him. Coxe eventually recovered his position in Philadelphia society and would later serve in numerous federal and state offices, including as assistant secretary of the treasury under Alexander Hamilton. When he was appointed a Pennsylvania delegate to the Continental

Congress in 1788, anonymous critics denounced the appointment of a notorious Tory.[135]

McKean's light treatment of Coxe reflected his general belief that the state would most likely pardon most offenders. Writing to his fellow justice William Augustus Atlee, McKean asserted that

> [a]fter a sufficient time has elapsed for discriminating, the Sta[te may?] no doubt grant a general pardon, excepting your cruel fellows & some men of property, whose estates really ought to be confiscated, tho' their lives are spared. Parricides should at least give some evidence of repentance before they are forgiven, and they deserve the punishment of suspense at any rate. The application and interest that will be made by the relatives & friends of the culprits for mercy will create respect to the Rulers, and their granting it on every reasonable occasion will reconcile & endear men to the Government: besides pardoning is a God-like power, and a God-like virtue.[136]

Even after the depredations of the British invasion, Pennsylvania's chief justice, at least, expected that no one would swing from the gallows in revenge.

Hiring Prosecutors and Court Employees

By August 1778, it was clear that numerous treason trials would be conducted that fall. The Council informed the Assembly that as "the professors of law are supposed to be making great sums of money by espousing the cause of the disaffected," a more liberal provision for the Attorney General would be required, including the appointment of "one or more able Gentlemen of the law" to assist him. This provision was the "more necessary as there is every reason to suppose that some of the persons who are charged with treasonable practices will endeavour to obtain, at any expense, the advice of the most experienced Council in this and the neighboring states. The bringing of traitors to justice is at all times an object of great importance, and more especially so in our present circumstances."[137] The Assembly agreed and authorized the Council to hire an additional lawyer. The position went to Joseph Reed (Figure 5.3), a Pennsylvania delegate to the Continental Congress, who, the Council concluded, could "render the state more essential service in the important trials now coming on, than any other person within our knowledge." Reed was offered two thousand pounds to focus on "the important trials of traitors, which will employ the Supreme Court during the next winter."[138] The thirty-five-year-old Reed had studied at Middle Temple and had developed a successful legal career, although he had little experience with

FIGURE 5.3 Attorney Joseph Reed prosecuted treason cases and later became President of Pennsylvania's Supreme Executive Council.
Credit: AR Collection/Alamy Stock Photo.

criminal cases.[139] He had served as president of Pennsylvania's 1775 Provincial Convention, as an aide to General Washington, and as adjutant general of the Continental Army[140]

In a curious twist, Reed's own loyalty would be called into question that fall. At the trial of William Hamilton, General John Cadwalader, noting the "force of [Reed's] declamation labored to inflame [Hamilton's] judge and jury against him," loudly exclaimed, "It argued the extremity of effrontery and baseness in one man to pursue another to death for taking a step, which his own foot had been once raised to take." Cadwalader claimed that prior to the Battle of Trenton, Reed had openly spoken of abandoning the American cause and joining the British.[141] Benedict Arnold, of all people, seized on this allegation in his January 1780 court-martial, claiming that Reed had considered "going over to the enemy."[142] Reed was also accused of having failed to take the required oath of allegiance until October 1778. An anonymous writer later mocked Reed, stating, "Posterity will review, as the greatest wonder of the revolution, a government administered for three years by a British subject . . . [E]ven Arnold himself will draw consolation, for the first time since his desertion, when he finds how much your conduct exceeds his own in baseness and malignity."[143] Reed unsurprisingly had a different view of his character, claiming in the fall of 1778 that "after fighting the open Enemies of our Country, I have now devoted my poor Talents to its Service in pleading its Cause against those Wretches who have secretly been endeavoring to ruin it."[144]

Shortly after Reed's appointment, and just ten days before the state's first treason trial was scheduled to begin, Attorney General Jonathan Dickinson Sergeant (Figure 5.4) suddenly announced his resignation. Sergeant claimed that he had found "the labour so great, and the compensation so very inadequate, that I have long wished to be discharged from it; but the shame of desertion in time of danger and the hope of more liberal appointments, when the legislature should have leisure to attend to it, have hitherto restrained me."[145] Sergeant's letter should probably not be taken at face value. Although his job was undoubtedly difficult, his labors had been reduced by the appointment of an assistant, and

FIGURE 5.4 Jonathan Dickinson Sergeant served as Pennsylvania's Attorney General from 1777 to 1780.

Credit: Jonathan Dickinson Sergeant, by Charles Willson Peale/Paul Fearn/Alamy Stock Photo.

abandoning his job on the eve of the most critical trials he had yet faced would surely open him to charges of desertion.[146] Perhaps he was frustrated by the large sum appropriated to Reed and was simply angling for more money for himself, by resigning at the time of his maximum value to the state. No surviving sources explain what happened next, but somehow Sergeant was persuaded to remain in his position.[147]

An additional appointment in August was equally important. The justices of the Supreme Court appointed attorney Edward Burd as prothonotary, or clerk, of the court.[148] Through his mother, Burd was a member of the prominent Shippen family, which had dominated the legal profession in Pennsylvania and held many of the leading positions in the colony's government. The Revolution found the family divided; many of Burd's relatives fled to the British and several of them were named in the first attainder proclamation. Before the British occupation, several prominent Shippens had been detained or subjected to parole.[149] Burd's brother-in-law, Peter Grubb, had been accused by Lancaster officials in October 1776 of toasting George III.[150] A few months later, commanding a battalion of Lancaster County militia, Grubb refused to march into New Jersey and instead took his men home.[151] He was later investigated for suspicious comments surrounding the explosion of a powder mill at French Creek.[152] Burd, by contrast, supported the Revolution, served in the army, and was briefly taken by the British as a prisoner of war. But even he had come under suspicion in April 1776 "for being that Monster a Tory," and been "attacked very warmly" by persons of a more radical disposition.[153] Shortly after his appointment as prothonotary, Burd married his first cousin Elizabeth Shippen, whose sister Margaret, known as Peggy, would marry Benedict Arnold a year later.[154]

Although Burd supported independence, he was a persistent critic of Pennsylvania's new government. The Council's rhetoric on freedom of speech was hypocritical, he felt, since that body so flagrantly violated the liberties of others, engaging in actions that violated "every idea I have of government." He strongly opposed the Test Act and the exiling of prominent Philadelphians to Virginia, a decision made on "base suspicion" only. Burd noted that treason and misprision of treason were extensively defined, and argued that if the exiles had been guilty of misprision, they should have been properly tried in a court of law. At the bottom of a 1777 letter to Jasper Yeates, he caustically added, "Since so little regard is paid to the laws perhaps I might be apprehended on suspicion and confined in jail if I travel to Lancaster this winter."[155]

Chief Justice McKean probably did not know that Burd had previously described him as behaving in "a violent and imperious manner."[156] But he and the other justices certainly knew that Burd was highly critical of the state government and that numerous members of his family had come under suspicion for disloyalty. Burd's appointment, shortly before the first treason trials were scheduled to begin, sent a strong message. The justices felt no need to hire a committed radical and felt perfectly comfortable with someone who might have every reason to be sympathetic to persons improperly charged with disloyalty.

Trial by Jury in Chester County

Before beginning the lengthy sessions for Philadelphia, the Supreme Court justices held their oyer and terminer session for Chester County. It was here, on September 18, 1778, over two years after independence was declared, that Pennsylvania's first official treason trial began. The common-law criminal jury, developed over hundreds of years in an island kingdom three thousand miles away, would here be deployed in a way Englishmen could never have imagined—to try as traitors those men who had remained loyal to their English king. The defendant was a wheelwright named Joseph Malin, who had been named in the June 15 attainder proclamation. This trial has posed difficulties for scholars because of peculiarities in the source material and failures to understand the legal background against which the attorneys were acting. The first problem is that the records for the Chester sitting of the court have not been preserved, and thus details of the trial must be gleaned from other sources. Historians have generally relied on Alexander Dallas, who included the Malin trial in his first volume of *Pennsylvania Reports*, published in the 1790s.[157] Dallas, however, erroneously placed the trial in Philadelphia County, a venue directly contradicted by the jurisdictional arguments raised in the case. Dallas also reported a motion made in the cases of Joshua Molder and John Taylor and attributed them to Philadelphia County. Dallas's errors have led to significant chronological confusion in several prominent accounts.[158] The unreliable "Black List" of persons attainted for high treason, published in 1802, also misdescribes the case, stating that Malin surrendered and was discharged, when he was actually tried and acquitted.[159] The most reliable sources for the Malin trial are a September 19, 1778 letter by Edward Burd to Jasper Yeates and a September 22, 1778 *Pennsylvania Packet* report.[160]

Malin was represented by two of America's finest attorneys, James Wilson and George Ross, and they fought the case "inch by inch," according to Edward Burd.[161] Wilson had immigrated to the United States from his native Scotland in his twenties, and practiced law in Reading and Carlisle before moving to Philadelphia. His 1774 pamphlet, *Considerations on the Nature and Extent of the Legislative Authority of the British Parliament*, had established his reputation as one of the leading political and legal thinkers of the Revolution. He would later serve as a key member of the Constitutional Convention and as a justice of the United States Supreme Court.[162] Ross was a prominent attorney from Lancaster, who had previously served on the state's Committee of Safety. It is unclear how Malin came to retain these attorneys or why they agreed to appear in the case, but their appearances at the Chester court and in the subsequent Philadelphia trials were among the most extraordinary events of the American Revolution. Connected through marriage, both Wilson and Ross had signed the Declaration of Independence as delegates to the Continental Congress from Pennsylvania, and had pledged their lives, fortunes, and sacred honor to the cause of American independence.[163] If the British were successful, there was a real risk that both men might be drawn and quartered as traitors who had violated their allegiance to George III.[164] As members of the Continental Congress, Wilson and Ross had served together on a five-member committee to "prepare an effectual plan for suppressing the internal enemies of America, and preventing a communication of intelligence to our other enemies."[165] Wilson had served on the Congress's Board of War, and the Board's July 1777 recommendation to exile prominent Philadelphians in anticipation of the British invasion was written in Wilson's hand.[166]

Although their patriot credentials were indisputable, Wilson and Ross were also strong opponents of the Pennsylvania constitution of 1776. Ross had been vice chairman of the constitutional convention and had served on the committee that drafted the ordinance on treason, but he ultimately refused to endorse the document the convention had adopted.[167] Wilson considered the constitution "the most detestable that ever was formed."[168] It has been suggested that Wilson and Ross took these cases as way of demonstrating their contempt for the state government. But if this factor played a role, it was likely a small one. There was nothing about the state judiciary that Wilson and Ross found particularly objectionable, and the prosecution of at least some traitors after the British invasion was almost inevitable, whatever the form of the Pennsylvania constitution. Moreover, the suggestion reduces an indisputable act of courage to mere political pettiness. Another uncharitable interpretation was offered by former Chief Justice Benjamin Chew, who speculated that "Ross is likely to make a fortune as counsel for the proscribed, whose numbers are already very great, some of them very fat clients too."[169]

The decision to defend the treason cases is more plausibly explained by the novel and fascinating questions raised by the cases and by the lawyers' general commitment to the rule of law. Although few lawyers in eighteenth-century Philadelphia found much of intellectual interest in the criminal law in general, treason cases were different. Treason law was the most complicated and subtle branch of English criminal law, an area in which legal expertise made a real difference. Because of this complexity, defense counsel were allowed to appear in English treason cases well before they were allowed to appear in cases of ordinary felony.[170] These were the first cases of high treason ever tried before a court in Pennsylvania and they attracted a considerable amount of attention. Moreover, appearing for the defendants demonstrated a deep commitment to the rule of law and to the idea that even the most unpopular defendants deserve a fair hearing in court. It would be very hard to argue that the trials were unfair if the defendants were vigorously represented by two signers of the Declaration of Independence. John Adams has received abundant praise for his work defending British soldiers in the Boston Massacre trial, but the work of Wilson and Ross during the Pennsylvania treason trials is even more exemplary, even though it is much less widely known. All three men took on unpopular causes, but Wilson and Ross, unlike Adams, defended their cases in the middle of a war and at far greater personal risk. Indeed, as noted in the Introduction, Wilson's role in the treason trials almost led to his death at the hands of an armed mob.

The Malin case opened with a significant procedural issue. Wilson and Ross made a motion that defendants in treason cases be provided a copy of the indictment, a list of the prosecution witnesses, and the names of the panel from whom the jury would be drawn at least five days before trial.[171] This motion invoked a long history. The famous Treason Trials Act of 1696, enacted in the wake of Stuart excesses in treason cases, had entitled a treason defendant to a copy of the indictment five days before trial and a copy of the jury panel two days before trial. A statute from the reign of Queen Anne, effective upon the death of the Stuart pretender, extended these protections by providing the defendant with a list of the prosecution witnesses, including their professions and place of abode, along with the jury panel and the indictment ten days prior to trial. Foster's treatise had expressed doubts about this statute, arguing that "furnishing the prisoner with the names, professions, and places of abode of the witnesses and jury so long before the trial may serve many bad purposes which are too obvious to be mentioned." At minimum, Foster felt, the Crown should be entitled to the same opportunity "of sifting the character of the prisoner's witnesses."[172] According to Edward Burd, Wilson and Ross had "insisted" on the benefit of this statute of Anne, even though they requested only the shorter time provided by the 1696 act.[173] After his appointment to the United States Supreme Court, Wilson would argue in a grand-jury charge that the "greatness of those advantages may be easily estimated by contemplating the hapless, the forlorn and anxious situation of a person, who is deprived of them in a trial for his life."[174]

The motion raised the question whether provisions of English treason law, intended to be beneficial to the defendant, were applicable in Pennsylvania. The justices concluded that the Pennsylvania Assembly had specifically repealed all provisions of English law respecting high treason, including the Treason Trials Act and the Statute of Anne. But the Assembly had not passed any legislation governing procedure in treason trials. The court was thus left to fashion a rule of its own. It concluded that the defendant could have the indictment and the panel list one day before trial, but was not entitled to the witness list at all.[175]

This was not an especially generous decision. Not only would the Statute of Anne not apply, but Pennsylvania treason defendants in 1778 would also lack even the procedural protections granted to English treason defendants under the 1696 act.[176] Nonetheless, it is possible that the court routinely provided this information earlier than the absolute minimum of one day. When sentencing Abijah Wright to death later that winter, Chief Justice McKean stated, "A copy of your indictment, and of the panel of the jury who were to try you, was delivered to you many days before your trial, that you might be prepared in the best manner for your defence and challenges."[177]

Wilson and Ross then moved that the prosecutor be endorsed, meaning personally subject to the costs if the prosecution failed. The court denied this motion, perhaps concluding that endorsement was appropriate for private prosecutors, but not for the state attorney general.[178]

There are no records of the witnesses or testimony in the trial, but Dallas reported mid-trial motions on two evidentiary issues. The first arose out of Malin's own incompetence. He had gone over to what he thought were British troops, but which turned out to be American. He had thus attempted to join the British army, but had failed. Pennsylvania law did not specifically criminalize attempted treason, and at the time of the Malin trial there was no generalized law of criminal attempt; the subject first appears in legal treatises in the nineteenth century.[179] Thus Malin's actions could not legally amount to treason.[180] Attorney General Sergeant sought to introduce words spoken by Malin to indicate his true intent. Wilson and Ross objected, arguing that as "words did not amount to treason, no general evidence could be given of a man's sentiments; but that the intention expressed by any words offered in evidence, must relate immediately to the overt act laid and proved on the indictment." Since adherence to American troops, "even under the supposition that they were British," did not amount to treason, no words relating to this evidence could be introduced. The attorney general agreed that "words alone do not amount to treason," but argued that the evidence could be admitted to show the defendant's intent.[181]

The court agreed with Wilson and Ross in part, ruling that "no evidence of words relative to the mistake of the American troops can be admitted; for any adherence to them, though contrary to the design of the party, cannot possibly come within the idea of treason." Nonetheless, since there was evidence that the defendant was "actually with the enemy at another time, words indicating his intention to join them, are proper testimony to explain the motives, upon which that intention was afterwards carried into effect." In other words, the overt act of treason could not be going to the Americans, but the subsequent act of being present with British troops. With respect to that overt act, the evidence was admissible.[182]

The second issue arose when Attorney General Sergeant sought to call a witness to testify that the defendant "had been seen parading with the enemy's light horse in the city of Philadelphia." According to Dallas's Reports, Wilson and Ross objected that the evidence could not be introduced, since overt acts of treason must be tried in the county where the act occurred. Sergeant replied that once an overt act had been proved in Chester County, "corroborative evidence may be given of overt acts committed in any other county." The court agreed with the attorney general, holding that "evidence might be given of an overt act, committed in another county, after an overt act was proved to have been committed in the county where the indictment was laid and tried."[183]

The trial had begun in the early afternoon and didn't end until the morning of the next day, when the jury returned with a verdict of not guilty.[184] The *Pennsylvania Packet* reported that the jury had been sworn "for twenty hours."[185] It is hard to know why the jury decided as it did. G.S. Rowe stated that "McKean's charge to the jury favored the defense," but no such jury charge survives.[186] Bradley Chapin, under the mistaken impression that the defense successfully managed to exclude evidence in both motions, claimed that the prosecution was "checked on both counts," leading to the not-guilty verdict.[187] But the motions reported by Dallas are only snapshots of a longer trial, and it is impossible to conclusively link the court's rulings to the verdict; if anything, the rulings were more favorable to the prosecution than to the defense. The court may have had its doubts about Malin's innocence, as it ordered him to provide security for his good behavior during the present war.[188]

Malin's acquittal nonetheless put the state on notice that convictions in treason trials would not be obtained easily. Every point would be fiercely contested by defense lawyers, and the court's rulings would not necessarily favor the prosecution. The savage popular rhetoric against traitors would carry little sway in the courtroom, where jurors would inevitably decide each case on its own merits.

* * *

A few days later, the justices, sitting as the Court of Oyer and Terminer for Philadelphia County, began the Revolution's lengthiest and most significant series of treason trials. Here, in the city where independence had been declared and where the British army had ruled just months earlier, the legal consequences of that independence would be played out in the most vivid manner imaginable. Twenty-three men would stand trial for their lives, accused of treason for remaining loyal to their English king.

6

The Philadelphia Treason Trials, 1778–1779

FORMING THE JURY

ON A COLD winter's day on December 15, 1790, James Wilson, now a justice of the United States Supreme Court, inaugurated his series of law lectures in a large hall at the College of Philadelphia. For Wilson, this moment, the summit of his professional career, nonetheless radiated warmth. Looking out into the hall, Wilson would see President George Washington, First Lady Martha Washington, Vice President John Adams, and numerous members of the United States Congress and the Pennsylvania legislature.[1] They were all there to hear Wilson, perhaps the most erudite legal mind in America, embark on his most ambitious intellectual project—a comprehensive overview of American law that bade fair to establish Wilson as the American Blackstone.[2]

The most distinctive procedural aspect of Anglo-American law, of course, was the jury system. To the audience that night, Wilson explained, "The rights and duties of jurors, in the United States, are great and extensive. No punishment can be inflicted without the intervention of one. . . . Is it not, then, of immense consequence . . . that jurors should possess the spirit of just discernment, to discriminate between the innocent and the guilty?"[3] The jury system would be one of Wilson's persistent themes; indeed, the published version of Wilson's lectures contains forty-six pages on juries (and only three on judges).[4] As he would put it in a later lecture, "To be tried only by men of one's own condition, is one of the greatest blessings—to know that one can be tried only by such men, is one of the greatest securities—which can be enjoyed under any government."[5] The jury was "the most excellent method for the investigation and discovery of truth; and the best guardian of both public and private liberty, which has hitherto been devised by the ingenuity of man."[6]

Wilson consistently lectured in the detached voice of the scholar and never referred to the particulars of individual cases or to his own experiences. When speaking of the jury, however, Wilson almost certainly had a particular set of trials in mind. It was in this very room, just twelve years earlier, that Wilson had defended the most significant capital cases of his career. Between September 1778 and April 1779, twenty-three men were tried for high treason for aiding the British during the British occupation of Philadelphia. Although these men were charged with attempting to undo the very Revolution to which Wilson had pledged his life, his fortune, and his sacred honor, Wilson appeared in court, as he had in Chester County, not to prosecute them, but to defend them. From the defense perspective, the results had been spectacular; Philadelphia juries acquitted nineteen of the twenty-three men, a high acquittal rate even in an age known for widespread jury leniency.[7] And in three of the four cases in which the jury convicted, the jurors petitioned the Supreme Executive Council for clemency. Even the judges who presided at the trials were surprised, attributing the verdicts, not to the actual innocence of the defendants, but to the "extreme lenity and tenderness of the Juries."[8]

These results raise a fundamental question: Why were Philadelphia jurors so willing to acquit defendants of treason in the middle of a convulsive civil war, the most violent and disruptive event any of them would ever know? To answer this question, we must begin with the jurors themselves. What type of person served on a Philadelphia jury? What prior experiences and preconceptions did he bring to the jury box? What processes were used to select the juries? These questions are usually unanswered by historians, who tend to focus on the more visible role of judges and speak only generically about "juries." Such reluctance is understandable, as the cliché of the jury as a black box remains powerful to this day. Yet with sufficient diligence the box can be opened, even after 240 years, and we can enter that room at the College of Philadelphia, where twelve men would sit in judgment of the allegiance of their peers.

The wheels of English criminal procedure, rusty from several years of disuse, began turning again in Philadelphia on August 21, 1778, when the three justices of the Supreme Court issued a precept to Philadelphia County Sheriff James Claypoole for holding a Court of Oyer and Terminer and General Gaol Delivery at the State House, beginning on Monday, September 21. The next day, Claypoole issued a proclamation announcing the court's sitting.[9] Claypoole presumably selected and summoned the grand jury and the panel of trial jurors sometime between August 21 and September 21.

The State House, now known as Independence Hall, was the most natural location for the trials, as it held the courtroom where the Pennsylvania Supreme Court had sat since 1743.[10] This courtroom was directly opposite the Assembly

Room, where the Continental Congress had approved the Declaration of Independence. Delays in restoring the State House courtroom from damage during the British occupation, however, meant that this highly symbolic location for treason trials would be unavailable. The trials were instead conducted at the College of Philadelphia.[11] The second floor of the College's New Building, known as "College Hall," would have been well suited to public trials. Over ninety feet long, it had a raised platform on the north end, where the judges presumably sat, and additional seating galleries on the south end. The Hall had become a major part of Philadelphia's cultural life, and was used for plays, concerts, lectures, and organ recitals.[12] Now the Hall would have to serve the very different purpose of trying the most contentious capital cases in Pennsylvania's history.

The Grand Jurors

The first hurdle on a prosecutor's path to conviction was the grand jury. In his Law Lectures, James Wilson celebrated the grand jury as "the peculiar boast of the common law." No institution, Wilson argued, was "so well fitted for avoiding abuses, which might otherwise arise from malice, from rigour, from negligence, or from partiality in the prosecution of crimes."[13] The grand jury of Wilson's day was a significant institution; in an era where private prosecutions were common, only the grand jury stood between a criminal defendant and the hazards of a baseless prosecution. The grand jury that sat in Philadelphia in the fall of 1778 took its screening function seriously, rejecting treason charges at a higher rate than it did for other crimes. The men who sat on this jury thus played an important, although underappreciated, role in the treason cases.

When the court of oyer and terminer convened on September 21, 1778, an eighteen-member grand jury was sworn in. It started work immediately, as the first treason trial, that of Abraham Carlisle, began just four days later.[14] The grand jurors continued to sit until October 16, and at one point petitioned the Pennsylvania Assembly for additional payments, noting that this "unusual length of time" had caused them to incur significant expenses, which ought to be borne by the public.[15] There is no direct documentation concerning where the grand jury met, what procedures it used, or what type of evidence it considered.[16] A few hints can be gleaned from a 1783 dispute over a grand jury's refusal to indict a newspaper publisher, Eleazar Oswald, for seditious libel.[17] Chief Justice McKean, the target of the alleged libel, had criticized the grand jury severely, prompting the grand jury to defend itself in the press. The foreman, Zebulon Potts, had served on the 1778 grand jury that heard the treason cases. Potts argued that the grand jury had the right to examine whatever witnesses it pleased, without prior approval of the court. The "whole truth" could not be established without "testimony on both sides."[18] McKean responded that no grand jury "before the present had ever treated the Court with so much contempt, as to send for and examine witnesses without their knowledge."[19] If McKean's statement is correct, witnesses before the treason grand jury would have been approved by the court before testifying.[20] The Oswald grand jury met at a tavern, and witnesses waited in the tavern's front room.[21] Chief Justice McKean sneeringly complained that the Oswald affair should not be "smothered in a corner in a tavern, as it appeared to be." The 1778 grand jury may have met in a tavern as well, although it may have met in a separate room at the College of Philadelphia.[22]

Over the course of its term, the grand jury considered at least forty-one separate cases.[23] Thirty-eight involved charges of treason. In the 1770s, Pennsylvania grand juries indicted at an average rate of 80%, but the Philadelphia grand jury found indictments in only twenty-four of the treason cases, yielding an indictment rate of 63.2%.[24] Without evidence of the internal deliberations, it is hard to know what factors led the grand jury to indict. A small hint, however, is provided by the attainder proclamations. Accused persons named in the attainder proclamation were indicted at a much higher rate (90%) than were persons who had not been named (53.5%). The evidence was perhaps stronger in the cases initiated by proclamation and there may have been less risk of manipulation by private prosecutors.

The relative lenity of the grand jurors toward persons accused of treason inevitably raises questions about the grand jury's composition. What type of person served on the grand jury, and do any personal characteristics help explain why the grand jurors reached the decisions that they did? William Blackstone memorably described English grand jurors as "gentlemen of the best figure in the county."[25] James Wilson agreed, stating in a 1790 grand-jury charge that grand juries should be "composed of men distinguished by their talents and their virtues—of men, entitled to the first grade of character in the country or state. . . . It is the duty of the returning officer, that such men be returned."[26] The Philadelphia grand jurors fit comfortably into these definitions. They were wealthy, prominent individuals with a deep commitment to the revolutionary cause. Table 6.1 sets forth basic demographic information about the grand jurors.

Although the grand jurors came from a wide range of backgrounds, their most distinguishing characteristic was their wealth. In 1779, the average assessed wealth in the City of Philadelphia was £29.19, and the median was £5.[27] By contrast, the seventeen grand jurors identifiable in the tax records had an average assessed wealth of £2262.47 and a median wealth of £450. Only two grand jurors had an assessed wealth below the 80th percentile, and ten were in the 90th percentile or higher. At least ten owned or had owned slaves. Some had inherited significant land holdings, while others had accumulated fortunes in various occupations.

Table 6.1 Grand Jurors, Philadelphia County Court of Oyer and Terminer, Fall 1778*

Name	Age	Occupation	Religion	Ethnicity
Ball, William	48	goldsmith/merchant	Baptist	English
Curry, Robert	44		Presbyterian	
Cuthbert, Thomas	65	retired mast-maker	Anglican	Scottish
Dean, Joseph	40	merchant	Presbyterian	Irish
Dorsey, John		shopkeeper	Quaker	
Fleeson, Plunket	66	upholsterer; justice of the peace	Anglican	Irish
Hasenclever, Francis		merchant	Lutheran	German
Hunter, James	49	merchant	Presbyterian	Scottish
Laughlin, Jacob		assessor		
Loxley, Benjamin	57	carpenter	Baptist	English
Moore, John	55	justice of the peace	Dutch Reformed	Dutch
Neff, Rudolph	50	wheelwright	German Reformed	Swiss
Potts, Zebulon	32	justice of the peace	Quaker	Welsh/English
Pryor, Thomas	42	baker/flour inspector	Quaker	
Purviance, John		merchant		
Quee, Seth	≤44	farmer; justice of the peace	Presbyterian	Scottish
Snyder, David		miller		German
Young, James	49	merchant; justice of the peace	Anglican	Scottish

*Full references for much of these data, and for Table 6.2, are in Larson, "Revolutionary American Jury," 1511–1512. The data in Tables 6.1 and 6.2 include corrections and additional genealogical information obtained through the Historical Society of Pennsylvania and online. The age column reflects age as of September 21, 1778.

Five were merchants, six were skilled artisans, and one, William Ball, was both an artisan and a merchant. Five were currently serving as justices of the peace and two others had served as justice of the peace in 1776.[28]

Grand-juror ethnicity and religion reflected the pluralistic nature of Pennsylvania society. Their numbers included at least four jurors of Scottish ancestry, two English, two Irish, two German, one Swiss, one Dutch, and one of mixed Welsh and English ancestry. Francis Hasenclever, born in Germany, had become a naturalized citizen only five years earlier.[29] Indeed, the grand jurors may have been more ethnically diverse than Pennsylvania's revolutionary leadership in general, which one historian has estimated as approximately 60% English.[30] Religious affiliations included four Presbyterians, three Anglicans, three Quakers, two Baptists, one Lutheran, one Dutch Reformed, and one German Reformed. Ages of the eleven grand jurors for whom age can be determined ranged from 32 to 66, with an average age of 49.75 and a median age of 49.[31]

The grand jurors were veteran players on Pennsylvania's revolutionary stage. Although Plunket Fleeson had been elected to the Pennsylvania Assembly in 1762,[32] most grand jurors rose to political prominence during the Revolution itself. By late 1774, fully a third of the grand jurors had assumed positions of leadership in the resistance movement. Two were named to an early committee of mechanics formed in June 1774 to "convince the world Americans were born and determined to live free, and that they will never be slaves; that liberty is their birthright—they cannot, they will not give it up."[33] Five were elected in the fall of 1774 to serve on the Philadelphia City Committee, and one was elected to the Philadelphia County Committee.[34] Six were also named in December 1774 to the city's Committee of Inspection and Observation, formed to enforce the resolutions of the First Continental Congress.[35]

In the months prior to independence, grand-juror political involvement increased significantly. Eight grand jurors served as delegates to the Pennsylvania Provincial Convention that met in January 1775.[36] The convention resolved that if Great Britain "should determine by force to effect a submission to the late arbitrary acts of the British Parliament, in such a situation we hold it our indispensable duty to resist such force, and at every hazard to defend the rights and liberties of America."[37] In the August 1775 elections for the Philadelphia Committee of Inspection, three "tickets" were pitted against one another: a radical "mechanics" ticket, a "moderate" ticket, and a "conservative" ticket, although many men were named on all three tickets.[38] Five grand jurors were named on the "mechanics" ticket,[39] six on the "moderate" ticket,[40] and four on the "conservative" ticket.[41] Of the seven grand jurors standing for election, all five named on the mechanics ticket were elected.[42] These five were re-elected in February 1776, along with Joseph Dean. They served alongside Benjamin Franklin, future Assistant

Attorney General Joseph Reed, and future Chief Justice Thomas McKean.[43] In June 1776, Joseph Dean and Benjamin Loxley were delegates to the provincial conference that called for a state constitutional convention.[44]

Several of the grand jurors had provided skilled services to the war effort. Thomas Pryor cowrote articles with Thomas Paine about saltpeter and ammunition in the fall of 1775.[45] Upholsterer Plunket Fleeson provided tents to George Washington, several of which still survive.[46]

There is little surviving evidence on the motivations for the grand jurors' embrace of resistance activity. The best source is the autobiography of master carpenter Benjamin Loxley. He later recalled that in 1775, "the inhabitants of America found that the Parliament of England was determined to oppress and chain down Americans to their arbitrary will." Loxley was hesitant to take up revolutionary activities "on account of the oaths I had taken to King George at the three times when I had received commissions under him (that I should be perjured)." But Loxley met with his fellow committee members, and they determined that "King George had broken his coronation oath with us, wherein he engaged to protect all his subjects in free liberty of conscience and lawful rights and now he had broken that promise."[47]

In the years following independence, the grand jurors continued to take a leading role in state and city affairs. Five of the grand jurors were named as justices of the peace for the City and County of Philadelphia County by the Pennsylvania Assembly in September 1776, and one was named a justice of the peace for the state of Pennsylvania.[48] In this capacity, they would have contact with many of the men later charged with treason. James Young, for example, issued the arrest warrant for defendant John Roberts.[49] Joseph Dean was named an assistant to the state's Council of Safety in December 1776, and later served as a member of the state's Board of War.[50] James Young was one of six men named by the Pennsylvania Assembly to discharge prisoners from the Philadelphia jail in August 1776.[51] John Purviance was named by the Continental Congress as a manager of the United States Lottery in November 1776 and served on a committee to arrest "such persons as are deemed inimical to the cause of American Liberty."[52] Robert Curry and Jacob Laughlin were elected as Philadelphia City Commissioners in 1777.[53] John Moore was elected a delegate to the Pennsylvania Assembly for Philadelphia County in 1777, although he resigned his seat later that year to take office as a Philadelphia County justice of the peace. Moore was also an agent for disposing of the confiscated estates of attainted and convicted traitors.[54] James Young and Plunket Fleeson were appointed as judges of the Philadelphia City Court in June 1777.[55]

Despite their embrace of revolutionary activity, the grand jurors had a mixed military record. Seven were fined at some point during the Revolution for failing to perform militia duties, a failure that was widespread among the Philadelphia population.[56] By contrast, three were named as militia officers in May 1775, when the Philadelphia militia was first formed.[57] Another three were appointed officers by Philadelphia County in July 1776 for the "Flying Camp," a "strategic reserve of militia troops for the Continental Army drawn from the Middle Atlantic States in 1776."[58] Grand jurors John Moore and Robert Curry were colonels of their respective battalions of Philadelphia County militia in 1777.[59] Moore also served as wagon master for Philadelphia County, as a commissioner of purchase, and as an agent for the forfeited estates of traitors.[60] James Young was wagon master for the state of Pennsylvania.[61] David Snyder was a lieutenant of the Light Dragoons, and Benjamin Loxley, who had led the Philadelphia Artillery in the defense against the Paxton Boys, was captain of an artillery company.[62]

The British invasion of 1777 brought significant disruption in its wake. Most of the grand jurors seem to have fled Philadelphia, although at least two, William Ball and Thomas Pryor, remained.[63] Ball's motivations are unknown, but Pryor may have remained because his wife was seriously ill.[64] Nonetheless he took the opportunity to engage in espionage, as he appears to have been arrested by the British for sending intelligence to Washington's army.[65] Many suffered significant deprivations at the hands of the British army. Benjamin Loxley, for example, had let his house in Philadelphia to Carey Brown, "second-captain of one of our gondolas." But, as Loxley explained, Brown "proved a villain, joined the British with his boat and crew, broke open my rooms where my furniture etc. were locked up, robbed me of them all, and assisted the enemy to destroy and damage sundry buildings and property of mine to a very great amount."[66] William Ball would later report damage to his estate of £1385.[67]

Most of the grand jurors would thus have had ample reason to be bitter and resentful to those Philadelphians who had assisted the British army during the occupation, and their early actions bore this out. Four of the grand jurors joined the "Patriotic Association," which sought to bring suspected traitors to trial.[68] In August 1778, William Ball accused Timothy Curby of calling him a rebel and was endorsed to prosecute Curby at the county quarter sessions.[69] The grand jurors ultimately indicted more individuals of treason than were convicted. But the rate of indictment for treason was still lower than that for other crimes. Was there something about treason that was different?

For the grand jury's foreman, James Young, the issue of treason struck very close to home.[70] Young's only surviving son, John, had fled Philadelphia to join the British in January 1776.[71] In New York, John was accepted into the royal army and sent on a ship to Boston. A shipwreck resulted in his quick capture by American forces.[72] The New York Committee of Safety, displaying considerable lenity, ordered him returned to Philadelphia. The committee noted that the "unhappy excursions of the son of any gentleman friendly to the general interests of America, give us great pain . . . [The] good sense of the parent, co-operating with filial piety, will bring the young gentleman to a proper sense of his duty."[73] In March, James Young requested that the Continental Congress parole his wayward son to a relative's estate approximately twenty miles from Philadelphia.[74] The Congress granted the request, but in September 1777 John broke his parole and rejoined the British at Germantown. He served in the British army until the end of the war, and was named as an attainted traitor in the proclamation of May 21, 1778.[75]

As a grand juror, James Young was confronted with indictments of people accused of doing precisely what his own son had done. Indeed, one of the indicted defendants, George Harding, served alongside John Young as an officer in the First Battalion of Pennsylvania Loyalists.[76] The other grand jurors almost certainly knew that Young's son, like Benjamin Franklin's, had sided with the British. This was probably not the only connection between the defendants and the grand jurors. Adam Stricker, indicted by the grand jurors for treason that fall, married the daughter of grand juror Rudolph Neff on July 18, 1779.[77] In October 1779, grand juror Francis Hasenclever was a surety on a bond for Peter Miller, indicted for treason. The other surety was Samuel Garrigues, Jr., the son of another indicted defendant.[78]

In short, although deeply committed to the revolutionary cause, the grand jurors were all familiar with people who had made the opposite choice. The British adherents could not be easily dismissed as unnatural monsters—they were family and friends with ties dating back for many years. In these circumstances, lenity for the accused might be justified in ways that would be unthinkable for cases of murder or rape. As we shall see, this tendency to treat treason differently from the way other capital crimes were treated was even more pronounced with the trial jurors, to whom we shall now turn.

Trial-Juror Selection: The Panel and Challenges

The sheriff of Philadelphia County played the initial role in jury selection by returning a panel of potential jurors, from which the jurors for each case would be selected. Assembling this panel was a significant power. As James Wilson later noted, "The selection and return of jurors is a most momentous part of the power and duty of a sheriff. It is that part, in which abuses are most fatal: it is that part, in which there is the greatest opportunity and temptation to commit them."[79] In 1783, the Council warned the Assembly that a "dangerous power is vested in sheriffs, by leaving the election of jurors totally dependent upon their pleasure."[80] This power may have been even more significant than the power to return the grand jury; the grand jury functioned by majority vote, but a single trial juror could force a hung jury.

Philadelphia's sheriff during the treason trials was James Claypoole (Figure 6.1), a fifty-seven-year-old Anglican house painter and glazier.[81] His 1779 tax assessment of £35 placed him in the top 20% of Philadelphia taxpayers, but he was significantly less wealthy than most of the grand jurors.[82] He appears to have been a serial office seeker, having previously sought the office of coroner in 1773 and recorder of deeds in 1776.[83] In February 1777, he was elected a Philadelphia City Commissioner, where he served alongside grand jurors Robert Curry and Jacob Laughlin.[84] Claypoole was appointed to the vacant office of sheriff of Philadelphia County in June 1777.[85] In the fall of 1777, Claypoole was elected sheriff, and he served in that office until 1780.[86] Claypoole was running for re-election during the treason trials, and he published newspaper advertisements seeking votes.[87]

FIGURE 6.1 James Claypoole, Sheriff of Philadelphia County, selected the grand jurors and the panel of trial jurors.

Credit: Portrait of James Claypoole, by Charles Willson Peale/Courtesy of the Pennsylvania Academy of the Fine Arts, Philadelphia, Henry D. Gilpin Fund.

Claypoole was not readily identifiable with Philadelphia's radical or conservative factions and he had not played a prominent role in revolutionary politics. It does not seem likely that he deliberately stacked the panel with certain kinds of jurors. Indeed, no defendant appears to have offered a challenge to the panel as a whole, despite the widespread use of such challenges.[88] Like most sheriffs, Claypoole probably returned individuals who were known to him personally or by reputation. Blair McClenachan, for example, had offered the financial bond for Claypoole's performance in office, both in 1777 and in 1778, in the middle of the trials.[89]

The qualifications for jury service in Pennsylvania in 1778 are not entirely clear, although traditional common-law requirements likely applied. No statute squarely addressed the issue, other than a 1777 statute excluding from jury service persons who had not taken the state's oath of allegiance, a limitation that excluded most practicing Quakers.[90] The Pennsylvania constitution granted voting rights to all free males twenty-one years and older who had paid taxes in the previous year, and these conditions most likely applied to jurors as well. When Pennsylvania enacted a statute on jury service in 1785, it did not explicitly impose age or property qualifications, although it did require that jurors be impartial and "sober and judicious persons of good reputation."[91]

The panel list unfortunately does not survive in its entirety. Nonetheless, it can be largely reconstructed from information in the court's docket book. In addition to the fifty-eight jurors who served in treason cases, the panel must have included an additional five members who served on a murder trial and an additional thirteen who were fined for failure to appear. The panel therefore included at least seventy-six members.[92]

The 22 treason trials for which jurors can be identified provided the opportunity to seat 264 jurors. The panel, of course, was significantly smaller than that, so it was inevitable that some jurors would serve more than once. If the panel members had been randomly assigned to the juries, we would expect each member to serve on roughly 3 to 4 juries. Instead, we see consistent multiple service on the part of a handful of jurors. Only 58 men served at all, and 19 of those served only once. The 39 other jurors filled the remaining 245 positions, for an average service of 6.28 juries.[93] (The full data are presented in Appendix 1). Each jury was uniquely composed, with the exception of the two trials on November 11, 1778, and the two trials on April 8, 1779, for which the same jury was used.[94] By the time of the later trials, the jurors brought substantial experience with treason cases to the jury box, in addition to familiarity with one another.

Serial jury service has been identified by other scholars, particularly in the English context, although it appears to vary considerably with time and place. In Hertfordshire in the late sixteenth and early seventeenth centuries, jurors rarely sat on more than one jury.[95] Repeat jury service was rare in Kent prior to 1650, but increased dramatically thereafter, a change that markedly increased the speed and efficiency of jury selection.[96] At the Old Bailey in the late seventeenth century, it was common for the same twelve men to serve on repeated juries, and many of these men served repeatedly in multiple sessions.[97] By contrast, in Staffordshire in the 1780s, there were a "large number of apparently wholly inexperienced jurors who served only once."[98] Scholars of early American law have found serial jury service in Virginia and Maryland state courts, and in New York federal courts.[99] By contrast, eighteenth-century jurors in Chester County, Pennsylvania, typically served on either one or two juries at most.[100]

The serial service in the Philadelphia treason trials was distinctive for two reasons. First, it involved a series of cases raising essentially the same issue—did the defendant aid the British during the British occupation of Philadelphia? The governing law was identical in each case; only the particular facts varied. Second, and more importantly, the serial service was produced by the adroit use of challenges by defense counsel to shape the jury in ways favorable to the defense.

Although both the state and the defendant were entitled to unlimited challenges for cause (claims that a juror was legally disqualified from serving), such challenges appear to have played little role in the Philadelphia trials. Far more significant were the thirty-five peremptory challenges that were granted only to the defendant and that could be used at the defendant's sole discretion.[101] As Blackstone pointed out, the law "wills not that he should be tried by any one man against whom he has conceived a prejudice, even without being able to assign a reason for such his dislike."[102] James Wilson later stated, "When on the voice of the jurors the prisoner's life is suspended, is it unnatural to suppose, that his mind, fluctuating, trembling, and solicitous, should conceive prejudices, even unaccountable ones, on the view of some, who are called, and appear to pronounce his fate?" Wilson's language suggests his personal experience, likely in the treason trials themselves. He continued, "Tender indulgence is shewn to human nature in that trying hour; and he, who has so many other embarrassments surrounding and pressing him, is relieved from the very excruciating one, however unfounded—an unfavorable opinion of his jury."[103] As he explained in his Law Lectures, "When [a juror] comes to the bar and looks upon the prisoner, a single supercilious look will produce a peremptory rejection."[104] Significantly, the prosecution was given no peremptory challenges.[105] Under English practice, the names of panel members were written on tickets and placed in a box or glass, and then drawn at random.[106] After each name was drawn, the defendant had the option of challenging for cause or offering a peremptory challenge. A 1785 statute codified this practice in Pennsylvania, but it was likely the procedure used in 1778 as well.[107] A 1746 English decision permitted the defendant to view the entire panel in order to know which panel members had actually appeared, a benefit that may also have been granted in Pennsylvania; the 1785 statute provided for public posting of the panel at least seven days before the return date.[108]

The Philadelphia treason defendants made extensive use of their right to peremptory challenges, and this right became especially useful in the context of a series of trials for essentially the same offense. The most direct evidence of this practice comes from the trial of John Roberts. When sentencing John Roberts to death, Chief Justice McKean stated, "though the law gives you a liberty to challenge thirty-five, you have challenged but thirty-three, so you allowed the rest to be an indifferent jury to pass between the state and you."[109] This evidence is consistent with the limited information we have about the use of challenges in other Pennsylvania cases. A rare document from a 1773 civil case in the Pennsylvania Provincial Supreme Court shows the defendant taking an active role in assessing potential jury members, focusing primarily on religion, but also on age, wealth, and sobriety.[110] Presumably, defendants on trial for their lives took at least as strong an interest in the composition of their jury.[111]

Moreover, there is strong circumstantial evidence indicating that peremptory challenges were used in a strategic manner to shape the jury in ways favorable to the defense. As we shall see when we take a detailed look at juror demographics, the composition of the juries was consistently nudged in certain directions and not others. Each of those directions favored the defense, a pattern that is explained most easily by the use of peremptory challenges.

In the earliest cases, defense counsel had little knowledge about juror behavior, but in later cases, that knowledge grew significantly. For example, when Joseph Bolton was tried on November 28, 1778, every member of the jury had previously served on a treason jury. Andrew Hathe's trial on December 4, 1778 included two jurors with no prior service, but the remaining ten jurors had combined experience of seventy-three trials. Several jurors had significant prior service. Juror John Drinker had served on sixteen previous juries, Isaac Powell on fifteen, Thomas Palmer on fourteen, and Cadwalader Dickinson on eleven. Defense counsel would have been readily familiar with these jurors and could have easily opted to strike them if they suspected they might be unfavorable. The persistent long-term service, however, suggests that these were jurors acceptable to the defense.

As the trials proceeded, defense attorneys could exercise their peremptory challenges with greater precision. The one-time jurors predominate in the earliest trials. Nine of the nineteen one-time jurors served in the first four trials. Moreover, two trials, those of Abijah Wright and John Huntsman, account for six of the remaining ten one-time jurors, suggesting that something distinctive occurred with jury selection in those trials. Nearly half of the one-time jurors served on juries that convicted—strong evidence that defense attorneys were especially cautious with respect to those jurors and had no desire to see them return to the jury box.

Trial-Juror Demographics

Table 6.2 sets forth the names, ages, occupations, religious affiliations, and ethnicities of the trial jurors, when known. Unfortunately, not all of the jurors can be identified with precision, since there were often multiple people with the same name, and the trial court records provide us with no identifying information other than the name. Although several people with the same name may have been included on the jury panel, it is more probable that each name represents a distinct person. The identification problems are particularly regrettable with respect to several of the most frequent jurors.

Consider, for example, the case of the juror named John Drinker. Since he served on twenty juries, more than any other juror, information on his identity would be particularly valuable. Unfortunately, there are three John Drinkers in the 1775 tax records: a bricklayer, a shipwright, and a merchant.[112] These three appear in the 1779 records, along with a fourth, who may be the 103-year-old cabinetmaker who died in 1782.[113] This cabinetmaker would have significantly exceeded the common law's requirement that jurors be no older than 70, and can thus be eliminated from consideration. Similarly, the merchant can be eliminated, as he was a well-known opponent of the revolution. A staunch Quaker, he had been publicly denounced as an "enemy to [his] country" in February 1776 by the Philadelphia Committee of Inspection and Observation for refusing to accept Continental bills of currency.[114] Moreover, he was one of the men sent by the Philadelphia Quaker Monthly Meeting in 1779 to persuade Cadwalader Dickinson of "the Evil of his conduct" in serving as a juror in the Carlisle case.[115] Thus the juror is either the bricklayer or the shipwright, both of whom were among the wealthiest men in Philadelphia.[116] The bricklayer possibility is particularly intriguing, because the bricklayer was the merchant's uncle.[117] He was also the uncle of Henry Drinker, who had been exiled to Virginia by the revolutionary government in 1777. Was the bricklayer particularly sympathetic to treason defendants because of his nephews' political difficulties? This family connection to prominent Tories might well explain why he would be a desirable juror for defendants. On the other hand, there appears to be no mention of the bricklayer in Henry's wife's extensive diaries, so it is possible that the families were estranged. Indeed, Quaker records indicate that a "John Drinker, the elder" was disowned in October 1772.[118] Conclusive identification, regrettably, remains impossible.

Table 6.2 Trial Jurors: Philadelphia County Court of Oyer and Terminer, 1778–1779

Name	# of juries	Age	Occupation	Religion	Ethnicity
Adcock, William	5	47	shopkeeper	Anglican	English
Albertson, Ricloff	4		carpenter	Anglican	
Barns, James	1				
Barnhill, John	4	49	merchant	Presbyterian	Irish
Beach, Edmund	1	49	cooper	Presbyterian	
Bitting, Lewis	1	49	innkeeper	German Ref.	German
Burkhard, Andrew	1	41	cordwainer	Lutheran	German
Campbell, John	4	52	merchant	Anglican	Scottish
Clumberg, Philip	1		surgeon	German Ref.	German
Corgee, Thomas	5	38	blacksmith	Anglican	
Dickinson, Cadwalader	15	42	cordwainer	Quaker (disowned)	English/Welsh
Dowig, George	6	54	silversmith/goldsmith		German
Drinker, John	20		[unidentified juror]		
Eckhart, William	5		baker	Lutheran	German
Esler, Henry	9		coachmaker		
Falconer, William	12	57	tavernkeeper	Presbyterian	
Forsberg, Nicholas	3	58	painter/glazier	Lutheran	Swedish
Forsyth, Andrew	1	34	merchant	Presbyterian	Scottish
Gamble, William	1		[unidentified juror]		
Gottier, James	2		[unidentified juror]		
Goucher, Thomas	3	28	cutler	Anglican	French

Gray, William	3	28	brewer	Quaker	English/Welsh
Grove, Samuel	1		shopkeeper		
Hale, Thomas	1		carpenter/bell-hanger	Anglican	English
Heidel, George	3		skinner	Lutheran	German
Hood, James	4		cooper	Quaker (disowned)	English
Humphreys, Whitehead	1	44	steel manufacturer	Quaker (disowned)	Welsh
Jackson, Matthew	3		shopkeeper		English
January, Peter	2	53	shoemaker	Presbyterian	French
Linnington, John	1		grocer	Baptist	
Lynn, John	1		[unidentified juror]		
McClenachan, Blair	1		merchant	Anglican	Irish
McLane, Samuel	1	28	leather worker/glover	Presbyterian	Scottish
McNeal, John	6		shopkeeper		
Merriam, Ezekiel	11		cordwainer	Baptist	
Palmer, John	9		[unidentified juror]		
Palmer, Thomas	18		[unidentified juror]		
Pancoast, David	4	50	carpenter	Quaker (disowned)	English
Pickering, George	3	28	joiner	Anglican	English
Piles, John	9		carpenter	Quaker	
Powell, Isaac	17		joiner	Baptist	
Pringle, John	6		merchant	Anglican/Presbyterian	Irish
Reese, David	11		[unidentified juror]		

(*continued*)

Table 6.2 Continued

Name	# of juries	Age	Occupation	Religion	Ethnicity
Rigden, William	1		painter		English
Ritter, Jacob	1		blacksmith		German
Roop, John	1		[unidentified juror]		
Roush, Isaac	2	44–47	stocking weaver	German Ref.	German
Roush, John	1	37	skinner	German Ref.	German
Rush, William	9	61	blacksmith	Presbyterian	English
Shields, Thomas	3	35	goldsmith/silversmith	Baptist	Irish/English
Simpson, Samuel	3	58	cordwainer	Anglican	English
Skinner, James	2		grocer	Anglican	Scottish
Steinmetz, John	4	38	merchant	Lutheran	German
Uttree, Jacob	4		potter	German Ref.	
Wilkinson, Anthony	2	27	stone-cutter	Anglican	
Wilson, Jr., George	7		[unidentified juror]		
Wilson, John	1		[unidentified juror]		
Zantzinger, Adam	3		merchant	Lutheran	German

Equally troublesome are Thomas Palmer, who served on eighteen juries, and John Palmer, who served on nine. There are five entries for "Thomas Palmer" in the 1775 tax records, and four in the 1779 tax records. He was most likely a gunsmith, but conclusive identification is impossible.[119] The most prominent John Palmer in Philadelphia was a bricklayer who had helped to build the State House steeple and the Christ Church steeple.[120] This man, however, cannot be the juror, as he had been hired to supervise the construction of the defenses of British-occupied Philadelphia, was named in the attainder proclamation of June 15, 1778, and was not discharged until December 1778.[121] There are two other John Palmers in the 1775 tax records, and three others in the 1779 records.[122] It is impossible to determine whether these entries reflect multiple people or simply multiple properties. The juror was quite likely the signatory to the agreement on providing information against suspected traitors, but further identification is impossible.[123] Similar identification problems plague eleven-time juror David Reese, seven-time juror George Wilson, Jr., two-time juror James Gottier, and one-time jurors William Gamble, John Lynn, John Roop, and John Wilson.

Uncovering information about the remaining jurors is not easy. As one scholar has noted, "Any direct study of jurors would require enormous time and effort."[124] None of the jurors were famous men, and their lives must be painstakingly reconstructed from tax records, court records, genealogical materials, manuscript sources, newspapers, and printed materials. Because the jury records contain the names of the jurors, but no other identifying information, it is particularly difficult to identify jurors when there are multiple individuals in Philadelphia with the same name, a problem compounded by the large number of sons who bore the same name as their fathers. Moreover, many names appear to have been spelled phonetically in court records and tax records, and do not always conform to other spellings. When identifying jurors I have erred on the side of caution, providing identifying information only in cases of reasonable certainty. Despite these problems, it is nonetheless possible to draw a general portrait of the jurors.

The trial jurors were drawn heavily from the city of Philadelphia. The majority of the jurors came from three central Philadelphia wards: Dock, Mulberry, and Middle. Only four came from wards outside of the City of Philadelphia, and even these, Southwark and Northern Liberties, were immediately adjacent to the city.[125] No juror came from the outlying county wards. This pattern differs strikingly from that of the grand jurors, at least a third of whom were drawn from the larger County of Philadelphia.[126]

The twenty-six jurors whose ages can be determined ranged in age from the 27-year-old Anthony Wilkinson to the 61-year-old William Rush, ages comfortably within the common-law requirement of jurors at least 21 and no older than 70.[127] As a group, the trial jurors were slightly younger than the grand jurors, with a median age of 44.75, and a mean of 43.48.[128] Defense counsel may have had a slight preference for older jurors. Of the jurors whose age can be identified, one-time jurors have a mean age of 40.28, jurors who served more than once have a mean age of 44.65, and jurors who served five times or more have a mean age of 49.83. The data for five-time or more jurors, however, include ages for only six of the sixteen jurors. The seeming preference for older jurors thus might be disproved with further data, but it does seem more likely than not.[129] Several reasons may have supported this preference. Older jurors had lived longer under the king and thus had a longer memory of loyalty. A study of Philadelphia merchants found that, on average, Tories were eight years older than Whigs.[130] A study of Poughkeepsie, New York, found that "Loyalism held a disproportionate attraction for men who had reached or passed their forty-fifth birthday," whereas "an unusually large number of men ranging in age from late twenties to the midforties firmly supported the movement for independence."[131] Age may also have inclined jurors to be more forgiving of youthful indiscretions.

The jurors represented a broad range of ethnicities, reflecting the ethnically diverse nature of Philadelphia itself.[132] Indeed, some scholars have suggested that revolutionary Philadelphia was "among the most ethnically heterogeneous cities in the western world" and was ethnically integrated even at the level of the city block.[133] Ethnicity is not necessarily easy to determine. Although it is tempting to assign ethnicities on the basis of last name, this is not a reliable method; the very English-sounding George Cook may well be Georg Koch from Germany. I have found independent evidence of ethnicity for thirty-four of the fifty-eight jurors, including eleven of German descent, nine of English descent, four of Scottish descent, three of Irish descent, two each of French descent and mixed English/Welsh descent, and one each of Swedish descent, Welsh descent, and mixed Irish/English descent.[134] German ethnicity seems to have played little role in juror selection. Six of the German jurors served in multiple trials; five served only once. Similarly, the four Scottish jurors split evenly between single and multiple service, and the others are of too small numbers to draw any conclusions. English ethnicity, however, was different. Of the nine jurors of English descent, seven served on multiple juries. Moreover, if one looks at English representation in the total number of seats, a preference for English jurors becomes unmistakable. The 34 jurors with identifiable ethnicities filled a total of 110 juror seats. Of these, persons with English ancestry (including mixed ancestry) occupied 54 of the seats (49%), despite constituting only 26.5% of the jurors as a whole. Indeed, these statistics almost certainly underrepresent the extent of service by English jurors. Significant multiple jurors John Drinker (20), Henry Esler (9), Thomas Palmer (18), John Piles (9), Isaac Powell (17), and George Wilson (7) are very likely of English descent as well, although that descent cannot be conclusively established.

Defense counsel may well have thought that jurors of English descent might be more sympathetic to persons accused of loyalty to their English king.[135]

We know more about occupation than any other juror characteristic, with identifiable occupations for 47 of the 58 jurors. Thirty of these, nearly two-thirds, were artisans. In addition, John Drinker, who served on twenty juries, was either a shipwright or a bricklayer, so he should also be included as an artisan juror. These men, sometimes called "mechanics," were self-employed craftsmen and constituted approximately half of Philadelphia's male residents in the early 1770s. Although artisans were considered of lower social status than merchants, many artisans were economically successful. Eric Foner points out that the typical artisan of revolutionary Philadelphia was "literate, self-educated, and often interested in science." Moreover, the artisans had played a leading role in pre-independence Philadelphia politics, and were often among the most ardent revolutionaries.[136] Among the artisan jurors, the most heavily represented occupations were cordwainer/shoemaker, with five; carpenter, with four; and blacksmith, with three. Artisan dominance of the jury box is revealed even more clearly when one looks not just at the number of jurors but also at the number of seats. Forty-one percent of the non-artisan jurors served only once, but only 22.6% of the artisan jurors served only once. The jurors with identifiable occupations (including John Drinker) filled 212 seats. Of those, 156, or 73.6%, were filled by artisans. These percentages would be even higher if, as is likely, eighteen-time juror Thomas Palmer was a gunsmith. Of the non-artisan jurors, eleven were merchants or shopkeepers.[137] The remaining six included two grocers, a steel manufacturer, a tavernkeeper, a surgeon, and an innkeeper. There were no clergymen jurors, as they were excluded from jury service under the common law. There were also no lawyers, no "gentlemen," and no farmers. Nor were there any identifiable jurors who were "laborers," a large group of men generally found at the bottom of Philadelphia's social structure.[138]

The occupational portrait of the jurors can be complemented by analysis of the jurors' wealth, as reflected in the Philadelphia tax lists for 1779.[139] These data in Table 6.3 reveal several points of interest.

First, on average, the trial jurors were wealthier than the average Philadelphia taxpayer. The mean wealth of the jurors was over nine times that of the city as a whole. The median wealth was £10.5, approximately the sixtieth percentile of Philadelphia taxpayers. These data are slightly distorted, however, by the presence of two exceptionally wealthy jurors, Ricloff Albertson and Samuel Simpson, with estates valued at £4000 and £6893, respectively. With those outliers removed, juror mean wealth drops to £34.11, still slightly above the city-wide mean. Similarly, the median drops to £10, which is still twice the city median of £5.[140]

Second, the multiple jurors were wealthier than the one-time jurors. The mean wealth of the multiple jurors was over ten times that of the one-time jurors, but

Table 6.3 Juror Wealth

	Mean Assessed Wealth (£)	Median Assessed Wealth (£)
Philadelphia City (n=3885)	29.15	5
Grand Jurors (n=17)	2262.47	450
Trial Jurors (n=46)	269.43	10.5
excluding outliers (n=44)	34.11	10
One-Time Jurors (n=14)	33.5	8
Multiple Jurors (n=32)	372.66	18
excluding outliers (n=30)	34.4	14
Ten or more trials (n=4)	9	4.5

with outliers removed, the difference in mean wealth between the multiple jurors and the one-time jurors is minimal. Median wealth is much more informative. The one-time jurors had a median wealth of £8, slightly above the city average, but the multiple jurors had a median wealth of £18, over twice as much. This discrepancy suggests at least some preference by defense counsel for wealthier jurors over poorer jurors. Although wealth in itself was hardly a predictor of political views in colonial America, a study of Philadelphia merchants found that the mean assessed wealth valuation of Tory merchants was three times that of Whig merchants.[141] It was at least plausible for defense counsel to imagine that wealthy jurors would be better jurors for the defense.

The seeming preference for wealthier jurors breaks down slightly when one focuses on the eight jurors who served in ten or more trials. The four of these who can be conclusively identified had tax assessments of £3, £3, £6, and £24, reflecting a mean of £9 and a median of £4.5, slightly below the mean and median for city tax payers as a whole. But of the four unidentified jurors in this category, three (John Drinker, John Palmer & Thomas Palmer) almost certainly were quite wealthy, with estates reaching into the hundreds, if not thousands, of pounds. Their absence is thus the likely explanation for the apparent dip in wealth for the most frequently serving jurors.

Third, the trial jury data place in bold relief the extraordinary wealth of the grand jurors. The median wealth of the grand jurors was over forty-two times the median wealth of the trial jurors. As in England, grand jurors and trial jurors seem to have been drawn from significantly different economic strata.[142]

Finally, the typical Philadelphia juror was by no means poor, but he was not especially wealthy or prominent, either. In this respect, he resembled the English juror. Blackstone had described the English jury as "chosen by lot from among those of the middle rank," and modern scholarship provides substantial support for this view.[143] Thomas Green concludes that in eighteenth-century English juries, "[t]he middling groups . . . constituted the trial jury class." There was "a firm upper limit on the status of persons eligible (in social, not legal, terms) for trial jury service."[144] Likewise, Staffordshire juries in the 1780s were composed largely of craftsmen and farmers.[145] Philadelphia juries were nonetheless open to a broader range of wealth than their English counterparts. For example, P.J.R. King found that in eighteenth-century Essex, "jurors were drawn exclusively from the top half of the spectrum of wealth and social status."[146] Douglas Hay concluded that English legislation effectively excluded "three-quarters of the adult males of England outside of London from jury service."[147] By contrast, twelve of the forty-six identifiable Philadelphia treason jurors had tax assessments below the fiftieth percentile.[148] Low wealth was not an insuperable barrier to jury service in revolutionary Pennsylvania.[149]

No issue was more divisive in Pennsylvania than religion. Since the march of the Paxton Boys, there had been intense hostility between Presbyterians, predominant in the western counties, and Quakers, heavily concentrated in the Philadelphia region. The Revolution heightened this hostility, as Quakers committed to the peace testimony refused to bear arms or to serve in the militia, and were far less likely to support the Revolution itself than were members of any other religious group.[150] By contrast, the new state government was perceived as dominated by Presbyterians, who were predominant in the Assembly, and also included officials such as Chief Justice McKean, Attorney General Jonathan Dickinson Sergeant, Assistant Attorney General Joseph Reed, and George Bryan, the Vice President of the Supreme Executive Council. A Hessian soldier complained in 1778 that the rebellion was "not an American Rebellion; it is nothing more than an Irish-Scotch Presbyterian Rebellion."[151] A Philadelphia Quaker later denounced "the Presbyterians [who] have been permitted to involve the whole British Empire in great distress and perplexity."[152] Charles Inglis, a New York Loyalist, claimed that in Pennsylvania, "The Presbyterian faction drive on in their career of persecution with the most unrelenting rigor."[153]

Historian Owen Ireland has argued that by 1778 Pennsylvania politics had polarized along religious lines, with members of the German Reformed and Dutch Reformed congregations, Presbyterians, and other Calvinists aligned against Quakers, Anglicans, and Lutherans. These groups differed significantly with respect to issues such as the acts of attainder and the treatment of loyalists, with the former group favoring harsh measures and the latter inclined to tolerance.[154] There were also significant disagreements over Pennsylvania's controversial 1776 constitution, which most Presbyterians supported, but which most Quakers and Anglicans opposed.[155]

The executions of Quakers Abraham Carlisle and John Roberts for treason have often been portrayed as the bloody denouement of longstanding Presbyterian-Quaker enmity. French writer J.P. Brissot de Warville, traveling in Pennsylvania in 1788, captured the typical Quaker view: "When the English evacuated this city and the Presbyterian party became its masters, the persecution of Quakers was renewed in an even more violent form, and two of them were condemned to be hanged for high treason." John Roberts, Warville claimed, "had strongly supported the party organized by Dr. Franklin in opposition to the Presbyterians, and this was undoubtedly the reason for their inveterate hatred of him, which brought about his death."[156]

Members of other religious affiliations were somewhat less polarized than the Presbyterians and the Quakers. In general, Anglicans were more supportive of the Revolution than Quakers. One study of Philadelphia merchants found that Anglican Whigs outnumbered Anglican Tories by a factor of nearly four to one.[157] Compared to Presbyterians, however, Anglicans were more likely to be supporters of the crown.[158] Lutherans may have been more aligned with the Presbyterians than Ireland suggests, but were still more likely than Presbyterians to remain loyal.[159] Members of the German Reformed and Dutch Reformed Churches were perhaps the closest to Presbyterians. Baptists were probably somewhere in the middle. Thus, for defense attorneys in treason cases, the ideal jurors would be Quakers, followed by Anglicans, and possibly Lutherans. The least desirable jurors would be Presbyterians, followed by members of the German and Dutch Reformed Churches. Again, the data suggest that the juries were selected according to defense preferences.

Thirty-nine of the fifty-eight jurors have an identifiable religious affiliation. Anglicans were the most numerous, with eleven jurors, followed by Presbyterians, with seven. There were also six Lutherans, six Quakers, five German Reformeds, and four Baptists. The Quaker jurors were not typical Quakers, as a Quaker in good standing could not take the oath required of jurymen. Most of the Quaker jurors had been previously disowned by the Philadelphia monthly meeting.[160] Jurors Cadwalader Dickinson and John Piles later became members of the "Free Quakers," a dissident group of Quakers who supported the Revolution.[161] The unidentified jurors may have had no religious affiliation at all, or may have floated between congregations. Philadelphians were not always consistent in church attendance, and sometimes chose different churches as fancy struck them.[162] Juror John Pringle is perhaps the best example of this practice. He was married in 1773 at Christ Church, Philadelphia's preeminent Anglican church.[163] In 1780, he remarried in a Presbyterian church and baptized his child in a Presbyterian church one year later.[164] When he died in 1792, however, he was buried at Christ Church, alongside his second wife.[165]

As with ethnicity, religious disparities in jury selection become more apparent by focusing on the total number of seats. The religiously identifiable jurors (excluding John Pringle) filled 159 seats. Of those, only thirty-nine, or 24.5%, were held by Presbyterians or German Reformeds, the least favored jurors from a defense perspective. Multiple service tracks predicted favorability almost exactly. Eighty-three percent of Quaker jurors served on multiple juries, as did 80% of Lutheran jurors, 77.8% percent of Anglican jurors, 75% of Baptist jurors, 57% of Presbyterian jurors, and 40% of German Reformed jurors. Similarly, the median Baptist juror served on seven juries, the median Quaker on four, the median Lutheran and Anglican on three, the median Presbyterian on two, and the median German Reformed on one.

Moreover, even these numbers are skewed by a peculiarity in the Presbyterian jurors. On first glance, it seems hard to understand why nine-time juror William Rush, a Presbyterian blacksmith who was a cousin to Dr. Benjamin Rush, a signer of the Declaration of Independence, would be a good juror for the defense.[166] But Rush had an extraordinary connection to the defendants. He was married to Esther Carlisle, the sister of defendant Abraham Carlisle, and the Carlisles and the Rushes lived in adjacent houses.[167] On October 26, 1778, Rush had personally appeared before the Supreme Executive Council to lobby for clemency in Carlisle's case.[168] Rush served on his first treason jury on November 11, 1778, one week after Carlisle's controversial execution. The common law forbade jury service by close relations of the defendant, but it said nothing about close relations to other defendants tried for the same offense. A prosecutor granted peremptory challenges would undoubtedly have used one on Rush. But in the absence of formal disqualification, there was nothing the prosecution could do. Rush would serve on nine consecutive juries, supporting acquittal in each case. He eventually served alongside seven of the twelve men who had voted to convict Carlisle, and in many cases was on a jury with five of them. In this case, family connections easily trumped religion; no defense counsel would pass up the remarkable opportunity to have the brother-in-law of an executed traitor sitting on the jury. William Rush alone accounts for nearly one-third of the Presbyterian seats on the juries.[169]

There are no reliable estimates for the proportions of different religious groups in Philadelphia in 1778. The best estimates for 1775 suggest that Anglicans constituted 17.8% of the population, Quakers 12.9%, German Lutherans 16%, German Reformed 6.7%, Baptists 1.2%, and Presbyterians 12.3%.[170] From this perspective, Presbyterians were slightly overrepresented on the juries relative to population size (a fact probably explicable entirely to William Rush) and

German Reformeds were slightly underrepresented. Quakers, however, were overrepresented, as were Anglicans and Baptists.

Trial-Juror Political Activity

Unlike the grand jurors, the trial jurors were not early or prominent revolutionists. Whereas eight of the eighteen grand jurors were prominent in resistance activities before 1775, only two of the fifty-eight trial jurors were. Carpenter Ricloff Albertson and blacksmith William Rush were elected to the Philadelphia City Committee in November 1774 and to the Pennsylvania Provincial Convention of January 1775. Rush had previously served on the Philadelphia City Council in the 1750s, and was a Philadelphia representative to a provincial meeting of deputies in July 1774.[171]

When the fighting broke out in April 1775, juror political involvement increased. William Adcock and Samuel Simpson played prominent roles on the Committee of Privates, an association of rank-and-file militiamen formed in September 1775. Adcock served as the first chair of the committee, and issued an address in October 1775 to the Pennsylvania General Assembly, arguing that Quakers should not be exempt from contributing to the defense of the province. The address concluded that the privates were "determined, to the utmost of our power, to support the liberties of America." In early 1776, Adcock served as a member of the Committee of Correspondence for the Committee of Privates.[172] In 1778, he joined the Patriotic Association and would serve on five treason juries, supporting acquittal in four cases, and conviction in one.[173] Cordwainer Samuel Simpson took over the chairmanship of the Committee of Privates in 1776. In an address to the Pennsylvania Assembly, Simpson warned that the "importance and necessity of defending our country against the ravages of a cruel and desolating enemy are so obvious, no arguments can be necessary to show it to be the duty of every good citizen to bear an equitable and proportional part of the public burden."[174] In November 1776 Simpson was appointed by the Council of Safety to a committee to enforce the state's salt regulations and he was elected a justice of the peace in February 1777.[175] In April 1778, his wife was ordered out of occupied Philadelphia by General Howe.[176] Simpson, too, joined the Patriotic Association, and would serve on three treason juries, supporting acquittal in each case.

Only a handful of other jurors held significant elective positions prior to independence. William Rush and John Linnington were elected to the Philadelphia Committee of Inspection in August 1775. Rush appeared on all three "tickets" that summer, although Linnington appeared only on the "mechanics ticket." They were re-elected along with James Barns and Samuel Simpson in February

1776. That same month, all four were appointed to subcommittees to superintend various districts of the city. Juror James Skinner was also appointed to a subcommittee.[177]

At least fifteen of the trial jurors provided military supplies or services to Pennsylvania's revolutionary government in the critical years of 1775 and 1776.[178] Thomas Goucher, for example, was paid "a premium for making public the art of grinding gun barrels."[179] Jacob Ritter provided work as a gunsmith, and Blair McClenachan produced niter for gunpowder.[180] William Rush provided blacksmith services.[181] Adam Zantzinger provided wagon services to the Continental Congress.[182] John Barnhill was appointed to purchase blankets and stockings.[183] David Pancoast submitted a proposal to Joseph Dean in regard to storage of artillery, and was directed to purchase wheels for gun carriages.[184] John Barnhill was one of four men who had established a relay stage line to New York, known as "The Flying Machine." It is quite likely that Barnhill (the great-great grandfather of President Theodore Roosevelt) used this stage during the Revolution to provide espionage services to General Washington.[185] By contrast, William Rigden failed to join the militia and refused to turn over his arms when requested to do so in May 1776.[186]

Like the grand jurors, the trial jurors had a mixed record of military service. Only two jurors appear to have served in the Continental Army. One-time juror surgeon Philip Clumberg was an ensign in 1775 and served in the Canadian operations, and four-time juror David Pancoast commanded a company in the Regiment of Artillery Artificers from February 1777 to April 1778.[187] Two jurors also held officer positions in their respective companies of City Guards.[188] At least ten jurors held officer positions in the Philadelphia militia.[189] With the exception of Ezekiel Merriam, who served on eleven juries, the militia officers did not have significant jury service. Five served only once; two served twice; and two, Anglican Ricloff Albertson and Quaker James Hood, served four times.

The overall militia record of the jurors was far from impressive. Six were noted in December 1776 as having failed to join their respective militia companies.[190] One of these, Andrew Forsyth, later married the daughter of a prominent colonel. According to a family history, her parents only grudgingly consented to her marriage to one who was not "an active revolutionist."[191] John McNeal was listed as having deserted his militia company on September 12, 1777.[192] Henry Esler was listed as "can't be found."[193] At least five of the jurors hired substitutes to perform their militia duties for them, including fifteen-time juror Cadwalader Dickinson and nine-time juror William Rush.[194] Over the course of the war, at least twenty-three of the jurors also paid fines rather than perform their militia service.[195] Fifteen of these twenty-three served on multiple juries.

In the years following the Declaration of Independence, the majority of the jurors continued to be relatively obscure. The few who were politically active played largely minor roles.[196] Samuel Simpson and John Barnhill attended the November 1776 meeting at the Indian Queen Tavern that investigated cases of disloyalty.[197] In April 1777, the Pennsylvania War Office appointed a Committee of Fifty to "have the direction and superintendence of the removal of all Provisions and other Stores . . . that will be useful to our enemies, should they get possession of them, or that may be necessary to the Army of the United States." Future jurors John Barnhill, Isaac Roush, Samuel Simpson, and Samuel McLane served on this committee.[198] William Gray signed an address to the Supreme Executive Council in May 1777, warning that "the emissaries of the enemy are busily employed in spreading the seeds and principles of disaffection to the American cause . . . There is no regular administration of justice, whereby the enemies of our country may be punished, and its friends protected."[199]

The British occupation of Philadelphia was undoubtedly the major event of the Revolution for the vast majority of the jurors. It is impossible to determine how many of the jurors fled the city, although at least five, including seventeen-time juror Isaac Powell, can be confirmed as remaining in the city. John Steinmetz remained, but one of his merchant ships was condemned by the British as a prize and taken to Halifax.[200] His decision to remain in the city was bitterly remembered six years later by Robert Morris, who thought it an indication of bad character.[201] John Barnhill, who may have remained to engage in espionage activities for General Washington, appears to have been arrested by the British shortly after the occupation.[202]

Several of the jurors incurred significant economic losses. After the British evacuation, Whitehead Humphreys advertised for the return of four tons of steel, stolen by "a certain Joseph Fox, a noted traitor."[203] Fifteen-time juror Cadwalader Dickinson apparently "lost everything during the economic dislocation of the Revolutionary War."[204] Three-time juror Adam Zantzinger reported damage of £1280 and nine-time juror William Rush reported damage of £2261.[205]

At least twenty of the jurors joined the Patriotic Association, formed in July 1778 to ensure that suspected traitors were brought to justice.[206] Members met regularly in August and September 1778, although the group appears to have dissolved shortly thereafter.[207] The defense attorneys might reasonably have assumed that members of this group would not be particularly favorable jurors, and there is some evidence that challenges were exercised against Association members. Overall, the average juror held 4.55 seats, but the average Patriotic Association member juror held 3.95 seats. Nonetheless, the predominance of Association members in the juries is striking. Identifiable Patriotic Association members constituted 34.5% of the jurors and filled 30% of the seats. Indeed, relative to the total population of eligible jurors, members of this Association, with approximately 250 members, were grossly overrepresented on the juries. But Patriotic Association members did not reflexively vote for conviction. The jury that tried Aubrey Harry on November 30, 1778, for example, included at least five Patriotic Association members, but Harry was acquitted. Four days later, another jury, with at least four Patriotic Association members, acquitted Andrew Hathe.

We thus have some initial answers to the puzzle of high acquittal rates in the Philadelphia treason cases. When the juries were finally seated, they had all been nudged in ways that consistently favored the defense. English jurors were preferred over non-English jurors; Quakers, Anglicans and Lutherans over Presbyterians and German Reformeds; wealthy jurors over less wealthy jurors; older jurors over younger jurors; and jurors who had paid fines or hired substitutes to perform their militia duties over those who had served directly. This jury composition is most plausibly explained by the adroit use of peremptory challenges. The thirty-five peremptory challenges granted to the defense, when none were given to the prosecution, provided the perfect opportunity for defense counsel to shape the jury. Juries selected in this manner were at least marginally more likely to acquit than juries selected without the use of defense peremptory challenges. But the results were certainly not foreordained by jury selection. The defendants would still face a large number of jurors who had joined the Patriotic Association and who would seem to have little desire to allow suspected traitors to escape justice. The trials themselves were critical, with defendants, witnesses, lawyers, and judges all playing an important role.

7

The Philadelphia Treason Trials, 1778–1779

TRIAL AND DELIBERATION

IN THE READING room of the Historical Society of Pennsylvania, where much of the archival research for this book was completed, hangs a large painting by the famed artist Benjamin West. It is a portrait of William Hamilton, one of the wealthiest men of late-eighteenth-century Philadelphia, and his niece Ann Hamilton Lyle (Figure 7.1). Hamilton's family had long been prominent in Philadelphia. His grandfather Andrew Hamilton, one of the first great "Philadelphia lawyers," had argued the famous Zenger case in New York and had led the design and construction of Independence Hall. His uncle James Hamilton had served several terms as the Lieutenant Governor of Pennsylvania. William graduated from the College of Philadelphia in 1762 and had inherited a large country estate known as "The Woodlands."[1] When the fighting with Great Britain erupted in 1775, he served as a colonel of the Philadelphia County Associated Battalion, and in March 1776, he was elected chairman of the Committee of Inspection and Observation for the County of Philadelphia.[2] Three months later, he served as a representative of the Philadelphia County Committee at the Provincial Conference of Committees.[3] The "Grand Federal Procession," staged by Philadelphia Federalists in support of the new Constitution in 1788, concluded with celebrations on the spacious lawn of one of Hamilton's homes.[4]

In his later years, Hamilton became a friend and regular correspondent of Thomas Jefferson. Hamilton's extensive botanical collection was of particular interest to Jefferson, and Jefferson forwarded specimens from the Lewis and Clark expedition to Hamilton in Philadelphia.[5] Hamilton introduced at least four new species of trees to America: the ginkgo, the Lombardy poplar, the Norway maple, and the tree of heaven.[6] Several buildings at the University of Pennsylvania are

FIGURE 7.1 William Hamilton, acquitted of treason in 1778, and his niece Ann Hamilton Lyle.

Credit: William Hamilton, 1745–1813, and His Niece Mrs. Lyle, by Benjamin West/Historical Society of Pennsylvania.

named after Hamilton, and his estate, The Woodlands, still stands in western Philadelphia, where it is a National Historic Landmark District.

By all accounts, Hamilton would seem to be a minor but distinguished participant in the Revolution. Yet at the critical moment Hamilton hesitated, unable to reconcile himself to the idea of American independence. He had readily denounced the "arbitrary and oppressive measures of the British ministry," but nonetheless argued that reconciliation with Britain was the only course "which can possibly give us happiness and security."[7] During the British occupation of Philadelphia, Hamilton allegedly joined the enemy and accepted "a superintendent's commission for keeping the Middle Ferry."[8] In the fall of 1778, he was one of the twenty-three men on trial for his life in College Hall on a charge of treason against the state of Pennsylvania. Hamilton was acquitted, but the experience soured him considerably. Several months later, he wrote to a friend that although once he had been anxious to have a view of Philadelphia through the woods of his country estate, "it is now absolutely disgusting to me. Judge by this what must be the frame of my mind."[9]

In many ways, William Hamilton was not a typical defendant in a treason trial. No others, so far as I know, continue to be honored in Philadelphia. But Hamilton's conflicting views on political matters were entirely consistent with those of his fellow defendants. This chapter first considers the demographic profile of the men tried for treason in Philadelphia. It then turns to the actual operation of the trials, including the testimony, the rulings from the bench, and the jury verdicts. In this regard, Hamilton's experience was entirely typical, as juries acquitted almost of all the men charged with treason. Finally, the chapter addresses the contested clemency proceedings for those few defendants who were convicted.

Defendant Demographics and Political Activity

The stereotypical "Tory" looms large in portrayals of the American Revolution. The "Tory" is a wealthy Anglican or Quaker merchant of English descent who stubbornly opposed resistance activities from the beginning and decisively cast his lot with the British. This stereotype is largely a myth; as Maya Jasanoff has pointed out, "loyalism cut right across the social, geographical, racial, and ethnic spectrum of early America."[10] Stereotypical loyalists certainly existed in Philadelphia, but most of them fled the city along with the British army in 1778. The treason defendants of 1778–1779 were of a different stripe. For the most part, they were ordinary Philadelphians of modest means who had much in common with the jurors who were to decide their fate. Indeed, if anything they were lower in the social and economic hierarchy than the jurors. Historian Ronald Hoffman found similar results in Maryland, where most people tried for treason, insurrection, or riotous behavior came from the lower echelons of society.[11] Table 7.1 sets forth basic demographic information about the treason defendants.

Occupations can be identified for eighteen of the twenty-three defendants. Of these, fourteen were artisans, including four carpenters, three millers, two blacksmiths, a ship joiner, a wheelwright, a yeoman, a wagoner, and a baker. Of the remaining four, William Hamilton was an independent gentleman of means, Samuel Garrigues engaged in trade, Andrew Hathe was an innkeeper, and Abijah

Table 7.1 Treason Defendants, Philadelphia County Court of Oyer and Terminer, 1778–1779

Name	Verdict	Trial Date	Age	Occupation	Religion	Ethnicity
Carlisle, Abraham	G	9/25/78		carpenter	Quaker	
Ming, Jacob	NG	9/28/78		wheel-wright		German
Roberts, John	G	9/30/78	57	miller	Quaker	Welsh
Turner, Joseph, Jr.,	NG	10/3/78				
Deshong, Peter	NG	10/7/78	41	miller	German Ref.	German
Cook, George, Jr.,	NG	10/9/78				
Hamilton, William	NG	10/18/78	33	gentleman	Anglican	Scottish/English
Woolfall, Charles	NG	11/11/78		blacksmith	Anglican	English
Piles, Samuel	NG	11/11/78		ship joiner		
Roberts, James	NG	11/13/78	32		Anglican	
Guion, Lewis	NG	11/16/78	c. 35	carpenter	Anglican	French/English
Wright, Abijah	G*	11/18/78		laborer		
Copeland, David	NG	11/21/78				
Devenderfer, George	NG	11/24/78				German
Huntsman, John	NG	11/25/78	61	miller	Anglican	
Stricker, Adam	NG	11/27/78	29	blacksmith	German Ref.	German
Bolton, Joseph	NG	11/28/78	41	carpenter	Quaker (disowned)	English
Harry, Aubrey	NG	11/30/78	50	wagoner	Quaker	Welsh/English
Hathe, Andrew	NG	12/4/78		innkeeper		
Garrigues, Samuel	NG	4/6/79	59	former clerk of the market/trader	Quaker	French
Whitefield, William	NG	4/8/79		yeoman	Quaker	
Harding, George	G	4/8/79		carpenter**		
Stevens, James	NG	4/?/79		baker	Quaker	

* Wright was indicted for treason and burglary. The jury convicted on the burglary charge, but court records do not indicate a resolution of the treason charge.

** Harding's indictment refers to him as an innkeeper, but Harding described himself as a carpenter from his arrival in Philadelphia in 1765 in papers later filed with the British government. Record of the Case of George Hardy, Clemency File, RG-27, PSA; Evidence in the Case of George Harding, late of Philadelphia, American Loyalist Claims, AO12.40.12, National Archives of the United Kingdom.

Wright was a laborer. John Roberts and George Harding were quite wealthy, but tax data are nonexistent or inconclusive for most of the other defendants, so aggregate wealth determinations are impossible.[12] The lack of data, however, is a strong indication that most of the defendants were not especially wealthy. Age can be identified for ten defendants, ranging from 29 to 61, with a mean age of 43.8.[13] Ethnicity can be identified for eleven defendants. Four defendants were of German descent, two of English descent, one of French descent, and one of Welsh descent. Three others had mixed descent—English combined with Scottish, Welsh, or French. Since the unidentified defendants were likely primarily of English descent, a majority of the defendants almost certainly had some English ancestry. Nonetheless, at least a quarter had none.

The defendants in the trials were all men, but the grand jury had indicted at least one woman, Catherine Devenderfer, likely the wife of defendant George Devenderfer. Although George stood trial and was acquitted, Catherine skipped bail and forfeited her recognizance, leaving no further trace in the records.[14]

The most striking demographic characteristic of the defendants is their religion. The fourteen defendants whose religion can be determined consisted of seven Quakers, five Anglicans, and two German Reformed.[15] Put another way, over 85% of the identifiable defendants were Quaker or Anglican. None of the defendants appear to have been Presbyterian. In a 1908 newspaper interview, Supreme Court Justice John Marshall Harlan asked, "Did you ever hear of such a thing as a Presbyterian Tory? I never did, and I have searched history very carefully. If there was one, he kept well out of view."[16] But Presbyterian Tories, although uncommon, certainly existed. In Philadelphia alone there were at least thirty, including members of the prominent Allen family, some of whom had been named in the attainder proclamations.[17] None of these Presbyterians, however, were tried for treason.

The demographic analysis of the defendants lends strong support to the thesis that defense counsel helped shape the juries through adroit use of peremptory challenges. The defendants undoubtedly wanted jurors who were as close to their peers as possible. The ideal juror would have been a Quaker or Anglican artisan of English descent. As Chapter 6 explained, that is precisely the type of juror that the defense counsel sought.

William Hamilton's early participation in resistance activities was far from unusual among the defendants. In June 1774, John Roberts was selected as a member of Philadelphia's Committee of Correspondence, formed to protest the closure of the port of Boston.[18] The next month, he was one of Philadelphia County's representatives to a colony-wide meeting of deputies.[19] In November 1774, he was elected to the Philadelphia County Committee.[20] In December 1774, he was named to represent Philadelphia County at the Provincial Convention that met in January 1775; at the Convention, he served alongside eight of the men who would serve on the grand jury that indicted him for treason.[21] At least five defendants had provided provisions or services to Pennsylvania's revolutionary government prior to the British occupation, including Lewis Guion, who had designed cheveaux-de-frise to protect the Delaware River against enemy ships.[22] Many were enrolled in the militia, although at least eight of them paid a fine to avoid militia service, as had many of the trial jurors.[23]

There were also connections between the defendants and the grand jurors and the trial jurors. Philadelphia was a city of approximately 30,000 people, so no one knew everyone, but many people were connected by only one or two degrees of separation.[24] Every juror almost certainly knew someone who had come under suspicion for treasonable activities. The most noteworthy connection is that between nine-time juror William Rush and defendant Abraham Carlisle, discussed in Chapter 6. Other connections are more difficult to document, but there are a few hints.

Consider, for example, the Carpenters' Company. This Company, under the leadership of grand juror Benjamin Loxley, built a headquarters known as Carpenters' Hall, which later served as the meeting place of the First Continental Congress. Loxley maintained a list of financial subscribers to the Hall, and this list included future defendants Abraham Carlisle, Charles Woolfall, and John Roberts, all of whom Loxley must have known personally.[25]

Juror John Piles paid the recognizance for defendant Samuel Piles.[26] The similarity in last names suggests that the two were familial relations, and, at minimum, the paying of the recognizance suggests a close connection between the two. John Piles did not serve on Samuel Piles's jury, but he did serve in nine other trials, supporting acquittal in each case. As with William Rush, John Piles would be an ideal juror from a defense perspective. The prosecution lacked any ability to exclude him for cause, because his legal ineligibility extended only to trials of his own relations.

A similar connection existed between juror Cadwalader Dickinson and defendant Abijah Wright. Two of Dickinson's brothers were married to two of Wright's sisters; indeed, Cadwalader Dickinson and Abijah Wright both appear as witnesses on the marriage certificate between Benjamin Dickinson and Isabel Wright.[27] Dickinson appeared on every jury between November 21, 1778 and April 8, 1779, with one exception—the trial of Abijah Wright; his family connection almost certainly disqualified him from service.

Other defendants had connections with prominent revolutionary leaders. Defendant James Roberts wrote to wealthy financier Robert Morris from the Philadelphia jail in October 1778, seeking Morris's help, based on his "Former Friendship," to "Extricate me from this Confinement, or Bring on my Tryal."

Roberts stated, curiously, that he was "Confin'd again in the same Circumstances as Once before (which you where [*sic*] acquainted with)."[28] Defendant Samuel Garrigues had named one of his sons after Benjamin Franklin, which suggests some relationship between Franklin and Garrigues.[29] In August 1778, Elias Boudinot, a New Jersey delegate to the Continental Congress, appeared at a bail hearing on behalf of defendant John Roberts.[30] This appearance on behalf of "an infamous tory" was denounced by an anonymous correspondent to the *Pennsylvania Packet* and later formed part of a complaint filed by the state of Pennsylvania, alleging that the Continental Congress had interfered with the state's internal affairs. The document, sent by Joseph Reed, charged that "last summer, a delegate in Congress, from the State of New Jersey, appeared as an Attorney in behalf of John Roberts, then under a charge and since executed for High Treason."[31]

Defense Counsel

The Pennsylvania constitution of 1776 guaranteed to each criminal defendant "a right to be heard by himself and his council," thereby guaranteeing the right of defense counsel to directly address the jury. Although England had recognized a right to counsel for defendants in treason cases in the famous Treason Trials Act of 1696, defense counsel did not appear in ordinary felony cases until the 1730s, and then only with special permission of the court.[32] By contrast, Pennsylvania's 1718 criminal justice statute permitted defense counsel to appear in all capital cases.[33] James Wilson applauded Pennsylvania's practices with respect to defense counsel, noting in his Law Lectures that the English common-law rule barring defense counsel in felony cases was a "hard one, and not . . . very consonant to the rest of the humane treatment of prisoners by the English law."[34] Chief Justice McKean pointedly noted when sentencing Abijah Wright to death, "Upon your trial, you have had two able Counsels assigned you by the Court to render you every possible assistance."[35] It appears that the court provided appointed counsel to defendants who could not afford it; in 1795, Hugh Henry Brackenridge noted that the "common law of the United States" permitted treason defendants to employ counsel, and if "not able himself to employ, counsel to be assigned by the court."[36] With regular experience in capital cases, the bar that represented treason defendants in Pennsylvania most likely had considerably more familiarity with criminal law than their counterparts in England.

Eighteenth-century court records generally do not state the names of defense counsel. As legal historian S.F.C. Milson put it, "It is a property of legal sources . . . that they will tell the investigator nearly everything except what he wants to know."[37] Nonetheless, other sources provide some hints. Attorney Jacob

Rush wrote on October 10, 1778, "Our Court of Oyer and Terminer has been sitting these two weeks for the trial of Tories, and I apprehend will continue to sit for three or four weeks to come." Rush continued, "the gentlemen of the bar (myself among them) are so entirely engaged in that way" it would be impossible for any other legal business to be heard for at least a month.[38] Rush's statement suggests that a wide variety of attorneys were employed. We can establish definitively only that Abraham Carlisle was represented by James Wilson, George Ross, and William Lewis; John Roberts by Wilson and Ross; William Hamilton by Wilson and Lewis; and Peter Deshong by Ross.[39]

These lawyers were among the best attorneys in America, and, as we shall see, they fought the cases ferociously, with challenges to indictments, challenges to the introduction of evidence, and motions in arrest of judgment. Lewis was only twenty-seven, but already a formidable lawyer; he later served as defense counsel in the Whiskey Rebellion cases and was appointed to the federal bench.[40] Rush was a graduate of Princeton and was later named to the Pennsylvania Supreme Court; as a brother of Benjamin Rush, the signer of the Declaration of Independence, he was also a cousin to juror William Rush.[41]

Charges and Defenses

The jury verdicts would ultimately turn on the facts produced at trial. It is possible that the jury verdicts correctly assessed guilt and innocence in each case. But this possibility requires us to accept an almost complete breakdown of criminal justice in revolutionary Philadelphia. These defendants had survived two significant sifting mechanisms—the state's initial decision to prosecute and the grand jury's decision to indict. If most of these people were factually innocent, there would have been serious abnormalities both in the charging decisions and in the grand-jury process. The more likely scenario is that most of the persons tried for treason committed acts that brought them within the technical scope of Pennsylvania's treason laws. Unfortunately, detailed evidence survives for only three of the trials, those of Abraham Carlisle and John Roberts, both of whom were convicted and executed, and Peter Deshong, who was acquitted.

Carlisle's indictment alleged that he had accepted a commission from the king of Great Britain to serve as a gatekeeper of the occupied city of Philadelphia, that he had levied war against the state of Pennsylvania, and that he had aided and assisted the enemy by joining his armies, by conspiring to betray the state of Pennsylvania, and by sending intelligence to the enemy. The indictment was hardly a model of legal precision, as Carlisle's attorneys pointed out. It failed to identify distinct overt acts, and the three separate charges led to considerable confusion as to what evidence was admissible with respect to each. Attorney General

Sergeant defended the indictment, noting that it was "similar to that against Eneas McDonald," one of the defendants in the English treason trials following the 1745 Jacobite uprising. Indeed, the indictment was copied almost verbatim from McDonald's indictment as reported in Foster's treatise. The court upheld the indictment, holding that the allegation of taking a commission was "certain enough" and that the charge of sending intelligence need not set "forth the particular letter, or its contents." Following Carlisle's conviction, his attorneys filed an unsuccessful motion for arrest of judgment, again arguing that the indictment was "vague and uncertain," did not expressly state an overt act, was drawn with insufficient precision, and lacked "form and substance."[42] The state later took full advantage of the court's permissiveness. By April 1779, it had created preprinted treason indictments that left blanks only for the defendant's name and the date and place of the offense. The rest was generic verbiage tracking the McDonald indictment.[43]

The trial testimony in Carlisle's case, which has been preserved in Chief Justice McKean's notes, was devoted almost entirely to the charge of accepting a commission. The prosecution witnesses testified that Carlisle had served as gatekeeper of the city of Philadelphia during the British occupation and issued the passes that were required for individuals to depart or to enter the city. They also testified to his vituperative attitude toward the Revolution, claiming that Carlisle had regularly cursed and damned the "rebels," had called Mary Sneider a "rebel bitch," and had boasted that he "could kill an hundred rebels and pity not." The defense witnesses did not deny that Carlisle had issued passes, but they testified that he had granted passes to almost everyone, that he was tired of his position, and that he was almost removed from office on account of his lenity. In their closing arguments, Carlisle's attorneys argued that no commission had been satisfactorily proved. The Assembly, they claimed, had intended only military commissions to be treasonous; Carlisle had held a civilian post, and it was not treason for civilians in a conquered city to join the conquerors.[44]

The indictment of John Roberts charged that he had levied war against the state and aided the state's enemies by joining the British army, serving as a guide to the army, and persuading others to enlist in the army, and sending intelligence to the enemy.[45] According to Chief Justice McKean's notes of the trial, the state presented seven witnesses, who testified that Roberts had been seen in the company of the British army, that he had committed depredations on American citizens, that he had sought to enlist people in the British army, that he had influence with the British army with respect to prisoners, and that he had sought to rescue the Pennsylvania detainees exiled to Virginia. The defense introduced at least twenty-nine witnesses, who testified Roberts had desired to remain neutral, had been compelled by the British to serve as a guide, had been under guard when seen with the British, and had revealed to the Americans that the journals of the Continental Congress were hidden at his farm, which allowed them to be saved. Numerous defense witnesses also testified that certain prosecution witnesses were of bad character and unreliable.[46] Overall, the Roberts defense seems stronger than the Carlisle defense and one observer noted that "those people who attended thought no evidence produced would authorize the jury to bring him in guilty."[47] Similarly, Quaker diarist Elizabeth Drinker noted surprise at the guilty verdict, "as they did not expect it."[48] On the other hand, Roberts's case was weaker than Carlisle's in one key respect, a point emphasized by Joseph Reed in his closing argument. Whereas Carlisle had simply remained in Philadelphia when the British arrived, Roberts voluntarily chose to leave his residence on the unoccupied outskirts of Philadelphia, leaving behind his wife and children, to enter the occupied city where he remained until the British departed.[49] The day after the British evacuation, Roberts hastily took the oath of allegiance to Pennsylvania before grand juror Zebulon Potts.[50]

Trial notes, in an unidentified hand, also survive for the case of Peter Deshong. Like Abraham Carlisle, Deshong had acted as a gatekeeper of the city during the British occupation.[51] Deshong was charged with "(1) granting passes in virtue of a commission to watch the gate; (2) disarming inhabitants; [and] (3) forming a plan to supply the enemy with provisions." Prosecution witnesses testified that Deshong issued passes to leave the city and had required various Philadelphians to surrender their guns. Defense witnesses testified that Deshong had sought to convey valuable military information to General Washington, that he had taken his post solely to assist impoverished people, and that he was generally friendly to the American cause.[52] These arguments were successful; according to a newspaper account, Deshong was acquitted because he "accepted the office with reluctance" and "was broke for his indulgence and lenity to the inhabitants."[53]

Although no testimony survives in full for any other trials, there are scattered references to the charges and defenses raised in other trials. The record book of justice of the peace Benjamin Paschall reveals that Joseph Turner, Samuel Piles, George Harding, and Charles Woolfall were charged with "collecting arms from the inhabitants of Southwark for the use of the enemy."[54] The recognizance records of the Court of Oyer and Terminer reveal that John Huntsman was charged with "having been a guide to the British Army," David Copeland with "recruiting men for the King of Great Britain," Aubrey Harry with "having been a Wagon Master to the British Army," and Lewis Guion with being a "Conductor of Wagons for the English Army."[55] The prison diary of Samuel Rowland Fisher records that James Stevens and Samuel Garrigues were charged with serving as bridge keepers, and George Harding and William Whitefield with "going about with the British soldiery to collect the Fire Arms of the inhabitants."[56] Fragmentary notes of testimony concerning Joseph Bolton indicate that he had allegedly assisted the British army in detaining several American prisoners.[57] A secondhand account claims that William Hamilton was acquitted "owing to a defect of proof, of a paper from Lord Cornwallis, the direction being torn off."[58]

Several defendants repeated Roberts's claim of compulsion. As Blackstone had explained, "in time of war or rebellion, a man may be justified in doing many treasonable acts by compulsion of the enemy or rebels, which would admit of no excuse in the time of peace."[59] A Philadelphia newspaper reported that George Cook, who had acted as a guide to the British, and Jacob Ming were acquitted because they had been compelled.[60] A Philadelphia woman in February 1779 claimed that many treason defendants had been acquitted "because they appeared to have acted a humane part, altho' submitting for a time, out of necessity, to the command of the enemy."[61] Others followed Deshong in arguing a hidden attachment to the American cause. Samuel Garrigues produced "[e]vidences in his behalf of things not consistent with the Trust reposed in him by the British."[62]

The scattered information concerning the defenses suggests that defendants did not generally argue factual innocence.[63] Rather, confronted with the reality that their actions technically fell within the scope of Pennsylvania's treason laws, defendants relied on compulsion defenses or on a parade of witnesses who could testify to their kindness and lenity to Americans.

Trial Witnesses

The surviving witness lists provide another window into the testimony offered at trial.[64] In his Law Lectures, James Wilson placed considerable emphasis on the jury's role in assessing the credibility of witnesses. "Truth will be estimated by the character, and not the number, of those, who give their testimony. . . . These advantages of a trial by jury are important in all causes: in criminal causes, they are of peculiar importance."[65] The jury, Wilson believed, was the "fittest to make the proper comparison and estimate" of the "character and conduct of the witnesses" and the "character and conduct of the prisoner."[66] The court's docket book lists both prosecution and defense witnesses and indicates whether the witness swore an oath or, as was customary practice for Quakers, offered an affirmation.

Witness lists survive for twenty-two of the twenty-three trials. In general, the defense called more witnesses. Overall, 174 witnesses testified for the prosecution and 262 witnesses for the defense.[67] The prosecution's mean number of witnesses per trial was 7.9, compared to 11.9 for the defense; medians were 6.5 for the prosecution and 11 for the defense. These statistics, however, are slightly skewed by several trials with high numbers of defense witnesses. If we look at individual trials, defense witnesses outnumbered prosecution witnesses in twelve of the twenty-two trials, prosecution witnesses predominated in eight trials, and two of the trials were equally matched. There appears to be no correlation between the predominance of defense witnesses and the likelihood of conviction. The number of prosecution witnesses ranged from 18, at the trial of Samuel Garrigues, to 2, at the trial of William Hamilton. The number of defense witnesses ranged from 31, at the trial of Peter Deshong, to zero, at the trials of Abijah Wright and Adam Stricker.

The prosecution and defense witnesses differ most strikingly with respect to gender and religion. Women constitute 12.8% of the prosecution witnesses whose gender can be determined, but 36.5% of the comparable witnesses for the defense. Overall, over four times as many women testified for the defense as for the prosecution. For its part, the state may have been reluctant to rely on female witnesses to prove a capital crime. Defendants, on the other hand, may have used female witnesses to testify to the defendants' acts of kindness or to their general character and family responsibilities.

Religious data are slightly less reliable, because in several trials the docket book does not indicate whether the witnesses were sworn or affirmed. Data on this point exist for 141 prosecution witnesses and 182 defense witnesses. Only 4 of the 141 prosecution witnesses were affirmed, an exceptionally small proportion given the large number of Quakers in Philadelphia. By contrast, 57 of the 182 defense witnesses, approximately 31.3%, were affirmed.

A number of witnesses appeared in multiple trials. Nine witnesses testified for the prosecution in more than one trial, not counting the identical witness list for the trials of George Harding and William Whitefield, who were tried on the same day. The most frequent prosecution witnesses were cordwainer and Patriotic Association member Peter Cooper and Alexander Hamilton, who both testified five times.[68] Defense witnesses were even more likely to be repeaters. The defense witnesses were identical in the two sets of trials held on the same day, those of Charles Woolfall and Samuel Piles and those of George Harding and William Whitefield. The most frequent defense witness was Richard Footman, who testified five times. Footman, a merchant and auctioneer, had been appointed a vendue master under the British occupation.[69]

Several of the grand jurors and trial jurors appeared as witnesses. For example, grand juror James Young testified against Lewis Guion, John Huntsman, Aubrey Harry, and Abijah Wright. Grand juror Benjamin Loxley testified against Peter Deshong. Trial jurors Thomas Hale and William Gamble testified against Abijah Wright and James Roberts, respectively. Trial juror William Gray testified for defendant Lewis Guion. By modern lights, the most unusual testimony was Cadwalader Dickinson's on behalf of John Huntsman while Dickinson was simultaneously serving as a juror in Huntsman's case. Eighteenth-century practice, however, permitted juror testimony without risk of disqualification.[70]

No defendant offered sworn testimony on his own behalf. Defendants were not permitted to offer sworn testimony in most American states until the mid-nineteenth century. A Pennsylvania lawyer stated the conventional view in 1831: "to confer a right upon a party to become a witness in his own cause, or in any way to legalize his oath, would only 'lead men into temptation,' without affording any additional advantages or security in the search after truth."[71] But defendants could testify at the trials of others. Adam Stricker, for example, testified on behalf of Andrew Hathe. Defendants also appear to have enlisted their relatives to testify on behalf of themselves or other defendants. Elizabeth Deshong testified for Peter Deshong, Samuel Garrigues's son testified for Jacob Ming, and Susanna Ming testified for George Cook and Andrew Hathe. Former Pennsylvania Lieutenant Governor James Hamilton testified on behalf of his nephew, William Hamilton.

Individuals of Hamilton's prominence were rare on the witness lists. Perhaps the most noteworthy were silversmith Philip Syng and General John Cadwalader. Syng, who testified for John Roberts, made the silver inkstand used for the signing of the Declaration of Independence and, later, for the Constitution.[72] Cadwalader, who testified for William Hamilton, was one of the most prominent American generals and one of the wealthiest men in Philadelphia.[73]

Evidentiary Objections

The surviving records of the Carlisle and Roberts cases indicate extensive objections by defense counsel to the introduction of certain evidence. It is likely that similar objections were raised in other trials. In the Carlisle case, the defense objected to the prosecution's first witness, who proposed to testify that Carlisle had taken salt from persons at the city gate and had the power of granting passes. This testimony, Carlisle's attorneys argued, was inadmissible because it did not directly relate to an overt act of accepting a commission. Until such an overt act was proved, no other testimony could be admitted. Chief Justice McKean, speaking for the court, ruled that the testimony did not support the charge of accepting a commission, but it could support the indictment's further allegation that Carlisle had joined the British army.[74] With respect to a different prosecution witness, however, the justices agreed with the defense that the evidence supported only the lesser charge of misprision of treason and was therefore inadmissible.[75]

The Roberts trial raised two contested evidentiary issues. The first involved a witness who was called to prove that Roberts had unsuccessfully attempted to convince him to join the British army. The act of the Assembly had declared that "persuading others to enlist" in the armies of an enemy was an act of high treason. Roberts's attorneys argued that "persuade" requires success. The Latin *suadeo* meant only advising; *persuadeo* meant an advising through, that is, a success. The justices agreed and ruled that the act applied only to those cases resulting in an actual enlistment. The evidence could be admitted, however, for the different purpose of showing that the defendant had joined the armies of the enemy.[76]

The second issue concerned the admissibility of the defendant's alleged confession, supposedly made in a Philadelphia tavern six months after the fact, that he sought to arrange the rescue of the prisoners exiled to Virginia. Roberts's attorneys argued that the evidence was inadmissible under common law and Pennsylvania statutes. Joseph Reed replied that "a dozen judges have settled this point. Confessions may be given in evidence to corroborate other proofs of overt acts by two witnesses." The court, according to McKean's notes, agreed with Reed, holding that the confession was "proper evidence to explain and corroborate the testimony of the two witnesses."[77] As reported in the Dallas volume, the court ruled that in the absence of other testimony, evidence of a confession could not support the charges of giving intelligence to the enemy; nevertheless, it was good for corroboration, and could be introduced to support other charges in the indictment.[78] After the defendant's conviction, Wilson and Ross moved for a new trial, arguing that the "evidence given respecting his declarations, or confessions, was altogether illegal, and ought not to have been allowed." The justices rejected this motion.[79]

Given the rudimentary state of evidence law in the 1770s, it is hard to argue that the justices consistently erred in favor of the prosecution or the defense. The inclination to allow prosecution evidence to be admitted, but only for limited purposes, arguably struck a reasonable balance between the prosecution and the defense positions.

Jury Deliberations

At the close of the evidence, the court charged the jury, with each judge possibly providing a separate charge. None of these charges have survived, although there is some indirect evidence of their content. A contemporary described McKean's charge in the Carlisle case as "favorable" to the defense.[80] Joseph Reed stated on October 23, 1778, that "[t]he Court began to think its charges give too much countenance to acquittals—I have thought so from the beginning, tho it is an error on the favorable side."[81]

After being charged, the jury began its deliberations, often very late at night.[82] Court prothonotary Edward Burd wrote to a friend that the Carlisle trial had lasted "all night" and that the Roberts trial would likely do the same. He noted,

"I expect we shall look like stewed witches before the Court is over."[83] John Roberts's trial took over two days, a very lengthy trial for the eighteenth century, including a "long" period of jury deliberation.[84] During the trial Attorney General Sergeant became so sick that he went home, leaving the prosecution in Joseph Reed's hands.[85] William Hamilton's trial lasted twelve hours, but the jury took only two minutes to acquit him.[86] George Harding later claimed that he had stood at the bar for twenty hours at his trial.[87]

As James Wilson explained in his Law Lectures, "When the jury retire, a bailiff is sworn to keep them together til they be agreed of their verdict."[88] The common law traditionally required that the jury be kept without "meat, drink, fire, or candle." The purpose was to hasten jury verdicts, but the requirements did not always have that effect. A juror in an April 1779 Philadelphia trial claimed that the verdict was delayed until the next morning, because "after it was dark we could do nothing, as we were deprived of candle by order of the Court."[89] Wilson pointed out that it was common to see a jury "worn down by thirst, and hunger, and want of sleep, distracted by altercations and debates . . . pale, anxious, dejected."[90] William Bradford, who would begin prosecuting treason cases for the state in 1780, later described the "looks of the prisoner," the "anxious attention and long deliberation of the jury," and "the awful silence which prevails while the verdict is given in by their Foreman."[91]

The jurors ultimately convicted four defendants, and acquitted the rest. The first two convictions, that of carpenter Abraham Carlisle and miller John Roberts, both Quakers, came in the first three trials. The third conviction came in December, when Abijah Wright was convicted of burglary for forcibly entering the house of Andrew Knox, a justice of the peace, with six other armed men; the court records are silent as to whether he was acquitted on his separate treason charge or whether the jury simply failed to reach that issue.[92] The fourth conviction came in April 1779, when George Harding was convicted of treason.

The only surviving account of deliberations in these trials comes from a somewhat questionable source. In the late 1780s, a few years before his own execution in the tumult of the French Revolution, the writer J.P. Brissot de Warville spent considerable time with the Philadelphia Quaker community. He was told that in the Roberts and Carlisle trials, "[o]nly two of the jurors thought Roberts and Carlisle guilty, and the ten others wished to acquit them. The two succeeded in persuading the other ten to change their votes only by promising that a pardon would be granted and by persuading the others of the necessity of a conspicuous example."[93] Much of Warville's subsequent account is inaccurate, as it asserts that Joseph Reed was President of the Supreme Executive Council that denied the men's petitions for clemency. Moreover, Carlisle's and Roberts's juries were composed of different people. Nonetheless, there may be a kernel of truth to this story, as it would explain why the jury in these cases both convicted and petitioned the Council for clemency. It was essentially a compromise verdict. It is noteworthy that two jurors in Roberts's case, James Barns and James Hood, did not sign the clemency petition. These two may well have been the two who argued for conviction, but then failed to carry out their side of the bargain. An unsavory episode of this sort may also partially explain James Wilson's forceful arguments in his Law Lectures for granting acquittals in cases in which only one juror supported acquittal.[94]

The deliberations were also shaped by the persistent pattern of serial jury service. In the later cases especially, the jurors had broad experience in treason cases and were familiar with one another from prior service. Modern empirical research offers several insights into the effects of serial service. Several studies have found that jurors with prior service in criminal cases are more likely to convict.[95] This insight supports the conventional wisdom among trial lawyers that inexperienced jurors are better defense jurors.[96] Other studies, however, have found the effect of prior service to be relatively slight.[97] One study clarified that "experience *does* tend to make jurors more likely to convict, but the bias seems to be suppressed unless experienced jurors are in the majority in the group."[98] If this effect was present in Philadelphia, it was minimal. Inexperienced juries convicted in two of the first three trials, and juries composed entirely of experienced jurors repeatedly acquitted.

A more promising theory is that jurors' initial trial experience is most strongly linked to later behavior. Jurors use their initial case as a sort of "anchor" by which to evaluate subsequent cases. Jurors who initially convicted in the face of a strong prosecution case will demand similarly strong cases in the future. Similarly, jurors who initially confronted a weak prosecution case will be more impressed with stronger cases in the future.[99] This theory provides a better explanation for the Philadelphia verdicts. If Sergeant and Reed led off with their strongest case, that against Abraham Carlisle, the jurors may have expected similar evidence in future cases. Even jurors who did not serve on Carlisle's jury may have been present in the courtroom or heard about it in subsequent deliberations from jurors who were. The evidence in later cases may well have seemed weaker than that against Carlisle, and perhaps that against Roberts as well, disposing experienced jurors in favor of acquittal.

The Death Penalty

The most significant factor in the long pattern of acquittals, however, was the death penalty, which shaped every decision the juries made. In England, juries often evaded the death penalty by finding defendants guilty of lesser offenses or by valuing stolen goods below the capital threshold.[100] The Philadelphia treason jurors lacked any such techniques. Pennsylvania law recognized a lesser offense of misprision of treason, but the treason juries did not have the option of convicting under that charge. And unlike in theft cases, there was no option of deliberately undervaluing particular goods.

The only intermediate sanction was the possibility that the court might impose a bond on an acquitted defendant. The defendant would be obligated to maintain good behavior or to keep the peace, and if he failed to do so, would owe the amount of the bond. Pennsylvania's early courts had made extensive use of such bonds, seemingly more so than other colonies, and the practice had remained vibrant into the 1780s.[101] Eleven of the acquitted treason defendants were ordered to sign bonds.[102] Ten of these bound the defendants to good behavior during the present war, or, in one case, for the next twelve months. Eight of these also bound the defendant to keep the peace.[103] Seven of these defendants were also ordered to pay the costs of prosecution. The bonds ranged in value from five hundred pounds to two thousand pounds, and the defendants were also obligated to provide two sureties who would collectively provide an amount equal to the defendant's obligation. These financial obligations were extremely burdensome, and many eighteenth-century Pennsylvanians denounced the bonds as unjust when levied on acquitted defendants.[104] Nonetheless, the court's widespread use of these bonds may have made some of the jurors more willing to acquit in treason cases. Indeed, two of the jurors in John Huntsman's trial, John Drinker and William Eckhart, were the sureties on Huntsman's bond.[105] Jurors could acquit marginal defendants secure in the belief that acquitted defendants would still be subject to judicial supervision.

The underlying calculus of the jury verdicts, however, did not change. A guilty verdict in a treason case guaranteed the death penalty, unless the Supreme Executive Council granted a reprieve. Under the 1776 constitution the Council had the power, in treason and murder cases, "to grant reprieves, but not to pardon till after the next session of the Assembly."[106] And there was, of course, no guarantee of what the Council would do. When the jurors were confronted with a case in which the evidence pointed to guilt, but the death penalty seemed a disproportionate punishment, the temptation to acquit would be strong. In a 1791 grand jury charge, James Wilson argued against mandatory severe punishments in criminal cases. In such cases, the "jury will probably find, or think they find, some decent ground, on which they may be justified, or at least excused, in giving a verdict of acquittal."[107]

The jurors convicted in the first case they heard, that of Abraham Carlisle, and the third case, that of John Roberts. But, surprisingly, the jurors had no desire to see either man hang. The jurors in Abraham Carlisle's case unanimously petitioned the Council for clemency, stating,

> [B]y the oath we had taken, and upon the whole of the evidence before us, we were constrained to give our verdict against him, agreeable to the laws of our country, yet from the knowledge we have of his former blameless character, the consideration of his advanced age, and our sympathy with his distressed family and reputable connexions, our sentiments of humanity lead us to wish that the rigor of the law may be abated in his case.[108]

Chief Justice McKean and Justice Evans favorably recommended this petition to the Council.[109] Justice Atlee did not sign the recommendation, but he did not issue any statement to the contrary. Similarly, ten of the jurors in John Roberts's case petitioned for clemency, stating "it appears to us . . . Roberts was under the influence of fear, when he took the imprudent step of leaving his family and coming to reside among the enemy, while they had possession of the city." Although the jurors were obliged by their oath "to pronounce him guilty," they knew that "juries are but fallible men," and the evidence "was of a very complicated nature, and some parts of it not reconcileable with his general conduct. . . ."[110] Even juror Andrew Burkhard, who named his newborn son after Assistant Attorney General Joseph Reed shortly after the Roberts trial (an action that guaranteed his exclusion from future juries), joined in this petition.[111] As in Abraham Carlisle's case, Chief Justice McKean and Justice Evans recommended the petition for "favorable acceptance."[112] These petitions were buttressed by a petition from eleven of the eighteen grand jurors, who stated that, "all circumstances considered," the men were "suitable objects of mercy."[113]

Curiously, prosecutor Joseph Reed stated that he had "always expected" such a petition from the jurors in both cases, suggesting that he knew he had not fully persuaded the juries of the heinousness of the defendants' offenses. Reed, however, expressed surprise at the actions of Chief Justice McKean and Justice Evans, which he felt "contributed largely to the Embarrassment which the Board must have upon the Occasion, and which taking into View all Circumstances must have been sufficiently great without the Addition."[114] McKean's actions were perhaps most surprising, as he had sentenced Roberts to death only one day before recommending the petitions. His sentence was a bombastic piece of theater that accused Roberts of "endeavour[ing] the total destruction of the lives, liberties, and property of all his fellow citizens" and supporting a cause "which has been complicated with the horrid and crying sin of murdering thousands, who were not only innocent, but meritorious; and aggravated by burning some of them alive and starving others to death." Roberts's acts of kindness to Americans, McKean argued, could "by no means compensate for treason."[115] Those acts of kindness, although legally immaterial to guilt or innocence of treason, were nonetheless relevant to sentencing and could be appropriately considered by the Council. McKean's published sentence of John Roberts was nonetheless far more publicized than his subsequent support of the petitions for clemency, and he was widely reviled as a hanging judge.[116] A few months later in New York, British Captain John André delighted his audience with an elaborate account of a dream about the rebels. André imagined himself in Hades, watching souls being tried:

> The first person to be called upon was the famous Chief-justice McKean, who I found had been animated by the same spirit which formerly possessed the memorable Jeffries. I could not but observe a flash of indignation in the eyes of the judges upon the approach of this culprit. His more than savage cruelty, his horrid disregard to the many oaths of allegiance he had taken, and the vile sacrifices he had made of justice to the interests of the rebellion, were openly rehearsed. . . . He was condemned to assume the shape of a blood-hound, and the souls of Roberts and Carlisle were ordered to scourge him through the infernal regions.[117]

In the same vein, a Philadelphia poet wrote, "Who guards McKean and Joseph Reed the vile / Help'd he not murder Roberts and Carlisle?"[118]

The jurors and the justices were not alone in their desire for clemency. Jasper Yeates noted that "the city is in the greatest ferment. Most good men hope for an act of oblivion."[119] Petitions flooded into the Council on behalf of Roberts and Carlisle. One petition in favor of John Roberts contained over 750 names, ranging from luminaries such as John Cadwalader and Benjamin Rush to Joseph Malin, recently acquitted of treason, and Samuel Garrigues, Jr., whose father was awaiting his own treason trial.[120] Petitioners presented a variety of reasons for leniency. One pointed to the hardships that execution would place on Roberts's wife and his nine children.[121] On another, 150 people asserted that Roberts had personally saved them from the plundering armies of the British.[122] Others testified to his many kindnesses to American prisoners.[123]

The issue seemed to cut to the core of what it meant to be an American. According to one petitioner, "the characteristic of the True Americans shall be humanity, mercy, charity and forgiveness."[124] Another hoped that "the foundation of our civil liberty may be firmly established without the blood of our fellow citizens."[125] One group of petitioners conceded the need "in every civilized state" for the "punishment of treasons and treasonable practices," but argued that mercy for Abraham Carlisle would not endanger the safety of the state.[126] There are no surviving records of any person petitioning the Council to let the sentences stand.[127]

The additional petitions included the signatures of numerous jurors from other treason trials.[128] Jurors Whitehead Humphreys, William Gray, and Anthony Wilkinson signed a petition stating that the British were unlikely to return to Pennsylvania and the executions would serve little deterrent value.[129] Cadwalader Dickinson, who served on Carlisle's jury, signed a separate petition on behalf of John Roberts.[130] Jurors Samuel Simpson, William Rush, and Adam Zantzinger signed a petition on behalf of John Roberts, stating that "however justly his conduct in legal construction may amount to that horrid crime," it did not "proceed from malevolence and a wicked disposition" but from "prejudices and attachments to the late government."[131] Another petition on behalf of John Roberts included jurors Thomas Shields and John Pringle, and grand juror Thomas Pryor.[132] Three other petitions for Abraham Carlisle were also signed by Pryor and at least sixteen trial jurors.[133] All told, at least thirty of the fifty-eight trial jurors signed a petition for Roberts, Carlisle, or both.

The petitions placed the Council in a difficult position. As Joseph Reed noted, "proceed how you will, the mouth of faction and censure will open upon you, either in a charge of unfeeling cruelty, mean timidity, or false compassion."[134] The claims of humanity in favor of clemency were strong, especially when presented by the juries and justices who had listened carefully to the evidence. Even Reed conceded that "the voice of the people will certainly justify Council in any act of mercy."[135] Going forward with the executions would be an insult to Pennsylvania's judicial system, inevitably alienate large segments of the community, and generate further antagonism between the state government and the Quaker population. General Cadwalader was willing to go so far to as to argue that "all distinction should be laid aside under a perfect oblivion for past offences."[136] By December 1778, Benjamin Rush had concluded the "time is now past when the least danger is to be apprehended to our liberties from the power of Britain, the art of commissioners, or the machinations of tories. Tyranny can now enter our country only in the shape of a whig."[137]

On the other hand, Rush's confidence that the British would never return to Pennsylvania was not universally shared. A blanket amnesty for persons like Carlisle and Roberts would have virtually guaranteed a profusion of similar treasonous acts in the event of a British return. Joseph Reed argued that whatever harm the executions might cause must be balanced against the "Lives & safety of officers & soldiers who are so often destroyed by these treacherous Practices."[138] Reed's prosecution of the treason cases may have even helped him politically. In October 1778, Reed resigned his seat in Congress and was elected to the Supreme

Executive Council.[139] In December, the Assembly elected him President of the Council by a nearly unanimous vote.[140]

Reed advised George Bryan, the acting president of the Council, that he supported "speedy execution of both the criminals," but suggested the Council defer the decision for several days to give time for the Assembly to weigh in.[141] Reed was unimpressed by the petitions, claiming, "Treason, Disaffection to the Interest of America & even assistance to the British Interest is called openly only Error of Judgment, which Candour and Liberality of Sentiment will overlook."[142] "Popular humanity (tho not mentioned in our Treason Law)," Reed argued, "is a Species of Treason of not the least dangerous kind."[143] Indeed the wealth and prominence of Roberts and Carlisle and their widespread public support were arguments for, not against, the executions. Carlisle and Roberts were "two of the most notorious" of "the great number of Pilots, Guides, Kidnappers, & other Assistants of the British Army." "None could be more guilty, but these being rich & powerful (both Quakers) we could not for shame have made an example of a poor rogue after forgiving the rich."[144]

Writing in 1795, Hugh Henry Brackenridge recalled, "The British at New York, and the tories, as they were called, in Philadelphia, were said to have insinuated that our government would not dare to execute these persons." The Council, Brackenridge felt, was inclined toward mercy in Carlisle's case, but "these ideas of the enemy at home and abroad, rendered it necessary to establish a conviction of our confidence in the event of our struggle, by hanging traitors: which would be as much to say, Do your worst; we are not afraid that you will ever have it in your power to hang us."[145]

Historians have continued to debate the propriety of the executions. Joseph Reed's grandson, William Reed, felt that the hangings were eminently just. Abraham Carlisle's behavior, for example, "was offensive in the extreme, and far beyond the line where technical treason begins."[146] Bradley Chapin agreed, claiming, "The justice of the sentences cannot be doubted . . . The pardon of Roberts and Carlisle would have amounted to a virtual guarantee of amnesty to all who contemplated treason."[147] In a measured analysis, David Maxey has argued that Carlisle was almost certainly guilty, but that Roberts's case raised more difficult questions.[148] At the other extreme, Raymond Werner has argued that "both men were undoubtedly innocent of the charges" and "were executed to appease the clamors of the extreme Whigs."[149] Steven Boyd contends that in 1778, "two Quakers became the victims of . . . politicized justice."[150] Geoffrey Seed describes the executions as a "miscarriage of justice."[151] In their monumental 1884 history of Philadelphia, Scharf and Westcott concluded, "Their execution . . . appear[s] at this day to have been dictated by the desire to satisfy popular clamor rather than a spirit of justice. The Whigs thirsted for revenge, and it seems to have been deemed expedient to supply them with at least two victims."[152] Richard Ryerson attributes the executions to raging patriot anger: "When Pennsylvania's Constitutionalists hanged Roberts and Carlisle, they were acting out the role of angry, frustrated, outsiders who had finally gotten through the doorway. . . . These apprehensive, deeply offended patriots lashed out . . . finally, and, most tragically, at Quakers."[153] Thomas Slaughter goes even further, claiming that "trials such as that of Philadelphia Quaker Abraham Carlisle reflected the blood lust endemic to the Revolutionary scene and the utility of treason trials for exacting judicial revenge."[154]

On balance, it is hard to find fault with the jury verdicts. There was ample evidence of treasonous behavior on the part of both men. Indeed, Joseph Galloway later testified to a British parliamentary committee that he had "positively advised [Carlisle] to leave the city [at the British evacuation], because I knew he would not be safe."[155] The men had received a fair trial and had been represented by excellent counsel. The question of a pardon, however, was much more difficult, as reasonable arguments could be made on both sides.

The controversy over the men's fate led many people to believe that the Council would grant a reprieve. Thomas Franklin initially doubted that the executions would go forward, as "their crimes is [*sic*] not so enormous or the evidence so full as was expected would appear against them."[156] The Council had issued death warrants for the two men on October 23, 1778, but Elizabeth Drinker noted in her diary on October 28 that "tis hoped and believed that their Lives will be spared, it would be terrible indeed should it happen otherwise."[157] On November 2, the Council again examined the petitions and studied McKean's notes from the trials. A man named Samuel Wallis appeared and offered to give evidence favorable to Roberts. The Council ordered him to prepare a deposition before a justice of the peace.[158] Wallis's deposition, taken the next day before grand juror Plunket Fleeson, asserted that Roberts "was a person in whom the enemy had no confidence," and that he had never been useful or reliable to the British.[159] Although the Council did not know it, Wallis was in fact a British agent and a spy, possibly sent by his British masters to plead for one of their own.[160] Wallis's last-minute appearance was unpersuasive, as were the personal appearances of the wives and children of the two men, and on November 3, the Council denied a reprieve.[161] Elizabeth Drinker still held out hope, confiding in her diary "that they will not be permitted, to carry this matter to the last extremity."[162]

On November 4, Carlisle and Roberts were marched to the scaffold with halters around their necks. Despite all the attention the trials and convictions had received, there were few spectators. Carlisle was too feeble to say anything, but Roberts, "with the greatest coolness imaginable, spoke for some time."[163] One account holds that Roberts claimed that his conscience acquitted him of guilt, that he "suffered for doing his duty to his sovereign," and "that his blood would one day be demanded at their hands," assertions wildly inconsistent with the defenses made at his trial.[164] The claim that four thousand people later marched in Abraham Carlisle's funeral procession is almost certainly exaggerated, but the burial services for both men, according to John Pemberton, who was present, were both "very large."[165]

The executions of Carlisle and Roberts were among the most divisive events of the American Revolution in Pennsylvania. We know of at least one Philadelphia woman whose sleep was disturbed by a nightmare of being hanged; there were probably many more.[166] As late as 1857, a Philadelphian could claim that the executions "created a feeling in the community that is not yet worn out."[167] That both men were Quakers raised considerable suspicion of religious bigotry. John Pemberton, a leading Quaker, found the quasi-military actions of Carlisle and Roberts to be an inappropriate violation of their peace testimony, but noted that the executions "alarmed and affected the inhabitants as neither had committed crimes worthy such severe treatment."[168] A Quaker committee appointed to examine the trials concluded that both Roberts and Carlisle had deviated significantly from Quaker principles, justifying the Meeting for Sufferings in declining to "interpos[e] in their favour or vindication, as is our duty and usual care." Nonetheless, the committee found the trial evidence "very contradictory" and discerned "clear indications of a party spirit" behind the prosecution, which had been conducted "with great severity and rigour."[169] Indeed, in a private letter written during the trials, prosecutor Joseph Reed had warned of the "Designs of a Tory, Proprietary Quaker Party" that needed to be "crushed in the Bud."[170] The Quaker committee also objected to the executions, which "far exceed[ed] the nature of the offense," and were inconsistent with the wishes of "great numbers of all ranks" who had signed the petitions.[171] Others denounced the executions as "murder."[172]

Yet the primary legal effect of the decision to execute Carlisle and Roberts was almost certainly not what the Council had expected: a virtual guarantee of acquittals in future treason cases. Jurors were now on clear notice that clemency could not be presumed, even if they unanimously petitioned the Council themselves. Compromise verdicts would be impossible. The jurors could either acquit or convict and risk death. On those terms, it wasn't a close question at all—juries acquitted the defendants in the next fourteen treason cases.

There would be no conviction until April 8, 1779, when George Harding (also called Hardy) was convicted. There can be little doubt about the accuracy of the verdict. Harding later claimed that during the British occupation of Philadelphia he had "rendered every service to the British in public and private to the utmost of his power, without a fee or reward for all of his trouble day and night." He was captured while attempting to flee with the British army when it departed Philadelphia.[173] But the entire jury nonetheless petitioned the Council for clemency, as did a number of other citizens.[174] The jury stated that it had "heard the testimony with candor, weighed it without partiality, and decided on it without prejudice." The jurors were constrained to convict by the law and by the evidence, but

> when they reflect on the part of the evidence offered on behalf of the prisoner, and give it a proper weight, when they take into consideration his acknowledged upright character as a citizen heretofore and view even in idea, the deep distress of an afflicted wife and her train of weeping children whose sole support rests upon the industry of their husband and parent they feel themselves under the most pressing obligation to declare that they unanimously at the time of agreeing on the verdict, and still do think the said George Hardy a fit object of mercy, and as such do with humility, but with fervor, recommend to your Honors for pardon.[175]

All three justices of the Supreme Court endorsed the petitions for Harding. They observed that Harding's character was good, his prospects for reformation were high, and "his death (being a man of small note or consideration) would afford little benefit by the example." They also stated that "more than one, at least equally criminal with this man, has been tried before us, and acquitted by the extreme lenity and tenderness of the Juries."[176]

The Council ultimately agreed to reprieve Harding, but not before giving him a serious fright. Harding later claimed that he "was led to the place of execution, bound like a Malefactor, and after being forty minutes under the gallows, was reprieved."[177] The *Pennsylvania Gazette* noted that the reprieve "gave satisfaction to the spectators, who were strongly moved by compassion toward the wife and children of this unhappy man."[178] Indeed, it is likely the Council deliberately delayed the reprieve for maximum effect. Harding's jail mate Samuel Rowland Fisher was informed shortly after the conviction that Harding would be reprieved, but Fisher was told to be prudent and not to inform Harding of this fact.[179] The reprieve was partly motivated by British commander Sir Henry Clinton, who apparently sought Harding's release. But the reprieve saved Harding only from the gallows. His property was confiscated, and he remained in prison until October 1779, when he was pardoned, on condition that he leave the state within two weeks and never return. Harding moved to New York and ultimately settled in Nova Scotia, where he sought compensation from the British government for his losses.[180]

The jurors' desire for clemency for convicted defendants did not stem from any general aversion to the death penalty. Pennsylvania executed more people in 1779 and 1780 than in any year prior to the nineteenth century.[181] More death warrants were issued in 1778 than in any previous year in Pennsylvania history.[182] Juries were more than willing to convict in capital cases. Indeed, none of the jurors from Abijah Wright's trial petitioned on his behalf, and only one of the fifty-eight jurors from any trial, Cadwalader Dickinson, Wright's relation through marriage, signed the meager petition circulated on Wright's behalf.[183] Wright had broken into the home of Andrew Knox, possibly with the intention of murdering him, or possibly, as his counsel argued, with the intent to carry him as a prisoner to the enemy (the basis of the treason charge).[184] Such conduct was unmistakably morally blameworthy and could not be justified or excused.

But the other cases were different, and they severely tested the law's traditional assumption that treason was the highest crime, worse even than murder. The jurors simply refused to believe that the allegations of aiding the British rose to the level of murder, or even of burglary. For many jurors (and grand jurors as well), individuals who made the wrong choice of allegiance in a convulsive civil war were not incorrigible criminals, but friends and neighbors with a high possibility of redemption. It is likely true, as Louis Masur has argued, that juries generally found it "easier to convict outsiders . . . of capital crimes, and governors felt less pressure to commute the death sentence of those with few ties to the community."[185] But the treason defendants were not easily defined as outsiders, and every juror knew someone who was potentially subject to Pennsylvania's treason laws.[186] Although treason merited punishment, death was not the answer. Through their strong aversion to capital punishment, Philadelphia jurors effectively nullified Pennsylvania's treason laws.

* * *

The Philadelphia cases weren't the only treason cases heard by the justices that fall. After hearing the first seven treason cases in Philadelphia County between September 25 and October 18, 1778, the Supreme Court had moved on to Bucks County, where six men were tried. The court records do not survive for these trials, so we lack the details that we have for Philadelphia, but the results are quite similar. Like the Philadelphia defendants, the Bucks defendants were relatively obscure. John Poor, William Davis, and John Ellwood were described as "watermen" in the proclamations of attainder.[187] Only one, fifty-seven-year old Thomas Yardley, was locally prominent. He had been disowned by the Quakers in 1756 for having joined a military company, but had served in elected office and was one of the county's wealthiest men.[188] In April 1774, he had served on the grand jury for the Court of Oyer and Terminer for Bucks County.[189] Joseph

Reed reported that Yardley's acquittal was "very much to the dissatisfaction of the Whigs who think him very culpable and a very dangerous fellow."[190]

The Bucks County juries acquitted five of the six defendants.[191] The only conviction came in the case of the waterman John Ellwood, charged with conducting the enemy up the Delaware.[192] The jury found that Ellwood had no "goods, chattels, lands, or tenements."[193] The next month, the Supreme Executive Council granted him a reprieve, as it was possible that he "for some years past hath been subject to fits of insanity."[194] In July 1779, he received a full pardon.[195]

* * *

As the Philadelphia treason trials finally wound to an end in April 1779, the jurors were undoubtedly satisfied with their verdicts. Despite popular hostility to persons accused of treason, they had taken their duties seriously and declined to engulf the city in a wave of executions. Politically, there were seemingly no consequences for the jury verdicts. In the Philadelphia city elections during the fall of the trials, grand juror John Dorsey and juror David Pancoast were elected street commissioners, juror Isaac Roush was elected a city assessor, and juror William Adcock was elected a warden.[196] In January 1779, grand juror William Ball and juror William Adcock were elected as justices of the peace for the city of Philadelphia.[197] Juror William Rush was elected a justice of the peace in May 1779.[198] Indeed, the Pennsylvania Assembly recognized the importance of jury service by quadrupling the fees paid to jurymen, "as the wages allowed them by the said laws were by no means adequate to their necessary expenses while they were attending on their respective business and duties."[199]

Only juror Cadwalader Dickinson initially suffered for his role in the verdicts. Dickinson, a Quaker shoemaker who served on the jury that convicted Abraham Carlisle, was expelled from the Philadelphia Monthly Meeting as a result of his jury service. Several leading Quakers initially met "with him on the painful subject of his case," but "found little satisfaction therein," as Dickinson "continued in a disposition to vindicate his conduct." Since he had "served as a juryman in the trial and condemnation of a fellow member in religious profession" and had acted in "a spirit of war," he was "separated . . . from religious fellowship with us."[200]

But to many of their fellow citizens the jurors amounted to little more than traitors themselves. As Philadelphia drifted into increasingly difficult economic times in 1779, the endless pattern of acquittals in treason cases began to infuriate many people. In March 1779, "A True Patriot," had warned in the *Pennsylvania Gazette* that "treasonable practices" were now being "ranked amongst [the state's] trivial affairs."[201] Diarist Christopher Marshall noted in April 1779 that "the honest inhabitants in Philadelphia were much displeased at the acquittal of G[arrigues] and S[tevens] as their behavior had been so atrocious while the enemy were in the city."[202] Joseph Reed, now president of the Supreme Executive Council, wrote to Chief Justice McKean, stating that "too easy an Ear has been given by the Ministers of Justice to the Applications of those who are disaffected to their country."[203] The verdicts would ultimately provoke ferocious debate over the nature of jury trial itself and a poisonous and violent reaction from those who were convinced that justice had not been done.

8

Resentment and Betrayal, 1779–1781

IN THE SUMMER of 1779, a young Quaker merchant named Samuel Rowland Fisher was sentenced to imprisonment by the Philadelphia Mayor's Court for misprision of treason. Fisher, one of the men who had been exiled to Virginia, would spend the next two years in the Philadelphia jail before receiving a pardon. Fisher's personal misfortune, however, has been historians' gain, for his imprisonment resulted in one of the most extraordinary surviving documents from revolutionary Philadelphia. For two years, Fisher kept a detailed diary of life inside the prison, noting his interactions with his fellow inmates and his observations on political developments. Fisher's sardonic perspective on the Pennsylvania government, which he bitterly opposed, remains gripping reading over two centuries later. The diary is one of our primary sources for the operation of the local courts and the fates and personalities of individual defendants. It also roughly tracks the period covered by this chapter, a convulsive period when juries came under bitter attack, culminating in the violence and bloodshed of the Fort Wilson incident; the state sought easier ways to convict the disloyal; the Council battled with Chief Justice McKean over executive detentions; and the discovery of Benedict Arnold's treason sent ripple effects through the state's legal system.

The Newspaper Debates over the Franks Trial

The first signs of serious repercussions from the treason trials arose in a series of newspaper exchanges triggered by the trial of David Franks, a Philadelphia merchant of Jewish descent, for sending intelligence to the enemy. On the basis of his prior experience provisioning the British army, the Continental Congress had permitted Franks to serve as commissary to British prisoners during the war. Because the British were expected to pay for the support of their own prisoners, Franks was required to have regular contact with the British army, and he remained in Philadelphia during the British occupation.[1] In the fall of 1778, Franks wrote a letter to his brother Moses in London, describing the costs of goods in Philadelphia and noting that William Hamilton, brother-in-law to Franks's daughter, had been acquitted of high treason. Franks claimed, "People are taken and confined at the pleasure of every scoundrel. Oh, what a situation has Britain left its friends." Franks sent this letter to a British officer in New York, requesting that the officer forward it to Moses. His cover letter described the Hamilton trial as an "ill-natured prosecution."[2]

The letters were intercepted and brought to the attention of the Continental Congress, which concluded that the letters manifested a "disposition and intentions inimical to the safety and liberties of the United States" and ordered Franks's arrest.[3] He remained under congressional custody until November 7, 1778, when, for reasons that are unclear, Congress transferred the matter to the state of Pennsylvania.[4] Attorney General Sergeant may well have taken personal offense at the description of the Hamilton prosecution and he was determined that Franks would not go unpunished. No legal documents of the subsequent proceedings survive, but the basic facts can be pieced together from other sources. Sergeant initially sought an indictment for high treason, but the grand jury returned it *ignoramus*.[5] In response, Sergeant adopted the novel course of pursuing the case as a common-law misdemeanor for disturbing the peace by raising sedition.[6] The trial was held before the justices of the Supreme Court on Saturday, April 24, and may have drawn on the same pool of jurors who served in the treason cases.[7] James Wilson and William Lewis conducted the defense.[8] They challenged the appropriateness of the misdemeanor charge, but the court upheld it, seemingly on the theory that if greater crimes include the lesser, the state was free to charge the lesser offense.[9] The jury sat until 8 a.m. the next morning before issuing a verdict of acquittal.[10]

Four days later, a blistering anonymous critique of the jury appeared in the *Pennsylvania Packet*. The author included the full text of David Franks's letters to Moses Franks and to the British officer and argued that had a similar "letter been wrote from General Washington's camp, the writer would have been hanged as a spy, and we should all have approved the sentence." He continued, "a juryman . . . is a public character" and the conduct of jurors "upon such interesting and important occasions" must be "open to the public eye." The names of the jury members should be widely published, so that if "there are any upon this occasion whose public conduct has suddenly altered to a very favourable turn towards these offenders, let them be known to their country."[11]

This attack prompted a swift response from one of the jurors, Davis Bevan, a former Quaker who had been disowned for his service as a captain in the Continental Army.[12] Writing under his own name, Bevan argued that the facts of the case failed to support a charge of giving intelligence to the enemy in New York, since the letter was intended to be opened in London and was clearly a "letter of negotiation for private emolument, and not to injure the states." The attacks in the *Packet* were little more than "the chimerical observations of any hot-headed scribbler."[13]

"Sidney" then joined the debate, with a terse two-sentence letter:

> In your paper of April 29th, I find an attack upon juries, the first that ever was made upon them in a free country. I wish the author of that publication would speak out and tell us at once that he means and wishes that Juries should be abolished as troublesome restraints upon our rulers, and that a few Tory-hunters should hang, burn or gibbet all who do not think with themselves, without Law, Judge or Jury.[14]

Davis Bevan's account of the jury deliberations was bolstered by Whitehead Humphreys, who had served on Franks's jury as well as the jury that had acquitted Joseph Turner of high treason. Writing as "A Juror," Humphreys accused Attorney General Sergeant of writing the April 29 attack, based on his "officiously listening at the window where the jury sat," his threat to publish Franks's letters, and his loud condemnations of the jury. "Do you really think," Humphreys asked," because you are Attorney General, that you have a right to insult in the public newspapers, the freemen of this state, especially those who are upon oath to do justice between the commonwealth of Pennsylvania and a person whom you thought proper to prosecute?" The jury had found "that neither the evidence, nor the law [Sergeant] dwelt so tediously upon, would support them in finding Mr. Franks guilty."[15]

But the attacks on the jury continued. "Diogenes" argued that juries had always been the subject of "free discussion and examination" and threatened that the "writ of *attaint*, which lies at common law against Jurors for a *false verdict*, is not yet forgotten."[16] "X" asserted that "juries have been in some instances sent out of Court again to amend and alter their verdict; that in other cases new Juries have been ordered to try causes again; and that the law not only supposed Jurors may be under undue influence or error, but provided punishments for corrupt, partial, and influenced Jurors." "X" was concerned that "two or three artful men, haughty in their sentiments, and loquacious loud and turbulent of tongue" could hijack a jury such that "confidence in the verdict of that Jury [would] be abated." He also stated that the judges in Franks's case had clearly directed the jury to convict.[17] "X" 's arguments were backed by "Cato," who argued, "Jurymen must expect like all other men, acting on public occasions, to stand or fall in the public opinion, by the rectitude and wisdom of their decisions. . . . There is no magic in the letters which compose the word Jury, that should charm or awe men into silence." The Franks verdict had given "great and general dissatisfaction." The "brave and gallant army" in the field expected "justice to punish traitors at home."[18]

On May 18, 1779, Timothy Matlack admitted in the *Packet* that he and another man were the primary authors of the initial attack on the jury, and that Attorney General Sergeant had nothing to do with it.[19] Matlack, a disowned Quaker and renowned cockfighter, was the secretary to the Supreme Executive Council and had played a leading role in the Pennsylvania constitutional convention. In his capacity as clerk to the Continental Congress, he had inscribed the parchment copy of the Declaration of Independence. Matlack reiterated his arguments against the Franks jury and claimed, "as the continuance of this inestimable mode of trial must depend on the wise and upright conduct of jurors—the importance and value of this mode of trial is the strongest possible reason why the conduct of Jurors ought to be strictly enquired into."[20]

These attacks in turn prompted further defenses of the Franks jury and the jury system more generally. "A.B." published a lengthy response, stating "the base attacks which I complain of . . . are leveled with a wicked intent, against the bulwark of our liberties, Trial by Jury, as well as against the safety of every citizen, who may hereafter be acquitted by the laws of his country, and the judgement of his peers." "What security," he asked, "can any freeman have in the due administration of wholesome laws, if it is in the power of prejudice to raise the resentment of the people, against both him and the jury who acquitted him, by publishing to the world such parts of the evidence only, as operated against him, and suppressing whatever made in his favour?" The trial, "A.B." reported, "was had by a struck Jury of reputable citizens, several of whom had faced the enemy in the hour of danger, and whose characters are too well-established to be hurt by the feeble efforts of narrow-minded men." Sergeant's decision to prosecute the case as a common-law misdemeanor foundered because "no violated law could be shewn to support the prosecution but, on the contrary, the 4th volume, page 5, of the learned Judge Blackstone's Commentaries was read, to prove that a 'misdemeanor is an act committed or omitted in violation of a public law, either forbidding it or commanding it,' and no such thing appeared in the case of Mr. Franks." Seeking to prevent "constructive engines of oppression in the hands of power," the jury had acquitted, "as by the law and their oaths they were bound to do." "Wherein," he asked, "does the excellency of trial by Jury consist, if by practices of this kind, Jurors are to be intimidated into convictions against both law and evidence, in order to support the character of Whigs?"[21]

Whitehead Humphreys joined the argument again, with a wry gesture toward *Hamlet*, noting a "Jury is composed of twelve Freemen, and they have a right to determine for themselves, according to law and evidence, and are not answerable for the blunders of men in office, who, God knows, are too often fond of ridiculously displaying the insolence of office." There was "more danger to be apprehended from the violence and partiality of Judges and the prejudices of State Officers than from a Jury legally impannelled and sworn, will be readily granted by every man of common understanding; and when once an Attorney General, or even the Judge can influence and direct the verdict of a Jury, according to their will and pleasure, we may then take leave of our liberty. . . ."[22] Another juror from the trial emerged under the pseudonym "A True Whig," stating emphatically the judges had not directed the jury to convict. He concluded, "Since these unhappy times, I have been in actual service for this my country, and am still willing, whenever called, to do what I can. And for all those low insinuations that have been hinted against the disaffection of the Jury pass by me, like the wind, unregarded."[23]

At the heart of these exchanges lay disagreements over the character of the jury—disagreements that would parallel later disputes over the character of judges. Was the jury an independent decision-making body that was intended to be free from public pressure? Or was it at least partly a representative body, owing certain duties to the community at large? The members of the jury feared that legitimate criticism of jury verdicts could easily devolve into improper pressure to issue particular verdicts—and that is exactly what happened next.

The Trial of Samuel Rowland Fisher

Disgust with the failure of the courts to convict traitors coincided with a precipitous economic decline throughout 1779. Inflation was the most pressing problem; the overall price level increased seven times between 1777 and 1779. In one month, prices rose 45%. The price of corn rose 1255% in calendar year 1779.[24] Suspected Tories, often wealthy, were quickly blamed for the increasing misery and poverty in Pennsylvania. The civil government seemed incapable of forcefully addressing these problems, and many people began seeking alternative methods of dealing both with the economic crisis and with the base traitors who supposedly lay behind it.[25] The memory of the committee system was still fresh, and to many people it seemed a preferable alternative. In May 1779, a citizens' committee met in the State House Yard to denounce "monopolizers and forestallers." Historian Eric Foner has described this meeting as "the most important extra-legal gathering in Philadelphia since pre-independence days."[26] Among other things, the committee resolved that "no person, who by sufficient testimony can be proved inimical to the interest and independence of the United States, be suffered to remain among us." Grand juror Joseph Dean and trial jurors Cadwalader Dickinson and James Skinner were appointed to a committee to carry these resolves into execution.[27] When the committee began detaining persons suspected of disloyalty, the Council intervened, requiring that the city magistrates enquire into the cases of persons imprisoned outside of the "ordinary course of justice." If there were reasonable grounds for apprehension, the magistrates could commit them or bind them to appear at the next court of quarter sessions; otherwise, the detainees would be released. The Council exhorted the public to "acquiesce in the decisions & determination of the said Justices," so as to "avoid giving the Common Enemies of our Liberty & Country grounds to rejoice & bring reproach on public authority."[28]

In July 1779, the committee justified its extra-legal actions by arguing that "written laws . . . in times of traitorous war" were "too slow in their operation, too uncertain in their effects." Committees, by contrast, were "not only a convenient but a necessary appendage to civil government." In particular, committees could punish offenders "for such parts of [their] conduct by which the public welfare appears to be injured or dishonoured, and for which no legal redress can be obtained."[29] Others took a dimmer view of committee action. One man noted, "we have no government . . . for every man who takes a club in his hand to town meetings (which, by-the-by, have been very frequent of late) undertakes to be governor; and our executive powers submit very patiently to their new masters."[30] A Loyalist poet, in the course of a lengthy poem mocking the May meeting, observed, "The Mob tumultuous instant seized / with venom'd rage on whom they please / The People cannot err / Can it be wrong in Freedom's Cause / To tread down Justice, Order, Laws / When all the Mob concur."[31]

Into this combustible atmosphere strode the principled and extremely prickly Quaker merchant and diarist Samuel Rowland Fisher, who had a long history of antagonism toward the revolutionary government. He been named as an "enemy to his country" in January 1776 by the Philadelphia Committee of Safety and was one of the men exiled to Virginia in 1777. Fisher was brought before Chief Justice McKean in late March 1779, after Pennsylvania authorities intercepted a letter sent by Fisher to his brother Jabez in British-occupied New York. Fisher admitted writing the letter and, after refusing to pay bail, was ordered jailed until the next meeting of the Mayor's Court, the Philadelphia equivalent of the county courts of quarter sessions. McKean entrusted Fisher to Sheriff James Claypoole, who told Fisher he was free to go home. Timothy Matlack later observed Fisher riding out to his father's farm and "was much displeased with it." Matlack brought the matter to the attention of the Council, which quickly issued an order to Claypoole directing Fisher's imprisonment.[32]

At the court's April sessions, Fisher was indicted for misprision of treason for conveying intelligence "to the enemies of this state and to the United States of America." Attorney General Sergeant was prosecuting the Franks trial, and had arranged for John Morris to represent the state in his absence. Fisher again refused to post bail, and rejected the assistance of attorneys William Lewis and Andrew Robeson, who offered to speak for him. Fisher's trial was then postponed until the July sessions; Fisher believed that Morris, "being an acquaintance of mine & lately one of our Society . . . did not chuse to be active therein." Despite his refusal to post bail, Fisher was released until his trial.[33]

The July 22 trial was held before three justices of the peace, John Ord, Benjamin Paschall, and Isaac Howell, none of whom were lawyers. Attorney General Sergeant appeared as prosecutor, but Fisher obstinately refused to recognize the jurisdiction of the court and refused to make any challenges to the jurors. William Lewis volunteered to serve as Fisher's counsel, but Fisher rejected his assistance, despite urging from the justices that he do so. Fisher admitted to writing the letter, and acidly noted that he did not "apprehend myself a person of any uncommon abilities, perhaps inferior to most present, but I must be a blockhead indeed to undertake to convey intelligence in an open letter with my name signed to it and send it subject to inspection before it could enter the British lines." Whether the letter conveyed any significant intelligence was doubtful. The two objectionable lines were one suggesting that the Quakers were resolute in their opposition to the currency, and one claiming that the grain supply might be depleted before harvest. Fisher offered a lengthy explanation of the letter, claiming that it was written with an innocent purpose. For his part, Sergeant called several witnesses, including Chief Justice McKean, who testified that Fisher had confessed the crime to him.[34]

The jury went "upstairs" and deliberated all evening "without Meat or Drink," but did not reach a verdict until the next morning. By that time a "great number" of what Fisher termed "the violent party" had arrived in the courtroom. The jury announced its verdict of acquittal, but Sergeant "would by no means admit of its' being received." The jury was sent back, but again returned with a verdict of acquittal. Fisher then argued that the verdict must stand, and Fisher's brother Miers argued that "by legal usage" Fisher had been properly cleared of the charge. Justice Isaac Howell "immediately joined in sentiment" with Miers.[35] This position had plausible legal support. In his prominent early-eighteenth-century treatise on criminal law, William Hawkins had noted the practice of ordering juries to reconsider verdicts before they were recorded, but stated "this is by many thought hard, and seems not of late years to have been so frequently practiced as formerly."[36] A Whig treatise on the rights of jurymen, first published in 1680 and reprinted throughout the eighteenth century, was more emphatic, arguing that a judge simply could "not refuse to accept the jury's verdict when agreed." Indeed, the treatise claimed that if a judge should "force the jury to return, and any one of them should miscarry for want of accommodation, it would be undoubtedly be murder: and in such case the jury may without crime force their liberty, because they are illegally confined, having given in their verdict, and thereby honestly discharged their office, and are not to be starved for any man's pleasure."[37] There is no clear evidence on how frequently judges ordered juries to reconsider verdicts in colonial Pennsylvania, but it seems unlikely that it was a common practice.

Sergeant, sensing his case slipping away, then tried, in Fisher's words, "to see if he could get some of the 12 Men to dissent from the Judgment, when one or two of them drew back a little," and the jury was again sent out, although juror John Brooks claimed "you may as well keep us here, for if we are kept six days & nights more I can never agree to anything else without wronging my conscience." Fisher noted that by this time, "the spirit of violence and rage appeared" and it was likely that "threats were made use of to the 12 Men," because, after an hour and a half of further deliberations, they now returned with a guilty verdict.[38]

Fisher was given the standard sentence of forfeiture of one-half of his property and imprisonment during the present war. Fisher suspected he might have received a lighter sentence, since "some moderation appeared with those on the bench," but "some of the Committee or Constitutional Society so called had frightened them & Sergeant continued very violent." Sheriff Claypoole was ill and absent from court, and his assistant, John O'Kelly, stated that he would be "very glad to let Mr. Fisher go home," but asked "what shall I do with Mr. Burns, pointing to him & saying there he is, he won't let me." Sergeant replied, "come Mr. Kelly enough of that, let us hear no more of that." Fisher concluded that a "Mob party had prevented the 12 Men from exercising their own Judgment & those on the Bench from shewing any Moderation, for it was evident that Burns had been sent by the party to make their Wills be put into execution."[39] "Mr. Burns" was Archibald Byrnes, a barber in the militia who was later captured by the British and died in 1781 on a prison ship in New York.[40]

Fisher later learned that "nine of them were of the judgment they gave the first and second time & some of them had said if they knew as much then as they do now of the rights of Jury Men, they would not have altered their verdict." "[V]ery few, if any at all of them had ever served under the character of Jury Men at any court before."[41] Unfortunately, the Mayor's Court docket book does not survive for the summer of 1779, so we do not know who served on Fisher's jury. It is unlikely that it included any of the experienced jurors who had previously served in the court of oyer and terminer.[42] The unusual events of the trial did not go unnoticed. Fisher's friend Elizabeth Drinker denounced the three verdicts as "fine liberty" in her diary.[43] Several years later, a writer noted "it is well known that the jury would not have found him guilty according to the indictment, if they had not been induced thereto by threats contrary to their judgment."[44]

Fisher's trial indicates the degree to which some Philadelphians were willing to intimidate juries in treason cases. Direct threats may well have been employed, but even the physical presence of large numbers of angry men at a trial might sway weak jurors to vote in a particular way. Such intimidation was undoubtedly easier at the Mayor's Court, presided over by the justices of the peace, than in the courts of oyer and terminer, presided over by the domineering Chief Justice McKean.[45]

In a curious footnote to the trial, Fisher was visited shortly afterward at the jail by Cadwalader Dickinson. Fisher described Dickinson as "one of the 12 men who brought in Abraham Carlisle Guilty" and as a "very active Statesman of the present times." Dickinson observed that "what a pity it was that there should be such a difference amongst Neighbours & fellow Citizens in sentiment, & how happy we should be if we could all unite with one Mind &c. I took no more notice of his Conversation apparently than if I had been asleep—he soon grew tired and went away." Shortly thereafter Fisher was moved to a different room in the jail and his liberties were more heavily restricted, a change that Fisher blamed on Dickinson.[46]

Fort Wilson

In early August, a mass election, involving "the greatest number of voters ever known on such an occasion" was held for a new extra-legal City Committee. One grand juror and ten trial jurors from the treason trials were among those elected.[47] Although three of the trial jurors had served only on one jury, Isaac Roush and James Skinner had served on two, George Pickering and Thomas Shields on three, James Hood and David Pancoast on four, and Cadwalader Dickinson on fifteen. Jurors who had repeatedly acquitted treason defendants could seemingly still obtain electoral support on a platform of popular radicalism. On the other hand, it is not entirely clear how well publicized the names of the jurors had been, and Dickinson in particular made efforts to ingratiate himself with all sides.

Philadelphia had become a steaming cauldron of resentments and mistrust. Shortly after the elections, "A Whig" published a blistering attack on Tories in the *Pennsylvania Packet*, claiming "[a]mong the many errors America has been guilty of during her contest with Great Britain, few have been greater, or attended with more fatal consequences to these States than her lenity to the Tories." Posterity, he argued, "will curse the memory of their forefathers for their shameful lenity." It was time "to rid ourselves of these bosom vipers" and "perpetual banishment should be their lot." [48] In late September, Samuel Rowland Fisher overheard a militia man state the "Militia were about to take up all the Tories & Quakers & would certainly create a most dreadful scene in the City."[49]

On the morning of October 4, 1779, a crowd composed primarily of Philadelphia militiamen began to form. A handbill urging a meeting "to drive from the city all disaffected persons, and those who supported them" had circulated that morning. By noon, the militia was ready to march and began taking prisoners, parading them through the streets to the strains of the "Rogue's March." Shortly thereafter, between twenty and forty men, including William Lewis, Robert Morris, and many other prominent opponents of Pennsylvania's 1776 constitution, gathered at the home of James Wilson to await the imminent arrival of the militiamen.[50] One witness described seeing "a number of desperate-looking men in their shirtsleeves, . . . moving toward Wilson's house, armed with bars of iron, and large hammers."[51] Another saw the militia bringing up pieces of artillery.[52] Captain Robert Campbell, who had lost an arm in combat two years earlier, leaned out of the third-story window of Wilson's house, waving a pistol. Harsh words were exchanged between the captain and the militiamen, and at that point someone fired a shot, although it is unknown whether the shot came from inside or outside the house. For ten minutes, the militiamen fired at the house, while the men holed up inside returned fire for fire. The militiamen had broken through the front door and were about to head upstairs when Joseph Reed, President of the Supreme Executive Council, arrived with an elite Philadelphia cavalry unit and quelled the fighting.[53] As one witness described it, Reed, Timothy Matlack, and James Claypoole, "not without many strokes of their swords," succeeded in forcing many of the militia members into jail.[54] Trial jurors Blair McClenachan and Adam Zantzinger were members of this cavalry troop and probably assisted in ending the riot.[55]

The fighting left six or seven men dead, including Captain Campbell, and between seventeen and nineteen seriously wounded.[56] The Supreme Executive Council ordered both the militia members and the defenders of Wilson's home to surrender themselves to the sheriff or a justice of the peace.[57] James Wilson thus found himself in the extraordinary position of signing a £10,000 bond to appear as a defendant at the next court of oyer and terminer.[58] His frequent co-counsel William Lewis was briefly imprisoned, but was quickly released.[59] The "Fort Wilson" affair, as it came to be known, placed the state government in an extremely awkward position. It had no desire to prosecute people such as Wilson and even less desire to provoke another riot by prosecuting the militiamen. The Council subsequently proposed an act of oblivion, exempting all participants in the Fort Wilson affair from criminal punishment, which the Assembly later passed.[60] The Council noted that such an act would "prove more beneficial to public interests than a rigorous enforcement of legal measures."[61]

The Fort Wilson incident had many causes, both economic and political. But numerous contemporary observers pointed to lenient treatment of disloyal individuals as a significant factor. Charles Wilson Peale stated that "among the militia were many Germans . . . whose resentment at this time was most violently intemperate against all Tories. They only looked straight forward, regardless of consequences."[62] On the day of the riot, Samuel Rowland Fisher learned that one of the militiamen had called out to his neighbors "to bring their spades with them for they were to hang & bury the Tories."[63] One participant later referred to "that damned Wilson that defended the Tory Hamilton" and stated that "[w]e were near breaking in and making short work of them."[64] Two days after the incident, the Council issued a proclamation stating, "The undue countenance and encouragement which has been shown to persons disaffected to the Liberty and Independence of America, by some whose rank and character in other respects, gave weight to their conduct, has been the principal cause of the present commotion."[65] A group of militiamen offered their own version of events, arguing that

> [t]he exceeding lenity which has been shown to persons notoriously disaffected to the Independence of the United States has rather tended to encourage them in their misconduct than to convert them to reason and sound Policy and although for the sake of order and good Government we cannot but disapprove every attempt to punish them otherwise than by the Laws of the State yet we humbly beg leave to represent in behalf of those of our fellow Citizens who lately assembled on the Commons for the purpose of removing such Obnoxious persons that their intended Conduct proceeded from an Attachment to the cause of their suffering Country, from a remembrance of the hardships they have endured in defense thereof and the numerous Grievances they at present undergo.[66]

This memorial was signed by one-time juror Thomas Hale and, curiously, by fifteen-time juror Cadwalader Dickinson.

The perception of lenity toward disloyal individuals, solidified by the 1778–1779 treason trials, would only have been enhanced by the most recent sitting of the Court of Oyer and Terminer for Philadelphia County. The court, now returned to its proper home in the State House, discharged nine men who had been named in the attainder proclamations and postponed one treason trial until December because the defendant was ill. Juries acquitted the defendants in the four treason cases that went to trial.[67] Edward Cutbush, an English-born stonecutter, was acquitted on charges that he had acted "officially under the British" and had taken arms and accoutrements from an inhabitant.[68]

The most prominent defendant was Robert Strettel Jones, a wealthy Anglican merchant who had served on several revolutionary committees and whom historian Richard Ryerson has described as an "important radical leader."[69] Jones had also been an officer of the American Philosophical Society, the Library Company of Philadelphia, and the Pennsylvania Hospital.[70] Jones attended college with

Attorney General Sergeant, who prosecuted the case, and it is possible that bad blood between the men dated back to their college days.[71] The case proved a debacle for Sergeant. His only witnesses were two German couples. The wives testified first, claiming that Jones had come to their houses to seize arms during the British occupation. The husbands then testified that their wives had made the same claims to them at the time. Under cross-examination, however, the lead witness, Christiana Beck, admitted that she did not know Jones by sight, and one of the husbands, Philip Aker, admitted that both of the men had sued Jones to recover their guns. For its part, the defense presented witnesses who testified that Jones had been out of the city at the time of the alleged events, that Jones at the time did not possess the distinctive green coat attributed to him by the prosecution witnesses, and that the British had chosen to store weapons in an outbuilding on Jones's lot, without his knowledge or permission. Under these circumstances, an acquittal was all but assured. The jury included Adam Zantzinger, who had served on three of 1778–1779 juries, but none of the other jurors had served during those trials.[72]

The most significant acquittal, however, may have been that of painter Joseph Wirt. An account from New York published in Edinburgh attributed the Fort Wilson incident to outrage over Wirt's acquittal two days earlier on October 2, 1779. James Wilson, the account noted, was Wirt's attorney.[73]

Many revolutionary leaders, although sharing the militia's concern about Tories, were deeply disappointed by the riot. General Arthur St. Clair felt that the targeting of Wilson was most improper, since "his advocating the causes of the accused persons should certainly not have been considered as a crime, as it is both a part and a consequence of that liberty we have been struggling to establish."[74] Timothy Matlack, who had strenuously denounced the Franks jurors, assisted Joseph Reed in breaking up the riot, and Charles Willson Peale, another radical, refused to participate in the procession as soon as it began.[75] Even Thomas Paine, the acknowledged master of anti-Tory rhetoric, who earlier that summer had seen a proposal to yield certain American fisheries to Britain as "a species of treason for which no punishment is too severe," found the entire Fort Wilson affair regrettable, claiming, "The difference is exceedingly great, between not being in favor and being considered as an enemy."[76]

The quelling of the Fort Wilson riot has been aptly described as the "major turning point in the history of popular radicalism in revolutionary Philadelphia."[77] It permanently divided radical leaders such as Joseph Reed and Timothy Matlack from the mass crowd activities favored by some members of the Philadelphia militia.[78] Although both Reed and Matlack were among the most strident critics of Tories and willing to criticize juries extensively, they were unwilling to condone violent attacks upon participants in the trials. The four years since the tumultuous months of late 1775 had significantly altered the revolutionary leadership's attitudes to such extra-legal crowd activity. Consider the many similarities between the Kearsley affair and Fort Wilson. Both began in the fall with a crowd taking up suspected Tories and marching them through the streets to the strains of the "Rogue's March." Both were motivated by a fear that established authority was not adequately dealing with Toryism and treason. Both ended at the home of a well-known opponent to radicalism. Both involved someone brandishing a pistol from a window inside the house. But the reactions to the two events clearly showed how much had changed between 1775 and 1779. The Kearsley affair ultimately led to the jailing of Kearsley and his associates on charges of treason against America. The crowd activity had the implicit, if not the explicit, sanction of many revolutionary leaders. Such actions were acceptable, even necessary, to deal with disaffection. After Fort Wilson, crowd activity was widely denounced by many of the people who had endorsed such actions only four years before. Equally important, after Fort Wilson, attacks on juries ceased almost entirely in Pennsylvania. The jury system had survived the first major challenge to its independence and would never again come under such sustained attack.

The Assembly nonetheless balanced the act of oblivion for the Fort Wilson participants with a repressive new law aimed at suspicious persons. The act's prologue announced that "there is reason to suspect that there are sundry persons within this commonwealth, who by their general conduct have manifested an enmity to the liberty and independence of their country," and added, a touch defensively, "the legislatures of countries most jealous of their liberties, have, in times of public danger, consented to a temporary suspension of laws." The act then empowered the Council and the justices of the Supreme Court to bind over, imprison, and even banish from the state any person who "in his general conduct manifested an enmity or disaffection to the liberty and independence of the United States of America."[79] Significantly, there was no requirement of a formal judicial proceeding or of a jury trial. Although the Council did not initially use this power extensively, it would eventually lead to serious conflict with Chief Justice McKean.

Modifications to Pennsylvania's Treason Law

The state's persistent failures to obtain convictions in treason cases led the Assembly to make a significant revision to the treason laws in March 1780. The Assembly authorized the Attorney General, with the permission of the court, in cases of "facts amounting to treason or misprision of treason," to proceed under a charge of misdemeanor. In these cases, there would no longer be a requirement of two witnesses, but the punishment would be the same as any other misdemeanor offense—a fifty-pound fine possibly coupled with imprisonment.[80] Although colloquially known as "treasonable misdemeanors," these cases would be entered as simple "misdemeanors" in the court docket books, making it difficult to determine which cases involved offenses tantamount to treason or misprision of treason.[81] Nonetheless, treason prosecutions dwindled after 1780, and a large number of misdemeanor cases began appearing in the courts of oyer and terminer. The handful of surviving indictment papers indicate that some of these involved conduct that was clearly treasonous under the 1777 statute, such as joining the king's armies.[82] Moreover, in some cases, the state had two witnesses, but nonetheless chose to prosecute under the misdemeanor charge.[83] The highest crime was starting to slip off its pedestal.[84]

The Assembly's revision also included a section on pardons. Existing law granted the Council the power to pardon, but was silent with respect to conditional pardons. Nonetheless, in 1778 the Council had remitted the fines of four men convicted of felony, provided that that they enroll in the Continental Army.[85] On January 6, 1780, the Council granted its first conditional pardon in a treason case. William Cassedy, convicted in Philadelphia in the fall of 1779, was pardoned on the condition that he "serve as a soldier during the present war, in one of the regiments of this state."[86] The March 1780 statute now explicitly authorized the Council to issue pardons for persons under a death sentence, provided that the person shall, "within a limited time, depart from this state to foreign parts beyond the seas, and . . . not return into this state or any of the United States of America." Failure to adhere to this condition would result in the reinstatement of the death sentence.[87] Although framed as an extension of the pardoning power, the language of the statute was arguably restrictive, limiting the type of conditions the Council could require in death cases. But the Council did not see it that way. A month later it again pardoned William Cassedy (for reasons that are entirely unclear), on the new condition that he enter "into the service of the United States, on board some ship."[88]

Perhaps encouraged by the state government's seeming new lenity, attorney Jasper Yeates went so far as to argue in court that the misprision statute should no longer be enforced. In a contentious 1779 case from Cumberland County, the lead prosecution witness testified that Thomas Kerr had "damned the states and their goddamn'd laws" and claimed that he "would remain as he was for the king." Another witness stated that Kerr had "damned the militia and their damn'd officers what did they do when they went to camp but run;" had claimed that "he and five Indians could kill all the Whigs in the valley," and had "damn'd the Congress and all their proceedings."[89] After the jury returned a guilty verdict, Yeates moved for a new trial and arguments were heard in April 1780. Although conceding that his client's political principles were not in tune with those of the majority of his countrymen, Yeates argued that "the character of the defendant as to politics has nothing to do with the present argument." Relying on the Supreme Court justices' handling of treason cases, he continued:

> The general indignation excited against disaffected persons will not control (or at least ought not to control) the court's judgment. The obsession of the Supreme Court in this point is extremely apposite, that the law and evidence should be the only guides in courts of justice, and not prejudices, or any opinions however popular or respectable.

After arguing that the prosecution had failed to prove the specific words in the indictment and challenging the credibility of the prosecution witnesses, Yeates argued that the statute against misprision was "perhaps necessary" at the time of enactment, but it was now much too severe. It created, Yeates claimed, "a new offense—a kind of constructive treason. The most innocent discourse may be misconceived."[90]

Asking the Cumberland County justices of the peace to effectively invalidate a Pennsylvania statute was a bold argument, to say the least, and it is not surprising that the motion failed. But it is of considerable interest that Yeates, a talented and experienced lawyer, thought it an argument worth making. "Constructive treason" still held much of the odium it had gained in the years preceding independence. Moreover, the motion raised tantalizing hints of future free-speech jurisprudence. Wartime restrictions on speech, Yeates seemed to argue, cannot be justified once the immediate danger has passed. In a November 1781 misprision case in Lancaster County, this time in the court of oyer and terminer (a procedure discussed in greater detail later), Yeates made a similar argument:

> [T]he law on which the indictment arose was new and could only be justified by the crisis of American affairs at the time of passing it, when it was necessary to seal the lips of the disaffected. The necessity no longer existed; and policy would admit, what legal authorities required, that, as a penal law, it should be strictly construed. . . . The act, indeed, has in this respect been thought so harsh by the legislature that the offense has since been reduced to the class of misdemeanors. . . . It is true that the words, in the present instance [praising the English government and claiming that the English king is our king], are exceptionable; but . . . they merely express a matter of opinion; and cannot fairly be converted into matter of treason.[91]

Chief Justice McKean agreed with Yeates that part of the misprision statute was poorly drafted, but instructed the jury that the defendant's statements, praising the English king and the English form of government, amounted to misprision under a different provision of the statute.[92] The defendant, George Weidel, was convicted, but was later pardoned by the Council.[93]

The Battle over Detentions

In early 1780, the Council began exercising the sweeping detention powers granted to it by the Assembly in the aftermath of the Fort Wilson affair. Elizabeth Fegan, the wife of an attainted traitor, had obtained permission to go to British-occupied New York, but had not yet departed. The Council concluded in February 1780 that Fegan was a "very suspicious character," and ordered her to depart immediately for New York or face imprisonment.[94] Joseph Richardson, charged with being "disaffected to the interests of America," was imprisoned in March 1780.[95] Abraham Harvey, charged with assisting British prisoners to escape and with "being a person of general disaffection to the American cause," was ordered in April 1780 to pay £10,000 surety for his good behavior and to be imprisoned until the payment was made. Similarly, John Coogler, also charged with helping British prisoners to escape, was ordered imprisoned in Philadelphia, and his wife, Susanna, charged with harboring spies for the British army, was ordered imprisoned in Bucks County, as there was "just reason to suspect she is an enemy to the American cause."[96] In May, Henry Lane, "charged with Enmity and disaffection to the United States," was brought before the Council, examined, and imprisoned after giving a "very unsatisfactory" account of his conduct.[97] In June, Phinas Paxton, charged with aiding British prisoners in their escape, was banned from keeping a public house and ordered imprisoned until he satisfied a £20,000 bond.[98] Alexander Mills, brought before the Council the same month on a charge of "discouraging the people from enlisting into the service of this Commonwealth and endeavouring to prevent the measures carrying on in support of the freedom and independence of the United States of America," was treated more leniently. After being examined, he was "reprimanded and dismissed, having promised to be more circumspect in the future."[99]

The procedural protections for the accused were minimal. John Coogler, for example, reported that he was examined "only for about ten minutes," that "no accuser had been brought to face him," and that he had been confronted with "sundry ensnaring questions." He learned the charge against him (entertaining and ferrying British soldiers on their way to New York) only from the course of the interrogation itself.[100] Unlike the proceedings in the court of oyer and terminer, the accused did not have access to an attorney and there was essentially no protection against completely arbitrary action.

These extrajudicial proceedings intensified in the summer of 1780. In June, the British landed in New Jersey, generating "great commotion," and Pennsylvania once again appeared at risk of invasion.[101] The Council responded with an extraordinary order, banishing all "wives and children of those persons who have joined the enemy" from the state, since their presence was now "too dangerous to be longer permitted." These individuals would be given ten days to depart, after which they would "not be deemed as entitled to any protection, but liable to be proceeded against as enemies of the state."[102] In its breadth and severity, this order exceeded anything previously issued by the Council. There was no opportunity for individualized hearings, which even persons such as the Cooglers had received. The women and children were being punished for the crimes of their relatives, an act perilously close to the discredited concept of corruption of blood. Moreover, by unilaterally declaring the women and children beyond the protection of the laws, the Council had effectively issued a declaration of outlawry. Samuel Rowland Fisher noted that "from these things many of the quiet inhabitants are much alarmed and under fearful apprehensions, of trials and sufferings falling to their lot shortly."[103] Not surprisingly, many of the wives did not depart within the allotted time, and in July the Council sent four women to the workhouse until they gave security to leave the state.[104]

By December, however, the Council's detention orders encountered a formidable obstacle in the person of Chief Justice McKean. In late November, Joseph Griswold and five other men were brought before President Joseph Reed and Vice President William Moore and were committed to jail for "treasonable practices," after examination on charges of conveying supplies and information to the enemy.[105] Samuel Rowland Fisher stated that "they were each separately examined by Joseph Reed & Timothy Matlack & demanded to confess every matter to them, if they expected mercy."[106] Griswold retained Jonathan Dickinson Sergeant, who had recently resigned as Attorney General, as his counsel, and Sergeant successfully persuaded Chief Justice McKean to admit Griswold to bail.[107]

The statute authorizing the Council to detain suspicious individuals was now up for extension in the Assembly and a draft statute included language authorizing the justices of the Supreme Court to grant bail. The Council was outraged, and responded to the Assembly with language that directly attacked McKean's actions in the Griswold case. "It has been the policy of all other States, and even of our enemy . . . to repose a confidence in the Executive powers to guard the public safety by commitments not subject to the examination of any other, and much less, an inferior authority, for such we deem the Justices of the Supreme

Court on this occasion." Habeas review by the justices would be "degrading" to the Council and "inconsistent with our ideas of law."[108]

Chief Justice McKean quickly learned of the Council's response, and wrote two forceful letters to President Reed. The first insisted that the bailing of Griswold was "strictly conformable to law and duty." In a footnote, he added that William Lewis had recently filed petitions for writs of habeas corpus for two of Griswold's confederates.[109] In the second letter, McKean noted that he and Justice Bryan had released the two confederates on bail, and he explained more fully the legal justification for releasing Griswold. McKean argued that commitments in England by justices of the peace, the Privy Council, or even the king himself, were all subject to inquiry by the twelve judges of the common-law courts on a petition of habeas corpus. Commitments by the Council were equally subject to scrutiny. "Justices of the Supreme court in this State," McKean added, "are intrusted with the personal liberty of the Subject; in brief, while the habeas corpus act remains in full force. . . . [W]hile those things are so . . . it will not be thought amiss in the Judges to proceed as they have done in cases of this sort."[110]

The Council fought back on Griswold's case, but ultimately conceded the larger point. On December 11, 1780, the Council issued a new warrant for Griswold's arrest, and two days later committed him to jail, as there was "just reason" to suspect that he was an enemy "to the American cause, and guilty of high treason, by holding an unlawful and dangerous correspondence with the enemy at New York."[111] Nonetheless, the Council withdrew from the larger field, informing McKean on December 15 that it had "resolved to make no more commitments subject to such hasty & imprudent control."[112] On December 27, President Reed admitted Griswold to bail. Samuel Rowland Fisher noted that "it seems as if Joseph Reed & his associates had been much vexed that Griswold should get out without petitioning them by the form of an Habeas Corpus Writ— & had therefore sent him to jail a second time, in order to make him humbly apply to them for a release."[113] The Assembly did not renew the Council's detention powers, and in March 1781 the cases of all detained persons were transferred to the "Chief Justice of the State, to be dealt with according to law."[114] The brief era of unbridled executive detention was over.

Misprision of Treason Cases before the Justices of the Pennsylvania Supreme Court

In 1779, misprision of treason cases started to appear on the dockets of the Pennsylvania Supreme Court as well as on the justices' dockets when sitting as a court of oyer and terminer. The 1777 treason statute vested jurisdiction over misprision cases in the county courts of quarter sessions, so the prosecution of this crime in other courts was unusual.[115] The cases arose from two mechanisms: removal from the county courts by writ of certiorari and original indictments in the court of oyer and terminer.

Under British practice, the Court of King's Bench could issue a writ of certiorari to transfer any criminal case initiated in a lesser jurisdiction. According to Blackstone, this was often done in cases where the validity of the indictment was at issue or if there was a risk that a "partial or insufficient trial will probably be had at the court below."[116] The Pennsylvania cases give no direct indication as to why the writ was sought or issued. In July 1779, Charles Humphreys petitioned for a writ of certiorari to remove an indictment from the Philadelphia City Sessions (the city analogue to the quarter sessions courts, also known as the Mayor's Court). Edward Burd wrote a short note to Attorney General Sergeant, asking him to note any objection he might have on the bottom of the note. Sergeant replied that he had no objections.[117] Humphreys's notoriety as an opponent of independence may have led him to question the fairness of a trial in the city court. A former member of the Pennsylvania Assembly, Humphreys had famously voted against American independence while serving as a Pennsylvania delegate to the Second Continental Congress.[118] His decision to remove the indictment proved wise, as he was acquitted at his trial before the Supreme Court. Sheriff James Claypoole testified against Humphreys; justice of the peace and former grand juror Zebulon Potts testified in his favor.[119] Writs were also used to remove three cases from the Lancaster County Court of Quarter Sessions, including the previously discussed case of George Weidel, the only misprision case of the war to make it into the formal law reports.[120] The records of the Westmoreland county court indicate that three misprision cases were removed by certiorari to the court of oyer and terminer, but I have found no further record of those cases.[121]

In one of the Lancaster cases, Peter Gottschalk had been charged in August 1780 with misprision for claiming, "The King of England is our King and will remain our King at last." His trial in the Supreme Court was set for April 1781, but the sheriff did not return his writ and so no jury was summoned. The trial was postponed until the fall of 1781, when Gottschalk was finally convicted.[122] Gottschalk petitioned the Supreme Executive Council for clemency, arguing that while "in the warmth of liquor" he had "sung a song (which he had learnt many years ago whilst a soldier) which is common for old soldiers who have been in different services to sing that is extolling or condemning the several nations of Europe." He had thus "sung a verse that was not politically proper at that time, and which ignorance and liquor prevented him from correcting."[123] The Council was persuaded and issued a pardon.[124]

Joseph Pritchard's case appears to have originated in the Philadelphia City Sessions and was removed to the Supreme Court. Pritchard, a Quaker, was tried on November 27, 1779, for having been employed by the British as an inspector at the Middle Ferry and for "having since used words greatly derogatory of the present Rulers."[125] Other men charged with aiding the British at Middle Ferry had been charged with high treason, so the state may have concluded that a misprision prosecution was more likely to be successful, even if it resulted in lesser penalties. According to Pritchard, at the trial Chief Justice McKean "had expiated largely on their Independence being most firmly fixed & established & was very bitter indeed in many expressions against him."[126] Pritchard was convicted, but was later pardoned with respect to his imprisonment.[127]

In one case, an indictment seems to have been brought directly in the court of oyer and terminer, without any prior proceedings in the county court. In March 1780, George Haughton was charged with treason at the Philadelphia Court of Oyer and Terminer. The grand jury refused to indict, but the court's docket book contains an unusual entry, stating "the grand jury found him guilty of misprision of treason."[128] Accordingly, the grand jury issued a separate misprision indictment charging Haughton with making a "huzza for King George," damning the rebels, and claiming that the American army was retreating. Haughton, an upholsterer, had arrived in America from London in early 1775, and in January 1776 was advertising military wares, particularly commending himself "to the several Committees and the Military Gentlemen."[129] Samuel Rowland Fisher reported that Haughton had provided "a great quantity of drums, as well as much camp furniture" to George Washington's army.[130] Haughton remained in Philadelphia during the British occupation and found that the British army was an equally good customer.[131] After a trial before a jury that included previous treason jurors Isaac Roush and John Roush, Haughton was convicted.[132] He was pardoned in August 1780, upon the condition that he serve on the warship *Confederacy* for the duration of the war.[133]

Overall, five misprision cases, two in Lancaster County and three in Philadelphia, went to trial before the justices of the Supreme Court.[134] Four defendants were convicted, and one acquitted. This conviction rate was higher than the 57% rate for misprision cases in the county cases, but one shouldn't make too much of this statistic, as changing one conviction to acquittal would yield a rate of 60%, nearly identical to the county rate. Two other initial misprision cases resulted in convictions for misdemeanor after removal. Peter Graybill, indicted for misprision in the Lancaster County Court of Quarter Sessions, was indicted for misdemeanor in the court of oyer and terminer and, after submitting to the court, was fined fifteen pounds, and ordered to pay costs and post a good behavior bond.[135] Similarly, John Martin, indicted for misprision in the Philadelphia

Mayor's Court in April 1779, saw his case continued until July 1781, at which point the Attorney General dropped the prosecution. At the same sessions, Martin was indicted for misdemeanor for speaking against the United States and the case was removed by certiorari to the Supreme Court, where Martin retracted his not guilty plea and was fined twenty-five pounds in April 1782.[136]

Benedict Arnold

On September 27, 1780, almost three years to the day since Philadelphia fell to the British, and almost two years to the day since the opening of the Philadelphia treason trials, horrifying news reached Philadelphia from New York. American general Benedict Arnold had fled to the British after the discovery of his plot to betray the fort at West Point. Arnold was a familiar figure in Philadelphia, as he had presided over the city's military establishment following the British evacuation. His stormy tenure led to frequent quarrels with the state's civilian leadership and to claims against him of mismanagement and favoritism toward known Loyalists. Joseph Reed, Arnold's next-door neighbor, was perhaps his fiercest antagonist and the driving force behind Arnold's eventual court-martial on corruption charges.[137] Arnold's marriage to Margaret ("Peggy") Shippen, the glamorous daughter of a family with Loyalist connections, made him a further object of suspicion. In February 1779, rumors had even circulated that Arnold "had left Philadelphia and gone over to the English."[138]

Nonetheless, few Pennsylvanians could have anticipated the magnitude of Arnold's current deception. As one writer put it, his actions were "treason of the blackest dye," and presented "such a scene of baseness and prostitution of office and character, as it is hoped that this new world cannot parallel."[139] On September 30, Philadelphians took to the streets in a massive procession, carting a two-faced effigy of Arnold through the streets. A large black devil appeared behind the effigy, offering it money. A sign in front of the effigy depicted two nooses hanging from the gallows and labeled "the traitor's reward." The procession lasted most of the day, and in the evening the effigy was hanged and burned. Although John Pemberton thought the crowd was composed mostly of "great rabble," the procession was an orderly, and even quasi-official, civic event. At the head of the procession were gentlemen on horseback. They were followed by officers of the Continental Army, a guard of the city infantry, and drums and fifes playing the "Rogue's March." It was a vivid demonstration of widespread hatred of a detested enemy.[140] Even avowed Tories were appalled by Arnold's actions. Samuel Rowland Fisher felt that "few men of virtue & integrity can esteem him or the principles upon which he has acted."[141] Grace Growden Galloway, whose husband Joseph had governed Philadelphia under the British occupation and was named in the first attainder proclamation, felt that Arnold had rendered himself "contemptible in the eyes of all good people" and demonstrated every mark of a "low creeping spirit." "The man who sells his honour," she wrote, "is entitled to nothing but contempt—let them be paid the price agreed on for their treachery but never them let them mix with the good subjects least they contaminate the manners and poison the minds of the unwary." Although she was "very sorry the affair miscarried," she nonetheless "hate[-d] all traitors."[142] The image of Arnold as Satan, as a freak of nature, pervaded much of the rhetoric surrounding the discovery of Arnold's plot.[143] The broadside depicting the procession (Figure 8.1) ended with the following lines: "Mothers shall still their children and say—Arnold! / Arnold shall be the bug-bear of their years. / Arnold!—vile, treacherous, and leagued with Satan."[144] Nearly a month after the revelation of Arnold's plot, Benjamin Rush noted, "Our streets ring with nothing but the execration of Arnold."[145]

Upon receipt of the news, Pennsylvania authorities moved into a state of high alert, concerned that some of Arnold's connections in Philadelphia may have been involved in the plot. Thomas McKean, Timothy Matlack, and the

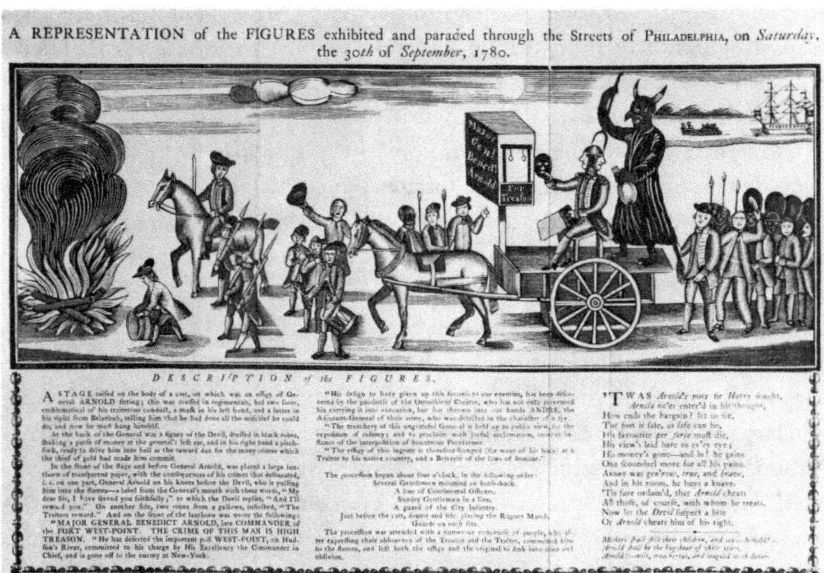

FIGURE 8.1 Benedict Arnold's betrayal prompted an elaborate Philadelphia street parade.

Credit: Representation of the figures exhibited and paraded through the streets of Philadelphia on Saturday 30th September 1780 (engraving) (black and white photo), American School (18th century)/Private Collection/Bridgeman Images.

Philadelphia sheriff appeared at the home of Tench Coxe. Coxe convinced them he had no role in the affair, but wrote to a friend that "suspicion flies like wildfire among [Arnold's] connections. . . . Do not mention this concerning me to any person."[146] An "Association, for the Purpose of preventing all intercourse with Tory and suspicious characters," quickly formed and met at the City Tavern.[147] The Council proclaimed ten more men, including Benedict Arnold himself, as attainted traitors, and issued arrest warrants for five men, including David Franks and William Hamilton, suspected of being "enemies to the American cause" and "holding an unlawful and dangerous correspondence with the enemy at New York."[148] On October 6, the Council invoked the statute enacted in the aftermath of Fort Wilson, subsequently extended by the Assembly, to issue banishment orders for both Franks and Hamilton, requiring them to depart the state and go to the enemy within fourteen days, pay a bond of £200,000, and never return to any of the United States during the present war.[149] In late October, the same authority was used to banish Arnold's wife.[150]

A letter from New York reprinted in the *Pennsylvania Gazette* summed up in striking terms what many people were feeling:

> The late horrible conspiracy . . . should stimulate us to . . . strain every nerve to prevent our yet becoming a sacrifice to the infernal machinations of those unwearied imps and fiends of darkness, that are permitted to continue amongst us; who, together with bosom traitors (those vilest of beings) are, and forever will be, plotting and executing schemes for our utter ruin and destruction. . . . [A]s we have found Judas in the field, where we little expected it, have we not abundant reason to suspect there are traitors in the cabinet, where their secret machinations are less liable to detection[?] . . . Can any man after the woeful experience we have had, be so lost to reason, as to plead for lenitive measures to be used towards the Tories that are amongst us; who are continually brooding in their dark corners, on schemes of destruction, and will ever be ready to put them in execution when opportunity offers[?] It were as reasonable to expect to transform the devil himself into an angel of light, as to change the principles and practices of a Tory.[151]

A Maryland man writing to Philadelphian Owen Biddle observed, "I am glad to see the spirit of vigor exercised by your Council in banishing old Franks and Billy Hamilton. I am no advocate for persecution, but it certainly is time to throw aside that lenity to the disaffected, which has been so constantly abused."[152]

In such an atmosphere, anyone might be a traitor. James Wilson was again accused of countenancing "toryism and tories," forcing Wilson to defend himself in the pages of the *Pennsylvania Gazette*. Wilson conceded that he had "indeed been council for many persons who were tried on indictments for treasons, and I have been council also for criminals of every other denomination," but, he asked, "have I, therefore, countenanced their crimes?" "The assistance of council, learned in the law," Wilson argued, "is thought necessary on the part of the Commonwealth. Is it less necessary for the prisoner? . . . Those who are acquainted with legal history know what dreadful engines of tyranny prosecutions have been, when the accused have not been allowed council to instruct and assist them in their defence." Wilson pointed out that criminal trial work was "neither the most profitable nor the most agreeable part of a Lawyer's profession," and that to be entrusted "with the defence of a man's life" produces "degrees of uneasiness and anxiety, not easily conceived by those who have not experienced it."[153]

The actions taken against Franks and Hamilton, however, provoked a significant response from many people who felt that the Council had gone too far. General John Cadwalader was "thunderstruck" at the news of Hamilton's arrest and blamed it on the abuses of "absolute power." Cadwalader agreed to exercise Hamilton's power of attorney and handle his affairs during his exile.[154] Isaac Gray wrote to the Council, arguing that even if Hamilton was "justly obnoxious to government," the bases of the banishment order should be publicized, lest the "lives and liberties of the people of Pennsylvania" hang by "a very slender and precarious tenure."[155] Over 150 Philadelphians signed petitions on behalf of William Hamilton arguing that "the Banishment of a Citizen . . . without due trial and process, and clear proof of guilt, must be highly unconstitutional, and dangerous to the Liberties of the People."[156] Tench Coxe blamed the banishment orders on "the ferment and suspicions which Arnold's baseness has produced."[157]

David Franks, although seeking extensions of time, accepted the order of banishment and departed for British-occupied New York with his daughter in late November.[158] William Hamilton, however, more adroitly played for time and as the ferment over Arnold's treason died down, his punishment became less and less severe. He initially intended to depart for the island of St. Eustatia in the Caribbean, but by November, he had still not left, and the Council agreed to permit him to "retire forthwith into a neighboring state," conditional upon entering into a £100,000 bond, and not returning to Pennsylvania or holding any correspondence with the enemy.[159] By January, he was on his way to Annapolis, and three months later, the Council relented even further, allowing him to remain in Pennsylvania.[160]

The Aftermath: The Executions of David Dawson and Ralph Morden

Benedict Arnold had escaped American jurisdiction, but his notorious betrayal sent ripple effects through pending treason cases. In November 1780, Pennsylvania undertook its last treason executions of the war. In the absence of the furor over Arnold, both David Dawson and Ralph Morden would likely have escaped the gallows. Their cases presented troubling aspects that in calmer times might have prompted clemency, but in the tense atmosphere of late 1780, the Council was in no mood for mercy.

David Dawson was a farmer from Chester County who had been named in a proclamation of attainder issued by the Council in May 1778.[161] He had allegedly joined the British during the occupation of Philadelphia, and, after following them to New York, had returned to Pennsylvania with the intent of spreading counterfeit Continental currency. After escaping from detention in New Jersey, he was recaptured in Chester County in May 1780. He was transferred to the Philadelphia jail in June, and was brought before the Philadelphia Court of Oyer and Terminer on September 26, 1780.[162]

Dawson's appearance triggered the brutal logic of the attainder proclamations. Since Dawson had not appeared for his trial by the specified date, he was formally an attainted traitor, and the only question before the court was whether there was any reason that judgment of "execution should not be awarded against him." For whatever reason, Dawson chose to say nothing. It is unclear whether Dawson had counsel, but it seems unlikely that the experienced defense lawyers of the Philadelphia bar would have allowed a man to effectively volunteer for suicide. Dawson's silence gave the court no choice; it was bound by the law to order his execution.[163]

This was not the first time the court had ordered an execution without a trial under the attainder proclamations. Like David Dawson, Edward Grizzle and John Wilson had joined the British army during the occupation of Philadelphia and had failed to surrender themselves after the time set forth in a proclamation. In May 1780, the Chester Court of Oyer and Terminer sentenced them to death, "without any sort of ceremony of a trial," as Samuel Rowland Fisher acerbically put it.[164] The Council gave their case considerable attention and ultimately concluded that both men should be pardoned. The equities of the case lay heavily in their favor. Grizzle and Wilson had deserted from the British army under the false impression that General Washington had promised pardons to such deserters, and both men were young and otherwise of good character.[165] In light of the leniency shown to other offenders, ordering the execution of these two without a trial would have been an act of remarkable cruelty and stupidity.

Dawson, by contrast, did not offer such a compelling story. According to Samuel Rowland Fisher, who knew Dawson in prison, Dawson had entered British-occupied Philadelphia "being in danger of his life from some of Washington's men," had "never acted in any manner under British [sic]," and had never gone to New York.[166] In his brief petition to the Council, however, Dawson made none of these arguments. He admitted the justice of the sentence and referred only vaguely to "inexperienced youth" and the "importunities of designing men." He did not request a trial, and instead suggested that his sentence be commuted to perpetual banishment from the United States.[167] The only other surviving petitions came from his mother and his sisters, and they did little to advance his cause. His mother described Dawson as a "thoughtless youth [who] was seduced to try the English market at Philadelphia as perhaps too many others had done."[168] His sisters admitted that Dawson was "justly culpable," but pointed out that they and his mother had always "demeaned themselves as good subjects to the state."[169]

But even the most compelling petitions might not have overcome the misfortune of timing. Dawson's sentence was entered on September 26, 1780. The next day, the news of Arnold's treason reached Philadelphia. His case thus arose in an atmosphere of vituperative rhetoric against Arnold in particular and against all traitors in general. The Council was placed in a difficult position. Execution without a trial did not violate Pennsylvania law in these circumstances, and refusing to apply the sanction of the attainder proclamation could reduce the effectiveness of both past and future proclamations. Moreover, it would open the Council to charges of weakness and irresolution in the face of clear treason. Nonetheless, the Council might still have hesitated. An execution without a trial was an extraordinary act and likely unprecedented in Pennsylvania's history. A reprieve of the death sentence, to be followed by an indictment and trial, was not beyond the realm of possibility. In the end, the Council chose the path of least resistance and confirmed Dawson's official death warrant.[170]

On November 25, 1780, a "dark windy day" in Philadelphia, David Dawson, accompanied by three siblings and "another woman," was marched to the scaffold with a rope around his neck and his arms tied behind him.[171] That night, Samuel Rowland Fisher, who had known Dawson in prison, wrote in his journal, "The taking the life of D. Dawson seems to me to be a greater act of cruelty in the present rulers than anything they have heretofore done, for they never gave him even a shadow of a trial in their own fashion & they executed him merely as what they call a proscribed person."[172]

Fifty-miles up the Delaware River, in Easton, Pennsylvania, on that same dark windy day, another executed traitor was hanging from the gallows. Ralph Morden's case, like David Dawson's, raised serious questions about the ability of

Pennsylvania officials to even-handedly apply justice in times of mass hysteria. Like Dawson, Morden was likely a surrogate for Benedict Arnold, but also for another dastardly villain, Robert Land, who had similarly escaped the jurisdiction of Pennsylvania.

Land had been captured by American forces in Minisink, New York, in March 1779 on suspicion of being a British spy, and was tried, convicted, and sentenced to death by a court-martial.[173] General Washington, however, vacated these proceedings when he learned that Land was "an inhabitant of one of the States," and therefore "not subject to military jurisdiction."[174] Washington ordered Land turned over to the civil authorities at Easton, and warned that "care should be taken that he does not escape."[175] Land was jailed at Easton until September 30, 1779, when he was surprisingly admitted to bail.[176] Land appears to have remained in Easton until May 12, 1780, when he jumped bail and departed for New York, apparently to join the Indians or possibly to reunite with the British. The departure was intercepted by American forces, and after a violent altercation, Land escaped, but several people who had assisted him were captured.[177]

One of those people was Ralph Morden, a thirty-eight-year-old English-born laborer.[178] In response to Land's escape, the state charged Land, Morden, and three others (James Griffin, Isaiah McCarty, and Elisha Barton) with the crime of high treason. When the Court of Oyer and Terminer for Northampton County convened on October 30, 1780, the grand jury declined to indict Barton, but indicted the four others. Of those, Land, Griffin, and McCarty had all escaped, leaving only Morden to stand trial.[179]

The trial of Ralph Morden, on November 2, 1780, was the first treason trial heard by the justices since the discovery of Arnold's betrayal.[180] The trial is not well documented, but the court's records indicate that seven men testified for the prosecution. Only Nicholas Depue testified for Morden, but he was a significant witness, a local notable who had represented Northampton County at the 1775 Provincial Conference of Committees and who was indicated as "Esq." in the court's records.[181] We do not know if Morden had counsel. The prosecutor, however, was court prothonotary Edward Burd—Benedict Arnold's brother-in-law. It is unclear how or when it was decided that Burd would prosecute the Northampton cases. The attorney general had offered the Northampton county prosecutions to Burd in September 1778, and he probably did so again in 1780.[182] Sending Burd to Easton would have removed an onerous duty from the attorney general's calendar, and would have imposed little extra burden on Burd, who was required to attend the court in any event.

Morden thus faced the extraordinary prospect of being prosecuted by Benedict Arnold's brother-in-law for the crime of high treason less than six weeks after Arnold's treason had been revealed. Arnold's actions had horrified

Burd, who denounced Arnold as a "vile monster."[183] Nevertheless, the Shippen family, of which Burd was a member by blood and by marriage, was coming under renewed suspicion of Toryism, and Burd may very well have felt the need to reassert his patriot credentials by vigorously prosecuting this treason case. Burd's efforts were successful, and Morden was convicted and sentenced to death.

The legality of this verdict is open to serious doubt. Because the indictment has not survived, we do not know the precise overt acts upon which the charge was based. Indirect evidence, however, suggests quite strongly that the offense was described as attempting to join the Indians. An observer described Morden's offense as "piloting some people through the back woods, to the Indians."[184] Chief Justice McKean, in a letter to his wife on the day of the trial, described it as "treason in joining the Indians."[185] Justice George Bryan described it as "attempting to join the Indian enemy."[186]

There were potentially two significant legal objections to the prosecution. First, if the offense was attempting to join the Indians, Pennsylvania law did not criminalize attempted treason, and, as noted with respect to the Malin prosecution, there was no generalized law of criminal attempt that prosecutors could have employed.[187] Second, if the offense was assisting Land in his attempt to join the Indians, it may not have been covered by Pennsylvania statutory law. The closest provision was the prohibition on "aiding or assisting enemies at open war with the state by joining their armies, or persuading others to join their armies." But Morden had not joined the armies of the enemy, nor had he persuaded anyone else to do so. Land, an American citizen, could not be an "enemy" under well-established understandings of treason law. Moreover, it was unclear whether even the Indians could amount to "enemies" under the statutory definition. Similar problems would have arisen if Morden had been charged with "furnishing enemies with arms, ammunition, or other provisions for their aid or comfort."[188]

Doubts about the verdict were raised almost immediately, but from a most unexpected source—the Supreme Court's junior justice, George Bryan. Bryan had joined the Pennsylvania Supreme Court in April 1780, when the Council concluded that the court would benefit from a fourth justice.[189] Bryan, the Council's vice president, was an unusual choice. Although he had served as a justice of the peace from 1764 to 1776, he had no formal legal training and, unlike his colleagues, had not been admitted to the bar.[190] He was a staunch supporter of the 1776 Pennsylvania constitution and had helped secure evidence against suspected traitors in the weeks following the reoccupation of Philadelphia.[191] As acting President of the Council, Bryan had supported the executions of Carlisle and Roberts, and a later anonymous critic claimed that Joseph Reed had stated that nothing "would induce George Bryan to pardon them, and that rather than pardon them he believed George Bryan would stand hangman himself." Bryan, according to this critic, had stated that "if a majority of the Council had agreed to pardon them after he had signed the death warrant, he would have set them at defiance, and ordered them out for execution."[192] Although secondhand, the claims may be well grounded. When Jacob Rush, who had served as counsel to accused traitors in the 1778 trials, joined the Supreme Court in 1784, Bryan's animosity towards Rush was so intense that Chief Justice McKean had to sit between them.[193]

Yet Bryan was concerned that the law had gone seriously awry in the Morden case. Writing to President Joseph Reed, Bryan observed that

> I had my doubts about the legality of the verdict at Easton against Morden. Something like his offense, which was attempting to join the Indian enemy, was prosecuted as a misdemeanor in England in the case of King against Cooper, 637 Skinner; but I am told Lord Preston for embarking for France was found a traitor. But is our treason law equally comprehensive? It is certain that the conviction of Morden is a stretch beyond the proceedings heretofore.[194]

It seems unlikely that Bryan would have independently researched this subtle point of English law, so his citations to English authority provide some indirect evidence that Morden had counsel. Bryan referred to "King against Cooper," an apparent reference to "King v. Cowper," a transcription error that makes perfect sense if the argument had been presented to the judges orally in court. If these arguments were raised in a challenge to the indictment, or in a motion for arrest of judgment, there is no surviving record of the court formally deciding them.

The report of *King v. Cowper*, like many late-seventeenth and early-eighteenth-century English law reports, is hardly a model of clarity.[195] The defendants appear to have been prosecuted for attempting to depart for France, during a period of open war between England and France, without a license from the king. The defendants argued that the relevant statute treated going to France as treason, but did not punish attempting to go to France. The Court of King's Bench appears to have agreed that the statute did not reach the defendants' conduct, but concluded that the offense could be charged at common law. The defendants were accordingly fined. For Morden, the case established the key point that attempted treason could not be punished as if it were a completed act of treason.

Bryan's second citation appears to come directly from Michael Foster's influential treatise on high treason. After discussing the case of Lord Preston, who was captured on the Thames River bearing proposals to the king of France to invade England in support of James II, Foster wrote,

> The Offence of Inciting Foreigners to invade the Kingdom is a Treason of Signal Enormity. In the lowest Estimation of things and in all Possible Events, it is an Attempt on the part of the Offender to render his Country the Seat of Blood and Desolation. And yet, unless the Powers so incited happen to be actually at War with Us at the Time of such Incitement, the Offence will not fall within any Branch of the Statute of Treasons, except that of Compassing the King's Death.[196]

As Bryan was undoubtedly aware, of course, "compassing the king's death" was no longer a part of Pennsylvania treason law, and there was no analogous provision in the Pennsylvania statute.

Chief Justice McKean may have anticipated Justice Bryan's concerns about the verdict. The day after the trial he forwarded the transcript of the record of conviction to the Council, since the justices had concluded that it should be sent as "soon as practicable."[197] Six days later, the Council confirmed the sentence and set the execution date for November 25.[198] An unsuccessful clemency petition from Morden soon followed, but it does not appear to have survived, so we do not know to what extent it relied on the legal arguments advanced by Justice Bryan.[199]

Ralph Morden, like David Dawson, was a victim of unlucky times. It is surely no coincidence that Pennsylvania's only executions for treason after 1778 occurred immediately after the Benedict Arnold affair. The Philadelphia trials had acquitted men who likely committed far more heinous offenses than either Morden or Dawson. Morden was a minor figure compared to the escaped Robert Land, and there were strong arguments that his conduct simply did not constitute treason under Pennsylvania law. The rage against Arnold ultimately settled on these two unfortunate, unknown men, the surrogate vessels for the hatred of a nation.

The Berks County Tax Revolt

During the uproar over Arnold, Pennsylvania was also confronted with the first hints of the tax resistance measures that would plague the state in the 1790s. Until this point, the state's actions with respect to disloyalty had all focused on cases of aiding the enemy. A conspiracy to resist the tax law in Berks County, however, raised significantly more difficult issues. In contrast to the firm actions taken against Dawson and Morden, the state's reaction to these tax protestors was relatively restrained.

According to the indictment ultimately entered in the case, a group of German residents of Berks County formed a seditious conspiracy in September 1780.

They agreed among themselves that they would not pay the state taxes for taxable property. Moreover, they agreed to use force to recover any property seized by state officials for nonpayment of taxes. Finally, they agreed that any conspirator who did not respond to the call to recover seized property would "be deemed an enemy to the liberties of his country."[200]

Joseph Reed took an active role in uncovering this plot and committed many of the offenders to jail, as he felt the "strength of government must depend upon decisive and even vigorous measures."[201] The problem was what charges to bring. The agreement, if made effective, was a fundamental assault on Pennsylvania's government. Justice George Bryan found it "very high and daring, bordering on treason."[202] But the agreement, standing alone, did not appear to violate any provision of Pennsylvania treason law, and the Germans had not taken up arms to enforce it. The initial recognizances granted to the men offered various descriptions, including misprision of treason and "entering into a treasonable association to oppose the laws."[203] The misprision statute prohibited "stirring up, exciting or raising tumults, disorders or insurrections," but, again, no actual tumult or disorder had ensued. The state ultimately chose to prosecute the case as a common-law seditious conspiracy under a heading of misdemeanor.

On November 6, 1780, 153 men were indicted in the Court of Oyer and Terminer for Berks County. In a lengthy letter to Joseph Reed, Justice Bryan explained the heavy judicial involvement in the resolution of the cases by plea bargain, a highly unusual procedure in the eighteenth century. Attorney General Sergeant and "even some of the judges" preferred to "single out the ringleaders" rather than "involve such a number." But it was impossible to identify the ringleaders, so the judges advised the attorney general to "strike at the whole, the whole sticking together, & all refusing to give evidence." The defendants had counsel, who pled not guilty for the 27 men who had appeared. Trial was set for the next day.[204]

Over dinner that night, the defendants' attorneys proposed that the 27 men would submit to the court, "if the rest might be let slip." The state rejected this proposal, arguing that "we could not, in a case like this suffer *nolo prosequi* to be entered. It was too serious a business to bargain about." Despite that confident assertion, the state then offered a different bargain: "if all would submit, upon security given for the absent, process against them should be rescinded, & the Court would consider of a fine, after hearing their excuses." The defendants accepted this proposal and agreed to assume the fines and fees of the absent men. The court imposed a fine of £300 per defendant.[205]

Justice Bryan regretted that the ringleaders escaped as lightly as the less culpable participants, but he could see no effective means of bringing them to justice. He was pleased to discover that the conspirators were "by no means popular in this county."[206] Joseph Reed pronounced himself satisfied with the compromise, noting, "We have happily suppressed the spirit of opposition in Berks County; we must act firmly and expeditiously in matters of taxation, or we are undone."[207] In December, the Council remitted the fines of those defendants who were unable to pay.[208]

The Trials of Justin McCarty and Samuel Chapman

In November 1780, Attorney General Jonathan Dickinson Sergeant submitted his resignation. The Council promptly named William Bradford to replace him.[209] A twenty-five-year-old graduate of Princeton, Bradford had studied law with Edward Shippen and had previously served as Pennsylvania's commissary of prisoners, but he had little experience as a prosecutor. He would later serve as a justice of the Pennsylvania Supreme Court and as the second Attorney General of the United States, where he died in office in 1795.

In late April 1781, Bradford complained to a friend about a "great deal of troublesome business in the Oyer and Terminer and the Supreme Court which has kept me closely employed these two weeks."[210] The "troublesome business" included two treason cases, both of which generated published reports.

The first case was that of Justin McCarty, who bears the distinction of being the only person tried twice for high treason during the Revolution in Pennsylvania. McCarty was initially charged with treason in Chester County, where he was acquitted on April 27, 1780.[211] The next day, he was committed to the Philadelphia jail by order of Edward Burd to stand trial for treason in Philadelphia.[212] The reasons behind this order have not been preserved, but it seems likely that the Chester trial disclosed that the relevant overt acts happened in Philadelphia County rather than in Chester County.

At the Philadelphia trial, Attorney General Bradford sought to introduce the confession McCarty allegedly made at his arraignment. McCarty's attorney, Jared Ingersoll, objected, arguing that the confession could be introduced only as corroboration and that the state was obligated to first prove an overt act. Bradford responded that a sufficient case of treason could be established by two witnesses testifying to the confession; moreover, the confession could be introduced without first proving an overt act.[213]

The justices found no controlling precedent and declined "giving an opinion at this time" as to whether the confession would be sufficient evidence to convict. But they agreed to receive the confession "in corroboration of any other evidence that may be adduced in support of the prosecution." In his charge to the jury,

Chief Justice McKean again declined to resolve the issue of admissibility and left the issue to the jury. McKean reviewed the relevant precedents and concluded that "most of the authorities on this point, seem to lean against the admission of the party's confession in the presence of two witnesses." The jury, which included previous Philadelphia jurors Andrew Burkhard (who served on John Roberts's jury) and David Reese (who served on eleven juries), acquitted.[214]

The second case, that of Samuel Chapman, produced the most significant judicial opinion in a revolutionary-era treason case. Chapman, a Quaker, left his home in Bucks County in December 1776 and joined the British army. On June 15, 1778, he was named in an attainder proclamation, and in early 1780, he was captured near Bermuda on a British ship and brought to Massachusetts. Upon learning of Chapman's capture, Pennsylvania President Joseph Reed wrote to Massachusetts officials, requesting Chapman's return to Pennsylvania "to be dealt with according to his demerits." Chapman, Reed asserted, "had been peculiarly obnoxious as an officer of a corps employed in harassing the inhabitants, stealing horses, & such like practices."[215] Chapman was finally returned to Pennsylvania in November 1780 and brought before Joseph Reed, who "threatened hanging him."[216] Chapman soon began devising a variety of schemes to escape from prison, including one in which he would escape while dressed as a woman.[217] None of these plans was successful, and Chapman was brought before the Supreme Court on April 17, 1781, to provide reasons that execution should not be awarded against him as an attainted traitor. Chapman's attorney contended that Chapman was a British subject from birth and had never been a citizen of the state of Pennsylvania, making it impossible for him to commit treason against it. Attorney General Bradford disagreed, and a jury was called the next day to determine whether Chapman was a British subject on December 26, 1776, the date he joined the British.[218]

Chapman's counsel made two arguments. The first was that "there was no government established in Pennsylvania" on December 26, 1776, "from which he could receive protection; and consequently there was none to which he could owe allegiance." In the chaotic interregnum that followed the collapse of the proprietary government in Pennsylvania, each person had a "right of election" and "dissenting from a majority, [a right] to retire with impunity unto another country." The second argument rested on statute. When Pennsylvania's new government finally passed an act for the revival of the laws, it explicitly stated that the laws were not in effect from May 14, 1776 to February 11, 1777, suggesting that there were no laws which Chapman could have violated. Moreover, the state's treason statute, passed on February 11, 1777, imposed a duty of allegiance only on those persons "now inhabiting" the state, or who "shall voluntarily come into the same hereafter." By that point, Chapman had long since departed.[219]

Attorney General Bradford countered the first argument by noting that throughout the period in question "a government under the authority of the people was administered by councils, committees, and conventions." Chapman was "certainly a subject of the state of Pennsylvania, under the constitution agreed to on the 28th day of September preceding, whatever doubts may be entertained with respect to the former establishments." With respect to the statutory argument, Bradford noted the legislature had attainted Joseph Galloway, who left the state in the fall of 1776; thus, the legislature clearly viewed persons in Chapman's situation as subjects of Pennsylvania.[220]

Chapman's case thus squarely raised the difficult question of who owed allegiance to the state of Pennsylvania. In his Law Lectures in the early 1790s, James Wilson complained, "on this subject, a great deal of learning, historical, legal, and political, might be displayed; and changes might easily be rung on the doctrines of natural, and local, and temporary, and perpetual allegiance. I purposely avoid them. The reason is that so much false is blended with so little genuine intelligence, as to render any discovery you would make an inadequate compensation for your trouble in searching for it."[221] But the distinction was vital, and various officials had grappled with it over the course of the war. Although Chapman was unaware of it, his position had been endorsed by none other than George Washington. In December 1777, Washington wrote,

> In my opinion, trying the Officers, taken by Gen. Dickinson on Staten Island, for High Treason, may prove a dangerous expedient. It is true they left the State after such an offense was declared treason, but as they had not taken the Oaths nor had entered into our Service, it will be said they had a right to chuse their Side. Again, by the same rule that we try them, may not the Enemy try any natural born subject of Great Britain taken in Arms in our Service. We have a great number of them, and I therefore think we had better submit to the Necessity of treating a few individuals, who may really deserve a severer fate, as prisoners of War, than run the Risque of giving an opening for retaliation upon the Europeans in our Service.[222]

Similarly, Elizabeth Graeme Ferguson, arguing against her husband's attainder in 1778, pointed out that although "in a severe construction of law" he "may be deemed an enemy," he was not a traitor, as he had left Pennsylvania before independence. Ferguson noted that "this idea I am allowed to suggest by gentlemen learned in the law."[223]

Chief Justice McKean, too, had grappled with the issue. In August 1779, the Council had requested McKean's opinion on the scope of the state's treason statute, with particular reference to persons who had departed the state prior to the Declaration of Independence or prior to the enactment of the treason statute.[224] McKean replied that "treason being an offense, against government and tending to its dissolution, could not be committed in Pennsylvania until a new government was formed." Because of the turbulence of 1776, it was a matter "of some doubt" when "a new government was formed in Pennsylvania." The convention to draft the constitution had issued a treason ordinance in the fall of 1776, but McKean concluded that the ordinance had not "been since confirmed or recognized by the legislature," and it was thus "not advisable to proceed upon it in the courts of justice." He concluded that, "in so unprecedented and doubtful a case," only those persons who resided in the state on February 11, 1777 (the date of the treason statute) were subject to the treason laws; those who had departed earlier should be treated as prisoners of war.[225] At the Council's request, McKean visited the new jail in Philadelphia to evaluate the status of the prisoners. McKean identified twenty men who were subject to the state's treason law because they had joined the British after February 11, 1777.[226]

Under the reasoning of McKean's 1779 opinion, Chapman's case was quite simple—he did not owe allegiance to Pennsylvania, since he had departed prior to February 11, 1777. But in his charge to Chapman's jury in April 1781, McKean offered a longer and more subtle analysis of the issues. McKean now concluded that government had not ceased to exist in Pennsylvania in 1776. Rather, "the powers of sovereignty were then lodged with Congress, under whose authority a council of safety had been elected by the people, and were employed, in conjunction with other committees, to conduct the war, and to secure . . . the life, liberty, and property within this state." Although there was no statute against treason, "treason is a crime known to the common law." After reviewing the events of 1776 in some detail, McKean concluded that allegiance was owed to the state at least by November 28, 1776, when the legislature under the new constitution convened.[227] Critically for Chapman's case, this date was one month *before* he left the state, so his first argument necessarily failed.

McKean was more receptive, however, to Chapman's second argument. The act for the revival of the laws seemed to suggest that the separation from Great Britain "worked a dissolution of all government," and extinguished not only colonial laws, but also "the common law and statute law of England." McKean then noted that in a civil war "every man chooses his own party," and the "minority have, individually, an unrestrainable right to remove with their property into another country" and a "reasonable time for that purpose ought to be allowed." But McKean doubted that one could enter another country "at open war with the country he leaves" without committing treason. Chapman's case, however, was different: "Pennsylvania was not a nation at war with another nation; but a country in a state of civil war; and there is no precedent in the books to show what might be done in that case." To solve this difficulty, McKean turned to the treason statute, which seemed to "allow a choice of his party to every man, until the 11th of February, 1777." "This construction," McKean observed, could be said to be "favorable to traitors," but we "cannot be influenced by observations of a political nature in the exposition of the law; it is our duty to seek for, and to declare, the true intention of the legislature." McKean concluded his charge by stating, "If there were no laws to be obeyed during that period, the prisoner could not be deemed a subject of the State of Pennsylvania on the 26th day of December 1776. . . . [A]t all events, it is better to err on the side of mercy, than of strict justice." Under such strong direction, the jury quickly found that Chapman was not a subject of Pennsylvania.[228]

Historian James Kettner viewed the *Chapman* decision as a prime example of what he termed the "idea of volitional allegiance"—an idea developed during the Revolution under which allegiance was determined by choice, rather than fixed immutably at birth. As he saw it, "Pennsylvania's definition of the time period in which individuals could choose or reject citizenship was perhaps the clearest of all the states."[229] As a description of *Chapman*'s holding, this is probably accurate. But it is important to note that this right was first recognized in 1781, not in 1776. As Chapter 4 explains, in August 1776, the Council of Safety routinely imprisoned civilians it viewed as inimical to the American states. Persons detained prior to independence, such as John Kearsley, were not released, but remained in prison. On September 5, 1776, the convention adopted a treason ordinance, which explicitly stated that all persons residing in Pennsylvania owed allegiance to the state. Most notably, on November 25, 1776, Thomas McKean himself presided over a meeting at the Indian Queen Tavern to investigate cases of suspected traitors—a meeting that resulted in the imprisonment of Joseph Stansbury. None of these actions were consistent with a right to choose one's allegiance free from state interference; rather, the state took significant steps to capture and punish those persons who maintained active allegiance to the British. A "right" to choose one's side could not be safely recognized in 1776; only after the danger had largely passed could courts consider recognizing such a right retrospectively. Moreover, when the "right" was recognized in 1781, it rested heavily on the peculiarities of the February 1777 treason statute. If the statute had been drafted differently, the court may well have found Chapman subject to Pennsylvania law.[230]

* * *

On October 24, 1781, the news of Cornwallis's surrender at Yorktown reached Philadelphia and the city erupted in celebration. Supporters of the Revolution fired their guns and illuminated their windows. Inevitably, attention turned to the Revolution's opponents. In the last significant crowd action of the Revolution, mobs attacked darkened homes, smashing windows, breaking down doors, and, in some cases, plundering belongings and throwing flaming materials.[231] A Quaker named Anna Rawle wrote in her diary, "In short, the sufferings of those they please to style Tories would fill a volume and shake the credulity of those who were not here on that memorable night."[232] Grand juror John Dorsey, appalled at the violence, saved fourteen Quaker houses by illuminating their windows before the mob could arrive.[233] Many of those "styled Tories," of course, were Quakers, and it seemed to them that an era was over. Two days after the surrender, Rawle wrote, "It seems universally agreed that Philadelphia will no longer be that happy asylum for Quakers that it once was. Those joyful days when all was prosperity and peace are gone, never to return; and perhaps it is as necessary for our society to ask for terms as it was for Cornwallis."[234]

Although the war would not formally end until the signing of the peace treaty in 1783, the threat posed by the British military was now minimal. Opponents of the Revolution were an annoyance, not a fundamental danger to the state. Even Joseph Reed, who had made his political career as a Tory hunter, recognized that the threat had dramatically diminished. In June 1781, Reed had written to General Nathanael Greene that Pennsylvania probably had more Tories than any other state, but they were "dastardly cowardly wretches who confer neither credit or strength on any cause to which they are attached." They had "neither the courage nor ambition which elevates men to great designs and makes them useful to the cause they espouse."[235]

The issue of treason, it would seem, was ready to fade away. And in some ways it did. But over the next two decades, the issue would re-emerge repeatedly, in new contexts that never could have been imagined at the beginning of the war.

9

Peace, the Constitution, and Rebellion, 1781–1800

IN MAY 1795, the United States Attorney for the District of Pennsylvania, William Rawle, commenced the first trials for treason under the United States Constitution. The defendants were men from western Pennsylvania who had opposed the federal excise tax on whiskey, and Rawle prosecuted the cases vigorously, arguing that the men's conduct clearly amounted to high treason against the United States. Rawle was joined at the counsel table by William Bradford, the United States Attorney General. Bradford, who had prosecuted treason cases during the war as the Pennsylvania Attorney General, was a natural for this role. But Rawle was not. Indeed, his presence at the trials suggested that the world turned upside down by the Revolution had perhaps turned upside down once more. Unlike President Washington and other high-ranking federal officials, Rawle was not a hero of the Revolution. Quite the opposite—he was a committed Loyalist from a deeply Loyalist family. His stepfather, Samuel Shoemaker, a former mayor of Philadelphia, had served as Philadelphia's magistrate of police during the British occupation, earning him the title of one of the Revolution's most detested Loyalists. When the British departed, Shoemaker and Rawle realized that their lives were in danger and they fled to British-occupied New York. While in New York, Rawle wrote letters lamenting the Revolution, and in 1781 he moved to London to study at Middle Temple. In late 1782, amid worries that he would be attainted for treason by the state of Pennsylvania, he returned to America and eventually developed a thriving law practice.[1]

The startling fact that a former Loyalist was now prosecuting American tax protestors for high treason shows just how much Pennsylvania and the United States had changed in the fourteen years since the victory at Yorktown. With Cornwallis's defeat, military hostilities largely came to a halt, and the pervasive fears of internal enemies that had consumed Americans for over six years diminished dramatically. Prosecutions for treason and misprision of treason did not immediately end in Pennsylvania, but it was clear that their days were numbered.

The issue of treason would now appear most prominently in the context of internal rebellions. Although the state prosecuted one man for levying war against the state, the primary actor would be the new federal government. When the Constitutional Convention met in Philadelphia in 1787, it authorized the federal government to try persons for treason, but adopted a restrictive definition in order to limit abuses. Within a few years, Pennsylvanians rising in arms to resist taxes and claiming to be the true heirs to the Revolution would fundamentally challenge the new government's ability to control internal dissent.

Treason Prosecutions after Yorktown

After Yorktown, the proclamations of attainder remained the greatest threat to British adherents. The David Dawson precedent of execution without a trial, however, would not be repeated. In January 1783, for example, Christopher Wilson was brought before the Supreme Court, charged with being a person named in an attainder proclamation and failing to report within the allotted time. Wilson "denied all the facts averred in the said suggestion," but a jury found for the government.[2] This was an unremarkable verdict, as Wilson's own wife had filed a petition to the justices in 1779, lamenting her "disagreeable and unhappy circumstance of being married to Christopher Wilson who has left the state in company with the common enemy of America."[3] A few days later, Wilson's attorneys, William Lewis and Jared Ingersoll, filed an unsuccessful motion to bar the judgment of execution. Although sentenced to death, Wilson was not executed and was eventually discharged.[4] In his clemency petition to the Council, Wilson admitted joining the British, but argued that he had "never borne arms with them." He had fled with the British to Long Island rather than "take the benefit of proclamation" because the "rage of war, and the injuries received from the British ran high in the passions of his countrymen," giving him but "small chance for his life at that time."[5] A similar procedure was used for Isaac Mitchenor and Samuel Burrowes in April 1783. The Supreme Court deferred their cases to the next session and admitted both men to bail, and it appears that they were never tried.[6]

In misdemeanor cases, defense attorneys began taking an increasingly dismissive tone. John Bulla, for example, was charged with misdemeanor at the Chester County Court of Oyer and Terminer in May 1783, for advising Thomas Woodward to steal a horse and supply it to the enemy during the British occupation. Jonathan Dickinson Sergeant, who had vigorously prosecuted traitors as the state's attorney general, appeared as Bulla's counsel, and noted that this was "a stale business. . . . The time was when these things were important—less now." Dredging up old charges was an opportunity for the airing of grudges, and "tories may now be disposed to hunt tory."[7] At another trial, Jasper Yeates stated, "This is, I hope the last time for such trials."[8] In a misdemeanor case in York County in 1782, even the prosecutor noted that "time has subdued the resentment of the people respecting the defendant. The zeal for prosecution has subsided."[9]

There were only three trials for high treason in Pennsylvania after the victory at Yorktown. George Clift was convicted in Bucks County in December 1781, but was later pardoned. His petition for clemency was supported by Chief Justice McKean and by the members of the jury that had convicted him.[10] Peter Kerr was tried in April 1782 in Chester County on a charge of having joined the enemy and capturing an American prisoner on October 6, 1777.[11] The tardiness of the prosecution, although not legally an impediment, may have contributed to the jury's verdict of acquittal.

The final treason trial was that of Joshua Buffington in September 1782. Buffington was no stranger to the justices. In September 1781, he had been brought before the Supreme Court as an attainted traitor who failed to surrender himself in a timely fashion. Buffington was represented by William Lewis and Jared Ingersoll, a Yale graduate and future signer of the United States Constitution. Lewis and Ingersoll argued that the proclamation of attainder had named Buffington's township as East Bradford, but they produced numerous affidavits demonstrating that Buffington had lived in West Bradford.[12] Accordingly, the accused, Joshua Buffington of West Bradford, had not been attainted of treason. An exasperated Attorney General Bradford insisted that Buffington was obviously named in the proclamation as the "description cannot apply to any other person."[13]

The court ruled in Buffington's favor: "Although it may be allowed, that the legislature is not bound to the same strictness, that is required in the description of all indictments; yet, we are inclined to think that the Executive Council is so bound." Even a pardon, the court noted, would be "extremely doubtful" if it named the wrong township. Thus, although "Joshua Buffington of East Bradford was called upon to surrender himself . . . Joshua Buffington of West Bradford certainly was not."[14]

A year later, Buffington was back, this time as the subject of an indictment by a grand jury in the court of oyer and terminer for serving as a soldier in the king's army.[15] The case was another debacle for the prosecution. Buffington was again represented by Jared Ingersoll, and he used nineteen of his peremptory challenges. Attorney General Bradford presented one witness, Elijah Wood, who testified that Buffington had come to him to buy molasses during the British occupation of Philadelphia. After presenting five affidavits stating that Buffington had lived in Chester County until 1780, Bradford sought to have Wood testify that Buffington had confessed to him. Ingersoll immediately objected, triggering a lengthy argument about the admissibility of the confession. The court ruled that the confession to Elijah Wood could not be admitted unless the state first presented two witnesses to a treasonous act. With that, the state's case appears to have collapsed, as the state produced no more witnesses. Buffington produced no witnesses on his behalf, and the jury returned a verdict of not guilty.[16] With that ignominious conclusion at the State House, treason prosecutions for aiding the British came to an end.

Treason Cases: Summary Data

Between September 1778 and September 1782, there were at least forty-five jury trials for treason in Pennsylvania's courts of oyer and terminer.[17] A full listing of these trials is provided in Appendix 2. As court records are incomplete, the possibility of additional trials cannot be completely eliminated.[18] The trials were heavily concentrated in the southeastern corner of the state. The vast majority of trials were in Philadelphia County. Of the remaining counties, Bucks County had seven trials, Chester and Bedford Counties had three, and Northampton had one.[19] Table 9.1 provides summary data from these trials.[20]

Overall, eighty-seven charges of high treason were presented to grand juries, which found indictments in 62% of the cases, a somewhat lower rate than the 86.5% indictment rate for misprision cases. Forty-five cases of high treason went to trial, but juries convicted in only 15.5% of them, a rate significantly lower than the 57% for misprision cases. Of the seven defendants who were convicted of high treason, four were pardoned and three were executed. Put another way, a person who was charged with treason before a grand jury in Pennsylvania between 1778 and 1782 had only a 3.4% chance of suffering execution.

On balance, it is hard to argue that Pennsylvania engaged in a reign of terror against opponents of the Revolution. Persons charged with treason were represented by skilled defense counsel, the courts did their best to ensure fairness at the trials, and conviction rates were surprisingly low. It seems far more likely that culpable people escaped than that innocent people were improperly convicted. The number of Pennsylvanians who actually provided some form of assistance to the British army in violation of the state's treason law almost certainly numbered in the thousands.[21] Yet only three were executed after a trial in a court of law. Admittedly, there is somewhat of a random quality to those three; Morden was a casualty of the fallout over Benedict Arnold, and Carlisle and Roberts probably suffered from being among the first of the Philadelphia

Table 9.1 Treason Cases: Pennsylvania Court of Oyer and Terminer, 1777–1782

County	Ignoramus/ True Bill	NG/G	Judgment Entered	Pardoned	Executed
Bedford	9/5	3/0			
Berks	0/0				
Bucks	0/7	5/2	2	2	
Chester	2/5	3/0			
Cumberland	0/0				
Lancaster	0/0				
Northampton	7/4	0/1	1	0	1
Northumberland	0/0				
Philadelphia	15/33	27/4	4	2	2
Westmoreland	0/0				
York	0/0				
TOTAL	33/54	38/7	7	4	3

prosecutions. But absent the pardoning of all convicted defendants, some element of randomness was probably inevitable.

How typical was the Pennsylvania experience compared to other states? Although most states shared an aversion to capital punishment for treason, the mechanisms by which that aversion was expressed varied significantly, as the experience of neighboring states demonstrates. The sharpest contrast can be found at a court of oyer and terminer in Morristown, New Jersey in the fall of 1778, at the height of the Philadelphia treason trials. Thirty-five men, many of whom were from Pennsylvania, were tried for high treason for marching to join the enemy in New York.[22] All thirty-five were convicted. New Jersey governor William Livingston argued that "sound policy will require the execution of the ring-leaders; so humanity and mercy will interpose in behalf of the more ignorant and deluded."[23] Most of the defendants were pardoned upon condition of serving in the Continental Army, and only two were executed.[24] A month later, at a court of oyer and terminer in Gloucester, New Jersey, seven men were convicted of high treason and sentenced to death, although most were later pardoned.[25]

In Delaware, eight men were convicted of high treason in 1780 alone, more than were convicted in Pennsylvania during the entire war. This figure is especially striking when one considers that Delaware's population was approximately 37,000 people, compared to approximately 300,000 in Pennsylvania.

No executions ensued, however, as all eight men were pardoned.[26] Similarly, at a court of oyer and terminer in Frederick, Maryland, in July 1781, seven people were convicted of high treason and sentenced to death, a figure equal to Pennsylvania's wartime total.[27] Only three of the defendants were executed.[28] Likewise, in 1782, ten men were convicted of treason in Virginia, but all were pardoned.[29]

What made Pennsylvania different? The answer almost certainly rests in the controversial executions of John Roberts and Abraham Carlisle in early November 1778. These executions put jurors on notice that clemency could not be routinely expected from Pennsylvania's executive authority. Jurors who may have been persuaded of the defendant's guilt, but were unwilling to expose the defendant to the death penalty, had no choice but to acquit. By contrast, in other states, jurors could confidently convict defendants, knowing that the likelihood of eventual capital punishment was low.[30]

Of course, the oyer and terminer data do not represent the totality of persons ensnared by charges of disloyalty in Pennsylvania. It does not include most of the hundreds of people named in the attainder proclamations who either fled the state entirely or who were later discharged (or, in the unusual case of David Dawson, executed). It does not include people jailed on suspicion of treason, but against whom charges were never filed. Nor does it include people brought before the committees of safety or the military in the years prior to 1778.

Some of the cases that never made it to court could nonetheless be quite disturbing. In April 1780 in Northumberland County, for example, a large number of armed men descended upon two Quakers, Moses Roberts and Job Hughes, and thirteen of their neighbors. Despite Roberts's plea that his wife was "great with child and near the time of her delivery," the men seized him and the others and placed them in a boat that took them to Sunbury. On the way, someone struck one of the captured men "on the head with a tomahawk which entered his skull and he shed much blood."[31] At Sunbury, the men were interrogated before a "Court of Private Sessions," on suspicion of aiding the Indians.[32] The sheriff freed ten of the men on the condition that they pay £10,000 bail and promise not to appear in the county during the war. The remaining men were ordered to Philadelphia, and were placed in a canoe that took them down the Susquehanna toward Lancaster, where they were arrested on suspicion of high treason and were committed to jail by Justice Atlee.[33]

President Joseph Reed was displeased by the actions of the Northumberland officials, stating to George Bryan that these were "really distressing cases when suspicion is made to stand for proof, and necessity makes the law. I am fearful that an entire discharge will have very bad effects, and it seems a stretch of power to hold them in confinement when no cause is shown."[34] Chief Justice McKean was willing to release the men on bail, but Roberts and Hughes refused, insisting that they were innocent and demanding an unconditional release, which angered McKean greatly.[35] The two men remained in jail, without indictment or trial, until they were released in late 1781.[36] Their case became a rallying cry for Quakers disillusioned with the state government.[37] John Pemberton felt that "judgment is turned backward, and equity cannot enter."[38] A Quaker committee reported that the men "were detained in prison without being charged with any crime, but merely for refusing to give bail, being entirely innocent of the breach of any law; and are therefore suffering for the testimony of a good conscience, having undergone great oppression & injustice from the hands of cruel men."[39] A case like this was not especially common, but it reminds us that not all significant legal proceedings were memorialized in the docket books of courts.

The Escaping-Prisoners Cases

As cases of treason and misprision disappeared after Yorktown, prosecutions for a different form of disloyalty—helping British prisoners of war to escape—began to occupy the courts. The presence of large numbers of prisoners of war in the state had long posed problems for Pennsylvania's government.[40] By 1781, over 800 prisoners were being held in Lancaster. As historian Ken Miller has noted, the prisoners "had access to an elaborate escape network consisting of loyalist guides and scattered safe houses stretching from Pennsylvania to New York."[41] In May, a "daring plot" by the prisoners to escape was fortuitously uncovered. Colonel Adam Hubley wrote despondently to President Reed, "the number of disaffected people through this country is very considerable so that our situation is truly alarming when I consider the state in which I find the militia, should the prisoners once clear themselves of the barracks, the few men on guard . . . would not be able to stop them."[42] By June, over 150 prisoners were sick with putrid fever, further increasing the desire of the healthier prisoners to escape from the crowded barracks where they were confined.[43]

Prisoners of war were not subject to the laws of Pennsylvania and, as the justices observed in a 1782 case, a "British prisoner may rightfully escape."[44] If captured, a prisoner would not be subject to criminal prosecution, but simply returned to confinement. But what about those Pennsylvanians who helped the escaping prisoners along the way, by offering them directions, a meal, or a place to sleep? Even though active hostilities had ended after Yorktown, British soldiers remained enemies for purposes of the state's treason law until a treaty of peace was concluded. Moreover, each British prisoner who successfully escaped was one fewer prisoner who could potentially be exchanged for an American prisoner. Accordingly, it would not be implausible to describe aid to escaping soldiers as a treasonous act of giving aid and comfort to the enemy.

Here, however, as elsewhere, the formal logic of the law yielded to realities. Prosecutors had found it almost impossible to win convictions from juries in cases involving far worse deeds. How likely was it that a jury in Lancaster County would convict someone of treason for giving food and a place in the barn to a young man trying to return to his family? Recognizing this problem, the Assembly passed an act in April 1782 providing for the punishment of "the base and treacherous practice of aiding, abetting, concealing or assisting" escaping prisoners of war. The act vested jurisdiction over the offense in the courts of quarter sessions, and imposed a punishment of a fifty-pound fine, half to be paid to the state, and the other half to the prosecutor, suggesting that private prosecutors would take the lead in these cases. Defendants unable to pay the fine would be publicly whipped with thirty-nine lashes.[45]

Curiously, however, no prosecutions were brought in the courts of quarter sessions. The statute did not create a new offense, but simply defined the parameters of an offense that was already subject to punishment as a common-law misdemeanor. The justices had been hearing similar cases prior to the statute's enactment and had been imposing stiffer sentences than those required by the statute. On May 27, 1782, for example, Nathaniel Forsyth was convicted in the Court of Oyer and Terminer for York County and fined £100 and ordered imprisoned until July 4, 1783.[46] Chief Justice McKean and Justice Bryan endorsed Forsyth's petition for clemency, noting that the statute, "which had passed before the trial of the prisoner, . . . was unknown to the Court, as they had been five weeks on the circuit."[47] The Council accordingly remitted the fine and the sentence of imprisonment.[48] The practice of prosecuting the escape cases in the courts of oyer and terminer continued, primarily in Lancaster, Chester, Philadelphia, and York Counties, and the charges included a common-law count as well as a statutory count. Attorney General William Bradford, occasionally assisted by Joseph Reed, argued personally for the state. Bradford may have seen these cases as opportunities to target opponents of the Revolution. As he pointed out in one case, "He is no good Whig who harbors prisoners of war."[49]

Justice George Bryan's notes for many of these cases survive, so we have better evidence of witness testimony, arguments by the attorneys, and rulings of the court than we do for the cases of high treason. Whereas the treason defendants were all men, the defendants accused of aiding escaping prisoners included several women, including Ann Shirk, acquitted in Lancaster County in October 1782; Susannah Longacre, convicted in Chester County in October 1782; and Rachel Hammer, convicted in Philadelphia in January 1783.[50] The cases were vigorously argued, and the defendants had the assistance of able counsel, including James Wilson, William Lewis, Alexander Wilcocks, Jasper Yeates, and Stephen Chambers.[51] The lawyers cross-examined witnesses, advanced evidentiary objections, and even attempted an insanity defense for one defendant.[52] At a Philadelphia trial in January 1783, the defense witnesses included former treason prosecutors Joseph Reed and Jonathan Dickinson Sergeant.[53]

Many of the cases stemmed from a clever sting operation, apparently initiated by General Moses Hazen, commander of the prison camp in Lancaster. Hazen arranged for Captain Noah Lee to pose as a British prisoner and provided three real British prisoners to assist him. The four men would then request help from various individuals to aid in their escape. When the assistance was provided, the trap was sprung. Misdemeanor charges followed, with Captain Lee and the British prisoners providing the sole testimony on behalf of the state. Each conviction yielded £25 for General Hazen (his half-share of the fine), and the fine could be assessed separately for each prisoner pretending to escape. Thus each person who fell for the plot could be fined up to £150, with General Hazen recovering £75. Although there is no direct evidence of Hazen's plans, it seems probable that he targeted persons suspected of active involvement in escape rings, rather than random individuals with no prior history of wrongdoing.

When these cases first reached the Court of Oyer and Terminer for Lancaster County in October 1782, defense counsel objected. In *Commonwealth v. Snyder et al.*, Stephen Chambers complained of a "plan laid to deceive these poor men and bring them to punishment."[54] Similarly, in *Commonwealth v. Meyers et al.*, defense counsel briefly argued that the "men were sent out by Lee for a particular purpose," and the defendants could therefore not be "guilty of harboring and aiding to escape." The point was buried in larger objections over evidentiary issues, however, and does not seem to have been squarely addressed by the court.[55]

When the court moved on to Chester County a few days later, however, defense counsel were ready to pounce. A modern attorney would consider some form of an entrapment defense, but this defense was not recognized until the nineteenth century.[56] The lawyers for Martin Usner and three other defendants instead argued that the alleged facts did not constitute a crime, as the men were not really British prisoners trying to escape. Alexander Wilcocks argued that "in the eye of law" the act did not apply "if these prisoners were permitted to go with intent to draw in these persons, and not to go off to New York." Similarly, William Lewis argued that the alleged offense lacked "the legal essentials," since these men could not "be considered as making an escape." It was analogous, Lewis suggested, to a "man shooting with malice at an object, supposed a man, yet proves a bear."[57]

An exasperated Attorney General Bradford complained that "this cause was advocated with as much zeal, as if the defendants were spotless." He asked, "Shall an offense bordering on treason go unchecked?" "Going to New York" is not necessary under the statute, he argued; "being at large is sufficient." Joseph Reed, assisting Bradford, argued, "it would disgrace us to suppose [this offense] not punishable." The court's decision, preserved in Justice Bryan's handwritten notes, is not entirely clear, but the court agreed with the state, noting that the statute must be construed "reasonably." Helping prisoners to escape was an offense before the statute was enacted, and the statute reached "any aid, that may help prisoners to escape, though not escaping at the moment."[58]

The court's approval of Captain Lee's entrapment plot would prove highly significant. At least twenty-seven people were convicted as a result of Lee's efforts. Three of these were on counts at common law, which did not provide a share of the fine to the prosecutor, but the twenty-four convictions under the statute would have yielded £1700 to General Hazen.[59]

In contrast to the treason cases, the state obtained convictions in a significant majority of the escape cases. The evidence of guilt was probably more straightforward than in the treason cases, and the punishment was relatively mild, giving juries less hesitation about convicting. Nonetheless, the convictions may have had a significant deterrent effect. A clemency petition from November 1782 suggested that the fines were designed "to strike terror in the generality to prevent further mischief, in which they succeeded so far that a stranger can get no more lodging or directions for the road."[60]

In many cases, however, the Council remitted the fine or a portion of the fines.[61] Christian Carpenter of Lancaster County, for example, petitioned the Council for clemency, arguing that he had thought "it proper, and consistent with the character of a Christian, to give what he could spare to those he thought in want. This principle, he is now convinced, was carried too far."[62] The Council agreed to remit one-third of his fine.[63] Jacob Grove similarly persuaded the Council to remit a portion of his fine by arguing that he could "scarcely understand one word of the English language" and thus could not be chargeable with knowledge of the prisoner's intended escape.[64] Frederick Buzzard successfully argued that he "was utterly ignorant of any law against lodging British prisoners" and pointed to the devastation of his farm by the British army, the loss of his wife, and the seven children he had to maintain.[65] John Evans persuaded the Council to remit the fine of his son, a minor convicted of giving prisoners directions to New York.[66]

The Returning Loyalists

With military hostilities over, attention turned to the fate of those who had fled to the British during the war. The terms of the articles of peace being negotiated in Paris were of significant concern. In August 1782, the Pennsylvania Assembly unanimously resolved that the restoration of the property of attainted traitors was "utterly incompatible with the future peace, interests, and safety" of the state and would "depreciate and weaken the independence gained at such a vast expense of blood and treasure.[67] A Philadelphia almanac published in late 1782 opened with a picture of a hanged man entitled "Tory turned Rope-Dancer." Doggerel verses stated that the Tory, who thought he was safe "from gallows and from rope," had made an improvident decision to return to Pennsylvania.[68] In June 1783, a group of militiamen met at the State House and issued resolves arguing that it was "inconsistent with the interest and dignity of the good people of this State, that any person who hath voluntarily withdrawn himself from this, or any of the United States of America, since the 19th day of April, 1775" and who had aided the British in any capacity "should be suffered to return to, or reside within the State of Pennsylvania." Such "unworthy men who would have rejoiced in the subjection of America" should not be allowed to "participate of the blessings of liberty and commerce." To enforce these resolves, the militiamen formed a committee "to use all means in our power, to expel with infamy, such persons who . . . shall presume to come among us."[69] Militiamen in Chester County resolved to do the same thing and vowed to "hereafter enquire into the character, and examine every suspicious person that comes within our knowledge."[70] A committee in Bucks County resolved against the return of any person who had aided the British, noting that "the re-admission of such infamous deserters into the bosom of our country would greatly dishonor and endanger the state."[71] Northampton County similarly instructed its representatives to support a law to prevent the return to Pennsylvania of anyone who had aided the British during the war.[72] An August 1783 circular letter by William Adcock (who had served on five treason juries, including that of John Roberts), warned that the "traitors, who joined the enemy, will also be creeping in amongst us." Many "people who call themselves Americans," Adcock warned, would "joyfully receive these men into our country, for the sake of strengthening their party, and promoting their own ambitious purposes."[73]

The Treaty of Paris, concluded on September 3, 1783, required the American states to terminate all treason prosecutions and property confiscations stemming from the war. It further required the Confederation Congress to recommend to the state legislatures the restoration of property of British subjects confiscated during the war and the revision of the laws "consistent not only with justice and equity but with that spirit of conciliation which on the return of the blessings of peace should universally prevail."[74] The British placed great emphasis on these provisions, but few Americans expected the states to comply. Not surprisingly, almost none did. New York, for example, enacted a law in 1784 that disenfranchised and barred from public office any person who had served in a British military unit or who had lived behind enemy lines after July 9, 1776.[75]

In Pennsylvania, resentment against the exiles nonetheless slowly dwindled and many of them eventually returned and were able to carry on their lives almost as if the Revolution had never happened. One of the most widely reviled exiles was Jacob Duché, the former minister of Christ Church in Philadelphia and chaplain to the Continental Congress, who had notoriously urged General Washington to negotiate for peace during the British occupation. Duché had been attainted in the original March 6, 1778 act of attainder, and his house was later occupied by Chief Justice McKean. Duché was desperate to return to Philadelphia, but feelers that he sent out in 1783 and 1789 discouraged him from doing so. In 1793, however, Duché finally received a pardon from Pennsylvania Governor Thomas Mifflin and was able to return. Memories of the war had faded, and Duché even had a cordial meeting with President Washington.[76]

In 1790, the Council considered a motion for a general pardon of all persons attainted for treason during the war. The motion was seconded by Zebulon Potts, who had served on the Philadelphia grand jury in 1778.[77] The Council had been regularly pardoning attainted traitors, but the motion was postponed and never received a vote.[78] When the new Pennsylvania constitution of 1790 took effect, the pardoning power was transferred to the governor, who continued to issue pardons regularly in treason cases. By 1792, Secretary of State Thomas Jefferson was able to assure the British ambassador that in Pennsylvania, "All persons were permitted to return . . . , and you see many of them living here to this day in quiet and esteem."[79]

In 1792, the Pennsylvania Assembly passed a law restoring the portions of the estates of John Roberts and Abraham Carlisle that were still held by the commonwealth to their heirs.[80] An Assembly committee found that "the critical circumstances of the late contest afford[ed] an ample justification for those proceedings, which were calculated to secure the allegiance of the citizens," but in the "present season of peace and prosperity," the state might exercise "its dignity and its mercy" to restore these small pieces of property.[81]

Leniency would eventually be extended to even the most notorious traitors. In late 1778 or early 1779, a Philadelphia broadside had warned about leniency toward the exiles, claiming that even "Samuel Shoemaker, Andrew Allen, and Joseph Galloway will have a beaten path to come back upon."[82] These three men were among the notorious adherents to the British and had been named in the state's first legislative attainder proclamation. Yet the broadside proved prescient, as all three men were eventually pardoned. Shoemaker, a former mayor of Philadelphia, had served as a magistrate of police during the British occupation. Upon the evacuation, he had fled to New York and then to England, where he met with George III.[83] But by 1791, Shoemaker was back in Philadelphia and was described in a city directory as a "gentleman" living on High Street.[84]

In 1793, he received a pardon from Pennsylvania Governor Thomas Mifflin.[85] Andrew Allen had served as Pennsylvania Attorney General, in the Pennsylvania Assembly, on the Pennsylvania Committee of Safety, and as a delegate to the Second Continental Congress before fleeing to the British in December 1776. Allen received a pardon in 1792, and he returned to Philadelphia, where he lived for approximately five years before returning to England.[86] Even Joseph Galloway, perhaps second only to Benedict Arnold in popular hatred, received leniency. The former speaker of the Pennsylvania Assembly, Galloway had defected to the British in the fall of 1776 and served as superintendent of Philadelphia during the British occupation.[87] A poem in a Philadelphia newspaper had described him as a "traitor to his country" and a "Lucifer on earth."[88] But by 1793, Thomas McKean had offered to help procure a pardon for Galloway.[89] In 1795 the pardon was issued, although Galloway chose not to return to Pennsylvania.[90] Only Benedict Arnold remained beyond possibility of redemption.

What made Arnold so distinctive? Unlike the other accused traitors, Arnold did not make his decision out of political principle at an early stage of the war. Instead, he sold out his country for money after five years of service in its army. This was no misguided neighbor, with simply a differing view of political issues. This was evil incarnate, the devil himself, as the Philadelphia street theater had so vividly demonstrated. Such a person was irredeemable, a foul villain who fully deserved to swing from the gallows.

The Continuing Threat of Internal Dismemberment

During the war, the most significant threat of treason came from the densely populated southeastern counties of the state. After the war, the threat shifted, and the state's greatest concerns over disloyalty arose in the sparsely settled frontier regions to the west and to the north, where loyalty to the government in Philadelphia was weakest. The controversies with Connecticut and Virginia that had consumed the colonial government prior to independence now threatened to erupt again. In November 1782, reports began circulating that the western settlers had "declared that the country within that space is independent of Pennsylvania." Some members of the Confederation Congress were sympathetic, concluding that Pennsylvania would "be large enough if it was confined to the Alleghany Mountains, and it would be wisdom to acquiesce in the proposition of an independent state."[91]

The Pennsylvania Assembly, however, had no desire to see the state dismembered. On December 3, 1782, it passed an act expanding the definition of high treason. It was now high treason to "erect or form, or . . . endeavor to erect or form any new and independent government within the boundaries of this commonwealth as described in the charter and settled between this state and the state of Virginia." Actions to accomplish this goal by force were probably already addressed by the 1777 statute's prohibition on levying war against the state, but the new provision made explicit that even attempts constituted high treason. Two separate sections extended the offense to meetings and discussions. It was now treason to "set up any notice, written or printed, calling or requesting the people to meet together for the design or purpose of forming a new and independent government as aforesaid" or to "assemble . . . for that purpose in consequence of such notice." It was also treason to "advisedly recommend or desire" the formation of a new government to the participants at such a meeting, or to "read to them any new form of a constitution with design to induce them to adopt the same as a new and independent constitution." The new statute followed the 1777 statute in requiring two witnesses and trial in a court of oyer and terminer, but it permitted trial "in any county within this commonwealth" at the Council's discretion, thus eliminating the advantages of a local jury. In a significant caveat, the Assembly stated that the act did not apply to the dispute between Pennsylvania and Connecticut.[92]

This statute, enacted as a panicked and hasty response to external events, is hardly a masterpiece of the legislative craft. It is easy to note just how many of the revolutionaries' own activities prior to independence would have been unlawful under the statute, and permitting the Council to remove a trial from a local jury was eerily reminiscent of the statute of Henry VIII that the revolutionaries had so ardently denounced. Two years later, a draft report of the Council of Censors singled out this statute as an unconstitutional infringement of the right of trial by jury.[93] But the legislative bark proved to be far greater than any executive or judicial bite. No person appears to have been charged or tried under this provision.

The border controversies did trigger a treason indictment, but not until several years later in the seemingly never-ending dispute with Connecticut. In November 1782, a congressional commission issued the so-called Trenton Decree, upholding Pennsylvania's jurisdiction over the Wyoming Valley, but many Connecticut settlers refused to accept this decision and the area again erupted in armed violence.[94] By 1786, Pennsylvania officials suspected that some of the Connecticut settlers intended to form an independent state.[95] In late August 1787, Chief Justice McKean issued an arrest warrant for John Franklin, the leader of the Connecticut settlers, who had been elected as Luzerne County's first representative to the Pennsylvania Assembly in February 1787.[96] The warrant charged Franklin with denying the jurisdiction of Pennsylvania and encouraging "diverse inhabitants of the said county to disobey our laws and to resist our government."[97] When Franklin was finally captured in early October 1787, he was brought to Philadelphia and placed under close confinement.[98] The *Pennsylvania*

Gazette approved of the arrest, describing Franklin as a "Western Shays, who . . . has uniformly labored to involve the county in civil war."[99] At Franklin's arraignment, Chief Justice McKean cited evidence that Franklin intended to erect an independent state and appointed a court to exercise its jurisdiction. Such facts, McKean stated, "would clearly constitute the crime of high treason, but that the laws of the government had prevailed upon them to institute a prosecution, for misprision of treason only." Franklin pleaded not guilty, and referred his defense to his attorneys, Daniel Clymer and James Biddle. McKean denied bail on the ground that information showing that the insurgents "had proceeded to acts of open rebellion" had recently come to light. Attorney General Bradford then argued that the new facts required that Franklin be committed on a charge of high treason, and the justices agreed.[100] By April 1788, Franklin had still not been tried, but the justices agreed to release Franklin on a two-thousand-pound bail, a sum he was unable to pay.[101]

In response to Franklin's continued detention, a group of Franklin's supporters, disguised as Indians, kidnapped Timothy Pickering, the leading Pennsylvania official in Luzerne County. Pickering was the former quartermaster general of the army and had been sent by the Pennsylvania government to organize the recently created county. The kidnappers initially intended to hold Pickering as a hostage for Franklin's release, but after a few weeks they concluded that the plan had failed and Pickering was released.[102]

The Council sought the advice of Chief Justice McKean and Justice Bryan on the best course of dealing with the kidnappers. The justices recommended charging them with riot, with the initial indictments brought in the court of quarter sessions, followed by removal by certiorari to the Supreme Court for trial. A charge of riot was preferable to high treason, as it was a noncapital offense, making convictions more likely.[103] Timothy Pickering felt that the kidnappers had clearly committed "high treason," a view confirmed by "gentlemen learned in the law," but the "great lenity and mercy" of the government led it to prosecute only for riot.[104] At the November sitting in Wilkes-Barre, three rioters were acquitted and the remainder received mild punishments. Chief Justice McKean, however, pointedly told them that "they were all guilty of high treason, and that in any country in Europe they would all be hanged, and it was to the mildness of the government of Pennsylvania that they were indebted for the light punishment now ordered."[105]

At the same sitting, John Franklin was finally brought before a Luzerne County grand jury, where he was indicted, along with two other men, on a charge of high treason. The indictment alleged that Franklin had endeavoured "to erect and form a new & independent government within the boundaries of this Commonwealth," had conspired to levy war against the state, and had endeavoured to persuade over two hundred to assemble with arms against the Commonwealth."[106] As a legal matter, the indictment was open to serious challenges. The 1782 act making it high treason to attempt to form a new government specifically excluded the Connecticut controversy from its scope, and the fact that the 1782 act was deemed necessary strongly suggested that the offense was not covered by the 1777 act. Moreover, conspiracy to levy war was not a form of high treason, and attempts to persuade had been seemingly excluded by the ruling in the Roberts case. These legal arguments were never raised, however, as Franklin successfully sought a postponement of the treason trial on the ground that three critical witnesses were missing.[107] He was returned to confinement, first in Easton, and then in Philadelphia.[108] In March 1789, an agreement was reached between members of the Assembly, the Council, and the justices that Franklin would be admitted to bail, and Franklin was released after seventeen months in confinement.[109] Upon his return to Luzerne County, he expressed an interest in election to the Assembly or the Council, a possibility that appalled Timothy Pickering. "Is it proper, is it consistent with common sense," he asked, "for the people of this county to elect a man to be a member of the government of the state, who now stands indicted for High Treason against that very government?" Such an election would indicate that Franklin could "never have an impartial trial among such men— . . . he will be acquitted, however clear the evidence may be against him."[110] Attorney General Bradford may well have agreed with this analysis, as Franklin was never tried and was discharged from his bail in May 1792.[111] Five months later Franklin was elected sheriff of Luzerne County.[112] In 1795, he was again elected to the Pennsylvania Assembly.[113] The failure of the Franklin prosecution marked the effective end of the offense of treason against the state of Pennsylvania.[114]

Treason and the United States Constitution

Although all of the Revolution's treason cases had been prosecuted at the state level, the rhetoric of treason was drenched in nationalism. The twin ideas of "treason against America" and of "treason against liberty" that had been enunciated prior to the Declaration persisted throughout the war. In indictments, in newspapers, in private correspondence, and in government records, the same phrase recurred over and over: "treason against the United States." The phrase "treason against Pennsylvania" tended to occur only in the context of "treason against the United States, and the state of Pennsylvania." In June 1782, David Ramsay, a South Carolina delegate to the Confederation Congress complained that "Treason in our governments may be committed by a state as well as an individual. That one which does not contribute its quota in men & money is guilty of treason in the worst sense; for it does that which in consequences tends to the destruction of the body politic."[115] In an item dated July 4, 1782, a writer in the *Pennsylvania Gazette* argued that "the man who grumbles at paying taxes" was "worse than a tory. He is an enemy to his own flesh and blood. He is a prophaner of the rites and worship of the sacred temple of liberty. He is a practical traitor against the independence and freedom of the United States."[116] A few months later, Thomas Paine argued for the creation of national treason laws, so that the continental government could define "treason against the United States."[117] In one of his final *American Crisis* papers, Paine wrote, "Our citizenship in the United States is our national character. Our citizenship in any particular state is only our local distinction . . . Our great title is Americans."[118] Similar nationalist ideals pervaded the address of the President and the Supreme Executive Council of Pennsylvania upon the arrival of the news of the preliminary articles of peace. The Council felt "impelled by a commanding sense of duty to country" to recommend the strengthening and improvement of the Union through a federal supremacy. The members called on "every man who truly loves his country" to stand up for this union, denounced as "treasonable cowardice" the selfish motives of those who opposed them, and concluded with the following lines: "We fervently pray that Almighty God will be pleased to inspire the people of this land with wisdom to make such choice as shall establish their felicity upon a durable basis, and till time shall be no more, afford just cause for an American to rejoice that he is a citizen of the United States."[119]

In 1787, the Constitutional Convention opened in the Assembly Room on the eastern side of the Pennsylvania State House, the same room where the Declaration of Independence had been signed eleven years earlier. Across the hall, on the State House's western side, sat the Pennsylvania Supreme Court chamber, where at least nine men had been tried for high treason during the war. The Pennsylvania delegation included two men with intimate knowledge of both sides of the building. As a member of the Continental Congress, James Wilson had signed the Declaration of Independence in the Assembly Room. As a lawyer, he had defended men accused of treason across the hall in the Supreme Court. Jared Ingersoll had similarly served in the Continental Congress in the Assembly Room and had defended men accused of treason in the Supreme Court.

The new Constitution eventually proposed by the Convention contained a significant provision on treason. Article Three, Section Three stated,

> Treason against the United States, shall consist only in levying War against them, or in adhering to their Enemies, giving them Aid and Comfort. No Person shall be convicted of Treason unless on the Testimony of two Witnesses to the same overt Act, or on Confession in open Court.

> The Congress shall have the Power to declare the Punishment of Treason, but no Attainder of Treason shall work Corruption of Blood, or Forfeiture except during the Life of the Person attainted.

This provision was innovative in three significant respects. First, none of the state constitutions contained any provisions addressing treason. By elevating the crime to constitutional significance, the framers prevented Congress, the President, and the judiciary from impulsively expanding the scope of treason. Second, under English law and Pennsylvania law, treason convictions required two witnesses and proof of an overt act. The Constitution significantly tightened this requirement by requiring two witnesses to the *same* overt act. Third, English law allowed convictions when two witnesses testified to an out-of-court confession.[120] The Constitution eliminated this possibility by requiring confession in open court.

Scholars have long speculated that James Wilson played a key role in the development of the Treason Clause. Although there is no direct evidence, the circumstantial evidence is suggestive. Wilson was the most distinguished lawyer at the convention, he was a member of the Committee of Detail that proposed the clause, and the clause addressed problems of particular professional interest to Wilson. In 1775, he had argued against broad readings of English treason law. In the Malin and Carlisle trials of 1778, Wilson had raised objections to the admissibility of certain overt acts, and in the Roberts trial, he had vigorously objected to the introduction of an out-of-court confession. In a careful study of Wilson's work at the Convention, William Ewald concludes, "Because treason had been a special concern of Wilson's since his unsuccessful defense of accused loyalists and Quakers during the war, this clause most likely represents his handiwork."[121] In subsequent speeches and writings, Wilson singled out the Treason Clause for special praise. As Willard Hurst argued, "Such continuing concentration on a clause which, whatever its merits, is certainly not one of the more conspicuously discussed parts of the Constitution, strongly suggests pride of authorship."[122]

One should be careful not to overstate the case, however. Wilson is likely responsible for the inclusion of a treason provision in the Constitution, but its precise contours bear the mark of other hands. The Committee of Detail's proposed treason provision emerged late in the drafting process, and did not include the requirement of two witnesses to the same overt act, nor did it define adhering to the enemy as "giving them aid and comfort."[123] These changes were introduced on August 20, 1787, when the Convention debated the specific language of the Treason Clause. In 1782, the Virginia General Court had ruled that no person could be convicted of treason without "two witnesses to one and the same overt act." Edmund Randolph complained about this requirement in a letter to James

Madison, arguing that "although it should be proved, that twenty or twenty hundred instances of adherence to the enemy be proved, each of them by a single witness, the punishment of treason cannot be executed upon their author."[124] An unnamed delegate now moved to insert the two witness requirement into the federal constitution, a motion that received prompt support from Benjamin Franklin, who argued "prosecutions for treason were generally virulent; and perjury too easily made use of against innocence." Wilson, by contrast, was more equivocal, noting that "much may be said on both sides. Treason may sometimes be practised in such a manner, as to render proof extremely difficult—as in a traitorous correspondence with an Enemy."[125] The motion was agreed to, eight states to three, with the Pennsylvania delegation voting in favor, and the Virginia delegation (which included Randolph and Madison), opposed. The "aid and comfort" language was proposed by Virginia delegate George Mason. Wilson felt the words were "explanatory, not operative; and that it was better to omit them," but the motion was agreed to, ten states to two, with the Pennsylvania delegation again voting in favor.[126]

In late November 1787, Pennsylvania convened the first ratifying convention for the federal constitution in the Assembly Room at the State House.[127] Many of the delegates had direct experience with Pennsylvania's treason trials. The strongest supporters of ratification were James Wilson, who had defended men accused of treason, and Thomas McKean, who had presided over the trials. Attorney Jasper Yeates, who defended cases of misprision of treason and assisting British soldiers to escape, spoke frequently in favor of ratification. Also supporting ratification, although less frequently, was attorney Stephen Chambers, who had been in James Wilson's house during the Fort Wilson incident and who later defended persons accused of assisting British soldiers to escape.[128] But the most surprising member of the convention was delegate Thomas Yardley of Bucks County, who had been acquitted of treason in October 1778 in a trial presided over by fellow delegate Thomas McKean. We do not know who defended Yardley, but James Wilson is certainly a possibility. There is no record of Yardley speaking during the convention, but he voted in favor of ratification.[129]

In the ratifying convention, Wilson praised the Treason Clause, stating that

> [y]ou will find the current running strong in favor of humanity. For this is the first instance in which it has not been left to the legislature, to extend the crime and punishment of treason so far as they thought proper. This punishment, and the description of the crime, are the great sources of danger and persecution, on the part of the government against the citizen. Crimes against the state! and against the officers of the state! History informs us, that more wrong may be done on this subject than on any

> other whatsoever. But under this constitution, there can be no treason against the United States, except such as is defined in this constitution. The manner of trial is clearly pointed out; the positive testimony of two witnesses to the same overt act, or a confession in open court, is required to convict any person of treason.[130]

In his handwritten notes of seventeen "Reasons for Adopting the Constitution" Wilson included "[t]he accurate description of treason—its consequences confined to the criminal."[131] In a later speech, Wilson stated, "If we have recourse to the history of the different governments that have hitherto subsisted, we shall find that a very great part of their tyranny over the people has arisen from the extension of the definition of treason. . . . Sensible of this, the Convention has guarded the people against it, by a particular and accurate definition of treason."[132]

The Status of State Treason Law

It remained an open question, however, just what this "particular and accurate definition" had in fact defined. As the United States Supreme Court put it in 1945, the Treason Clause's "superficial appearance of clarity and simplicity . . . proves illusory when it is put to practical application. There are few subjects on which the temptation to utter abstract interpretive generalizations is greater or on which they are more to be distrusted. The little clause is packed with controversy and difficulty."[133]

One source of difficulty was whether the clause effectively eliminated the treason laws of the states. The issue was extensively debated at the convention itself. Connecticut delegate William Johnson took the most extreme position, arguing that states had no power over treason, even under the Articles of Confederation, "the Sovereignty being in the Union." Virginia delegate George Mason disagreed, pointing out that "an act may be treason against a particular state which is not so against the United States," such as Bacon's Rebellion in Virginia. Massachusetts delegate Rufus King moved to give Congress the "sole" power to punish treason. James Wilson then pointed out that in "cases of a general nature, treason can only be against the United States, and in such they should have the sole right to declare the punishment—yet in many cases it may be otherwise." He noted, however, that the subject was "intricate" and that he "distrusted his present judgment on it." The motion was defeated, six states to five, and the final document defined "treason against the United States," rather than treason generally.[134]

Questions began to arise almost immediately. Shortly before his nomination to the United States Supreme Court in 1789, Massachusetts Chief Justice William Cushing wrote to John Adams, asking "whether there be any kind of treason which may be tried by a particular state, consistent with the Constitution, & if any what kind."[135] Adams responded that "a more important question . . . never was proposed upon any part of the constitution: and upon the right decision of it will, in my opinion, depend the existence of government. Two sovereignties against which treason can be committed can never exist in one nation or in one system of laws." In particular, Adams worried that state officials might punish federal officials for discharging their duties under federal law.[136] This concern was not entirely misplaced, as just a few years later Thomas Jefferson suggested that the state of Virginia convict and execute the employees of the Bank of the United States for treason against Virginia.[137]

The most plausible reading of state treason laws is that they are preempted by federal treason law with respect to the offense of adhering to enemies.[138] Only the nation, not states, can be said to have "enemies" in the way that treason law has traditionally contemplated. By contrast, an attempt to overthrow a state government by force, while otherwise maintaining allegiance to the United States, would constitute treason against the state by levying war against it. Subsequent state prosecutions for treason would prove extremely rare. There have been a handful of indictments, but only a few convictions: those of Thomas Wilson Dorr in 1844, convicted in Rhode Island in the wake of the Dorr Rebellion; John Brown and Edwin Coppoc, convicted in Virginia after the Harper's Ferry raid of 1859; and Walter Allen, convicted in West Virginia during the Mine Wars of the 1920s.[139]

After the adoption of the Constitution, Pennsylvania maintained its laws against treason, but modified the punishment significantly in 1794. As part of a broader penal law reform, Pennsylvania eliminated the death penalty for a variety of offenses, including treason. In an influential 1793 pamphlet, former Attorney General William Bradford had argued that capital punishment should be eliminated in all cases other than the "higher degrees of treason and murder."[140] The legislature went even further, eliminating capital punishment for treason, and replacing it with imprisonment at hard labor for six to twelve years.[141] This lenity went too far for Thomas McKean, who later sneeringly complained that "the crime of high treason is considered as less injurious to society than a rape, though committed on a courtesan."[142] Justice Edward Shippen of the Pennsylvania Supreme Court (and Benedict Arnold's father-in-law), however, argued that this modification would increase the number of convictions. Shippen noted that there is "a tenderness in jurymen where death is the consequence of their verdict, that inclines them to suffer trivial doubts to operate too much in favor of the accused" and that "the calls of mercy are frequently loud in the ears of the pardoning power." By contrast, a sentence of lengthy imprisonment would stir no such sympathy from the jury or the governor.[143]

The Whiskey Rebellion

A more pressing issue would prove to be the meaning of the phrase "levying war against the United States."[144] In his 1778 grand-jury charges, Chief Justice McKean had interpreted "levying war" broadly, in accordance with English precedents, and he continued to do so through the late 1790s.[145] Similarly, in his Law Lectures in the early 1790s, James Wilson followed Michael Foster's treatise almost word for word. Although Wilson noted that the "line of division" between levying war and "an aggravated riot is sometimes very fine and difficult to be distinguished," he argued that "insurrections in order to throw down all inclosures, to open all prisons, to enhance the price of all labour, to expel foreigners in general, or those from any single nation living under the protection of government, to alter the established law, or to render it ineffectual—insurrections to accomplish these ends, by numbers and an open and armed force, are a levying of war against the United States."[146] According to Foster, these acts were in "construction of law" high treason, for "though they are not levelled at the person of the king, they are against his royal majesty."[147] Former Pennsylvania Attorney General William Bradford agreed, arguing in a 1793 essay that the phrase "levying war" originated with the treason statute of Edward III and had "been settled by the judicial construction of more than four centuries."[148]

Internal rebellions in Pennsylvania, however, would quickly test these confident assertions. In 1794, the Whiskey Rebellion erupted in western Pennsylvania, triggered by opposition to the federal excise tax on whiskey. Although the tax had been deeply unpopular from the moment of its enactment, the opposition took a decidedly violent turn in July 1794, when a group of between 400 and 800 men attacked the opulent mountaintop mansion house of excise collector and staunch Federalist John Neville. The attack resulted in several deaths, and although Neville successfully escaped, the attackers burned Neville's house and many of his outbuildings to the ground. On August 1, 1794, a group of approximately 7000 armed men met at Braddock's Field, with the intent of marching on Pittsburgh. The next day, President Washington convened a high-level conference of advisors, including Pennsylvania Chief Justice Thomas McKean, who argued that the state's judiciary was fully capable of dealing with the crisis and that "employment of a military force" would be "unconstitutional and illegal."[149] But the military option proved irresistible. On August 4, 1794, James Wilson, now an Associate Justice of the United States Supreme Court, issued a declaration stating that the laws of the United States could not be executed by ordinary judicial proceedings in Washington and Allegheny Counties.[150] Wilson's declaration allowed the Washington Administration to invoke the Militia Act of 1792, and Washington, aided by Alexander Hamilton, assembled a force of nearly

13,000 militiamen to crush the rebellion. By the time this force reached western Pennsylvania, however, organized opposition had collapsed, and Hamilton had to be content with bringing twenty men back to Philadelphia for trial.[151]

At no time did the administration consider a wholesale trial of the rebels. As their British predecessors had learned long before, such trials would serve no useful purpose and only inflame western sentiment against the federal government. Nonetheless, the administration hoped to prosecute the most prominent leaders of the rebellion. Unfortunately, the rebellion did not have an obvious leadership structure, and the most prominent men had fled in advance of Washington's army. The men brought back to Philadelphia were all fairly obscure.[152] More humiliating for the government, the prosecutions that were brought degenerated into a complete fiasco.

Before any indictments were formally issued, several of the prisoners, represented by William Lewis, filed petitions in the United States Supreme Court arguing that any trials should be held at a special session in western Pennsylvania, rather than in Philadelphia. Such a session would allow for more westerners to be represented on the jury and would facilitate the easier attendance of witnesses. The court's ruling was announced by Justice James Wilson, who had stood side by side with William Lewis during the Philadelphia treason trials. The court, Wilson stated, had "a wish, if possible, to grant" the petitions, but felt that insurmountable difficulties rendered it impractical.[153]

United States Attorney General William Bradford sought indictments against the twenty men brought from western Pennsylvania as well as against sixteen others. But the grand jury, as had its predecessor during the Philadelphia trials of 1778–1779, viewed the proposed indictments with some skepticism, rejecting one-third of the charges and issuing indictments in only twenty-four of the cases. The grand jury was chaired by Samuel Miles, a prominent Philadelphia businessman and politician, and included Davis Bevan, who had served on Samuel Rowland Fisher's jury and had stoutly defended the jury's independence in the newspaper wars of 1779. Eleven of the indicted defendants were never found. Several others successfully argued that they fell within President Washington's amnesty proclamation. Only ten defendants went to trial; in two cases, two defendants were tried together, so there were only eight jury trials in total.[154] All were held at Philadelphia's City Hall (Figure 9.1), where the restored courtroom can now be seen at Independence National Historic Park.

Jury selection played an important role in the Whiskey Rebellion trials, just as it had in the Philadelphia trials during the war. William Lewis, a seasoned advocate who had represented a number of the Philadelphia defendants, now appeared on behalf of many of the Whiskey Rebellion defendants. In addition to arguing that the return of the jurors did not comply with Pennsylvania law

FIGURE 9.1 Philadelphia's Old City Hall, site of the Whiskey Rebellion and Fries's Rebellion treason trials.
Credit: Nikreates/Alamy Stock Photo.

(which would have limited the number of prospective jurors from the eastern counties), he also argued the defendants had not been provided the caption to the indictments, which would include the names of the grand jurors. Moreover, he argued that the lists of prospective jurors and witnesses that the prosecution had provided to the defense were inadequate, since they specified residence only by county and did not specify occupations. United States Supreme Court Justice William Paterson, presiding over the case with District Judge Richard Peters, concluded that Pennsylvania law did not control federal jury practice in all its particulars, thus ensuring a larger number of easterners in the jury pool. He agreed with Lewis, however, that the caption was required; the caption and the indictment "seem naturally to form but one instrument" and adopting such a rule would "avoid much difficulty and controversy." Although he declined to require the prosecution to provide the occupation of the prospective jurors and witnesses, he did require the prosecution to provide the township of residence, to "enable the party accused to prepare for his defense." The trials were accordingly suspended for three days to enable the prosecution to comply with this order.[155]

As in the Philadelphia trials of 1778–1779, the defendants' ample use of the thirty-five peremptory challenges shaped the jury in significant ways. In the first trial, that of Robert Porter, the whole panel was drawn "out of the balloting box without furnishing twelve names unchallenged."[156] In the six trials that were held in May and June 1795, a total of forty jurors filled seventy-two jury seats. Twenty-one jurors served only once, ten jurors served twice, six jurors served three times, two jurors served four times, and one juror, a hatter named Benjamin Scull, served five times. Defense attorneys learned from experience. Of the twelve jurors who convicted Philip Vigol, six did not serve again; of the twelve who convicted John Mitchell, seven did not serve again. A similar pattern occurred in the two trials that were delayed until October. After the first jury acquitted, eight of the jurors reappeared in the second jury (with one of them testifying as a defense witness).[157]

Future United States Secretary of the Treasury Albert Gallatin concluded that the shrewd use of challenges contributed heavily to the verdicts. Defendant John Mitchell, Gallatin noted, was defended by a "young, unexperienced, impudent and self conceited" lawyer, who made the baffling decision to challenge all the prospective jurors from the western counties and was left with a jury of "12 Quakers," apparently "on the supposition that Quakers would condemn no person to death." He was "utterly mistaken" and the jury found Mitchell guilty. By contrast, defendant John Barnet, who, Gallatin felt, was equally as guilty as Mitchell, was defended by the savvy William Lewis, who "got a jury of a different complexion." Though the trial lasted sixteen hours, Barnet's jury took only fifteen minutes to acquit.[158] Court records bear out Gallatin's observation. Although there was significant overlap between many of the juries, there were only two jurors who served on both Mitchell's and Barnet's juries, and Mitchell's jury included the highest number of jurors who were never chosen again.[159] As it had in 1778–1779, religion played a significant role, although this time with the polarities reversed. As Gallatin explained, he agreed with the opinion of Hugh Henry Brackenridge that defendants should "always choose a jury of Quakers or at least Episcopalians in all common cases such as murder, rape & so forth, but in every possible case of insurrection, rebellion & treason, give him Presbyterians in the jury, by all means."[160]

Although Justice Paterson and Judge Peters have often been criticized for excessively partisan rulings in the cases, their actual conduct was reasonably even-handed. They postponed the trial of two men, over the prosecution's objection, so that the defense would have a reasonable time to respond to the government's witness list as well as time to bring their own witnesses from the western counties.[161] In one case, they excluded two pieces of evidence that the prosecution sought to present to the jury.[162] In another case, the jury requested a copy of Foster's *Crown Law* and the *Acts of Congress*, which the court willingly provided.[163]

The prosecution does not appear to have been expertly managed. In several cases, the prosecution struggled to satisfy the two witness requirement.[164] The most embarrassing debacle for the government came in the first trial, when "after a long examination of the witnesses, it was discovered, that the defendant . . . had taken no part in the insurrection, that, in fact, he was not the person, liable to the charge, but another person of the same name." The court accordingly directed a verdict of acquittal.[165] Prosecutor William Rawle later described it as a "circumstance not very pleasing" and blamed the incident on perjured testimony in an earlier affidavit.[166]

In the end, juries acquitted eight men and convicted only two, William Mitchell and Philip Vigol. One observer noted, "I do not think two more insignificant figures could be found in the western country."[167] Mitchell was described as a simpleton with no active role in leading the rebellion.[168] The jurors in Mitchell's case unanimously signed a petition to President Washington, stating that Mitchell was a "proper object of mercy," but providing no further explanation.[169] Mitchell's attorneys transmitted the petition, noting that it was "the unsolicited act of the jurors."[170]

Vigol, for his part, was described as a "rough ignorant German"[171] and as "a very ignorant man, said to be of an outrageous temper, and subject to occasional fits of insanity."[172] Six of the twelve jurors in Vigol's case signed a memorial to President Washington, stating only that Vigol was a "proper object of mercy."[173] The other six jurors, including the foreman, signed a more extensive memorial. These jurors had "felt themselves obliged by their oaths and affirmations to give a verdict" against Vigol, but they could not "help thinking his case, although within the letter of the law, to be a hard one, and his crime, although great, not be such as in their opinion should forfeit his life." They noted that Vigol did not play a prominent role in the rebellion, had been induced by others, had a wife and five children who depended on him, and was an "ignorant and harmless man whose existence can in no way be dangerous to security and government." Significantly, they also pointed to Pennsylvania's abolition of the death penalty for treason: "By what is generally conceived to be, and in the opinion of the jury is, a valuable improvement of the penal laws of Pennsylvania murder of the first degree alone is punished with death and high treason only with imprisonment and hard labour. The laws of the United States are not yet arrived to an equal degree of perfection and the Constitution has left to you alone the power to correct the hardships of the law."[174] William Lewis transmitted both memorials to the President, noting that the court had assigned him as Vigol's counsel. Lewis felt that the second memorial "fairly stated" the facts, but he strongly opposed the statement about the abolition of the death penalty, claiming, "had it come to my hands before the jurors who have subscribed it left the city, I should have declined any interference unless that part had been omitted."[175]

The jurors' argument about the abolition of the death penalty, however, resonated with the larger community. Alexander Hamilton later recalled that the "sentiment that their punishment ought to be remitted was universal."[176] Petitions flowed to the Washington Administration seeking mercy for both men. One petition argued, "The influence of Christian and Republican principles have lately rendered a belief almost universal throughout the United States, that the punishment of death is disproportionate to all crimes, except murder. Your petitioners therefore believe that the feelings of a majority of the Citizens of the United States will revolt at the execution of the prisoners now under sentence of death."[177] One of the most notable petitions was from the grand jury for the City of Philadelphia, chaired by William Adcock. Adcock had served as a trial juror on five of 1778–1779 Philadelphia treason trials, including the jury that convicted John Roberts. The grand jury noted that it "was forcibly impelled by a reference in the Penal Code of Pennsylvania, and to the universal horror of their fellow-citizens, at the idea of inflicting the punishment of death. If high treason had been committed against this Commonwealth, the legal sentence would only have amounted to a long imprisonment at hard labour." The grand jury urged President Washington to accommodate the "laudable sentiments" of his fellow citizens.[178]

Unsurprisingly, President Washington pardoned both men. The Whiskey Rebellion cases thus reflected a pattern similar to the cases from the 1770s. Pennsylvanians in the mid-1790s were no more willing to indict, convict, or execute people for treason than were their predecessors fifteen years earlier. With several trials still ahead of him, William Rawle explained that "a great unwillingness to say too much against their fellow citizens, a reluctance in the jury to convict the smaller engine on the testimony of their ringleaders, and a natural repugnance to capital convictions, occasioned some unexpected acquittals; and in some instances, bills were returned ignoramus, equally contrary to what appeared a grounded expectation."[179]

The trials nonetheless offered federal judges the first opportunity to construe the phrase "levying war" in the Treason Clause of the United States Constitution. In August 1794, Attorney General William Bradford had provided a legal opinion to President Washington, arguing that the resistance activities to the excise tax constituted treason. "It has been settled by uniform judicial construction," Bradford argued, "that all insurrections, risings, or armed combinations to withstand the authority or alter the lawful measures of government, to change the established law—to redress a real or pretended grievance of a public nature, and to effect other innovations of a general concern by their own authority & with force—are in construction of law high treason within the clause of levying war."[180] Treasury Secretary Alexander Hamilton agreed, more colorfully arguing in an anonymous newspaper contribution that the resistance to the excise tax was "treason against society, against liberty, against every thing that ought to be dear to a free, enlightened, and prudent people."[181]

The federal judiciary readily agreed with the Washington Administration. In October 1794, Supreme Court Justice William Cushing argued in a grand-jury charge that the Whiskey Rebellion was an act of high treason "by rising in arms to control or oppose the laws."[182] In his charge to the Philadelphia grand jury in May 1795, Justice William Paterson similarly embraced English law, arguing that "all persons, who rise in rebellion, and take up arms against the government, or who in a violent and forcible manner resist and prevent the regular administration of justice, and due execution of the laws, come within the description of levying war." Moreover, persons who "make insurrections under the pretence of redressing national or public grievances . . . or who attempt, by intimidation and violence, to force the repeal of a law, or an alteration in governmental measures" were equally guilty of levying war. An "insurrection with an avowed design to pull down all inclosures, to open all prisons, and the like" was also treasonous. The line between treason and riot was drawn by the "universality of the intention."[183]

This theme was forcefully articulated by United States Attorney William Rawle, assisting Attorney General Bradford in the prosecutions, who argued that "so frequently and fully has the offence of levying war against the government been defined, that a doubt can hardly be raised upon the subject." English precedents were fully applicable, allowing the court "in the first stage of our own experience, to acquire precise and satisfactory ideas upon the subject, from the matured experience of another government, which has employed the same language to describe the offence, and is guided by the same rules of judicial exposition." Those precedents confirmed that "raising a body of men to obtain, by intimidation or violence, the repeal of a law, or to oppose and prevent by force and terror, the execution of a law, is an act of levying war."[184]

The few surviving reports of the trials indicate that the defendants took differing approaches with respect to this definition. At the trial of Philip Vigol, for example, William Lewis conceded that the offense charged in the indictment (attacking excise officers and burning their papers) amounted to levying war against the United States and based his defense instead on the sufficiency of the evidence and a duress claim.[185]

By contrast, the lawyers for John Mitchell accepted the English precedents but sought to narrow them as much as possible.[186] They conceded that "to compel Congress to repeal a law, by violence, or intimidation, is treason," but argued that merely "resisting the execution of a law, or attempting to coerce an officer into the resignation of his commission" was not. Even if an "insurrection for the avowed purpose of suppressing all the excise offices in the United States" was an act of levying war against the United States, it did not follow "that an attempt to oblige one officer to resign, or suppress all the offices in one district, will be a crime of the same denomination." The federal government's position was a "constructive, or interpretative, weapon, which is calculated to annul all distinctions heretofore widely established in the grades and punishments of crimes; and by whose magic power a mob may be easily converted into a conspiracy; and a riot aggravated into high treason." Such "constructive or interpretative treasons must be the dread and scourge of any nation that allows them."[187]

In reply, Attorney General Bradford argued, "If it is meant by this argument, that the insurgents of Pennsylvania must have contemplated a march from Georgia to New Hampshire, it is extravagant and absurd." The requirement of universality was satisfied because "it was intended that, by their lawless career and example, Congress should be forced into a repeal of the obnoxious law, it necessarily followed, that, from the same cause, the offices of excise would be suppressed throughout the Union." The "universality of object, which the books require, was inseparable from the nature of the opposition, for it was impossible to contemplate the repeal of the excise law in one survey, or one state, without effecting it in every survey, and in every state."[188]

Justice Paterson's charge to the jury sided with Bradford. Paterson concluded that an insurrection "to suppress the excise offices, and to prevent the execution of an act of Congress, by force and intimidation" was an act of "High Treason by levying of war." The key distinction was that the rebels did not attack Neville's house because of private motives or a personal hatred; they rose to address issues of a "general and public nature."[189]

At least one member of the audience would have made an even more audacious claim for the defendants. Hugh Henry Brackenridge, a lawyer from western Pennsylvania, had been involved in various aspects of the Whiskey Rebellion, and thus was precluded from serving as a defense counsel. But he later published the arguments he would have made if he had appeared in court. Brackenridge accepted that under the English precedents the attack on Neville's house and the gathering at Braddock's field amounted to treason. But those precedents, Brackenridge argued, should be rejected. Only risings with the direct intent of overthrowing the government entirely should be considered treason by levying war against the United States: "I would therefore understand our law, as having in view only a fixed, formed, deliberate intention of subverting the government, as that offence which it will consider high treason, and punish with the loss of life itself. The accused had meditated death to the government, and the law in this case, and this case only, will meditate death to him."[190] In 1795, no lawyer had yet made that argument in court. But a few years later, after another rebellion in Pennsylvania, someone would.

Fries's Rebellion

The events that became known as "Fries's Rebellion" originated with the enactment of a federal property tax in 1798, the first direct tax imposed by the federal government. Partisan conflict was at a boiling point, and the tax proved highly controversial; for many Americans it was as contemptible as the Alien and Sedition Acts of the same year. In several Pennsylvania counties, primarily Northampton and Bucks, federal tax assessors encountered significant threats and harassment.[191]

After a federal marshal arrested a number of the tax protestors, a group of nearly four hundred armed men confronted the marshal at a tavern and successfully demanded the release of the prisoners. The men were led by a German-American Revolutionary War veteran and Federalist named John Fries, who had marched with President Washington against the Whiskey Rebels in 1794.[192] Fries and his comrades believed that the federal property tax was unconstitutional and that rescuing the prisoners was a justifiable method of countering unconstitutional governmental actions.[193] President John Adams, however, took a very different view of the matter and ordered a federal military force to march to Bucks and Northampton Counties to arrest the leading figures on charges of treason by levying war against the United States.[194]

The cases came before the April 1799 sitting of the Circuit Court for the District Court of Pennsylvania, which was presided over by United States Supreme Court Justice James Iredell, and District Judge Richard Peters, who had previously presided over the Whiskey Rebellion cases. Justice Iredell opened the court with a charge to the grand jury, denouncing the French Revolution and offering a lengthy defense of the Alien and Sedition Acts. He touched on the issue of treason only briefly, noting that if "the intention was to prevent by force of arms the execution of any act of the congress of the United States altogether . . . any forcible opposition calculated to carry that intention into effect was a levying of war against the United States." By contrast, if the intention was "merely to defeat its operation in a particular instance" because of "some private or personal motive," the defendants' actions would not amount to treason.[195]

Prosecutors submitted eleven charges of treason to the grand jury, which, curiously, included one member who had served on the jury that had convicted John Mitchell during the Whiskey Rebellion. This time, the grand jury was far more receptive to prosecutors' pleas. The grand jurors issued indictments in ten of the cases, and rejected the charges in only one.[196]

Only John Fries's case went to trial during the court's spring 1799 sitting. Fries was represented by William Lewis, Alexander Dallas, and William Ewing.[197] In an opening motion, they argued that the trial should be held in Northampton County, where the alleged overt act of treason occurred, rather than in Philadelphia.[198] The right to a local jury, Lewis insisted, "was one of the grounds of complaint to the United States, which promoted their separation from the mother country, and this was one cause of her taking up arms."[199] The court rejected this argument, but the jury that was ultimately selected included six jurors from the city of Philadelphia, four from Bucks County, and two from Northampton County. The Northampton County jurors were Germans, with limited English proficiency, and were allowed to have an interpreter.[200]

Since the facts were largely undisputed, the primary issue in the case was whether the alleged acts constituted treason by levying war against the United States. In his opening statement, prosecutor Samuel Sitgreaves, assisting William Rawle, stated the government's theory that it was treason to raise "a military force from among the people for the purpose of attaining any object with a design of opposing the lawful authority of the government by dint of arms, in some matter of public concern in which the insurgents have no particular interest distinct from the rest of the community." Such an interpretation, Sitgreaves argued, was firmly rooted in English precedents.[201]

The defense sought to parry this argument in two ways. First, in an argument advanced by William Ewing, the defense argued that Fries's views were "not of a general nature" and that he had sought only to rescue particular prisoners. After the rescue was complete, he went home and caused no further disturbance. Even accepting the English precedents, such conduct could not amount to high treason.[202]

But the second argument, advanced by William Lewis, went much further. Lewis squarely rejected the idea that English interpretations of English treason law governed the interpretation of the United States Constitution. Most of the English precedents, Lewis argued, dated from before the reforms of the 1696 Treason Trials Act and before the period of functional judicial independence. Accordingly, "[a]s we have enacted laws of our own, and have not extended the laws of England to this country, we must put our own construction on them, and not the determination of an English court."[203] Lewis proposed a fundamentally different definition of levying of war, limited to three particular acts: (1) "where a body of men take up arms, and array themselves in a martial manner against the government, with a view to put an end to its existence"; (2) "if a part of the Union throw off all allegiance and authority of the United States"; and (3) if a number of a people should "take possession of the legislative or executive authority, and by this force of arms or numbers should undertake to compel either of the departments of government to act as they dictate." Expanding the definition of levying war beyond these narrow categories would "make the constitution anything or nothing—a mere nose of wax, to be molded into any form."[204] Under this interpretation, forcible resistance to one particular law, even if animated by general, rather than private, concerns, could not amount to treason.

This argument, the narrowest interpretation of treason yet offered in an American courtroom, proved, not surprisingly, unpersuasive to the judges. In his charge to the jury, Judge Peters followed English precedents and concluded that "to oppose or prevent by force, numbers, or intimidation, a public and general law of the United States, with intent to prevent its operation, or compel its repeal" was treason by levying war."[205] Similarly, Justice Iredell advised the jury that it was treason to "oppos[e], by force of arms, an act of congress, with a view of defeating its efficacy, and thus defying the authority of the government."[206]

The trial had lasted for nine days, most likely the longest criminal trial to that point in the history of the United States. When not in court, the jury had been sequestered "in the same room at a tavern," and Justice Iredell observed that "we must be all very much fatigued."[207] After three hours of deliberation, the jury returned with a guilty verdict.[208] Justice Iredell later wrote to his wife that "though Mr. Peters and myself were clear that such ought to be the verdict, we both felt a great deal when it was actually pronounced. I could not bear to look on the poor man, but I am told he fainted away. . . . I dread the task I have to perform in pronouncing sentence on him."[209]

Five days later, however, William Lewis returned to court with a bombshell motion. He produced affidavits showing that John Rhoad, one of the German-American jurors from Northampton County, had declared before the trial that John Fries "ought to be hung." The court held an evidentiary hearing, and numerous witnesses testified that the juror had uttered these prejudicial comments.[210] Rhoad denied making the statements, and insisted that he "went to the trial . . . with a mind perfectly open . . . as to his guilt or innocence and that before I assented to the verdict I deliberately weighed and considered all that had been adduced in his favor."[211] But Justice Iredell concluded that the verdict had to be rejected. The juror may have had a "predisposed opinion of the guilt of the man"; accordingly, it was the justice's duty to "vote for a new trial in the present case, as the fact appears too clear to be controverted."[212] Judge Peters, by contrast, was not persuaded by the motion, noting that "the juror said no more than all friends to the laws and the government were warranted in thinking and saying as the facts appeared then to the public." But to prevent "a division in the court," he yielded "with some reluctance" to the opinion of Justice Iredell.[213]

Fries's retrial was delayed until the April 1800 sitting of the Pennsylvania Circuit Court. William Rawle again appeared for the government. Judge Peters was joined on the bench by Supreme Court Justice Samuel Chase. Before the jury was empaneled, Justice Chase announced that the court had issued an opinion on the meaning of levying of war. The opinion noted that although the jury had the ultimate power to decide all questions of law and fact, it was the duty of the court to offer its opinion on questions of law. And the law, Chase and Peters, declared, was clear: "[A]ny insurrection or rising of any body or people, within the United States, to attain or effect by force or violence, any object of a great public nature, or of public and general (or national) concern, is a levying war against the United States." Moreover, "any such insurrection or rising to resist or prevent by force or violence, the execution of any statute of the United States . . . is a levying of war against the United States."[214]

Pretrial rulings on contested points of law were highly unusual, and Chase's conduct in the Fries case would eventually be used against him in his 1805 impeachment trial.[215] As Stephen Presser has pointed out, "Chase's hair-trigger temper, his stubbornness, and his sense of his own judicial prerogative led him to rush precipitously into a confrontation on a sensitive jurisprudential point for which he had little support."[216] The ruling deprived the defense of its primary argument, and Fries's attorneys, William Lewis and Alexander Dallas, concluded that the best strategy was to protest the court's decision by withdrawing from the case. The withdrawal placed both Chase and Rawle in an awkward position, and after a meeting at Rawle's house, Chase offered to withdraw the opinion. But Lewis and Dallas concluded that the case had been irreparably damaged. They continued to refuse to serve as counsel and advised Fries to refuse the court's offer of appointing substitute counsel. According to Dallas, this unusual strategy was designed to maximize the likelihood of a presidential pardon in the likely event of a conviction.[217] Hanging a man who had been convicted without the assistance of counsel would be a public relations disaster for the Adams Administration, and Dallas and Lewis knew it.

The case proceeded with Chase stating that the court would act as counsel for the defense.[218] Although Fries used thirty-four of his thirty-five peremptory challenges, he asked only a few pointed questions of the witnesses and Chase did little to assist him.[219] In his charge to the jury, Chase echoed the points of his pretrial opinion, and after two hours of deliberation, the jury returned with a guilty verdict.[220]

Fries's trial was followed by several others. Rawle had brought nine treason cases to the 1800 grand jury, which issued indictments in all nine. Rawle later declined to prosecute two cases, and in two other cases, the defendant could not be found. The trials of the remaining four defendants produced mixed results.

Conrad Marks was acquitted on April 28, 1800. John Gettman and Frederic Heany were tried together, and were convicted on April 29. Finally, Anthony Stähler was acquitted on May 1. Jury challenges may have played some role in the verdicts. Of the twelve men who served on Fries's jury, ten were challenged in later cases. By contrast, none of the jurors who acquitted Conrad Marks were subsequently challenged.[221]

At the conclusion of Stähler's trial, the issue of juror misconduct arose again in Fries's case. The court was informed that juror Charles Deshler had become lost in the crowd outside of City Hall on the first night of the trial and was separated from his fellow jurors. Unsure what to do, Deshler went to the house of his brother-in-law Isaac Roush, who had served as a juror in two of the Philadelphia treason trials. Roush asked whether the jury had been discharged, and Deshler replied that it had, but that he was not supposed to speak with anyone on the subject of Fries's trial. Roush found this surprising and stated that "it did not use to be so; for the jury used to be kept together by a constable." Roush later said that "he supposed the evidence would go hard against Fries," to which Deshler replied, "Don't say anything about it for I am sworn." Deshler then returned to his house for the night, and rejoined the jury the following morning. The court concluded that the error was an innocent one and that it did not affect the validity of the verdict. The court then pronounced the death sentence on John Fries, as well as on Frederic Heany and John Gettman.[222]

As there were no criminal appeals in 1800, the defendants' only hope of escaping the gallows rested with President Adams. The president requested that Lewis and Dallas provide him with the points and authorities upon which they would have relied had they been allowed to present a full defense.[223] The two attorneys responded with a detailed letter setting out their principal arguments: (1) The trial was improper because it was held in Philadelphia County, rather than Northampton County, where the alleged events took place; (2) levying war under American law was limited to attempts to overthrow the government, and even under the English precedents, a riot to oppose a particular law had never been prosecuted as treason; and (3) Charles Deshler's separation from the jury on the first night of the trial and his conversation with Isaac Roush necessarily voided the proceedings.[224]

After receiving the defense attorneys' arguments, Adams posed fourteen pointed questions to several members of his Cabinet. Among other questions, Adams asked, "Is the execution of one or more so indispensably demanded by public justice and by the security of the public peace, that mercy cannot be extended to all three or any two or one?" "Was it any thing more than a riot, high handed, aggravated daring and dangerous indeed, for the purpose of a rescue? This is a high crime, but can it strictly amount to treason?" "Will not a career of capital executions for treason, once opened, without actual bloodshed or hostility against any military force of government inflict a deep wound in the minds of the people, inflame their animosities, and make them more desperate in sudden heats and thoughtless riots, in elections and on other occasions where political disputes run high, and introduce a more sanguinary disposition among them?"[225]

The Cabinet members responded immediately. In a brief letter, Attorney General Charles Lee, Treasury Secretary Oliver Wolcott, and Navy Secretary Benjamin Stoddert all agreed that the crimes "amounted to treason, and that no danger can arise to the community from the precedents already established by the judges upon this subject." Lee and Stoddert suggested that Fries alone should be hanged, but Wolcott favored the execution of all three defendants.[226]

Adams was unpersuaded, and the next day he directed his attorney general to issue pardons to all three convicted men, noting that he "must take on myself alone the responsibility of one more appeal to the humane and generous natures of the American people."[227] In an 1815 letter, Adams explained, "What good, what example would have been exhibited to the nation by the execution of three or four obscure, miserable Germans, as ignorant of our language as they were of our laws, and the nature and definition of treason? . . . My judgment was clear, that their crime did not amount to treason. They had been guilty of a high-handed riot and rescue, attended with circumstances hot, rash, violent, and dangerous, but all these did not amount to treason. And I thought the officers of the law had been injudicious in indicting them for any crime higher than riot, aggravated by rescue."[228]

Adams's pardon, contrary to the advice of his Cabinet, exacerbated a growing divide between Adams and the Hamiltonian faction of the Federalist Party.[229] In his notorious 1800 pamphlet attacking John Adams, Hamilton singled out the Fries pardon for special criticism. Hamilton claimed that previous lenity to persons accused of treason had led too many Pennsylvanians to assume that "neither the general nor the state government dared to inflict capital punishment."[230] Fries's execution was required, Hamilton argued, to "repress this dangerous spirit" and to teach the people that "they were the dupes of a fatal illusion."[231] "A striking demonstration" was required to prove that "condign punishment would be the lot of the violent opposers of the laws."[232] Hamilton sneered at Adams's interpretation of treason law, which he claimed was "disavowed by every page of our law books."[233]

The debate between Adams and Hamilton over the scope of the levying war provision has never been conclusively resolved. No Supreme Court decision has explicitly rejected the idea that an armed rising with the intent of suppressing a particular law is an act of high treason. In his 1964 book *The American Law of Treason: Revolutionary and Early National Origins*, Bradley Chapin went so far as to claim that the interpretation of the law by "Iredell, Peters, Patterson, and Chase . . . remains good law to this day."[234] Formally, this claim may be true. On the other hand, as James Willard Hurst argued in 1971, "this branch of the crime has become obsolete by nonuse and by critical reaction against it at the bar and in the courts."[235] Hurst probably has the better of the argument, given the tendency of early-nineteenth-century lower-court opinions to interpret the crime narrowly and the complete disappearance of such prosecutions in the twentieth century. The likelihood of a modern prosecutor seeking a treason indictment on facts similar to those of Fries's Rebellion seems vanishingly small. To that extent, at least, Adams, rather than Hamilton, has been vindicated by history.

* * *

The Fries cases marked the end of the trials of allegiance in Pennsylvania. The issue of treason did not disappear completely—there would later be indictments for treason in Pennsylvania arising from opposition to the Fugitive Slave Act, from the Homestead Strike, and from World War I.[236] But the issue of treason would not dominate political and legal events in the way that it had from 1765 to 1800. The imprecation of treason would no longer hang over the head of every American. The convulsive civil war had ended, and a new nation, formed by people from around the world, willingly shedding their old allegiances in favor of a new one, could finally emerge.

Conclusion

THE PENNSYLVANIA THAT greeted the nineteenth century was a very different place from the one that had greeted William Penn as he disembarked from the *Welcome* nearly 120 years earlier. The peaceable kingdom in which Penn had invested such hopes had become the scene of bloody, fratricidal warfare that fundamentally transformed the colony's identity. The Pennsylvanians once ferociously loyal to their English king were now citizens of the United States of America, a new nation that, like its English predecessor, would demand allegiance from all within its borders.

As this book has sought to demonstrate, the American Revolution cannot be fully understood without careful attention to the role of the law of treason. Prior to independence, arguments over British policies and the rights of British subjects were drenched in the rhetoric of treason. The question posed in February 1775—"What is treason in relation to the present contention, and who are the traitors, those who oppose or those who endeavor to support and enforce the new-fangled laws?"—was perhaps the most fundamental question of American politics.[1] When the war erupted a few months later, the men tried by the committees of safety could be confident that the question had already been answered. Rather than being celebrated for their loyalty to their English king, they were imprisoned for treason against America. When the Declaration of Independence cleared away any remaining legal obstacles to the execution of traitors, the states responded aggressively, by enacting new treason legislation and ferreting out perceived disloyal individuals. When cases of treason finally appeared in the courts of law, Americans of all social classes played a role in the legal proceedings, whether as judges, jurors, defendants, witnesses, or bondsmen.

In answering the question of who was the traitor, revolutionary Americans necessarily had to grapple with the concept of allegiance. The rhetoric uncovered in this volume was unmistakably nationalist. Even prior to the Declaration of Independence it was common to speak of "treason against America." By late 1776, people were being imprisoned for "treason against the United States of America." This terminology was not merely the accidental byproduct of thirteen independent nations temporarily allied together against a common enemy. No one in World War II spoke of treason against the Allies; no one in the Korean War pointed to the dangers of treason against the United Nations. The phrase "treason against the United States of America" necessarily implied that there was a legally binding allegiance to the United States, reflecting both a common national citizenship and a common national identity.

But the new allegiance would ultimately not be enforced by the gallows. Even in the midst of a tumultuous, violent civil war drenched with vicious rhetoric against Tories and traitors, revolutionary Americans were unwilling to see their fellow citizens executed for crimes of disloyalty. No state engaged in wholesale executions of traitors or political dissidents during the war. As Bradley Chapin observed, "Drastic purges and violent assizes were not a part of the Revolution. There was no reign of terror. The record is one of substantial justice done."[2]

The states varied, however, in how this aversion to capital punishment was expressed. In Pennsylvania, there were few executions because grand juries refused to indict and trial juries refused to convict. But in other states, jury lenity was less significant. The more typical pattern was that juries regularly convicted defendants of treason, but the executive authority intervened with a pardon.

The aversion was not to capital punishment as such. The states did not hesitate to execute murderers, rapists, and burglars. Treason was different. Although in theory the highest crime a person could commit, the theory collapsed upon contact with reality. A person who made the wrong choice in a bitterly divisive civil war was a serious threat, but not an incorrigible criminal beyond possibility of redemption. Every American knew someone, perhaps even a family member or a close friend, who had chosen the other side. As such, British adherents could not be viewed as sinister and alien beings, but as fundamentally normal people who had made a political mistake.[3]

The war necessarily required a balancing of the demands of security with the protection of basic civil liberties. In this regard, revolutionary Pennsylvania produced a highly mixed record. The roster on the negative side includes the trials by committees of safety without juries prior to independence; the execution of at least one civilian by military authority; the suspension of habeas corpus and the exile of prominent Quakers to Virginia, a move clearly tainted by religious bigotry; the widespread use of proclamations of attainder; the legislature's authorization of unreviewable executive detentions; and the state-sanctioned execution of a man without a trial. From this perspective, the state government appears to have run wild, unrestrained by traditional legal norms and fundamentally subverting the fundamental rights of citizens.

On the positive side, however, the worst problems disappeared once a functioning court system was in place. Courts enforced the right of individuals to challenge their detentions through the writ of habeas corpus. Military jurisdiction over civilians was recognized as an anomaly, justifiable only in the absence of regularly constituted courts. Once courts were operating, Americans who joined or aided the British army were generally not subject to military jurisdiction, but were handed over to the civil courts for trial and punishment.[4] Persons accused of treason were tried by juries of their peers; they were provided with experienced, competent counsel far superior to that provided to most capital defendants today; judicial rulings were reasonably balanced; and most defendants escaped with an acquittal.

Institutions thus mattered greatly. Whereas the Assembly and the Supreme Executive Council were frequently inclined to impulsive actions, the courts functioned in a more deliberate manner. Much credit, of course, goes to Chief Justice McKean, who maintained a deep commitment to the rule of law even in the midst of a tumultuous civil war. But one should be careful not to overstate McKean's role. One scholar has argued that "[t]he personality of Chief Justice Thomas McKean combined with the political interests of the state explain why only Abraham Carlisle and John Roberts suffered the hangman's noose."[5] McKean was important, but the juries were equally important. Juries in revolutionary Pennsylvania were independent, deliberative bodies that played a major role in shaping the administration of criminal justice. All the evidence indicates that jurors took their responsibilities seriously and were perfectly willing to make unpopular decisions. As the democratic branch of the judicial department, juries reflected community values, but they did not mindlessly yield to the passions of the moment.

Both judges and juries operated largely within well-established English legal norms. Despite the overthrow of English government, English procedures dominated the treatment of treason. Lawyers and judges relied on English precedents and English treatises, and they employed the jury trial as it had developed in England. The procedures included the thirty-five peremptory challenges granted to the defense, which were skillfully employed by Pennsylvania defense counsel to create more favorable juries. Peremptory challenges enabled certain jurors to serve repeatedly and to draw on significant prior experience during deliberations. The jurors did not operate in a vacuum, but against the informative backdrop of numerous similar cases.

The attentive reader will have no doubt noted the numerous resonances that many of the debates in revolutionary Pennsylvania have with the present day.

When I began researching this subject in 1996, it was almost entirely of historical interest. After September 11, 2001, the issues discussed during the revolution seemed almost eerily prescient of modern concerns. Were there hidden enemies in the United States just waiting to launch a nefarious plot? If so, what tools could we use to identify them? If we captured them, could we use military authority to detain them? What process, if any, should such detainees receive? What was the role of courts in safeguarding civil liberties? History never repeats itself, but it does echo, and there is much to learn from the experience of our predecessors addressing issues not entirely dissimilar to our own. If we listen closely, we can hear the drums beating on the streets of Philadelphia as furious men march a suspected Tory through the streets. We can hear the guns of the British army as it marches on the Pennsylvania capital. And we can hear the lawyers, arguing and debating in Independence Hall. In the Assembly Room, they are declaring independence and framing the Constitution. Across the center corridor, in the courtroom, they are prosecuting, defending, and presiding over the trials of allegiance, deeply committed to the fundamental American ideal that the laws do not go silent, even in time of war.

APPENDIX I

Juror Assignments: Philadelphia Treason Trials, 1778–1779

Key: A: Carlisle; B: Ming; C: John Roberts; D: Turner; E: Deshong; F: Cook; G: Hamilton; H: Woolfall; I: Piles; J: James Roberts; K: Guion; L: Wright; M: Copeland; N: Devenderfer; O: Hunstman; P: Stricker; Q: Bolton; R: Harry; S: Hathe; T: Garrigues; U: Whitefield; V: Harding*

Juror	Total #	Trials
Adcock	5	C, H, I, P, S
Albertson	4	H, I, M, N
Barns	1	C
Barnhill	4	H, I, N, S
Beach	1	L
Bitting	1	O
Burkhard	1	C
Campbell	4	N, P, Q, R
Clumberg	1	A
Corgee	5	C, K, S, U, V
Dickinson	15	A, H, I, J, K, M, N, O, P, Q, R, S, T, U, V
Dowig	6	E, F, M, P, Q, T
Drinker	20	A, B, C, D, E, F, G, H, I, J, K, M, O, P, Q, R, S, T, U, V
Eckhart	5	E, O, Q, S, T
Esler	9	B, F, G, J, L, N, P, R, T

Juror	Total #	Trials
Falconer	12	D, F, G, H, I, K, N, P, Q, R, U, V
Forsberg	3	D, U, V
Forsyth	1	C
Gamble	1	D
Gottier	2	F, K
Goucher	3	A, O, T
Gray	3	D, E, F
Grove	1	O
Hale	1	M
Heidel	3	H, I, L
Hood	4	C, H, I, J
Humphreys	1	D
Jackson	3	A, R, S
January	2	U, V
Linnington	1	L
Lynn	1	A
McClenachan	1	G
McLane	1	M
McNeal	6	C, G, H, I, J, T
Merriam	11	D, E, H, I, J, K, L, M, N, P, Q
J. Palmer	9	A, D, E, F, G, L, T, U, V
T. Palmer	18	A, B, D, E, F, G, J, K, M, N, O, P, Q, R, S, T, U, V
Pancoast	4	B, C, G, R
Pickering	3	S, U, V
Piles	9	E, F, G, J, K, N, O, Q, T
Powell	17	A, B, C, D, E, G, H, I, J, K, L, M, P, Q, R, S, T
Pringle	6	B, D, G, J, M, Q
Reese	11	A, B, D, F, K, M, O, P, Q, U, V
Rigden	1	C
Ritter	1	S
Roop	1	L
I. Roush	2	B, L
J. Roush	1	B
Rush	9	H, I, J, K, L, M, N, O, P

Juror	Total #	Trials
Shields	3	A, F, R
Simpson	3	E, F, G
Skinner	2	L, N
Steinmetz	4	C, K, L, R
Uttree	4	A, B, U, V
Wilkinson	2	B, E
G. Wilson	7	N, O, R, S, T, U, V
J. Wilson	1	O
Zantzinger	3	B, E, J

* For full information on the defendants and their trials, see Table 7.1. The data presented here exclude the trial of James Stevens, for which no juror information is available. The oyer and terminer docket book appears to be in error with respect to Abraham Carlisle's jury. The court clerk appears to have erroneously copied the jury list for Peter Deshong into the court's docket book under Carlisle's name. For the accurate jury list, see Notes of C.J. McKean in *Case of Ab'm Carlisle,* 1778, *Pa. Archives*, 7:44; Memorial of Jurors and Judges in Favor of Ar'm Carlisle, *Pa. Archives*, 7:52.

APPENDIX 2

Jury Trials for High Treason in Pennsylvania during the American Revolution

Date	*County*	*Location*	*Defendant*	*Verdict*
Sept. 18, 1778	Chester		Joseph Malin	NG
Sept. 25, 1778	Philadelphia	College of Philadelphia	Abraham Carlisle	G
Sept. 28, 1778	Philadelphia	College of Philadelphia	Jacob Ming	NG
Sept. 30, 1778	Philadelphia	College of Philadelphia	John Roberts	G
Sept. 28–Oct. 2, 1778	Bedford		Peter Potmercer	NG
Sept. 28–Oct. 2, 1778	Bedford		Jacob Yost	NG
Sept. 28–Oct. 2, 1778	Bedford		Adam Potmercer, Jr.	NG
Oct. 3, 1778	Philadelphia	College of Philadelphia	Joseph Turner, Jr.	NG
Oct. 7, 1778	Philadelphia	College of Philadelphia	Peter Deshong	NG
Oct. 9, 1778	Philadelphia	College of Philadelphia	George Cook, Jr.	NG

Date	*County*	*Location*	*Defendant*	*Verdict*
Oct. 18, 1778	Philadelphia	College of Philadelphia	William Hamilton	NG
Oct. 20–27, 1778	Bucks	Newtown Courthouse	Thomas Yardley	NG
Oct. 26, 1778	Bucks	Newtown Courthouse	John Ellwood	G
Oct. 20–27, 1778	Bucks	Newtown Courthouse	John Tomlinson	NG
Oct. 20–27, 1778	Bucks	Newtown Courthouse	Richard Tomlinson	NG
Oct. 20–27, 1778	Bucks	Newtown Courthouse	William Davis	NG
Oct. 20–27, 1778	Bucks	Newtown Courthouse	John Poor	NG
Nov. 11, 1778	Philadelphia	College of Philadelphia	Charles Woolfall	NG
Nov. 11, 1778	Philadelphia	College of Philadelphia	Samuel Piles	NG
Nov. 13, 1778	Philadelphia	College of Philadelphia	James Roberts	NG
Nov. 16, 1778	Philadelphia	College of Philadelphia	Lewis Guion	NG
Nov. 18, 1778	Philadelphia	College of Philadelphia	Abijah Wright	G*
Nov. 21, 1778	Philadelphia	College of Philadelphia	David Copeland	NG
Nov. 24, 1778	Philadelphia	College of Philadelphia	George Devenderfer	NG
Nov. 25, 1778	Philadelphia	College of Philadelphia	John Huntsman	NG
Nov. 27, 1778	Philadelphia	College of Philadelphia	Adam Stricker	NG
Nov. 28, 1778	Philadelphia	College of Philadelphia	Joseph Bolton	NG
Nov. 30, 1778	Philadelphia	College of Philadelphia	Aubrey Harry	NG

Date	*County*	*Location*	*Defendant*	*Verdict*
Dec. 4, 1778	Philadelphia	College of Philadelphia	Andrew Hathe	NG
April 6, 1779	Philadelphia		Samuel Garrigues	NG
April 8, 1779	Philadelphia		William Whitefield	NG
April 8, 1779	Philadelphia		George Harding	G
April?, 1779	Philadelphia		James Stevens	NG
Sept./Oct. 1779	Philadelphia	State House	John Holder	NG
Sept. 28, 1779	Philadelphia	State House	Robert Strettel Jones	NG
Sept./Oct. 1779	Philadelphia	State House	Edward Cutbush	NG
Oct. 2, 1779	Philadelphia	State House	Joseph Wirt	NG
Nov./Dec. 1779	Philadelphia	State House	Peter Miller	NG
Nov./Dec. 1779	Philadelphia	State House	William Cassedy	G
Nov./Dec. 1779	Philadelphia	State House	Richard Mason	NG
April 27, 1780	Chester		Justin McCarty	NG
Nov. 2, 1780	Northampton	Northampton County Court House, Centre Square, Easton, PA	Ralph Morden	G
April 1781	Philadelphia	State House	Justin McCarty	NG
Dec. 29, 1781	Bucks		George Clift	G
April 29, 1782	Chester		Peter Kerr	NG
Sept 30, 1782	Philadelphia	State House	Joshua Buffington	NG

* Wright was indicted for burglary and treason, and convicted on the burglary charge. There is no record of a verdict on the treason charge.

APPENDIX 3

Jury Trials for High Treason, United States Circuit Court for the District of Pennsylvania, 1795–1800, Held at City Hall in Philadelphia

Date	*Defendant(s)*	*Verdict*	*Defense Counsel*
May 18, 1795	Robert Porter	NG	?
May 22–23, 1795	Philip Vigol	G	William Lewis/ Moses Levy
May 25, 1795	John Mitchell	G	Edward Tilghman/ Joseph Thomas
May 28, 1795	Marmaduke Curtis	NG	?
May 29, 1795	John Barnet	NG	?
June 1, 1795	Thomas Miller	NG	William Lewis/ Joseph Thomas
Oct. 16, 1795	David Bolton & Ebenezer Gallagher	NG	William Lewis/ William Clark
Oct. 19–22, 1795	James Stewart & Edward Wright	NG	William Lewis
May 1–9, 1799	John Fries	G	William Lewis/ Alexander Dallas/ William Ewing
April 24–25, 1800	John Fries	G	None

Date	*Defendant(s)*	*Verdict*	*Defense Counsel*
April 26–28, 1800	Conrad Marks	NG	Thomas Ross/ Joseph Hopkinson
April 28–29, 1800	John Gettman & Frederic Heany	G	Moses Levy/ Edward Tilghman
April 30–May 1, 1800	Anthony Stähler	NG	Thomas Ross/ Joseph Hopkinson

Abbreviations

MANUSCRIPT COLLECTIONS

APS	American Philosophical Society, Philadelphia, PA
HSP	Historical Society of Pennsylvania, Philadelphia, PA
PSA	Pennsylvania State Archives, Pennsylvania Historical and Museum Commission, Harrisburg, PA

PUBLISHED MATERIALS

Col. Records	*Colonial Records of Pennsylvania,* 16 vols. (Harrisburg, PA: Pennsylvania Historical & Museum Commission, 1851–1853)
LDC	*Letters of Delegates to Congress, 1774–1789,* 25 vols. (Washington, DC: Library of Congress, 1976–2000)
JCC	*Journals of the Continental Congress,* 34 vols. (Washington, DC: Library of Congress, 1904-1937)
Pa. Archives	*Pennsylvania Archives,* 119 vols. (Harrisburg, PA: Pennsylvania Historical & Museum Commission, 1852–1935)
Pa. Stat.	*The Statutes at Large of Pennsylvania,* 18 vols. (Harrisburg, PA: State Printer of Pennsylvania, 1896–1915)
PMHB	*Pennsylvania Magazine of History & Biography*
SCP	*The Susquehannah Company Papers,* 11 vols. (Ithaca, NY: Cornell Univ. Press, 1962–1971)

Notes

INTRODUCTION

1. James Wilson, *Considerations on the Nature and Extent of the Legislative Authority of the British Parliament* (Philadelphia: William Bradford, 1774).
2. The Memorial and Representation of a Deputation from the Several Battalions of Militia of the City and Liberties of Philadelphia, Oct. 8, 1779, Stauffer Collection, 9:633, HSP.
3. See generally Holger Hoock, *Scars of Independence: America's Violent Birth* (New York: Crown, 2017).
4. Hector St. John de Crevecouer, *Sketches of Eighteenth Century America*, ed. Henri Bourdin, Ralph Henry Gabriel & Stanley Thomas Williams (New Haven, CT: Yale Univ. Press, 1925), 178.
5. Robert Ferguson, *Reading the Early Republic* (Cambridge, MA: Harvard Univ. Press, 2004), 120.
6. The best twenty-first-century work on Loyalism is Maya Jasanoff, *Liberty's Exiles: American Loyalists in the Revolutionary World* (New York: Knopf, 2011). For a military perspective see Thomas B. Allen, *Tories, Fighting for the King in America's First Civil War* (New York: Harper, 2010). Classic older works include William H. Nelson, *The American Tory* (Oxford: Oxford Univ. Press, 1961), and Robert Calhoon, *The Loyalists in Revolutionary America, 1760–1781* (New York: Harcourt, 1973). On spies and plots, see Carl Van Doren, *The Secret History of the American Revolution* (New York: Viking Press, 1941).
7. For a study of similar shifting loyalties and trials of treason in the Netherlands in the late 1500s, see Henk van Nierop, *Treason in the Northern Quarter: War, Terror, and the Rule of Law in the Dutch Revolt*, trans. J.C. Grayson (Princeton, NJ: Princeton Univ. Press, 2009).

8. Eric Foner, *Tom Paine and Revolutionary America* (New York: Oxford Univ. Press, 1976), 19, 21.
9. Billy G. Smith, "Philadelphia: The Athens of America," in *Life in Early Philadelphia*, ed. Billy G. Smith (College Station: Penn. St. Univ. Press, 1995), 3.
10. Eminent legal historian John Philip Reid has noted a similar problem in his study of the New Hampshire judiciary. Reid observes that we lack "the scholarly research to make comparative studies of the state judiciaries between the colonial period and the Civil War. . . . By necessity, the story that the three books tell has to be one with little comparisons." John Philip Reid, *Legitimating the Law: The Struggle for Judicial Competency in Early National New Hampshire* (DeKalb, IL: NIU Press, 2012), 3–5. Reid notes, however, that the "the most interesting jurisdiction will be Pennsylvania." Ibid., 4.
11. Harold M. Hyman & Catherine M. Tarrant, "Aspects of American Trial Jury History," in *The Jury System in America: A Critical Overview*, ed. Rita James Simon (Beverly Hills, CA: Sage Publications, 1975), 23; see also Albert W. Alschuler & Andrew G. Deiss, "A Brief History of the Criminal Jury in the United States," *U. Chi. L. Rev.* 61 (1994): 867, 867–869 (noting general lack of historical scholarship on American juries).
12. John M. Murrin, "Magistrates, Sinners, and a Precarious Liberty: Trial by Jury in Seventeenth-Century New England," in *Saints & Revolutionaries: Essays on Early American History*, ed. David D. Hall, John M. Murrin & Thad W. Tate (New York: Norton, 1984), 152, 153.
13. Such works include Daniel D. Blinka, "Trial by Jury on the Eve of the Revolution: The Virginia Experience," *UMKC L. Rev.* 71 (2003): 529-581; Daniel D. Blinka, "Jefferson & Juries: The Problem of Law, Reason & Politics in the New Republic," *Am. J. Legal Hist.* 47 (2005): 35-103; James D. Rice, "The Criminal Trial before and after the Lawyers: Authority, Law and Culture in Maryland Jury Trials, 1681–1837," *Am. J. Legal Hist.* 40 (1996): 455-475. On civil juries in colonial Connecticut, see Bruce H. Mann, *Neighbors & Strangers: Law and Community in Early Connecticut* (Chapel Hill: UNC Press, 1987), 67–81.
14. J.R. Pole, "Further Reflections on Law in the American Revolution," *Wm. & Mary Q.* 50 (1993): 594, 597. On the importance of juries in late-eighteenth-century America, see also Akhil Reed Amar, *The Bill of Rights* (New Haven, CT: Yale Univ. Press, 1998), 81–118.
15. Bruce H. Mann, "The Evolutionary Revolution in American Law: A Comment on J.R. Pole's 'Reflections,'" *Wm. & Mary Q.* 50 (1993): 168, 169.
16. James Willard Hurst, *The Law of Treason in the United States: Collected Essays* (Westport, CT: Greenwood Publishing Corp., 1971), 11. Hurst's work, originally developed for briefs in a 1944 treason case in the United States Supreme Court, nonetheless relied almost entirely on published sources. Hurst argued that "records of trials for treason are scant and do not contribute as much as statutory material to

outlining the attitudes taken towards the crime." Ibid., 83. This book contends that far more attention to trials is warranted.

17. Steven Wilf, *Law's Imagined Republic* (Cambridge: Cambridge Univ. Press, 2010), 196.
18. On this problem, see James H. Merrell, "'Exactly as They Appear': Another Look at the Notes of a 1766 Treason Trial in Poughkeepsie, New York, with Some Musings on the Documentary Foundations of Early American History," *Early American Studies* 12 (2014): 202–237.
19. The case for "disaffected" is forcefully made in Anne Ousterhout, *A State Divided: Opposition in Pennsylvania to the American Revolution* (New York: Greenwood Press, 1987), 1–7. On the general problem, see also Robert Calhoon, *The Loyalists in Revolutionary America, 1760–1781* (New York: Harcourt Brace Jovanovich, 1973), xi–xii.

CHAPTER 1

1. Hans Fantel, *William Penn: Apostle of Dissent* (New York: William Morrow, 1974), 1.
2. Bushel's Case, 124 Eng. Rep. 1006 (C.P. 1670).
3. See generally Craig W. Horle, *The Quakers and the English Legal System 1660–1688* (Philadelphia: Univ. of Penn. Press, 1988), 101–120. On Pennsylvania's early criminal-law and judicial system, see Jack D. Marietta & G.S. Rowe, *Troubled Experiment: Crime and Justice in Pennsylvania, 1682–1800* (Philadelphia: Univ. of Penn. Press, 2006), ch. 1; G.S. Rowe, *Embattled Bench: The Pennsylvania Supreme Court and the Forging of a Democratic Society, 1684–1809* (Newark: Univ. of Delaware Press, 1994), chs. 1–3; William H. Loyd, *The Early Courts of Pennsylvania* (Boston: Boston Book, 1910); John Smolenski, *Friends and Strangers: The Making of a Creole Culture in Colonial Pennsylvania* (Philadelphia: Univ. of Penn. Press, 2010), ch. 3; William E. Nelson, "Government by Judiciary: The Growth of Judicial Power in Colonial Pennsylvania," *SMU L. Rev.* 59 (2006): 3–53.
4. Act of 1690, ch. 197, *Pa. Stat.*, 1:138, 139; Act of May 31, 1693, ch. 88, *Pa. Stat.*, 1:192; Act of Nov. 27, 1700, ch. 100, *Pa. Stat.*, 2:134; Act of Oct. 28, 1701, ch. 106, *Pa. Stat.*, 2:148, 151; Act of Feb. 28, 1711, ch. 168, *Pa. Stat.*, 2:301, 310; Act of May 28, 1715, ch. 202, *Pa. Stat.*, 3:33; Act of May 28, 1715, ch. 203, *Pa. Stat.*, 3:65, 68–69.
5. Act of 1684, ch. 171, *Pa. Stat.*, 1:122.
6. Act of Nov. 27, 1700, ch. 47, *Pa. Stat.*, 2:52; Act of Nov. 27, 1700, ch. 14, *Pa. Stat.*, 2:14.
7. For a thorough overview of the problem, see Joseph H. Smith, "The English Criminal Law in Early America," in *The English Legal System: Carryover to the Colonies* (Los Angeles: William Andrews Clark Memorial Library, Univ. of Cal., 1975), 3–60; see also Herbert A. Johnson, "English Statutes in Colonial New York," in Herbert A. Johnson, *Essays on New York Colonial Legal History* (Westport, CT: Greenwood, 1981), 193–212.

8. Andrew R. Murphy, *Liberty, Conscience, and Toleration: The Political Thought of William Penn* (New York: Oxford Univ. Press, 2016), 62–69.
9. Loyd, *Early Courts*, 52.
10. Act of May 31, 1718, ch. 236, *Pa. Stat.*, 3:199, 200.
11. For background and subsequent implementation of the Statute of Treasons, see J.G. Bellamy, *The Law of Treason in England in the Later Middle Ages* (Cambridge: Cambridge Univ. Press, 1970). For an eighteenth-century defense of acts of attainder under 25 Edward III, see Richard West, *A Discourse Concerning Treasons, and Bills of Attainder*, 2d ed. (London: J. Roberts, 1717).
12. Edward Coke, *The Third Part of the Institutes of the Laws of England*, 5th ed. (1671), 2.
13. David Cressy, *Dangerous Talk: Scandalous, Seditious, and Treasonable Speech in Pre-Modern England* (Oxford: Oxford Univ. Press, 2010); John Bellamy, *The Tudor Law of Treason: An Introduction* (London: Routledge, 1979).
14. The development of the idea of treason against the state is carefully and thoughtfully traced in D. Alan Orr, *Treason and the State: Law, Politics, and Ideology in the English Civil War* (Cambridge: Cambridge Univ. Press, 2002). A related argument is made in Lisa Steffen, *Defining a British State: Treason and National Identity, 1608–1820* (Basingstoke, UK: Palgrave, 2001). Cf. *A Short Review of a Late Pamphlet, Intituled, Some Considerations on the Law of Forfeitures for High Treason* (London: J. Roberts, 1746), 62 ("Treason against our Country is Treason against our King, and Treason against our King is Treason against our Country").
15. Orr, *Treason and the State*, 30.
16. Ibid., 173.
17. For a vigorous defense of the proceedings against Charles I, arguing that they represent the first modern trial of a head of state for waging war against his own people, see Geoffrey Robertson, *The Tyrannicide Brief: The Story of the Man Who Sent Charles I to the Scaffold* (London: Random House, 2005).
18. The interregnum between the flight of James II and the declaration of William and Mary as joint monarchs raised the question whether treason could be committed in the absence of a king. Although an argument was made that treason could be made "against the people or the state," several judges concluded that the offense of treason required a king. Richard S. Kay, *The Glorious Revolution and the Continuity of Law* (Washington: Catholic Univ. of Am. Press, 2014), 260.
19. "Pine's Case," *A Complete Collection of State Trials*, ed. T.B. Howell (London: T.C. Hansard, 1816), 3:359, 367.
20. William Hawkins, *A Treatise of the Pleas of the Crown* (London: Elizabeth Nutt, 1716), 38–39; Michael Foster, *A Report of Some Proceedings on the Commission of Oyer and Terminer and Goal Delivery for the Trial of the Rebels in the Year 1746 in the County of Surry, and of Other Crown Cases, To Which are Added Discourses upon a Few Branches of the Crown Law* (Oxford: Clarendon Press, 1762), 200–207; William Blackstone, *Commentaries on the Laws of England* (Oxford: Clarendon

Press, 1769), 4:79–81. Nonetheless, a New York grand jury charge from 1727 asserted that "learned Lawyers are on both Sides of the Question" whether words amounted to treason. Lewis Morris's Charge, New York City, March, 1727, in *Gentlemen of the Grand Jury: The Surviving Grand Jury Charges from Colonial, State, and Lower Federal Courts before 1801*, ed. Stanton D. Krauss (Durham, NC: Carolina Academic Press, 2012), 1:645.

21. For a detailed explication of this point, see Carlton F.W. Larson, "The Forgotten Constitutional Law of Treason and the Enemy Combatant Problem," *Univ. of Penn. Law Review* 154, no. 4 (2006): 863, 874–878.
22. Edward Coke, *The Third Part of the Institutes of the Laws of England* (1644), excerpted in *The Selected Writings of Sir Edward Coke*, ed. Steven Sheppard (Indianapolis, IN: Liberty Fund, 2003), 2:958.
23. William Hawkins, *A Treatise of the Pleas of the Crown* (London: Eliz. Nutt, 1716; reprint, New York: Garland Publishing, 1978), 35.
24. Larson, "The Forgotten Constitutional Law of Treason," 878–900.
25. On the Treason Trials Act, see generally John H. Langbein, *The Origins of Adversary Criminal Trial* (Oxford: Oxford Univ. Press, 2003), ch. 2.
26. Act of May 31, 1718, ch. 236, *Pa. Stat.*, 3:199, 201.
27. The Charter of Privileges to the Province and Counties (1701), in *The Earliest Printed Laws of Pennsylvania 1681–1713*, ed. John D. Cushing (Wilmington, DE: Michael Glazier, 1978).
28. Blackstone, *Commentaries*, 4:92.
29. Bellamy, *Tudor Law of Treason*, 201.
30. David William Vorhees, "The 'Fervent Zeale' of Jacob Leisler," *William & Mary Q.* 51 (1994): 447–472.
31. *N.Y. Gazette*, Sept. 1, 1766; *N.Y. Gazette*, Feb. 23, 1767.
32. See, e.g., *N.Y. Gazette*, July 15, 1771; *Mass. Spy*, July 25, 1771; *N.H. Gazette*, July 26, 1771; *Pa. Gazette*, July 18, 1771.
33. Marjoleine Kars, *Breaking Loose Together: The Regulator Rebellion in Pre-Revolutionary North Carolina* (Chapel Hill: UNC Press, 2002), 1, 207. Although most American states changed the punishment to hanging during the Revolution, the old punishment occasionally reappeared. The Maryland General Court imposed the sentence on John Tims in 1778, but he was eventually pardoned. Ronald Hoffman, *A Spirit of Dissension: Economics, Politics, and the Revolution in Maryland* (Baltimore: Johns Hopkins Univ. Press, 1973), 238–239. In 1779, the sentence was delivered to Joseph Judson in Delaware, but he was subsequently reprieved. G.S. Rowe, *Thomas McKean and the Shaping of American Republicanism* (Boulder, CO: Associated University Press, 1978), 435 n.44. Delaware imposed the sentence again on eight convicted traitors in 1780, but they all received pardons. Harold B. Hancock, *The Loyalists of Revolutionary Delaware* (Newark: Univ. of Delaware Press, 1977), 92; Jeffery M. Dorwart, *Invasion and Insurrection: Security, Defense, and War in the Delaware Valley, 1621-1815* (Newark: Univ. of Delaware

Press, 2008), 154. Maryland imposed the sentence on seven convicted traitors in 1781, but the sentences were later commuted. Harry M. Ward, *The War for Independence and the Transformation of American Society* (London: UCL Press, 1999), 44; Bradley Chapin, *The American Law of Treason: Revolutionary and Early National Origins* (Seattle: University of Washington Press, 1964), 70. The Maryland sentence was reproduced, in both English and German, in a broadside published in Philadelphia. *Sentence of Death for High Treason* (Philadelphia: 1781). A former resident of Pennsylvania was convicted of high treason in Quebec and was executed under the British punishment in 1797. *The Trial, Condemnation and Horrid Execution of David McLean* (Windham, CT: John Byrne, 1797), 11–12. During the War of 1812, British officials imposed the punishment in Canada, but allowed the defendants to die from hanging before mutilating their bodies. Alan Taylor, *The Civil War of 1812: American Citizens, British Subjects, Irish Rebels, & Indian Allies* (New York: Knopf, 2010), 316.

34. Edwin Wolf II, *The Book Culture of a Colonial American City: Philadelphia Books, Bookmen, and Booksellers* (Oxford: Oxford Univ. Press, 1988), ch. 4; *The Charter, Laws, and Catalogue of Books, of the Library Company of Philadelphia* (Philadelphia: B. Franklin & D. Hall, 1764), 13, 16–17.
35. On the 1715 rebellion and the fate of captured Jacobites, see Margaret Sankey, *Jacobite Prisoners of the 1715 Rebellion: Preventing and Punishing Insurrection in Early Hanoverian Britain* (Aldershot, UK: Ashgate, 2005); Daniel Szechi, *1715: The Great Jacobite Rebellion* (New Haven, CT: Yale Univ. Press, 2006), ch. 8.
36. See, e.g., Commonplace Book of James Wilson, James Wilson Papers, HSP, which contains a detailed explication of English treason statutes, particularly the famous statute of 25 Edward III.
37. *Am. Weekly Mercury*, Oct. 20, 1720, 3. Hunt's wife was convicted for "uttering the said Money, knowing it to be counterfeit." She was fined five hundred pounds and sentenced to life imprisonment. Ibid. She was pardoned several years later. Minutes of the Provincial Council, March 13, 1724/1725, *Col. Records*, 3:244.
38. Bellamy, *Tudor Law of Treason*, 60. James Wilson noted this statute in his commonplace book. James Wilson, Commonplace Book, 33, James Wilson Papers, HSP.
39. *Am. Weekly Mercury*, Nov. 24, 1720, 2. In 1757, English legal officials concluded that the Statute of Mary did not apply in Nova Scotia. Smith, "English Criminal Law," 15. The statute's application to Pennsylvania in 1720 would have rested on the 1718 statute adopting English law. In the 1760s, it was still viewed as an open question whether the English counterfeiting laws applied in Massachusetts. Thomas Hutchinson's Charge, Suffolk County, August, 1766, in *Gentlemen of the Grand Jury*, 1:319.
40. Minutes of the Provincial Council, Nov. 5 & 9, 1720, *Col. Records*, 3:103–105. For an analysis of Hunt's gallows address, see Michael Meranze, *Laboratories of Virtue: Punishment, Revolution, and Authority in Philadelphia, 1765–1835* (Chapel Hill: UNC Press, 1996), 39–41.

41. Blackstone, *Commentaries*, 4:93.
42. *Pa. Chronicle*, April 16, 1770; *The Life and Confession of Herman Rosencrantz, Executed in the City of Philadelphia, on the 5th Day of May, 1770, for Counterfeiting and Uttering the Bills of Credit of the Province of Pennsylvania* (Philadelphia: James Chattin, 1770); *Pa. Packet*, April 18, 1774, 4; *Pa. Packet*, June 5, 1775, 3.
43. E.g., Act of Sept. 28, 1773, ch. 686, *Pa. Stat.*, 8:339 (punishing as a capital crime the counterfeiting of the paper money of other colonies); see also Herbert Fitzroy, "The Punishment of Crime in Provincial Pennsylvania," *PMHB* 60 (1936): 242, 256 n.56; Harold Gillingham, *Counterfeiting in Colonial Pennsylvania* (New York: American Numismatic Society, 1939); Kenneth Scott, *Counterfeiting in Colonial America* (New York: American Numismatic Society, 1955).
44. William Bradford, *An Enquiry How Far the Punishment of Death is Necessary in Pennsylvania* (Philadelphia: T. Dobson, 1793), 27–28.
45. *Pa. Gazette*, September 30, 1731. Petty treason was still a distinct crime in Pennsylvania in 1793, and, although other states had banned the punishment of burning, Pennsylvania had not. William Bradford denounced burning as a "barbarity" and urged the state to punish such crimes as ordinary murders. Bradford, *Enquiry*, 42. Eighteenth-century English law tended to treat the offense as a form of homicide rather than of treason. Matthew Lockwood, "From Treason to Homicide: Changing Conceptions of the Law of Petty Treason in Early Modern England," *J. Leg. Hist.* 34 (2013): 31–49. In his law lectures of 1790 and 1791, James Wilson referred to the crime as "treasonable homicide." James Wilson, *The Works of James Wilson*, ed. Robert Green McCloskey (Cambridge, MA: Harvard Univ. Press, 1967), 2:661.
46. On these issues, see generally David L. Preston, *The Texture of Contact: European and Indian Settler Communities on the Frontiers of Iroquoia, 1667–1783* (Lincoln: Univ. of Nebraska Press, 2009); Matthew G. Ward, *Breaking the Backcountry: The Seven Years' War in Virginia and Pennsylvania, 1754–1765* (Pittsburgh, PA: Univ. of Pittsburgh Press, 2003); Peter Silver, *Our Savage Neighbors: How Indian War Transformed Early America* (New York: Norton, 2008).
47. C. Hale Sipe, *The Indian Wars of Pennsylvania* (Harrisburg, PA: Telegraph Press, 1929), 203–275. In 1755, Conrad Weiser, a Pennsylvania justice of the peace and Indian agent, was meeting with Iroquois Indians when a large number of men gathered and denounced Weiser as a "traitor of the country who held with the Indians." Weiser feared for his life, but violence was averted when news of a fresh Indian attack sent the crowd hurriedly away. Silver, *Our Savage Neighbors*, 97.
48. *Pa. Gazette*, April 15, 1756.
49. Silver, *Our Savage Neighbors*, 162.
50. Sipe, *The Indian Wars of Pennsylvania*, 283.
51. For analysis of Indian legal status in colonial Pennsylvania, see John Smolenski, "Murder on the Margins: The Paxton Massacre and the Remaking of Sovereignty in Colonial Pennsylvania," *J. of Early Modern History* 19 (2015): 513–538.

52. Articles of Agreement between William Penn & Susquehannah Indians 1701, *Pa. Archives*, 1:144–146.
53. In a 1766 grand jury charge, Edward Shippen emphasized that provincial laws against murder extended to the murder of an Indian. Edward Shippen's Charge, Northampton County, Sept. 18, 1766, in *Gentlemen of the Grand Jury*, 2:761.
54. *A Court Martial Held at Newport, Rhode Island, In August and September 1676, For the Trial of Indians, Charged with being Engaged in King Philip's War* (Albany, NY: J. Munsell, 1858), 3, 4. For the larger context of these trials, see Jenny Hale Pulsipher, *Subjects unto the Same King: Indians, English, and the Contest for Authority in Colonial New England* (Philadelphia: Univ. of Penn. Press, 2005); Jenny Hale Pulsipher, "'Subjects . . . unto the Same King': New England Indians and the Use of Royal Political Power," *Mass. Hist. Review*, 5 (2003): 29–57.
55. *A Court Martial Held at Newport*, 5, 6, 8, 9. On this point, I disagree with Pulsipher's unqualified characterization of these trials as treason trials. Pulsipher, *Subjects unto the Same King*, 129. I am similarly unpersuaded by her claim that "English leaders also charged Philip, the sachem of the Wampanoags, with treason." Ibid. The English colonists certainly used the rhetoric of treachery and breach of allegiance to describe various Indian actions, but they did not institute formal treason charges in a court of law.
56. Gregory Evans Dowd, *War under Heaven: Pontiac, the Indian Nations, and the British Empire* (Baltimore: Johns Hopkins Univ. Press, 2002), 181. A 1744 Pennsylvania statute had provided that Indians could be tried in Philadelphia for capital offenses: "murders, manslaughters, homicides, felonies, and offenses whatsoever." Despite this broad language, the statute omitted the offense of treason, perhaps reflecting a sense that this offense did not apply easily to members of the Indian tribes. Act of Oct. 19, 1744, ch. 362, *Pa. Stat.*, 5:5.
57. On the difficulties of determining Indian legal status in the nineteenth-century Indian wars, see John Fabian Witt, *Lincoln's Code: The Laws of War in American History* (New York: Free Press, 2012), 328–338; Carol Chomsky, "The United States-Dakota War Trials: A Study in Military Injustice," *Stan. L. Rev.* 43 (1990): 13–98.
58. New York, by contrast, charged several persons with treason for trading with the enemy during the war. Thomas M. Truxes, *Defying Empire: Trading with the Enemy in Colonial New York* (New Haven, CT: Yale Univ. Press, 2008), 88, 148.
59. Minutes of the Provincial Council, Nov. 24, 1756, *Col. Records*, 7:344. A nineteenth-century history quotes an unnamed source for the proposition that Dr. Hugh Mathews was suspected of having suspicious company at his house and that "many letters and papers had been read and handed about in the said company which there was great reason to suspect contained some traitorous and treasonable matter." J. Thomas Scharf & Thompson Westcott, *History of Philadelphia* (Philadelphia: L.H. Everts, 1884), 2:1370.
60. In 1755, the justices of Berks County warned the Provincial Council of possible disloyalty by priests and parishioners, suspecting some of having gone to the enemy at

Fort Duquesne. Justices of Berks County to Provincial Council, July 23, 1755, *Col. Records*, 6:503. The provincial government concluded that there was "very little foundation" for these fears. *Col. Records*, 6:534.

61. Jack D. Marietta, *The Reformation of American Quakerism, 1748–1783* (Philadelphia: Univ. of Penn. Press, 1984), 156.
62. *Lawmaking and Legislators in Pennsylvania*, ed. Craig W. Horle, Jeffrey L. Scheib, Joseph S. Foster, David Haugaard, Carolyn M. Peters & Laurie M. Wolfe (Philadelphia: Univ. of Penn. Press, 1997), 2:76–78; Marietta, *Reformation*, 158.
63. Kevin Kenny, *Peaceable Kingdom Lost: The Paxton Boys and the Destruction of William Penn's Holy Experiment* (Oxford: Oxford Univ. Press, 2009), 134–140. On the background to the Paxton Boys, see generally George W. Franz, *Paxton: A Study of Community Structure and Mobility in the Colonial Pennsylvania Backcountry* (New York: Garland, 1989); see also Thomas P. Slaughter, "Crowds in Eighteenth-Century America: Reflections and New Directions," *PMHB* 115 (1991): 3–34.
64. *Pa. Gazette*, Jan. 12, 1764.
65. *Col. Records*, 9:129, 132; Act of Feb. 3, 1764, *Pa. Stat.*, 6:325.
66. Kenny, *Peaceable Kingdom Lost*, 152, 162.
67. Foster, *A Report of Some Proceedings*, 211.
68. *A Dialogue, Containing some Reflections on the late Declaration and Remonstrance, Of the Back-Inhabitants of the Province of Pennsylvania* (Philadelphia: 1764), in *The Paxton Papers*, ed. John R. Dunbar (The Hague: Martinus Nijhoff, 1957), 111, 118.
69. *The Quaker Vindicated* (Philadelphia: 1764), in Dunbar, *The Paxton Papers*, 231.
70. *The Quakers Assisting, To Preserve the Lives of the Indians in the Barracks, Vindicated* (Philadelphia: Anthony Armbruster, 1764), in *The Paxton Papers*, 353, 355.
71. Ibid., 120.
72. *The Conduct of the Paxton Men* (Philadelphia: A. Steuart, 1764), in *The Paxton Papers*, 267, 269.
73. *The Address of the People call'd Quakers* (Philadelphia: Andrew Steuart, 1764), in *The Paxton Papers*, 133.
74. *A Looking-Glass for Presbyterians* (Philadelphia: 1764), in *The Paxton Papers*, 243, 246.
75. *A Declaration and Remonstrance* (Philadelphia: 1764), in *The Paxton Papers*, 101. On the various Paxton pamphlets, see Alison Olson, "The Pamphlet War over the Paxton Boys," *PMHB* 123 (1999): 31–55.
76. Szechi, *1715*, 207–208.
77. Geoffrey Plank, *Rebellion and Savagery: The Jacobite Rising of 1745 and the British Empire* (Philadelphia: Univ. of Penn. Press, 2006), 3.
78. *The Prisoners of the '45*, ed. Bruce Gordon Seton & Jean Gordon Arnot (Edinburgh, Scottish History Society, 1928), 1:7–11.
79. On the failure to prosecute Confederate soldiers and leaders, see William A. Blair, *With Malice toward Some: Treason and Loyalty in the Civil War Era* (Chapel Hill: UNC Press, 2014), 234–261.

80. *Pa. Gazette*, July 12, 1764; Kenny, *Peaceable Kingdom Lost*, 202.
81. Dowd, *War under Heaven*, 183.
82. Thomas Gage to Henry Bouquet, Oct. 15, 1764, *The Critical Period, 1763–1765*, ed. Clarence Alvord & Clarence Carter (Springfield, IL: Illinois State Historical Library, 1915), 347–349.
83. Henry Bouqet to Asher Clayton, Dec. 1, 1764, *The Papers of Colonel Henry Bouquet*, ed. Sylvester K. Stevens & Donald H. Kent (Harrisburg, PA: Pa. Hist. Comm., 1940–1943), 21653:338.
84. James R. Williamson & Linda A. Fossler, *The Susquehanna Frontier: Northeastern Pennsylvania during the Revolutionary Years* (Wilkes-Barre, PA: Wilkes Univ. Press, 1997), 70; John A. Nagy, *Spies in the Continental Capital: Espionage across Pennsylvania during the American Revolution* (Yardley, PA: Westholme, 2011), 136.
85. John Penn to John Armstrong et al., June 27, 1765, *Pa. Archives* (4th Ser.), 3:302.
86. John Penn to Thomas Gage, June 28, 1765, *Pa. Archives* (4th Ser.), 3:304–305.
87. For an overview of the decades-long Connecticut controversy, see Paul Moyer, *Wild Yankees: The Struggle for Independence along Pennsylvania's Revolutionary Frontier* (Ithaca, NY: Cornell Univ. Press, 2007). In the 1730s, violence had erupted along the disputed Maryland-Pennsylvania border, but no treason prosecutions ensued. Patrick Spero, "The Conojocular War: The Politics of Colonial Competition, 1732–1737," *PMHB* 136 (Oct. 2012): 365–403.
88. Daniel P. Barr, *A Colony Sprung from Hell: Pittsburgh and the Struggle for Authority on the Western Pennsylvania Frontier, 1744–1794* (Kent, OH: Kent State Univ. Press, 2014), 142–144.
89. Ibid., 145–146.
90. Glenn F. Williams, *Dunmore's War: The Last Conflict of America's Colonial Era* (Yardley, PA: Westholme, 2017), 19.
91. Ibid., 151.
92. Arthur St. Clair to John Penn, Feb. 2, 1774, *Pa. Archives*, 4:476; Aeneas McKay to John Penn, April 4, 1774, *Pa. Archives*, 4:484.
93. John Penn to [Henry Wilmot], May 1, 1774, *SCP*, 6:234.
94. John Penn to Earl of Dunmore, June 28, 1774, *Pa. Archives* (4th Ser.), 3:480–481; John Penn to Pennsylvania Assembly, July 18, 1774, *Pa. Archives* (4th Ser.), 3:483, 484.
95. See generally Williams, *Dunmore's War*.
96. Barr, *Colony Sprung from Hell*, 170.
97. Ibid., 177.
98. Ibid., 230–232.
99. Minutes of the Pennsylvania Council, March 2, 1754, *SCP*, 1:55.
100. Opinion of the Attorney General of Pennsylvania, March 18, 1754, *SCP*, 1:70.
101. James Hamilton, Proclamations Against the Connecticut Settlers, Feb. 20, 1761 & Sept. 16, 1761, *SCP*, 2:62, 116.

102. Opinion of Charles Yorke, Solicitor General, March 30, 1761, *SCP*, 2:67–69; Proclamation of Thomas Fitch Against the Susquehannah Company, June 8, 1762, *SCP*, 2:135; Earl of Egremont to Thomas Fitch, Jan. 27, 1763, *SCP*, 2:194–196; Order of the King in Council, June 15, 1763, *SCP*, 2:255.
103. Thomas Fitch to the Board of Trade, Nov. 10, 1763, *SCP*, 2:281–282.
104. Eliphalet Dyer to William Samuel Johnson, March 10, 1769, *SCP*, 3:87.
105. Ibid., 3:88.
106. Presentment of Isaac Tripp and Others by the Northampton County Grand Jury, *SCP*, 3:92–93.
107. John Penn to Charles Stewart, May 16, 1769, *SCP*, 3:124–125.
108. Proclamation of Governor John Penn, May 16, 1769, *SCP*, 3:125–127.
109. Deposition of Joseph Morris, June 1, 1769, *SCP*, 3:134.
110. Edward Shippen to James Burd, June 25, 1769, *SCP*, 3:139.
111. John Penn to John Jennings, Aug. 24, 1769, *SCP*, 3:168–169; *SCP*, 3:184, 21.
112. Eliphalet Dyer to William Samuel Johnson, Aug. 8, 1769, *SCP*, 3:161.
113. Agreement Between Connecticut and Pennsylvania Settlers at Wyoming, Nov. 14, 1769, *SCP*, 3:200–202.
114. Warrant for the Arrest of Benjamin Shoemaker and Others, Dec. 21, 1769, *SCP*, 3:214–216.
115. Kenny, *Peaceable Kingdom Lost*, 220.
116. John Penn to Richard Penn, May 22, 1770, *SCP*, 4:67.
117. Proclamation of John Penn, June 28, 1770, *SCP*, 4:88–89; Presentment of Lazarus Stewart and Others by the Northampton County Grand Jury, *SCP*, 4:92–93.
118. Kenny, *Peaceable Kingdom Lost*, 223.
119. Deposition of John Philip de Haas, Sept. 26, 1770, *SCP*, 4:121–123.
120. A Message to the Governor from the Assembly, Sept. 27, 1770, *CR*, 9:685. G.S. Rowe asserts that Pennsylvania authorities charged Stewart with "arson and treason." Rowe, *Embattled Bench*, 114. His sources, however, indicate only an arson charge, and I have located no other evidence of a treason charge.
121. Charles Stewart to John Penn, Jan. 21, 1771, *SCP*, 4:152–153.
122. Minutes of the Pennsylvania Council, Feb. 8, 1771, *SCP*, 4:170.
123. Eliphalet Dyer et al. to Jonathan Trumbull, March 27, 1771, *SCP*, 4:194.
124. Eliphalet Dyer to William Samuel Johnson, Aug. 8, 1770, *SCP*, 4:107 ("we should have been glad if you had pointed out the danger to the Colony for if it is got to be Treason in England for a Colony to pretend to claim according to the express words of their grant it may soon be so in a particular person what state then must the property of an English subject be in").
125. Resolution of the Connecticut Legislature Concerning the Western Claim, May 1771, *SCP*, 4:215.
126. Proclamation for Removing the Connecticut People, July 10, 1771, *SCP*, 4:221–223; Minutes of the Pennsylvania Council, July 16, 1771, *SCP*, 4:223–225.

127. *Conn. Courant*, Aug. 6, 1771, *SCP*, 4:339 n.3.
128. *Conn. Courant*, Aug. 20, 1771, *SCP*, 4:339–342.
129. Articles of Capitulation, Aug. 15, 1771, *SCP*, 4:241.
130. Message from the President and Council to the Assembly, Sept. 18, 1771, *SCP*, 4:261–263.
131. Act of Feb. 9, 1771, ch. 618, *Pa. Stat.*, 8:5, 6; Proclamation of Richard Penn, July 22, 1772, *SCP*, 5:3–4.
132. William Plunket and Others to the Governor and Council of Pennsylvania, June 11, 1773, *SCP*, 5:148–149.
133. The State of the Case, with Legal Opinions of Wedderburn and Others, *SCP*, 5:229–244; Act of the Connecticut General Assembly Erecting the Town of Westmoreland, *SCP*, 5:268–269.
134. Proclamation by John Penn, Feb. 28, 1774, *SCP*, 5:304–307.
135. Act of Jan. 22, 1774, ch. 690, *Pa. Stat.*, 8:366.
136. Eliphalet Dyer et al. to Zebulon Butler et al., Aug. 2, 1775, *SCP*, 6:337–338.
137. John Montgomery to James Wilson, Oct. 9, 1775, *SCP*, 6:367.
138. Joseph Shippen et al. to William Plunket et al., Oct. 13, 1775, *SCP*, 6:371.
139. Extract from the Minutes of the Pennsylvania Assembly, Nov. 23, 1775, *SCP*, 6:391–392.
140. Deposition of Daniel Saint John, Dec. 12, 1775, *SCP*, 6:410–11.
141. Resolution of the Continental Congress, Dec. 20, 1775, *SCP*, 6:420–421; Extract from *Conn. Courant*, Jan. 22, 1776, *SCP*, 6:422.
142. In 1748, Governor Thomas Penn had complained that Benjamin Franklin's organization of a colonial militia was a "contempt to government" and "little less than treason." Thomas Penn to Richard Peters, March 30, 1748, quoted in *The Papers of Benjamin Franklin*, ed. Leonard W. Labaree (New Haven, CT: Yale Univ. Press, 1961), 3:186.
143. Minutes of a Meeting of the Susquehannah Company, June 2, 1773, *SCP*, 5:139.
144. Reports of the Lords of the Committee of Council, May 25, 1771, *SCP*, 4:213.
145. Edward Shippen, Charge to Grand Jury, June 1762, Balch-Shippen Papers, HSP, 2:85.

CHAPTER 2

1. John Adams to Hezekiah Niles, Feb. 13, 1818, *The Works of John Adams*, ed. Charles Francis Adams (Boston: Little, Brown, 1856), 10:282–283.
2. Edmund S. Morgan & Helen M. Morgan, *The Stamp Act Crisis: Prologue to Revolution* (Chapel Hill: UNC Press, 1953), 250–251.
3. *N.Y. Mercury*, Sept. 14, 1767.
4. *New London Gazette*, Nov. 8, 1765.
5. *Conn. Courant*, Oct. 1–8, 1771.

6. *The New Year's Verses of those Who Carry the Pennsylvania Journal to the Customers* (Philadelphia: 1775).
7. Chapin, *American Law of Treason*, 14.
8. Blackstone, *Commentaries*, 4:85–86.
9. *Proceedings and Debates of the British Parliaments Respecting North America, 1754–1783*, ed. R.C. Simmons & P.D.G. Thomas (White Plains, NY: Kraus, 1986), 5:382. This statement was reprinted in the *Pennsylvania Gazette* on the auspicious date of April 19, 1775.
10. Nick Bunker, *An Empire on the Edge: How Britain Came to Fight America* (New York: Knopf, 2014), 65–69.
11. Report of the Attorney & Solicitor General, Aug. 10, 1772, available at The Anglo-American Legal Tradition, http://aalt.law.uh.edu/AALT7/G3/PC1no55Pt69_1772/Gaspee/IMG_0810_3.htm.
12. Richard West, *A Discourse Concerning Treasons, and Bills of Attainder* (London: J. Roberts, 2d ed., 1717), 101. West suggested that a parliamentary act of attainder would be appropriate to fill the statutory gap.
13. An Act for the better securing and preserving his Majesty's dock yards, magazines, ships, ammunition and stores, 12 Geo. III, ch. 24 (1772).
14. See generally Steven Park, *The Burning of His Majesty's Schooner Gaspee: An Attack on Crown Rule before the American Revolution* (Yardley, PA: Westholme, 2016); Neil L. York, "The Uses of Law and the Gaspee Affair," *Rhode Island History* 50 (1992): 3–21; Lawrence J. DeVaro, "The Impact of the Gaspee Affair on the Coming of the Revolution, 1772–1773" (Ph.D. diss., Case Western Reserve Univ., 1973). On July 4, 1826, four of the surviving raiders were guests of honor at a Rhode Island Independence Day celebration. Bunker, *Empire on Edge*, 67.
15. Attorney- and Solicitor-General to Earl of Dartmouth, Feb. 11, 1774, in *Documents of the American Revolution* (Colonial Office Series), ed. K.G. Davies (Shannon, Ireland: Irish Univ. Press, 1975), 8:46–48.
16. Earl of Shelburne to Earl of Chatham, April 4, 1774, in Lord Fitzmaurice, *Life of William, Earl of Shelburne* (London: Macmillan, 2d ed., 1912), 1:473. English critics ridiculed Mansfield for the bellicose nature of this speech. Norman S. Poser, *Lord Mansfield: Justice in the Age of Reason* (Montreal: McGill-Queen's Univ. Press, 2013), 309.
17. Attorney- and Solicitor-General to Earl of Dartmouth, Feb. 12, 1775, in *Documents of the American Revolution* (Colonial Office Series), 7:259.
18. James Wilson, "Speech Delivered in the Convention for the Province of Pennsylvania, Held at Philadelphia, in January, 1775," in Kermit L. Hall & Mark David Hall, eds., *Collected Works of James Wilson* (Indianapolis, IN: Liberty Fund, 2007), 1:32, 41–42.
19. *N.Y. Mercury*, Aug. 26, 1765.
20. *Pa. Gazette*, March 1, 1770.

21. The Petition of William Bollan, *Boston Post-Boy*, April 17, 1769.
22. *Pa. Gazette*, Aug. 24, 1774.
23. *Pa. Gazette*, March 8, 1770.
24. *N.Y. Gazette*, May 22, 1769 (reprinting material from *Md. Gazette*, May 4, 1769).
25. *The Crisis Number XVIII*, reprint (New York: John Anderson, 1775), 153.
26. John Phillip Reid, *Constitutional History of the American Revolution: The Authority of Rights* (Madison: Univ. of Wisconsin Press, 1986), 1:54–55; William R. Leslie, "The Gaspee Affair: A Study of its Constitutional Significance, *Mississippi Historical Review* 39, no. 2 (1952): 233, 245–46. The 1772 statute prohibiting the burning of the king's dockyards and stores also provided for trial in England if the offense was committed outside of the realm. 12 Geo. III, ch. 24.
27. *Proceedings and Debates of the British Parliaments Respecting North America, 1754–1783*, ed. R.C. Simmons & P.D.G. Thomas (New York: Kraus, 1984), 3:90.
28. *N.Y. Gazette*, July 17, 1769.
29. John Adams, Proposed Resolutions, Sept. 30, 1774, *LDC*, 1:131.
30. John Adams to a Friend in London, Feb. 10, 1775, *LDC*, 1:308, 310.
31. "From Lloyd's Evening Post of June 16," *Pa. Chronicle*, Sept. 11–18, 1769.
32. *N.Y. Gazette*, June 5, 1769.
33. *N.Y. Journal*, Jan. 18, 1770.
34. *Pa. Gazette*, July 20, 1774.
35. *Pa. Gazette*, June 22, 1774.
36. Christopher Marshall to J-n P-e, April 13, 1775, Letterbook of Christopher Marshall, HSP.
37. Benjamin Franklin, "Rules By Which a Great Empire May be Reduced to a Small One," *Public Advertizer*, Sept. 11, 1773.
38. *Pa. Gazette*, Aug. 9, 1770.
39. Matthew Hale, *Historia Placitorum Coronae* (London: Nutt & Gosling, 1736), 1:154–156.
40. *Proceedings and Debates of the British Parliaments*, 3:95.
41. Ibid., 3:68.
42. Ibid., 3:77.
43. John Philip Reid, *Constitutional History of the American Revolution: The Authority to Legislate* (Madison: Univ. of Wisconsin Press, 1991), 3:283.
44. *Proceedings and Debates*, 3:65–66.
45. Ibid., 3:92.
46. Ibid., 3:94.
47. *N.Y. Gazette*, July 17, 1769.
48. *Pa. Gazette*, July 20, 1774.
49. Foster, *Report*, 238.
50. Attorney- and Solicitor-General to Earl of Dartmouth, Feb. 11, 1774, in *Documents of the American Revolution* (Colonial Office Series), 8:46–48.

51. Earl of Dartmouth to Lieut.-General Thomas Gage, April 9, 1774, in *Documents of the American Revolution* (Colonial Office Series), 8:86–90.
52. See generally Neil L. York, "Imperial Impotence: Treason in 1774 Massachusetts," *Law and History Review* 29 (2011): 657–701; Bernard Donoughue, *British Politics and the American Revolution: The Path to War, 1773–75* (London: Macmillan, 1964), 53–63.
53. Reid, *Authority to Legislate*, 284.
54. "Remarks on the King's Speech," *N.Y. Journal*, Jan. 18, 1776.
55. *JCC*, 1:76 (Oct. 20, 1774).
56. *JCC*, 2:146 (July 6, 1775).
57. Pauline Maier, *American Scripture: Making the Declaration of Independence* (New York: Knopf, 1997), 118.
58. *Conn. Journal*, July 1, 1774; *Conn. Gazette*, June 3, 1774.
59. *Conn. Gazette*, Aug. 20, 1774.
60. Blinka, "Jefferson and Juries," 56.
61. *N.Y. Weekly Journal*, Jan. 2, 1737. In the 1670s, Nathaniel Bacon, leader of Bacon's Rebellion in Virginia, had argued that the colonial governor had committed treason against the people of Virginia. Holly Brewer, "Subjects by Allegiance to the King? Debating Status and Power for Subjects—and Slaves—through the Religious Debates of the Early British Atlantic," in *State and Citizen: British America and the Early United States*, ed. Peter Thompson & Peter S. Onuf (Charlottesville: UVA Press, 2013), 25, 31.
62. Bernard Bailyn, *Ideological Origins of the American Revolution* (Cambridge, MA: Harvard Univ. Press, enl. ed., 1992 (1967)), ch. 3.
63. *Pa. Gazette*, Dec. 26, 1765.
64. *Conn. Gazette*, Nov. 8, 1765.
65. *Pa. Gazette*, June 28, 1770.
66. *Pa. Gazette*, May 18, 1774.
67. John Philip Reid, *Constitutional History of the American Revolution*, 4 vols. (Madison, WI: Univ. of Wisconsin Press, 1986–1993).
68. *N.Y. Mercury*, Aug. 26, 1765.
69. [John Allen], *An Oration upon the Beauties of Liberty* (Boston: D. Kneeland & N. Davis, 1773), 9.
70. *Pa. Gazette*, April 20, 1774.
71. [John Dickinson], *An Essay on the Constitutional Power of Great Britain over the Colonies in America* (Philadelphia: William & Thomas Bradford, 1774), 62.
72. Wilson, "Speech Delivered in the Convention for the Province of Pennsylvania," 1:32, 43–44.
73. *Mass. Spy*, Feb. 9, 1775.
74. Thomas Coombe, *A Sermon Preached before the Congregations of Christ Church and St. Peter's, Philadelphia, on Thursday, July 20, 1775* (Philadelphia: John Dunlap, 1775).

75. *Pa. Gazette*, April 17, 1766.
76. *Pa. Journal*, April 3, 1766.
77. John Hughes to Commissioners, Nov. 2, 1765, *N.Y. Mercury*, Sept. 8, 1766.
78. *Pa. Gazette*, July 20, 1769.
79. *Pa. Gazette*, June 28, 1770.
80. James Wilson's commonplace book described high treason as an offense "against the Security of the King *or Kingdom*." James Wilson, Commonplace Book, James Wilson Papers, HSP, 33 (emphasis added).
81. *Pa. Gazette*, Oct. 20, 1773.
82. The Committee for Tarring and Feathering, *To the Delaware Pilots* (Philadelphia: 1773).
83. *Pa. Gazette*, Dec. 8, 1773. On both the power and the ambiguity of the term "liberty" in revolutionary Pennsylvania, see Stephen Lucas, *Portents of Rebellion: Rhetoric and Revolution in Philadelphia, 1765–1776* (Philadelphia: Temple Univ. Press, 1976), 85–86.
84. *A Sermon on Tea* (Lancaster, PA: Francis Bailey, 1774), 6.
85. *Pa. Gazette*, Nov. 17, 1773.
86. *JCC*, 1:79 (Oct. 20, 1774).
87. *Pa. Gazette*, Jan. 4, 1775.
88. [John Drinker], *Observations on the Late Popular Measures* (Philadelphia: 1774), 24.
89. *Mass. Spy*, Feb. 16, 1775.
90. Thomas Gage, *A Proclamation* (New York: 1775).
91. George III, *Proclamation, for Suppressing Rebellion and Sedition* (Aug. 23, 1775), in *The Declaration of Independence in Historical Context: American State Papers, Petitions, Proclamations, and Letters of the Delegates to the First National Congresses*, ed. Barry Alan Shain (New Haven, CT: Yale Univ. Press, 2014), 358–359.

CHAPTER 3

1. *Pa. Gazette*, April 10, 1776.
2. Burton Alva Konkle, *Benjamin Chew* (Philadelphia: Univ. of Penn. Press, 1932), 143–144.
3. Eric Nelson, *The Royalist Revolution: Monarchy and the American Founding* (Cambridge, MA: Harvard Univ. Press, 2014), 4–5.
4. Resolves of the Assembly, June 30, 1775, *Pa. Stat.*, 8:485–486; Richard Alan Ryerson, *The Revolution Is Now Begun: The Radical Committees of Philadelphia, 1765–1776* (Philadelphia: Univ. of Penn. Press, 1978), 99–100. On the early committees, see T.H. Breen, *American Insurgents, American Patriots: The Revolution of the People* (New York: Hill & Wang, 2010), 160–240; Harold M. Hyman, *To Try Men's Souls: Loyalty Tests in American History* (Berkeley: Univ. of Cal. Press, 1959), 64–77; Peter Thompson, "Social Death and Slavery: The Logic of Political Association and the Logic of Chattel Slavery in Revolutionary America," in *Between Sovereignty*

and Anarchy: The Politics of Violence in the American Revolutionary Era, ed. Patrick Griffin, Robert G. Ingram, Peter S. Onuf & Brian Schoen (Charlottesville: UVA Press, 2015), 139–164. Brendan McConville argues that these committees launched the "American Terror," but that term is somewhat overstated; although there were many instances of rough treatment, no dissident was ever executed by a committee. Brendan McConville, *The King's Three Faces: The Rise and Fall of Royal America, 1688–1776* (Chapel Hill: UNC Press, 2006), 291–300.

5. The Pennsylvania Committee occasionally heard some lesser charges. For example, in February 1776, the committee heard the case of Thomas Austin, a member of the Philadelphia Committee of Inspection & Observation who was accused of being "inimical to the liberties of America." Austin signed a recantation, resigned his membership on the committee, and pledged not to speak against resistance measures. Minutes of the Committee of Safety, Feb. 14, 1776, *Col. Records*, 10:485. Similarly, a month later the committee head the case of Henry Yelverton Price, who had tried to discourage service on armed boats, had "declared himself a Tory, & inimical to the American cause," and had "damned the Congress and wished that the wagons carrying powder for the Continental Congress were blown up." Yelverton did not deny the charge and was detained at the committee's pleasure. Minutes of the Committee of Safety, March 4, 1776, *Col. Records*, 10:503.
6. Chapin, *American Law of Treason*, 29.
7. Stephen Payne Adye, *A Treatise on Courts-Martial* (New York: H. Goyne, 1769; reprint, Philadelphia: R. Aitken, 1779), 50. On the development of English martial law, see John M. Collins, *Martial Law and English Laws, c. 1500–c.1700* (Cambridge: Cambridge Univ. Press, 2016).
8. [Isaac Hunt], *A Looking-Glass for Presbyterians* (Philadelphia: 1764).
9. Benjamin Franklin to Isaac Hunt, Dec. 24, 1767, *Papers of Benjamin Franklin*, ed. Leonard W. Labaree (New Haven, CT: Yale Univ. Press, 1970), 14:343.
10. Isaac Hunt, *The Political Family* (Philadelphia: James Humphreys, 1775).
11. James Hutchinson to Jabez Maud Fisher, Oct. 24, 1775, Fisher Collection, HSP.
12. *Pa. Gazette*, Sept. 6, 1775.
13. To the Printers of the Pennsylvania Journal, n.d., *American Archives* (4th Ser.), ed. Peter Force (Washington, DC: M. St. Clair Clark & Peter Force, 1840), 3:172.
14. Ibid.; James Hutchinson to Jabez Maud Fisher, Oct. 24, 1775, Fisher Collection, HSP; *Extracts from the Diary of Christopher Marshall*, ed. William Duane (Albany, NY: Joel Munsell, 1877), 41.
15. Memorial of Isaac Hunt, American Loyalist Claims, AO13.102A.339, National Archives of the United Kingdom.
16. Examination Relative to Tories, July 11, 1776, *Pa. Archives* (2d Ser.), 1:611. Isaac Atwood, a comb maker, later revealed Kearsley's secret meetings. Immediately after Atwood's revelations, Christopher Marshall and six other people were appointed to a Committee of Secrecy to "examine all inimical and suspected persons that came to their knowledge." *Diary of Christopher Marshall*, 80–81.

17. Alexander Graydon, *Memoirs of His Own Time with Reminiscences of the Men and Events of the Revolution*, ed. John Stockton Littell (Philadelphia: Lindsay and Blakiston, 1846), 126.
18. James Hutchinson to Jabez Maud Fisher, Oct. 24, 1775, Fisher Collection, HSP.
19. *Diary of Christopher Marshall*, 41.
20. James Hutchinson to Jabez Maud Fisher, Oct. 24, 1775, Fisher Collection, HSP. Hunt soon made his way to New York, where he denounced the "Measures, Plots, and Treason" of the revolutionary leaders. Isaac Hunt, *Faction: A Sketch; or, a Summary of the Causes Of the present most unnatural and indefensible of all Rebellions* (New York: 1777), 4. He later became an Anglican clergyman in England and was the father of the noted poet Leigh Hunt. Graydon, *Memoirs*, 127 n*. In 1794, Hunt was arrested for uttering "seditious expressions" at the Swan Tavern in London. *Pa. Gazette*, July 16, 1794. He was "acquitted and discharged," however, after demonstrating "that in the year 1775, he risked his life, lost his property, and fair prospects of wealth and eminence in America, in defence and support of the King and Constitution of Great Britain." *Morning Chronicle* (London), May 29, 1794.
21. Graydon, *Memoirs*, 126.
22. James Hutchinson to Jabez Maud Fisher, Oct. 24, 1775, Fisher Collection, HSP; Memorial of Mary Kearsley, American Loyalist Claims, AO13.102A.323, National Archives of the United Kingdom; see also Steven Rosswurm, *Arms, Country, and Class: The Philadelphia Militia and "Lower Sort" during the American Revolution, 1775–1783* (New Brunswick, NJ: Rutgers Univ. Press, 1987), 46–48.
23. "To the Printers of the Pennsylvania Journal," n.d., *American Archives* (4th Ser.), ed. Peter Force (Washington: M. St. Clair Clark & Peter Force, 1840), 3:175.
24. Caesar Rodney to Thomas Rodney, Oct. 9, 1775, *LDC*, 2:151, 152; Christopher Marshall to SH, Oct. 31, 1775, Christopher Marshall Letterbook, Christopher Marshall Collection, HSP.
25. *Pa. Chronicle*, April 26, 1773.
26. Christopher Marshall to SH, Oct. 31, 1775, Christopher Marshall Letterbook, Christopher Marshall Collection, HSP.
27. *Diary of Christopher Marshall*, 45.
28. "A Friend to your Friend Coriolanus" to Charles Jenkinson, Oct. 1775, Intercepted Letters of the Revolutionary War, Box 15C, Society Miscellaneous Collection, HSP.
29. Caesar Rodney to Thomas Rodney, Oct. 9, 1775, *LDC*, 2:151, 152.
30. *JCC*, 3:280 (Oct. 6, 1775).
31. John Adams, Notes of Debates in the Continental Congress, in ibid., 3:482–484.
32. Blackstone, *Commentaries*, 3:133.
33. Minutes of the Committee of Safety, Oct. 7, 1775, *Col. Records*, 10:359; *Diary of Christopher Marshall*, 45.

34. Minutes of the Committee of Safety, Oct. 7, 1775, *Col. Records*, 10:359.
35. *Diary of Christopher Marshall*, 45.
36. Minutes of the Committee of Safety, Oct. 7, 9, 1775, *Col. Records*, 10:360–361.
37. *Diary of Christopher Marshall*, 46.
38. Christopher Marshall to SH, Oct. 31, 1775, Christopher Marshall Letterbook, Christopher Marshall Collection, HSP.
39. *Diary of Christopher Marshall*, 46.
40. Christopher Marshall to SH, Oct. 31, 1775, Christopher Marshall Letterbook, Christopher Marshall Collection, HSP. The previous month the Philadelphia committee had resolved that no one should be held out as an enemy without "full and sufficient evidence of guilt, after a fair and impartial examination." *Pa. Packet*, Sept. 25, 1775 (quoted in Ousterhout, *State Divided*, 120).
41. Memorial of Christopher Carter, American Loyalist Claims, AO13.70C.209, National Archives of the United Kingdom.
42. Extract from the Minutes of the Pennsylvania Committee of Safety, Oct. 11, 1775, Peter Force Collection, Series 9, Manuscript Division, Library of Congress. This item does not appear in the published *Colonial Records* volume.
43. Memorial of Mary Kearsley, American Loyalist Claims, AO13.102A.323, National Archives of the United Kingdom.
44. Christopher Marshall to SH, Oct. 31, 1775, Christopher Marshall Letterbook, Christopher Marshall Collection, HSP. The committee later agreed to allow Kearsley both a servant and a clerk. Minutes of the Committee of Safety, Oct. 19, 1775, *Col. Records*, 10:373; Minutes of the Committee of Safety, Oct. 20, 1775, *Col. Records*, 10:374.
45. Miers Fisher to Jabez Fisher, Oct. 29, 1775, Fisher Collection, HSP.
46. Ibid.
47. Christopher Marshall to SH, Oct. 31, 1775, Christopher Marshall Letterbook, Christopher Marshall Collection, HSP. Both Snowden and Carter apparently failed to pay their bonds, perhaps disputing the Committee of Safety's jurisdiction. Snowden remained in jail for seventeen months and Carter for four months. Ousterhout, *State Divided*, 119–120. Kearsley was later moved to the Carlisle jail, where he died in 1777, still widely reviled. The burial of Kearsley in the Carlisle church "disgusted many of the church party in that place, so they declared against going to that church anymore." *Diary of Christopher Marshall*, 143–144. Kearsley's wife later fled with her three children to the British, but lost all her property in a shipwreck en route. David Kearsley to Phineas Bond, Dec. 26, 1778, Phineas Bond Correspondence, Cadwalader Collection, HSP.
48. *Conn. Journal*, Oct. 25, 1775; *Wochentliche Philadelphische Staatsbote*, Oct. 20, 1775.
49. Extract from the Minutes of the Committee of Safety, Oct. 11, 1775, Pennsylvania Manuscripts, Peter Force Collection, Series 9, Manuscripts Division, Library of Congress.

50. The General Committee to the Lancaster Committee, Oct. 19, 1775, *Pa. Archives* (2d Ser.), 13:503–504.
51. Ibid.
52. Mittimus for Michael Immel, Oct. 7, 1777, *Pa. Archives*, 5:649.
53. *Diary and Autobiography of John Adams*, ed. L.H. Butterfield (Cambridge, MA: Harvard Univ. Press, 1961), 354–356.
54. Rules and Regulations for the better Government of the Military Association in Pennsylvania, *Pa. Archives* (8th Ser.), 8:7369, 7374.
55. *Rules and Constitutions of the Society of Englishmen, and Sons of Englishmen* (Philadelphia: Benjamin Towne, 1774).
56. *Pa. Gazette*, Oct. 25, 1775.
57. *Pa. Gazette*, March 6, 1776.
58. Minutes of the Committee of Safety, Oct. 14, 1775, *Col. Records*, 10:367.
59. George Washington to Jonathan Trumbull, Nov. 15, 1775, *Papers of George Washington: Revolutionary War Series*, ed. W.W. Abbot (Charlottesville: UVA Press, 1987), 2:379.
60. On Connolly's early activities, see Patrick Griffin, *American Leviathan: Empire, Nation, and Revolutionary Frontier* (New York: Hill & Wang, 2007), 107–123; Douglas MacGregor, "Double Dishonor: Loyalists on the Middle Frontier," in *Pennsylvania's Revolution*, ed. William A. Pencak (University Park: Penn. State. Univ. Press, 2010), 144–150; Douglas MacGregor, "The Ordeal of John Connolly: The Pursuit of Wealth through Loyalism," in *The Other Loyalists: Ordinary People, Royalism, and the Revolution in the Middle Colonies, 1763–1787*, ed. Joseph S. Tiedemann, Eugene R. Fingerhut & Robert W. Venables (New York: SUNY Press, 2009), 161–178.
61. Examination of A. Cameron, Dr. Smith and John Connolly, Nov. 23, 1775, *Pa. Archives*, 4:682–683.
62. Francis Lightfoot Lee to Landon Carter, Oct. 21, 1775, *LDC*: 2:227.
63. Committee of Frederick County, Md., to John Hancock, Nov. 24, 1775, *Pa. Archives*, 4:681–682; J.F.D. Smyth, *A Tour in the United States of America* (Dublin: T. Henshall, 1784), 2:159. One of Connolly's letters denounced the revolutionaries as "enemies to their country, to good order, and government." John Connolly to John Gibson, Aug. 9, 1775, *Pa. Archives*, 4:683–684.
64. *JCC*, 3:415 (Dec. 8, 1775).
65. *JCC*, 4:29 (Jan. 3, 1776).
66. Minutes of the Committee of Safety, Jan. 3, 1776, *Col. Records*, 10:444–445.
67. Minutes of the Committee of Safety, Jan. 18, 1776, *Col. Records*, 10:461.
68. *JCC*, 4:20 (Jan. 2, 1776).
69. Minutes of the Committee of Safety, Jan. 27, 1776, *Col. Records*, 10:469.
70. Minutes of the Committee of Safety, Jan. 30, 1776, *Col. Records*, 10:472;
71. Minutes of the Committee of Safety, Jan. 29, 1776, *Col. Records*, 10:470.

72. Minutes of the Committee of Safety, Jan. 3, 1776, *Col. Records*, 10:445; Minutes of the Committee of Safety, Jan. 30, 1776, *Col. Records*, 10:472.
73. The Continental Congress continued to supervise the conditions of the detainees' imprisonment after the Pennsylvania Committee's examination. E.g., *JCC*, 4:311 (April 26, 1776). For Connolly's side of the story, see "A Narrative of the Transactions, Imprisonment, and Sufferings of John Connolly, An American Loyalist and Lieut.-Col. in His Majesty's Service," *PMHB* 12 (1888): 310–324, 407–420; *PMHB* 13 (1889): 61–70, 153–167, 281–291. In March 1776, the men detained as "enemies to this country" rioted in the Philadelphia jail. Minutes of the Committee of Safety, March 12, 1776, *Col. Records*, 10:512–13. An informant notified the Continental Congress that a plan "for a general escape of the State or Tory prisoners" had been in contemplation for some time. Intelligence Received by Congress, *Pa. Archives*, 4:728–729. The Congress ordered that Connolly and Smyth be confined in separate apartments and that the Philadelphia sheriff provide a guard of fifty men for additional security. *JCC*, 4:239 (March 28, 1776).
74. Smyth, *Tour*, 2:120.
75. Connolly, "Narrative," 13:63; Smyth, *Tour*, 2:268.
76. *JCC*, 12:1128–1129 (Nov. 12, 1778).
77. Connolly, "Narrative," 13:157.
78. J.F.D. Smyth to Continental Congress, Dec. 17, 1778, in Smyth, *Tour*, 2:273, 275.
79. Connolly, "Narrative," 13:166–167, 281, 283, 286.
80. *Pa. Archives* (8th Ser.), 8:7476. During the eighteenth century, the use of the term "American" steadily increased in colonial newspapers. The term was used more frequently, however, in articles that originated in Great Britain. Richard L. Merritt, *Symbols of American Community, 1735–1775* (New Haven, CT: Yale Univ. Press, 1966), 130–133.
81. Cf. Breen, *American Patriots*, 185 ("Long before Congress declared independence, committees spoke to Americans of an imagined collectivity—a country of the mind—and so, by aggressively monitoring popular allegiance to a common cause, they laid the foundation for a shared identity that later generations would celebrate as nationalism."). A convention in Virginia in December 1775 formally adopted an "Enemies to America Act." Blinka, "Jefferson and Juries," 64. Similarly, in January 1776, the Continental Congress asserted that that "those who refuse to defend their country, should be excluded from its protection, and be prevented from doing it injury" and warned against "enemies to the American cause." *JCC*, 4:26–27 (Jan. 3, 1776).
82. Minutes of the Committee of Observation and Inspection of Northampton County, PA, in *Two Hundred Years of Life in Northampton County, Pa.* (Easton, PA: Mack Printing, 1976), 4:33, 37.
83. See, e.g., Lancaster Committee to John Henry and Edward Cowan, June 6, 1776, Jasper Yeates Papers, HSP (ordering a search of Thomas Prichard's papers, but excluding papers of merely private concern).

84. In Committee, at Carlisle, June 28, 1776, *Pa. Archives* (2d Ser.), 14:470.
85. Notes concerning a charge of Toryism against James Sullivan—In Committee, Feb. 28, 1776, Miscellaneous Legal Papers, Jasper Yeates Collection, HSP. The notes are similar to the notes that Yeates took in criminal trials.
86. *Pa. Journal*, Jan. 3, 1776.
87. *Pa. Gazette*, June 7, 1775,
88. *Depositions Charging William Moore* (Philadelphia: 1775).
89. *Pa. Gazette*, June 14, 1775.
90. "Minutes of the Committee of Safety of Bucks County, Pennsylvania, 1774–1776," *PMHB* 15 (1891): 257, 263.
91. Ibid., 266.
92. Ibid., 266–267.
93. Minutes, *Two Hundred Years*, 4:47–48 (June 13, 1776). On Michael Ohl, see Francis S. Fox, *Sweet Land of Liberty: The Ordeal of the American Revolution in Northampton County, Pennsylvania* (Univ. Park: Penn. St. Univ. Press, 2000), 69–72.
94. Minutes, *Two Hundred Years*, 4:48–50 (June 15, 1776). Joseph Romig was later charged with high treason in an attainder proclamation and his estate was confiscated. Fox, *Sweet Land of Liberty*, 105–111.
95. Chester, In Committee, April 2, 1776, *Pa. Archives* (2d Ser.), 14:137.
96. Berks County, May 11, 1776, *Pa. Archives* (2d Ser.), 14:310; *Pa. Gazette*, May 22, 1776.
97. Committee of Cumberland County to Committee of Safety, April 6, 1776, *Pa. Archives* (2d. Ser.), 1:593–595.
98. Berks County, June 15, 1776, *Pa. Archives* (2d Ser.), 14:312.
99. Testimony of William Caldwell, Feb. 7, 1787, American Loyalist Claims, AO12.40.235, National Archives of the United Kingdom.
100. Charles Willson Peale to Benjamin West, Aug. 31, 1775, Charles Willson Peale Papers, APS.
101. *Pa. Evening Post*, Oct. 7, 1775.
102. Miers Fisher to Jabez Fisher, n.d., Fisher Family Papers, HSP. Fisher had been providing information on American affairs to Lord North. Lord North to Miers Fisher, Sept. 10, 1775, Miers Fisher Collection, HSP.
103. Robert Proud to William Proud, Sept. 7, 1775, Robert Proud Collection, HSP.
104. Notes, Memorandums and Observations on different Subjects, Robert Proud Collection, HSP, 104.
105. Tory Letter to Col. Roberdeau, Dec. 23, 1775, *Pa. Archives* (2d Ser.), 1:561.
106. Minutes of the Committee of Safety, Sept. 16, 1775, *Col. Records*, 10:336–337.
107. Rules and Regulations for the better Government of the Military Association in Pennsylvania, *Pa. Archives* (8th Ser.), 8:7369, 7374.
108. *JCC*, 4:49 (Jan. 11, 1776).
109. *Pa. Gazette*, April 3, 1776.

110. Minutes of the Committee of Safety, Feb. 15, 1776, *Col. Records*, 10:486–487; Thomas Fisher to Jabez Fisher, March 11, 1776, Fisher Collection, HSP.
111. Joseph Shippen to Edward Shippen, July 3, 1776, Shippen Papers, HSP.
112. Records of the Berks County Committee, *Pa. Archives* (2d Ser.), 14:309.
113. *JCC*, 4:205 (March 14, 1776).
114. *Pa. Archives* (8th Ser.), 8:7505–7507.
115. J. Paul Selsam, *The Pennsylvania Constitution of 1776: A Study in Revolutionary Democracy* (Philadelphia: U. of Penn. Press, 1936), 136.
116. *The Proceedings Relative to Calling the Conventions of 1776 and 1790* (Harrisburg: John S. Wiestling, 1825), 38–39; see generally Selsam, *Pennsylvania Constitution*, ch. 4. An earlier proposal to similarly limit the suffrage in Assembly elections was denounced as "treason—the worst of treason—treason against the Constitution" by an anonymous writer in the *Pennsylvania Gazette*. *Pa. Gazette*, May 1, 1776. This writer was in turn denounced as a "bloody minded traitor" by another anonymous writer. *Pa. Gazette*, May 15, 1776. On the many newspaper exchanges in March, April, and May 1776, see Ryerson, *Revolution*, 166–175.
117. *JCC*, 4:464 (June 18, 1776).
118. *Pa. Evening Post*, June 15, 1776.
119. Ibid.
120. *Pa. Evening Post*, April 20, 1776.
121. Thomas Paine, *Common Sense*, in *The Complete Writings of Thomas Paine*, ed. Philip S. Foner (New York: Citadel Press, 1945), 2:43–44.
122. A New York newspaper approvingly noted in February 1776 that Lord Mansfield had issued a writ of habeas corpus with respect to an individual charged with "treasonable practices." *N.Y. Journal*, Feb. 1, 1776.
123. Jasper Yeates to Edward Burd, Aug. 15, 1775, Edward Burd Papers, HSP.
124. Some Americans disputed this, asserting that the Prohibitory Act of December 1775 effectively removed the Americans from the king's protection and thus eliminated any reciprocal duty of allegiance. See, e.g., William Henry Drayton's Charge, Charlestown District, Oct. 15, 1776, in *Gentlemen of the Grand Jury*, 2:1194.
125. Willard Sterne Randall, *Ethan Allen: His Life and Times* (New York: Norton, 2011), 375–401.
126. Amanda L. Tyler, *Habeas Corpus in Wartime: From the Tower of London to Guantanamo Bay* (New York: Oxford Univ. Press, 2017), 64–78.
127. George Washington to Thomas Gage, Aug. 11, 1775, *Papers of George Washington: Revolutionary War Series*, ed. Philander D. Chase (Charlottesville: UVA Press., 1985), 1:289. Washington's letter specifically referred to the differing treatment of officers and common soldiers, but his comments had obvious implications for executions of American prisoners.
128. *JCC*, 3:412 (Dec. 6, 1775) ("whatever punishment shall be inflicted upon any persons in the power of our enemies for favouring, aiding, or abetting the cause of

American liberty, shall be retaliated in the same kind, and the same degree upon those in our power, who have favoured, aided, or abetted, or shall favour, aid or abet the system of ministerial oppression").

129. Randall, *Ethan Allen*, 402–409.
130. 17 George III, ch. 9; Paul D. Halliday, *Habeas Corpus: From England to Empire* (Cambridge, MA: Harvard Univ. Press, 2010), 251–252; Steffen, *Defining a British State*, 95–96; Tyler, *Habeas Corpus in Wartime*, 80–98.
131. *Pa. Evening Post*, May 14, 1776.
132. Extract of a letter from a gentlemen of Philadelphia, to his friend in London, dated Philadelphia, May 18, 1776, *Gazetteer and New Daily Advertiser* (London), July 13, 1776.
133. John Adams to John Sullivan, June 23, 1776, *Letters of Delegates to Congress*, 4:296.
134. *JCC*, 4:475 (June 24, 1776).
135. "The Declaration of the Deputies of Pennsylvania met in Provincial Conference at Philadelphia, June 24, 1776," *Pa. Gazette*, June 26, 1776. For a detailed examination of the Provincial Conference and the politics surrounding it, see Ryerson, *Revolution*, ch. 9. A few weeks earlier the city of Boston had resolved that "loyalty to [the king] is now treason to our country." *Pa. Evening Post*, June 8, 1776.
136. Joseph Hawley to Elbridge Gerry, July 17, 1776, in *The American Tory*, ed. Morton Borden & Penn Borden (Englewood Cliffs, NJ: Prentice-Hall, 1972), 73.
137. *Pa. Evening Post*, April 20, 1776.
138. John Adams to Jonathan Dickinson Sergeant, July 21, 1776, *Papers of John Adams*, ed. Robert J. Taylor (Cambridge, MA: Harvard Univ. Press, 1979), 4:397–398.
139. *Pa. Evening Post*, June 29, 1776.
140. For an analysis of the Declaration of Independence as a legal document, see Carlton F.W. Larson, "The Declaration of Independence: A 225th Anniversary Re-Interpretation," *Wash. L. Rev.* 76 (2001): 701–791.
141. A week before the adoption of the Declaration, for example, the Committee of Safety ordered David McCutcheon to be held in the Philadelphia jail "as a person dangerous to the safety of American Liberty." *Col. Records*, 10:616.
142. [Thomas Paine], *Four Letters on Interesting Subjects* (Philadelphia: Styner & Cist, 1776), 3.

CHAPTER 4

1. John W. Jackson, *With the British Army in Philadelphia, 1777–1778* (San Rafael, CA: Presidio Press, 1979), 120.
2. James Allen, "Extracts from the Diary of James Allen," Jan. 25, 1777, in John K. Heyl, *James Allen: Builder of Trout Hall* (Allentown, PA: Lehigh County Historical Society, 1962), 74.
3. Thomas Hartley to James Wilson, Dec. 22, 1776, Gratz Collection, HSP, quoted in Selsam, *Pennsylvania Constitution*, 239.

4. Selsam, *Pennsylvania Constitution*, 146–147, 149–150.
5. Ordinance of Sept. 5, 1776, ch. 782, *Pa. Stat.*, 9:18–19. The New Jersey convention enacted a similar ordinance on July 18, 1776. *Pa. Gazette*, July 24, 1776.
6. James Kettner, *The Development of American Citizenship, 1608–1870* (Chapel Hill: UNC Press, 1978), 8. The leading British decision was Calvin's Case, 77 E.R. 377 (K.B. 1608).
7. *Pa. Gazette*, Sept. 4, 1776.
8. Ordinance of Sept. 12, 1776, ch. 783, *Pa. Stat.*, 9:19–21.
9. *Votes and Proceedings of the House of Representatives of the Province of Pennsylvania* (Philadelphia: Henry Miller, 1776), 6:764.
10. Minutes of the Council of Safety, Aug. 2. 1776, *Col. Records*, 10:666–667.
11. Minutes of the Council of Safety, Aug. 5, 1776, *Col. Records*, 10:670. In 1770, the younger Hatton had been brutally assaulted by a Philadelphia crowd for assisting with his father's duties as Customs Collector of New Jersey. Rosswurm, *Arms, Country & Class*, 32–33.
12. Minutes of the Council of Safety, Aug. 5, 1776, *Col. Records*, 10:669.
13. Minutes of the Council of Safety, Aug. 8, 1776, *Col. Records*, 10:676.
14. Minutes of the Council of Safety, Nov. 22, 1776, *Col. Records*, 11:12. This may be a transcription error for John Hales, who was imprisoned on a charge of "treasonable practices" in August 1776. Petition of John Hales, Clemency File, RG-27, PSA.
15. Minutes of the Council of Safety, Dec. 22, 1776, *Col. Records*, 11:59. The Council also ordered the arrest of Samuel Biles, former sheriff of Bucks County. Order for the Arrest of Samuel Biles, Oct. 4, 1776, *Pa. Archives* (2d Ser.), 1:629.
16. Minutes of the Council of Safety, Oct. 31, 1776, *Col. Records*, 10:773; Order for the Removal of Dr. Kearsley, Oct. 31, 1776, *Pa. Archives* (2d Ser.), 1:640; see also Minutes of the SEC, April 2, 1777, *Col. Records*, 11:196 (review of John Connolly's confinement).
17. Deposition of Francis Mills, Aug. 30, 1776, *Pa. Archives*, 5:15.
18. Minutes of the Northumberland Co. Committee of Safety, April 17, 1777, *Pa. Archives* (2d Ser.), 14:363, 365.
19. Minutes of the Council of Safety, Dec. 7, 1776, *Col. Records*, 11:38.
20. Council of Safety to Committee of Chester, Feb. 1777, *Pa. Archives* (2d Ser.), 1:699–700.
21. Minutes of the Council of Safety, Dec. 17, 1776, *Col. Records*, 11:54.
22. Record of the Council of Safety, Jan. 18, 1777, *Pa. Archives* (4th Ser.), 3:623.
23. Council of Safety to John Hancock, Dec. 22, 1776, Papers of the Continental Congress, State Papers, Pennsylvania, 1: 277, available at http://www.fold3.com.
24. Minutes of the Council of Safety, Oct. 31, 1776, *Col. Records*, 10:774.
25. Minutes of the Council of Safety, Jan. 1, 1777, *Col. Records*, 11:70–71. There is a variant text of this resolution in *Pa. Archives*, 5:147–148. The *Colonial Records* text, however, was published in the *Pennsylvania Packet*, Jan. 4, 1777, suggesting that the *Pa. Archives* text was an earlier draft.

26. Minutes of a Meeting held at the Indian Queen, 1776, *Pa. Archives*, 5:73–75. Arping later claimed that he had been imprisoned for five months. Ousterhout, *State Divided*, 157.
27. Joseph Stansbury to Council of Safety, Dec. 6, 1776, *Pa. Archives*, 5:94–95.
28. Joseph Stansbury to Council of Safety, Dec. 10, 1776, *Pa. Archives*, 5:98–99. The original document is preserved in the Clemency File, RG-27, PSA.
29. Minutes of the Council of Safety, Dec. 10, 1776, *Col. Records*, 11:43.
30. Minutes of the Council of Safety, Jan. 28, 1777, *Col. Records*, 11:106.
31. "In Council of Safety," Oct. 5, 1776, Society Collection, HSP.
32. Minutes of the Committee of Observation and Inspection of Northampton Co., Aug. 2, 1776, *Pa. Archives* (2d. Ser.), 14:611.
33. Minutes of the Committee of Observation and Inspection of Northampton Co., Feb. 15, 1777, *Pa. Archives* (2d. Ser.), 14:625–627. The resemblance to a docket book is more obvious in the manuscript, which can be found in the Northampton County Papers, HSP, 64.
34. Minutes of the Committee of Observation and Inspection of Northampton Co., Dec. 9 & Dec. 13, 1776, *Pa. Archives* (2d Ser.), 14:617–618.
35. Minutes of the Committee of Observation and Inspection of Northampton Co., Aug. 2, 1776, *Pa. Archives* (2d. Ser.), 14:611.
36. Commitment Order for Matthew McHugh, Dec. 16, 1776, *Pa. Archives* (2d Ser.), 13:538–539.
37. Minutes of the Committee of Observation and Inspection of Northampton Co., Dec. 9, 13, & 24, 1776, *Pa. Archives* (2d Ser.), 14:617–619.
38. Minutes of the Committee of Observation and Inspection of Northampton Co., Dec. 27, 1776, *Pa. Archives* (2d Ser.), 14:620–621.
39. James Read to Council of Safety, Dec. 27, 1776, *Pa. Archives*, 5:138–139.
40. Petition of John Wilson, American Loyalist Claims, AO13.17.338, National Archives of the United Kingdom; Statement of Daniel Batwelle, American Loyalist Claims, AO13.17.341, National Archives of the United Kingdom. The committee was either from York or Cumberland County; Wilson was from York County, but he was imprisoned in Carlisle, the seat of Cumberland County.
41. Committee of Safety Minutes, Northumberland Co., *Pa. Archives* (2d Ser.), 14:352–358. It is unclear what, if anything, the Council did with Robb. In 1780, he was acquitted of misprision of treason for similar behavior. Docket Book of the Northumberland County Court of Quarter Sessions, Northumberland County Courthouse, Sunbury, PA. He was later appointed a justice of the peace. *History of Lycoming County, Pa.*, ed. John F. Meginness (Chicago: Brown, Runk, 1892), 101.
42. Committee of Safety Minutes, Northumberland Co., April 17, 1777, *Pa. Archives* (2d Ser.), 14:366.
43. Thomas Paine, "The American Crisis," in *The Complete Writings of Thomas Paine*, ed. Philip S. Foner (New York: Citadel Press, 1945), 2:53.

44. Ibid., 2:62–63.
45. John Cadwalader, Address to the Council of Safety, Jan. 15, 1777, Cadwalader Collection, HSP.
46. *Pa. Archives*, 5:186–188.
47. John Armstrong to Council of Safety, Jan. 5, 1777, *Pa. Archives*, 5:164.
48. George Stevenson to James Wilson, Jan. 30, 1777, Pennsylvania Collection, MG- 8, PSA. On Stevenson, see Roland M. Baumann, *George Stevenson (1718–1783): Conservative as Revolutionary* (Carlisle, PA: Cumberland Co. Hist. Soc., 1978).
49. Act of Jan. 28, 1777, ch. 737, *Pa. Stat.*, 9:29.
50. Act of Feb. 11, 1777, ch. 740, *Pa. Stat.*, 9:45.
51. Paine, "American Crisis," 1:94. In a separate publication, Paine argued, "the union must be supported. . . . it would be treason in any one province to act separately from the rest." [Thomas Paine], *Four Letters on Interesting Subjects* (Philadelphia: Styner & Cist, 1776), 9.
52. On the development of the two-witness rule in English law, see L.M. Hill, "The Two-Witness Rule in English Treason Trials: Some Comments of the Emergence of Procedural Law," *Am. J. Leg. Hist.* 12 (1968): 95–111.
53. Foster, *Report*, 211.
54. Hurst, *American Law of Treason*, 93.
55. Blackstone, *Commentaries*, 4:120.
56. Act of Feb. 11, 1777, ch. 740, *Pa. Stat.*, 9:46–47.
57. SEC to Sheriffs and Magistrates of Bucks Co., April 2, 1777, *Pa. Archives*, 5:291.
58. Examinations in the Case of James Molesworth, *Pa. Archives*, 5:270–281.
59. Pa. War Office to Gen. Lincoln, March 31, 1777, *Pa Archives*, 5:281; Pa. War Office to Gen. Putnam, March 31, 1777, *Pa. Archives*, 5:282.
60. *JCC*, 5:693 (Aug. 21, 1776).
61. James Wilkinson, *Memoirs of My Own Times* (Philadelphia: Abraham Small, 1816), 1:159.
62. Wilkinson, *Memoirs*, 1:159.
63. *JCC*, 7:210 (March 31, 1777).
64. John Adams to Abigail Adams, March 31, 1777, *LDC*, 6:512. Christopher Marshall noted in his diary that Molesworth had been executed for "treasonable practices against this state." Marshall, *Diary*, 118.
65. Memorial of Thomas Davidson, American Loyalist Claims, AO12.42.388, National Archives of the United Kingdom.
66. Wilkinson, *Memoirs*, 1:159.
67. Roger Sherman to Jonathan Trumbull, Sr., May 25, 1777, *LDC*, 7:134. Sherman had made a similar point in a separate letter four days earlier. Roger Sherman to Oliver Wolcott, May 21, 1777, *LDC*, 7:101. For more on the distinction between military jurisdiction over prisoners of war and civilian jurisdiction over traitors, see Abraham Clark to William Livingston, Dec. 11, 1777, *LDC*, 8:403.

68. George Washington to Preudhomme de Borre, Aug. 3, 1777, in *The Papers of George Washington: Revolutionary War Series*, ed. Frank E. Grizzard, Jr. (London & Charlottesville: UVA Press., 2000), 10:495.
69. Ex parte Milligan, 71 U.S. (4 Wall.) 2, 80 (1866).
70. John Hancock to Horatio Gates, April 18, 1777, *LDC*, 6:610.
71. *JCC*, 7:374.
72. *JCC*, 8:382; John A. Nagy, *Spies in the Continental Capital* (Yardley, PA: Westholme Publishing, 2011), 39–41. This Brown may be the same John Brown who was later charged with treason in New Jersey. *Pa. Gazette*, Jan. 27, 1778.
73. Court Martial Records, May 26, 1777, *Pa. Archives*, 5:389.
74. *Pa. Gazette*, July 2, 1777.
75. War Office to SEC, April 2, 1777, *Pa. Archives*, 5:290–291. At least one other woman, Jane Cooper, was initially imprisoned on suspicion of aiding Molesworth. Jane Cooper to Thomas Wharton, April 1, 1777, Clemency File, RG-33, PSA.
76. SEC to James Young, May 9, 1777, *Pa. Archives*, 5:336; James Young to Timothy Matlack, May 13, 1777, *Pa. Archives*, 5:337.
77. Minutes of the SEC, July 2, 1777, *Col. Records*, 11:236.
78. Paine, "The American Crisis," 1:91.
79. Act of June 18, 1777, ch. 756, *Pa. Stat.*, 9:110–114.
80. Ousterhout, *State Divided*, 161–162; Robert L. Brunhouse, *The Counter-Revolution in Pennsylvania, 1776–1790* (Harrisburg, PA: Pa. Hist. Comm., 1942), 40–41.
81. Archibald McClean to George Bryan, Oct. 11, 1777, *Pa. Archives*, 5:662–663.
82. Robert Strettel Jones to ?, July 19, 1777, Jonah Thompson Collection, HSP, 3:99.
83. See, e.g., Mittimus in case of Henry Funk, Aug. 9, 1777, *Pa. Archives*, 5:508–509; Minutes of the SEC, Aug. 15, 1777, *Col. Records*, 11:269; see also Examination and Commitment of Thomas Patterson, June 13, 1777, Clemency File, RG-27, PSA. Loyalty oaths similar to those mandated by the Test Act would eventually be adopted by all of the states by 1778. Hyman, *To Try Men's Souls*, 85.
84. "An Address presented to the Honourable President of the Executive Council, and the Board of War, on the sixth instant," *Pa. Gazette*, May 21, 1777.
85. "To the Honourable House of Assembly of the State of Pennsylvania, *Pa. Gazette*, May 21, 1777.
86. Gouvernor Morris to Alexander Hamilton, May 16, 1777, in *The Works of Alexander Hamilton*, ed. John C. Hamilton (New York: Charles S. Francis, 1851), 1:27–28.
87. Brunhouse, *Counter-Revolution*, 37.
88. Minutes of the SEC, March 20, 1777, *Col Records*, 11:186; Minutes of the SEC, April 9, 1777, *Col. Records*, 11:202; Minutes of the SEC, July 23, 1777, *Col. Records*, 11:249; Council to Joseph Reed, July 23, 1777, *Pa. Archives*, 10:157–158.
89. G.S. Rowe, *Thomas McKean: The Shaping of an American Republicanism* (Boulder, CO: Colorado Associated Univ. Press, 1978), 93.
90. Pa. Const. of 1776, § 23.

91. On later controversy over these dual appointments, see Rowe, *Thomas McKean*, 164–169.
92. Minutes of the SEC, Aug. 16, 1777, *Col. Records*, 11:270.
93. Qualification of Chief Justice McKean, *Pa. Archives*, 5:621.
94. *Pa. Gazette*, July 30, 1777.
95. Marshall, *Diary*, 122 (Aug. 5 & 8, 1777).
96. Rowe, *Thomas McKean*, 102.
97. Archibald McClean to George Bryan, Aug. 13, 1777, *Pa. Archives*, 5:514–520.
98. Archibald McClean to George Bryan, Oct. 11, 1777, *Pa. Archives*, 5:662–663.
99. Robert Levers to Timothy Matlack, Nov. 15, 1777, *Pa. Archives*, 6:5.
100. Minutes of the SEC, July 26, 1777, *Col. Records*, 11:252.
101. Minutes of the SEC, Feb. 28, 1777, *Col. Records*, 11:432.
102. Francis S. Fox, "The Prothonotary: Linchpin of Provincial and State Government in Eighteenth Century Pennsylvania," *Pa. History* 59, no. 1 (Jan. 1992): 41, 48; Brunhouse, *Counter-Revolution*, 35–36.
103. James Allen, "Diary," 78 (June 6, 1777).
104. William Duer to John Jay, May 28, 1777, *LDC*, 7:138.
105. Graydon, *Memoirs*, 283–285.
106. *JCC*, 8:591 (July 31, 1777).
107. Warrant to Arrest Certain Persons, Aug. 1, 1777, *Pa. Archives*, 5:478.
108. Authority to Call in Aid in Arresting Certain Persons, Aug., 2, 1777, *Pa. Archives*, 5:480.
109. Warrant to Arrest Certain Persons, Aug. 4, 1777, *Pa. Archives*, 5:484.
110. James Tilghman to SEC, Aug. 8, 1777, *Pa. Archives*, 5:502–503. Tilghman later claimed, "I have said nothing that any Attorney General of any state can make out to be treason nor even misdemeanor nor anything injurious to the United States." James Tilghman to Benjamin Chew, Oct. 31, 1777, Chew Family Papers, HSP.
111. James Hamilton to SEC, n.d., *Pa. Archives*, 5:611.
112. Benjamin Chew, Account of his Arrest, n.d., Chew Papers, HSP.
113. Benjamin Rush to John Adams, Aug. 8, 1777, *Letters of Benjamin Rush*, ed. L.H. Butterfield (Princeton, NJ: Am. Phil. Soc., 1951), 1:152.
114. *JCC*, 8:633–634 (Aug. 12, 1777).
115. Parole of Benjamin Chew, Aug. 14, 1777, Chew Papers, HSP.
116. *JCC*, 8:641 (Aug. 14, 1777).
117. *JCC*, 8:678–679 (Aug. 26, 1777).
118. *JCC*, 8:694–695 (Aug. 28, 1777).
119. John Adams to Abigail Adams, Sept. 8, 1777, *LDC*, 7:626, 627.
120. *JCC*, 8:695 (Aug. 28, 1777).
121. Minutes of the SEC, Aug. 31, 1777, *Col. Records*, 11:283–284.
122. Minutes of the SEC, Sept. 3, 1777, *Col. Records*, 11:287–289.
123. *JCC*, 8:707–708 (Sept. 3, 1777).

124. Minutes of the SEC, Sept. 4, 1777, *Col. Records*, 11:290.
125. *JCC*, 8:713 (Sept. 5, 1777).
126. *Pa. Eve. Post*, Sept. 4, 1777.
127. *JCC*, 8:718–719 (Sept. 6, 1777).
128. Remonstrance of Israel Pemberton, John Hunt, and Samuel Pleasants, *Pa. Eve. Post*, Sept. 4, 1777.
129. *JCC*, 8:718–719 (Sept. 6, 1777); Henry Laurens to? Sept. 5, 1777. Laurens described the issue as a "silly point."
130. Minutes of the SEC, Sept. 6, 1777, *Col. Records*, 11:293.
131. Minutes of the SEC, Sept. 8, 1777, *Col. Records*, 11:294.
132. *JCC*, 8:722–723 (Sept. 8, 1777).
133. Minutes of the SEC, Sept. 9, 1777, *Col. Records*, 11:295–296.
134. *An Address to the Inhabitants of Pennsylvania, by those Freemen of the City of Philadelphia who are now confined in the Mason's Lodge* (Philadelphia: 1777), 16–17, 20.
135. Ibid., 35.
136. "Observations on the Charges," in Thomas Gilpin, *Exiles in Virginia* (Philadelphia: Society of Friends, 1848), 242. When officers came to arrest John Pemberton, citing "orders," he sarcastically asked them "whether if they had orders to Hang me whether they would do it." Diary of John Pemberton, Pemberton Papers, HSP, 1.
137. "Journal and Transactions of the Exiles," in Gilpin, *Exiles*, 69.
138. "Diary of James Allen," 293. On the exiles' deliberate use of the rhetoric of liberty, see Paige L. Whidbee, "The Quaker Exiles: 'The Cause of Every Inhabitant,'" *Pa. Hist.* 83 (2016): 28–57.
139. *Journal and Proceedings of the General Assembly of the Common-wealth of Pennsylvania* (Philadelphia: John Dunlap, 1777), 88.
140. Act of Sept. 16, 1777, ch. 762, *Pa. Stat.*, 9:138.
141. *Pa. Eve. Post*, Sept. 6, 1777.
142. Thomas McKean to John Adams, Sept, 19, 1777, in *LDC*, 7:574–575. A draft of the letter is in the Thomas McKean Papers, HSP, 1:11.
143. *Pa. Packet*, Nov. 7, 1778 (death sentence for John Roberts).
144. Robert Morton, "The Diary of Robert Morton," *PMHB* 1 (1877): 6.
145. McKean to Adams, *LDC*, 7:575.
146. Robert Oaks, "Philadelphians in Exile: The Problem of Loyalty during the American Revolution," *PMHB* 96 (July 1972): 298, 316; Minutes of the SEC, Jan. 5, 1778 & Feb. 24, 1778, *Col. Records*, 11:395, 427.
147. *JCC*, 10:238 (March 10, 1778).
148. Thomas Wharton, Jr., to Henry Laurens, March 7, 1778, Papers of the Continental Congress, State Papers, PA, 1:481.
149. *JCC*, 10:260 (March 16, 1778).

150. Oaks, "Philadelphians in Exile," 298–325; Theodore Thayer, *Israel Pemberton: King of the Quakers* (Philadelphia: HSP, 1943), 207–233.
151. Minutes of the SEC, April 8, 1778, *Col. Records*, 11:461.
152. Konkle, *Benjamin Chew*, 161. For the Council's defense of the Penn and Chew detentions, see SEC to Abraham Clarke, March 27, 1778, *Pa. Archives*, 6:389–390 ("The arrest of those Gentlemen was unquestionably proper. At a time of great confusion, when the enemy was advancing to our Capitol, it was in their power to have done us a great injury by heading a party against the few Whigs which remained in it, and by other means, which are now wholly out of their power").
153. Richard Bauman, *For the Reputation of Truth: Politics, Religion, and Conflict among the Pennsylvania Quakers, 1750–1800* (Baltimore: Johns Hopkins Univ. Press, 1971), 164.
154. Leonard W. Levy, *Original Intent and the Framers' Constitution* (New York: Macmillan, 1988), 239–240.
155. Edward Burd to Jasper Yeates, Sept. 16, 1777, Jasper Yeates Papers, HSP.
156. Allen, "Diary of James Allen," 293.
157. Robert Morton, "The Diary of Robert Morton," *PMHB* 1 (1877): 5.
158. Owen Jones, Jr., to James Duane, *Pa. Archives*, 6:102.
159. Observations respecting the Memorial presented to Congress on behalf of Israel Pemberton and others Prisoners at Winchester tending to shew that the Prayer of the said Memorial ought to be complied with; on the principles of Humanity, Justice, & Policy, Clemency File, RG-27, PSA.
160. British practice is summarized in Halliday, *Habeas Corpus*, 247–256.
161. Typescript of James Pemberton's Diary, Pemberton Papers, HSP, 1, 4.
162. Oaks, "Philadelphians in Exile," 309–312.
163. *Report of the Committee of the Council of Censors . . . as Adopted by the Said Council* (Philadelphia: Francis Bailey, 1784), 6.
164. Joseph F. Foster, "James Pemberton," in *Lawmaking and Legislators in Pennsylvania: A Biographical Dictionary*, ed. Craig W. Horle, Joseph S. Foster & Laurie M. Wolfe (Harrisburg, PA: Commonwealth of PA, 2005), 3:1020–1038, 1034.
165. Joseph F. Foster, "James Rankin," in *Lawmaking and Legislators in Pennsylvania*, 3:1148–1155. Rankin later fled to the British and was named in the first legislative attainder proclamation.
166. SEC to John Creigh & John Agnew, Sept. 16, 1777, *Pa. Archives*, 5:628–629; Minutes of the SEC, Sept. 15, 1777, *Col. Records*, 11:307–308. In a petition to the Continental Congress, Shelley stated that he "could neither read Dutch nor English writings, and has been always been accustomed to hard Labour." Daniel Shelley to Continental Congress, Oct. 16, 1777, Clemency File, RG-27, PSA.
167. Deposition of Daniel Shelly, Sept. 22, 1777, Pa. Provincial Conference Box, Simon Gratz Collection, HSP.

168. John Carothers to William Henry, Sept. 25, 1777, *Pa. Archives*, 5:634. On the clergymen, see James P. Myers, Jr., "Homeland Security in the Pennsylvania Backcountry, 1777–1778: The Example of the Reverend Mr. Daniel Batwelle, SPG," *Penn. History* 78 (2016): 247–271; William Pencak, "Out of Many, One: Pennsylvania's Loyalist Clergy in the American Revolution," in *Pennsylvania's Revolution*, ed. William Pencak (Univ. Park: Penn. St. Univ. Press, 2010), 113.
169. Edward Burd to Jasper Yeates, Sept. 8, 1777, Jasper Yeates Papers, HSP.
170. *JCC*, 9:777 (Oct. 6, 1777).
171. Rosswurm, *Arms, Country and Class*, 149.
172. *JCC*: 9:784 (Oct. 8, 1777); *JCC*: 9:1068 (Dec. 30, 1777).
173. Act of Oct. 13, 1777, ch. 765, *Pa. Stat.* 147–148.
174. Act of Oct. 13, 1777, ch. 766, *Pa. Stat.* 149–151. In 1784, the Pennsylvania Council of Censors concluded that the formation of the Council of Safety, which combined legislative and judicial powers, was "inconsistent" with the constitution and "subversive of it." *Report of the Committee of the Council of Censors*, 13.
175. Proclamation of the Council of Safety, Oct. 17, 1777, *Col. Records*, 11:325, 327.
176. Minutes of the Council of Safety, Oct. 21, 1777, *Col. Records*, 11:328–331.
177. Minutes of the Council of Safety, Nov. 20, 1777, *Col. Records*, 11:344; Minutes of the Council of Safety, Dec. 1, 1777, *Col. Records*, 11:352.
178. *JCC*, 9:937–938 (Nov. 18, 1777); Minutes of the Council of Safety, Nov. 21, 1777, *Col. Records*, 11:344–345.
179. Minutes of the Council of Safety, Nov. 21, 1777, *Col. Records*, 11:344–345.
180. Charles Rappleye, *Robert Morris: Financier of the American Revolution* (New York: Simon & Schuster, 2010), 128–129; George Washington to the Continental Congress, Nov. 23, 1777, *Pa. Archives*, 6:30; Robert Morris to Thomas Wharton, Jr., Nov. 30, 1777, *Pa. Archives*, 6:45.
181. George Stevenson to Thomas Wharton, Jr., Dec. 15, 1777, *Pa. Archives*, 6:94.
182. Minutes of the Council of Safety, Dec. 4, 1777, *Col. Records*, 11:352–353.
183. *JCC*, 9:1069 (Dec. 30, 1777).
184. Board of War to Thomas Wharton, Jr., Dec. 20, 1777, *Pa. Archives*, 6:118.
185. General Roberdeau to George Bryan, Dec. 28, 1777, *Pa. Archives*, 6:144.
186. John Bayard to Thomas McKean, Feb. 28, 1778, Thomas McKean Papers, HSP.
187. *JCC*, 10:204–205 (Feb. 27, 1778).
188. U.S. Continental Congress, *The deluded tools of the enemy . . .* (n.p., 1778). There were also calls to punish counterfeiting by court-martial. As one Pennsylvanian put it in March 1778, counterfeiters should be sent "to camp to be tried for their lives, as the law of the land requires their execution for examples to evil-doers." Alex? to Captain Chambers, March 18, 1778, William Henry Papers, HSP.
189. William Bradford to Tacy Bradford, March 15, 1778, Wallace Collection, HSP.
190. *Pa. Gazette*, March 21, 1778.
191. List of Persons Tried before the General Court-Martial at Lancaster, Court Martial Papers, 1777–1805, Box 15c, Society Miscellaneous Collection, HSP.

192. Examination of Henry Mansin, Feb. 2, 1778, *Pa. Archives*, 6:221–224.
193. *Pa. Gazette*, March 21, 1778; Examination of Wendle Meyer, Feb. 3, 1778, *Pa. Archives*, 6:225–226.
194. George Washington to Adam Hubley, Feb. 14, 1778, *Papers of George Washington: Revolutionary War Series*, ed. Edward G. Lengel (Charlottesville: UVA. Press, 2003), 13:537–538.
195. *Pa. Gazette*, March 21, 1778.
196. List of Persons Tried before the General Court-Martial at Lancaster, Society Collection, HSP.
197. Minutes of the SEC, April 25, 1778, *Col. Records*, 11:472.
198. John Lacey, Jr., to George Washington, April 12, 1778, *Papers of George Washington: Revolutionary War Series*, ed. David R. Hoth (Charlottesville: UVA Press, 2004), 14:486–488.
199. John Lacey, Jr., to George Washington, April 20, 1778, ibid., 14:569–570.
200. George Washington to John Armstrong, March 17, 1778, ibid., 14:326–328.
201. George Washington to Joseph Kirkbride, April 20, 1778, ibid., 14:568.
202. SEC to John Lacey, March 12, 1778, *Pa. Archives*, 6:361.
203. SEC to John Lacey, March 27, 1778, *Pa. Archives*, 6:390.
204. George Washington to Brig. Gen. Lacey, April 11, 1778, *Pa. Archives*, 6:410.
205. The military regularly exercised jurisdiction over its own members for traitorous acts. For example, in August 1778, Lieutenant Samuel Ford was sentenced to death by a Philadelphia court-martial for deserting to the enemy during the siege of Fort Mifflin. *Pa. Archives*, 6:697–699. The Council rejected Ford's request for clemency, and he was publicly executed in Philadelphia. Minutes of the SEC, Sept. 1, 1778, *Col. Records*, 11:566; *Pa. Eve. Post*, Sept. 2, 1778.
206. Benedict Arnold to Henry Laurens, Aug. 15, 1778, Papers of the Continental Congress, Letters from General Officers, 1:142, available at http://www.fold3.com.
207. *JCC*, 11:797–798 (Aug. 15, 1778).
208. SEC to Henry Laurens, Aug. 22, 1778, *Pa. Archives*, 6:713.
209. Minutes of the SEC, Aug. 22, 1778, *Col. Records*, 11:561.
210. Petition of Frederick Verner, Dec. 7, 1778, Papers of the Continental Congress, Petitions, 8:33–36, available at http://www.fold3.com.
211. Joseph Reed to John Jay, March 13, 1779, *Pa. Archives*, 7:246; see also Nagy, *Spies in the Continental Capital*, 100–101.

CHAPTER 5

1. Elizabeth Drinker, *The Diary of Elizabeth Drinker*, ed. Elaine Forman Crane (Boston: Northeastern Univ. Press, 1991), 1: 270.
2. Ibid.
3. *Pa. Packet*, Sept. 26, 1778.

4. *Pa. Packet*, Oct. 6, 1778.
5. Marshall, *Diary*, 201 (Oct. 9, 1778). Two disowned Quakers later claimed that Quaker officials had entered a "formal written order" for Molesworth's burial and that Molesworth's "funeral was attended by a very great number of the people of that society, which is too notorious to need proof." Memorial and Remonstrance of Isaac Howell and White Matlack, *Minutes of the First Session, of the Sixth General Assembly, of the Commonwealth of Pennsylvania* (Philadelphia: John Dunlap, 1781), 668.
6. Thomas Paine, "American Crisis: V," March 21, 1778, in *Complete Writings of Thomas Paine*, ed. Philip S. Foner (New York: Citadel Press, 1945), 1:106, 126.
7. Jasper Yeates to James Burd, Feb. 15, 1778, Burd-Shippen Family Collection, MG-30, PSA. Yeates was admitted to the bar of the Court of Quarter Sessions for York County in July 1778. Docket Book of the York County Court of Quarter Sessions, York County Historical Society, York, PA.
8. Jonathan Dickinson Sergeant to Thomas Wharton, May 13, 1778, Pennsylvania Committee and Council of Safety Box, Simon Gratz Collection, HSP.
9. Memorial of Justices of Northumberland, *Pa. Archives*, 7:72–73.
10. Justices of Berks County to Council, 1778, *Pa. Archives*, 6:722–723.
11. Robert Galbraith to Thomas Wharton, May 16, 1778, *Pa. Archives*, 6:511–512.
12. Blackstone, *Commentaries*, 4:368–369.
13. Robert Galbraith to Thomas Wharton, Feb. 6, 1778, *Pa. Archives*, 6:238–239.
14. Docket Book of the York County Court of Quarter Sessions, York County Historical Society, York, PA (Jan. Sessions 1778; April Sessions 1778).
15. Pennsylvania v. McKinley, Docket Book of the York County Court of Quarter Sessions, York County Historical Society, York, PA (April Sessions 1778; April Sessions 1779).
16. Minutes of the SEC, Jan. 20, 1779, *Col. Records*, 11:673. The surviving city court docket book begins in October 1779, so the number of cases at issue is not known.
17. Docket Book of the Cumberland County Court of Quarter Sessions, Cumberland County Historical Society, Cumberland, PA, 6:16.
18. Ibid., 6:22.
19. Ibid., 6:20.
20. Ibid., 6:34.
21. Ibid., 6:18, 54.
22. Recognizance of Michael Ohl, Recognizances taken before Judge Robert Levers, Court of Quarter Sessions of Northampton County, Dec. 19, 1777–Nov. 1, 1779, Pennsylvania Collection, MG-8, #884, PSA.
23. Indictment of Michael & Jacob Mossinger, March Sessions 1778, Winthrop Sargent items, Simon Gratz Collection, HSP, 179; Indictment of Philip Lumbach, Dec. Sessions, 1778, Northampton County Papers, HSP; Indictment of Adam Rosnick, June Sessions, 1779, Miscellaneous Box, Northampton County Papers, HSP.

24. Minutes of the SEC, Aug. 31, 1777, *Col. Records*, 11:285.
25. Minutes of the SEC, Oct. 18, 1777, *Col. Records*, 11:357.
26. SEC to Assembly, May 18, 1778, *Pa. Archives*, 6:518.
27. Edward Burd to Jasper Yeates, Sept. 30, 1778, Yeates Family Collection, HSP. Burd later prosecuted treason cases at the Northampton Oyer and Terminer Court in 1780. See Chapter 8.
28. Docket Book of the Cumberland County Court of Quarter Sessions, Cumberland County Historical Society, Carlisle, PA, 6:71.
29. Docket Book of the York County Court of Quarter Sessions, York County Historical Society, York, PA (Jan. Sessions, 1779).
30. Docket Book of the Bedford County Court of Quarter Sessions, Bedford County Courthouse, Bedford, PA (Oct. Sessions, 1780); Docket Book of the Westmoreland County Court of Quarter Sessions, Westmoreland County Courthouse, Greensburg, PA, 182 (July Sessions, 1782).
31. Docket Book of the Westmoreland County Court of Quarter Sessions, Westmoreland County Courthouse, Greensburg, PA, 88 (Jan. Sessions, 1779).
32. Record Book of Benjamin Paschall, Esq., Justice of the Peace for the City and County of Philadelphia, HSP (Commonwealth v. Stephen Blunt; Commonwealth v. Edward Bowell; Commonwealth v. Robert Black; Commonwealth v. George Amor; Commonwealth v. Alexander Corbet; Commonwealth v. Timothy Curby; Commonwealth v. Samuel Gillodey; Commonwealth v. Samuel Coalston); Docket Book of the Philadelphia County Court of Quarter Sessions (1777–1780), Philadelphia City Archives, Philadelphia, PA.
33. Docket Book of the York County Court of Quarter Sessions, York County Historical Society, York, PA (Jan. Sessions, 1779).
34. Respublica v. Robb, Miscellaneous Papers, Northumberland County Court of Quarter Sessions, Northumberland County Courthouse, Sunbury, PA (Nov. 1780).
35. Grand Inquest against Daniel Lee, Miscellaneous Papers, Northumberland County Court of Quarter Sessions, Northumberland County Courthouse, Sunbury, PA (May 1779).
36. Indictment of James Molesworth, Miscellaneous Papers, Northumberland County Court of Quarter Sessions, Northumberland County Courthouse, Sunbury, PA (Feb. 1778).
37. Indictment of Daniel Fields, Miscellaneous Papers, Northumberland County Court of Quarter Sessions, Northumberland County Courthouse, Sunbury, PA (n.d).
38. Indictment of Philip Lumbach, Northampton County Papers, HSP (Dec. Sessions, 1778).
39. Indictment of Samuel Stroud, Northampton County Papers, HSP (Sept. Sessions, 1779).
40. Indictment of Michael & Jacob Mossinger, Winthrop Sargent items, Simon Gratz Collection, HSP, 179 (March Sessions, 1778).

41. Deposition of Gilbert Clark, Nov. 15, 1777, Miscellaneous Papers, Lancaster County Court of Quarter Sessions, Lancaster County Historical Society, Lancaster, PA.
42. Record of Benjamin Paschall, Esq., Justice of the Peace for the City and County of Philadelphia, HSP (Commonwealth v. Stephen Blunt; Commonwealth v. George Amor; Commonwealth v. Timothy Curby; Commonwealth v. Samuel Gillodey; Commonwealth v. Samuel Coalston).
43. Docket Book of the York County Court of Quarter Sessions, York County Historical Society, York, PA.
44. Docket Book of the Philadelphia County Court of Quarter Sessions, 1777–1780, Philadelphia City Archives, Philadelphia, PA, 123–124, 130.
45. Minutes of the SEC, Sept. 22, 1778, *CR*, 11:583. In December 1778, the SEC also remitted the fine of a "Marlon Carvel" (possibly a transcription error), convicted of going to Philadelphia while in possession of the enemy. I have been unable to determine in what court this charge was tried. Minutes of the SEC, Dec. 12, 1778, *Col. Records*, 11:642.
46. These data differ from those of the two scholars who have previously examined Pennsylvania's court records in misprision of treason cases. Henry J. Young concluded that the state "charged" eighty-one men with misprision of treason. Henry J. Young, "Treason and Its Punishment in Revolutionary Pennsylvania," *PMHB* 90 (1966): 287, 295. Young appears to have included every entry in a docket book or court paper, regardless of whether the case was formally presented to a grand jury. Young found forty cases going to trial; I found twenty-one. Young found twenty-five acquittals; I found nine. Young found fifteen convictions, I found twelve. A small number of these discrepancies are explained by Young's inclusion of trials of misprision of treason in the Supreme Court, whereas my data are solely from the county courts, but the rest is inexplicable. I have examined all the records Young examined as well as others he did not find (the records of Northampton and Berks County), and can only conclude that he misinterpreted the evidence in front of him. Anne Ousterhout's data are closer to mine, although she, too, did not locate the Northampton County records. She finds twenty-four trials, with seven acquittals and seventeen convictions, along with eight pardons. Ousterhout, *State Divided*, 320. Her data, like Young's, include the handful of misprision of treason cases tried in the Supreme Court (a procedure discussed more fully in Chapter 8), whereas mine focus solely on the courts of quarter sessions. Although Ousterhout's numbers are clearly preferable to Young's, the data presented here are preferable to both.

As the table indicates, not every case moved smoothly through the system. Some indictments never went to trial, because the defendant disappeared or died or prosecutions were declined. Some cases were removed to the court of oyer and terminer or to the Pennsylvania Supreme Court. Similarly, not every conviction led to judgment; some convictions were subject to successful motions in arrest of judgment. It is possible that there were more indictments than the chart indicates;

charges entered into the docket book without an explicit finding of a "true bill" or an "ignoramus" are excluded. The records of Northampton County are incomplete.

The information in Table 5.1 is derived from the following: Docket Book of the Bedford County Court of Quarter Sessions, Bedford County Courthouse, Bedford, PA; Docket Book of the Berks County Court of Quarter Sessions, Berks County Historical Society, Reading, PA; Docket Book of the Bucks County Court of Quarter Sessions, Mercer Museum Library, Bucks County Historical Society, Doylestown, PA; Docket Book of the Chester County Court of Quarter Sessions, Chester County Archives, West Chester, PA; Docket Book of the Cumberland County Court of Quarter Sessions, Cumberland County Historical Society, Carlisle, PA; Docket Book and Miscellaneous Papers of the Lancaster County Court of Quarter Sessions, Lancaster County Historical Society, Lancaster, PA; Northampton County Papers, HSP; Docket Book and Miscellaneous Papers of the Northumberland County Court of Quarter Sessions, Northumberland County Courthouse, Sunbury, PA; Docket Book of the Philadelphia County Court of Quarter Sessions (1777–1780), Philadelphia City Archives, Philadelphia, PA; Docket Book of the Philadelphia County Court of Quarter Sessions (1780–1785), Court Records Collection, HSP; Docket Book of the Mayor's Court (1779–1783), Philadelphia City Archives, Philadelphia, PA; Docket Book of the Westmoreland County Court of Quarter Sessions, Westmoreland County Courthouse, Greensburg, PA; Docket Book of the York County Court of Quarter Sessions, York County Historical Society, York, PA; High Court of Error and Appeal Papers, RG-33, PSA; Winthrop Sargent items, Simon Gratz Collection, HSP, 179; "Journal of Samuel Rowland Fisher, of Philadelphia, 1779–1781," *PMHB* 41 (1917): 145–197, 274–333, 399–457; *Col. Records*, Vols. 11–13.

47. Several of these were partial pardons near the end of the war relieving that part of the judgment that required imprisonment until the end of the war. These might be viewed more as clerical declarations of the end of the war rather than true pardons.
48. Act of March 6, 1778, ch. 784, *Pa. Stat.*, 9:201.
49. In 1806, Daniel Clymer, after a visit to McKean, stated that McKean "drew the act of attainder in 1777." Daniel Clymer to Matthias Aspden, *Letters and Other Documents Produced in the Case of the Succession of Matthias Aspden* (Philadelphia: 1837), 249. The initial draft of the legislation was drawn in 1777, so Clymer's date is plausible. *Minutes of the Second General Assembly of the Commonwealth of Pennsylvania* (Lancaster: John Dunlap, 1778), 31. McKean's assistance to the legislature in drafting legislation in other cases is well documented. Thomas McKean to George Read, April 3, 1778, *LDC*, 9:363–366.
50. Opinion of Thomas McKean, June 23, 1777, *Pa. Archives*, 5:400.
51. Blackstone, *Commentaries*, 4:301.
52. Act of May 31, 1718, ch. 236, *Pa. Stat.*, 3:205–206.
53. In 1782, the Pennsylvania Supreme Court used the proclamation technique to attaint members of the notorious Doan gang, provoking considerable outcry as to

the propriety of this measure. See generally G.S. Rowe, "Outlawry in Pennsylvania, 1782–1788 and the Achievement of an Independent State Judiciary," *Am. J. Leg. Hist.* 20 (1976): 227–244.

54. The state's attorney general later concluded that any property held by traitors "in right of their wives during coverture, & by courtesy" is forfeited to the state "so far as such traitors have title during coverture, or in right of courtesy." Minutes of the SEC, Sept. 29, 1778, *CR*, 11:587. On the relation between women's rights and treason laws more generally during the Revolution, see Linda K. Kerber, *No Constitutional Right to Be Ladies: Women and the Obligations of Citizenship* (New York: Hill & Wang, 1998), 16–33. On land forfeitures in revolutionary New York, see Howard Pashman, *Building a Revolutionary State: The Legal Transformation of New York, 1776–1783* (Chicago: U. of Chicago Press, 2018).
55. *Pa. Archives* (4th Ser.), 3: 669–672, 676–688.
56. Of the nearly 500 people proclaimed, only 120 suffered forfeiture of real property. Anne Ousterhout, "Pennsylvania Land Confiscations during the Revolution," *PMHB* 102 (1978): 328–343, 339. In November 1778, the Assembly repealed the attainders of Reynold Keen and Albertson Walton, prompting complaints that only the Council should exercise the pardoning power. A Whig Citizen, "To the Freemen of Pennsylvania," Broadside, Evans 43709, Broadsides Collection, HSP.
57. *JCC*, 10:381–382 (April 23, 1778).
58. Henry Laurens to Jonathan Trumbull, Sr., April 26, 1778, *LDC*, 9:497.
59. Henry Laurens to George Washington, April 24, 1778, *LDC*, 9:481–482.
60. SEC to Assembly, May 18, 1778, *Pa. Archives*, 6:518–519.
61. Act of April 1, 1778, ch. 796, *Pa. Stat.*, 9:238.
62. Journal of Sarah Wister, June 2, 1778, HSP.
63. Coleman, *Thomas McKean*, xii–xiii.
64. Notes of Charges delivered to Grand Juries by Chief Justice Thomas McKean, in his own writing, 1777–1779, Thomas McKean Papers, HSP, 51. See generally John Coleman, "Thomas McKean and the Origin of an Independent Judiciary," *Penn. History* 34 (1967): 111–130.
65. Thomas McKean to John Adams, Nov. 8, 1779, Thomas McKean Papers, HSP.
66. Loyd, *Early Courts of Pennsylvania*, 139.
67. SEC to Delegates in Congress, Feb. 7, 1778, *Pa. Archives*, 6: 242–243.
68. Thomas Wharton to Thomas McKean, Feb. 15, 1778, *Pa. Archives*, 6: 266–268.
69. *JCC*, 13:453–454, n.2.
70. Nathanael Greene to Thomas McKean, June 3, 1778, *The Papers of General Nathanael Greene*, ed. Richard K. Showman (Chapel Hill: UNC Press, 1980), 2:424–425.
71. Thomas McKean to Nathanael Greene, June 9, 1778, Thomas McKean Papers, HSP.
72. Robert Hooper to George Bryan, Aug. 31, 1778, *Pa. Archives* (2d Ser.), 3:236; see also Charles Henry Hart, "Colonel Robert Lettis Hooper," *PMHB* 36 (1912): 60–91.
73. Edward Burd to Jasper Yeates, Nov. 16, 1777, Jasper Yeates Papers, HSP.

74. William Rawle to "Margaret," May 3, 1780, William Rawle Letters, HSP.
75. [Jonathan Dickinson Sergeant], "To A.F.," *Freeman's Journal*, Aug. 15, 1781, 2. Sergeant's authorship is revealed in Thomas McKean, "To the Printer," *Freeman's Journal*, Aug. 22, 1781, 2.
76. Thomas McKean to George Washington, April 12, 1789, Thomas McKean Folder, Hampton L. Carson Collection, HSP.
77. Burton Alva Konkle, *George Bryan and the Constitution of Pennsylvania, 1731–1791* (Philadelphia: William J. Campbell, 1922), 225–226.
78. Thomas McKean to Sally McKean, April 9, 1778, Thomas McKean Papers, HSP.
79. McKean's notebook of grand jury charges is in the holdings of the Historical Society of Pennsylvania. However, it is not filed with the bulk of McKean's papers and has thus been regularly overlooked. The title, "Notes of Charges delivered to Grand Juries by Chief Justice Thomas McKean, in his own writing, 1777–1779," is misleading. No grand jury charges were delivered until 1778; moreover, in several places the phrase "President of the Supreme Executive Council" has been deleted and replaced with the word "Governor," strongly suggesting that McKean was still using these charges after 1790, when the new Pennsylvania constitution replaced the Council with a governor. As late as 1806, without mentioning that he was doing so, he included verbatim elements of one charge in a letter to Paul Hamilton, the Governor of South Carolina. Thomas McKean to Paul Hamilton, Sept. 1, 1806, Society Collection, HSP.
80. Thomas McKean, *Charge Delivered to the Grand-Jury, By the Honourable Thomas McKean, Esquire, Chief Justice of Pennsylvania, At a Court of Oyer and Terminer, and General Goal Delivery, held at York, on the 21st Day of April, 1778; and published at the special request of the said Grand-Jury* (Lancaster, PA: Francis Bailey, 1778).
81. McKean, *Charge*, 6–7, 9–11. I follow the published York charge here. For the particulars of the crime of treason, the York charge is identical to the material in the unpublished book of charges.
82. Thomas McKean, Notes of Charges delivered to Grand Juries by Chief Justice Thomas McKean, in his own writing, 1777–1779, Thomas McKean Papers, HSP, 1–3, 13, 25–29.
83. Michael Foster, *A Report of Some Proceedings on the Commission of Oyer and Terminer and Goal Delivery for the Trial of the Rebels in the Year 1746 in the County of Surrey, and of other Crown Cases. To Which are Added Discourses upon a Few Branches of the Crown Law* (Oxford: Clarendon Press, 1762).
84. McKean, Notes of Charges, 28–29.
85. Ibid., 25–26.
86. Ibid., 26–27.
87. John Kelyng, *A Report of Divers Cases in Pleas of the Crown, Adjudged and Determined; in the Reign of the late King Charles II* (London: Isaac Cleave, 1708), 70–79.

88. Hayes McKinney, "Treason under the Constitution of the United States," *Ill. L. Rev.* 12 (1918): 381, 387. The defendants in the brothel case had also opened a prison and attacked the king's troops, which is the likely explanation for why a treason indictment was initially sought. Kelying, *Report*, 70–74.
89. Letter of Thomas McKean, Aug. 15, 1777, Thomas McKean Papers, HSP, cited in Thomas R. Meehan, "The Pennsylvania Supreme Court in the Law and Politics of the Commonwealth., 1776–1790" (Ph.D. diss., Univ. of Wisc., 1960).
90. Hale explained his disagreement in his posthumously published treatise. Matthew Hale, *Historia Placitorum Coronae* (London: E. & R. Nutt & R. Gosling, 1736), 134–135. Foster's summary of the case law is at Foster, *Report*, 211, and the passing reference is at ibid., 215. An unpaginated prefatory addendum also appears to cast doubt on the case.
91. John Popham, *Reports and Cases, Collected by the Learned, Sir John Popham, Knight, Late Lord Chief-Justice of England* (London: Thomas Roycroft, 1656), 122–123.
92. McKean, Notes of Charges, 27.
93. Ibid., 29.
94. McKean, *Charge*, 18.
95. John Piper to Thomas Wharton, May 4, 1778, *Pa. Archives*, 6:469–470.
96. Thomas McKean to George Bryan, May 27, 1778, *Pa. Archives*, 6:569.
97. Minutes of the SEC, Aug. 18, 1778, *Col. Records*, 11:556–557.
98. SEC to Gen. Armstrong et al., Aug. 24, 1778, *Pa. Archives*, 6:715–716.
99. SEC to John Hubley, Sept. 19, 1778, *Pa. Archives*, 6:750.
100. Robert Galbraith, Names of Those who were Under Arms in Bedford County Against the United States, Aug. 2, 1778, *Pa. Archives* (5th Ser.), 5:78.
101. Summary Extracts of the Proceedings of the Special Court of Oyer and Terminer held at Bedford 28th Sept. 1778 by Archibald McLean Esq., Executive Correspondence and Petitions, 1777–1790, Records of Pennsylvania's Revolutionary Governments, RG-27, PSA.
102. Barnard Dougherty to Joseph Reed, April 6, 1779, *Pa. Archives*, 7:297. The justices of the Supreme Court would not sit as an oyer and terminer court for Bedford County until 1783. Rowe, *Embattled Bench*, 185–186.
103. Jackson, *With the British Army*, 259–260.
104. Stephen R. Taaffe, *The Philadelphia Campaign, 1777–1778* (Lawrence: Univ. Press of Kansas, 2003), 192.
105. Jackson, *With the British Army*, 265–273.
106. Diary of Charles Willson Peale, June 17, 1778, Charles Willson Peale Papers, APS.
107. Ibid.
108. Timothy Matlack to Jonathan Dickinson Sergeant, July 9, 1778, *Pa. Archives*, 6:630.
109. SEC to Thomas Hale & N. Weaver, July 7, 1778, *Pa. Archives*, 6:628.
110. Ibid.
111. Diary of Charles Willson Peale, June 17, 1778, Charles Willson Peale Papers, APS.

112. Robert Oaks, "The City under Military Occupation: Philadelphia, 1777–1778," in Robert F. Oaks, Margaret F. Morris & Elliott West, eds., *Essays on Urban America* (Austin: University of Texas Press, 1975), 24, 43. For a bitter complaint of a Philadelphia Quaker who claimed he was unlawfully imprisoned by British military authorities, see Stephen Collins to Joseph Galloway, May 23, 1778, Joseph Galloway Papers, Thompson Family Collection, HSP.
113. William Lewis to Timothy Matlack, July 14, 1778, *Pa. Archives*, 6:641. An even more extreme example was described by Hector St. John de Crevecouer. In July 1778, Butler's Rangers, a British military unit, had destroyed homes and killed hundreds of frontier settlers along the Wyoming River in an incident that came to be known as "Butler's Massacre." The local militia suspected that Joseph Wilson, a well-known Tory, had harbored some of the Rangers, an act of treason under Pennsylvania law. Militia members arrived at Wilson's house and hanged him by the toes and thumbs to force a confession. When he refused to confess, the militia announced a death sentence. But Wilson's subsequent hanging was not expertly handled; the militia failed to secure his arms or cover his face, resulting in a "most dreadful spectacle." Wilson had almost expired when the militia resolved to take him down again and he "gradually recovered." Upon further reflection, though, the militia decided that Wilson still deserved to hang. A maudlin prayer by Wilson, in which he insisted on his innocence and forgave his persecutors, however, persuaded the militia to send him for a "fair trial" by the "law of the land." Crevecouer reported that Wilson was later acquitted after this trial, but I have been unable to document this trial in any surviving court records. Hector St. John de Crevecouer, "The Man of Sorrows," in *Sketches of Eighteenth Century America*, ed. Henri L. Bourdin, Ralph H. Gabriel & Stanley T. Williams (New Haven, CT: Yale Univ. Press, 1925), 178–191.
114. *Pa. Evening Post*, July 16, 1778.
115. *Pa. Evening Post*, July 25, 1778.
116. Ibid.
117. Rosswurm, *Arms, Country, and Class*, 155.
118. Thomas McKean to William Augustus Atlee, June 5, 1778, *LDC*, 10:31–33.
119. SEC to Samuel Potts, June 11, 1778, *Pa. Archives*, 6:595. On Pennsylvania bail practices generally, see Paul Lermack, "The Law of Recognizances in Colonial Pennsylvania," *Temple L.Q.* 50 (1977): 475–512.
120. Thomas McKean to William Augustus Atlee, July 7, 1778, *LDC*, 236–237.
121. Minutes of the SEC, June 15, 1778, *Col. Records*, 11:512–513.
122. Memorial of Anthony Yeldall, American Loyalist Claims, AO13.95B.171, National Archives of the United Kingdom.
123. *Pa. Packet*, Dec. 12, 1778; Minutes of the SEC, Oct. 3, 1780, *Col. Records*, 12:496; Memorial of Anthony Yeldall, n.122.
124. Thomas McKean to Caesar Rodney, May 31, 1778, Hampton L. Carson Collection, HSP.

125. Thomas McKean to George Bryan, May 21, 1778, *Pa. Archives*, 6:555.
126. Thomas McKean to William Augustus Atlee, June 5, 1778, *LDC*, 32.
127. Jacob E. Cooke, *Tench Coxe and the Early Republic* (Chapel Hill: UNC Press, 1978), 21–29.
128. Benjamin Yard to Tench Coxe, Nov. 2, 1777, Tench Coxe Correspondence, Coxe Family Collection, HSP.
129. Cooke, *Tench Coxe*, 41.
130. Tench Coxe to John Cox, June 10, 1778, Tench Coxe Letterbook, Coxe Family Collection, HSP.
131. Tench Coxe to William Tilghman, July 13, 1778, Tench Coxe Correspondence, Coxe Family Collection, HSP.
132. Cooke, *Tench Coxe*, 29.
133. Joseph Reed to Tench Coxe, Jan. 29, 1779, Tench Coxe Correspondence, Coxe Family Collection, HSP.
134. Cooke, *Tench Coxe*, 14, 40, 42.
135. Ibid., 126–127.
136. Thomas McKean to William Augustus Atlee, June 5, 1778, *LDC*, 10:31–33.
137. SEC to Assembly, Aug. 7, 1778, *Pa. Archives*, 6:685–686.
138. SEC to Joseph Reed, Aug. 21, 1778, *Pa. Archives*, 6:712.
139. John F. Roche, *Joseph Reed: A Moderate in the American Revolution* (New York: Columbia Univ. Press, 1957), 23, 30.
140. Ibid., 54, 59–84.
141. John Cadwalader, *A Reply to General Joseph Reed's Remarks on a Late Publication in the Independent Gazetteer* (Philadelphia: T. Bradford, 1783), 25–26.
142. *Proceedings of a General Court Martial for the trial of Major General Arnold* (New York: 1865), 133.
143. *Pa. Gazette*, Feb. 26, 1783. The allegations figured prominently in a bitter press war in the early 1780s. On this later dispute, see Roche, *Joseph Reed*, 203–213. The issue continued to generate controversy many decades later. In 1856, it was reported that "within the last twenty years all the copies [of Cadwalader's pamphlet], or nearly so, have been spirited away—where or by whom no one knows. They have been stolen from public libraries and from the book cases of private individuals." The publisher of a second edition was "threatened with prosecution." Horace W. Smith, *Nuts for Future Historians to Crack* (Philadelphia: Horace W. Smith, 1856), 13.
144. Joseph Reed to John Armstrong, *LDC*, 11:25–26.
145. Jonathan Dickinson Sergeant to George Bryan, Sept. 8, 1778, *Pa. Archives*, 6:740.
146. Sergeant's successor William Bradford described the job this way in 1784: "I have been for three days past smothered in the Court House amidst a crowd of rogues and c. It was the criminal court, where the refuse of our species is gathered together. But it is over and I will engage no more in such scenes." William Bradford to [Rachel?], Sept. 10, 1784, Wallace Collection, HSP.

147. In the 1830s, the elderly Jacob Mordecai recalled Sergeant as a "good republican, rather short & stout, an easy fluent speaker & the dread of evil doers. . . . He was a powerful advocate." "Addenda to Watson's Annals of Philadelphia: Notes by Jacob Mordecai, 1836," ed. Whitfield J. Bell, Jr., *PMHB* 98 (1974): 131, 144.
148. Appointment of Edward Burd, Aug. 12, 1778, *Pa. Archives*, 6:695. The appointment was officially confirmed by the Council on Sept. 1, 1778. Minutes of the SEC, Sept. 1, 1778, *Col. Records*, 11:566. On Burd's early career, see *Neddie Burd's Reading Letters: An Epic of the Early Berks Bar*, ed. J. Bennett Nolan (Reading, PA: Berks Co. Bar Assoc., 1927).
149. Randolph Shipley Klein, *Portrait of an Early American Family: The Shippens of Pennsylvania across Five Generations* (Philadelphia: Univ. of Penn. Press, 1975), 171–172.
150. John Hubley to President Wharton, Oct. 28, 1776, *Pa. Archives* (2d Ser.), 13:528–529. A month earlier, Grubb had been "run the gauntlet for a Tory & a coward" and he referred to the members of the state constitutional convention as "fools" and "numskulls." Sarah Yeates to Jasper Yeates, Sept. 14, 1776, Jasper Yeates Papers, HSP.
151. Selsam, *Pennsylvania Constitution*, 233.
152. It was determined that Grubb was "greatly in liquor and behaved very madly." Deposition of Col. William Dewees, March 15, 1777, *Pa. Archives*, 5:261. Grubb committed suicide in 1786, after a lifetime of "long and immoderate use of drink." Edward Burd to Jasper Yeates, Jan. 18, 1786, quoted in Samuel E. Dyke, "The History of a Flintlock Pistol and the Peter Grubbs of Cornwall," *Papers of the Lancaster Co. Hist. Soc.* 59, no. 4 (1955): 96.
153. Edward Burd to Jasper Yeates, April 15, 1776, Jasper Yeates Papers, HSP.
154. Klein, *Portrait of an Early American Family*, 187–189.
155. Edward Burd to Jasper Yeates, Sept. 16, 1777, Jasper Yeates Papers, HSP.
156. Edward Burd to Jasper Yeates, Nov. 16, 1777, Jasper Yeates Papers, HSP.
157. Alexander J. Dallas, *Reports of cases ruled and adjudged in the courts of Pennsylvania, before and since the Revolution* (Philadelphia: T. Bradford, 1790). This volume was later included as Volume 1 of the *United States Reports*, the official collection of United States Supreme Court decisions. It nonetheless contains only decisions of Pennsylvania state courts.
158. The leading biography of James Wilson, for example, claims that the trials of Molder, Taylor, and Malin were held in Philadelphia following the trial of Abraham Carlisle, and that Molder and Taylor were acquitted. Smith, *James Wilson*, 121. G.S. Rowe makes a similar error of chronology in his biography of Thomas McKean and in his history of the Pennsylvania Supreme Court. Rowe, *Thomas McKean*, 116; Rowe, *Embattled Bench*, 144. By October 12, 1778, Molder and Taylor had not yet been tried, and it is probable that they were simply discharged. See Recognizance of John Molder and John Taylor, Oct. 12, 1778, Records of the Supreme Court, Eastern District, RG-33, PSA.

159. *Black List: A List of Those Tories Who Took Part with Great-Britain, in the Revolutionary War, and Were Attainted of High Treason, Commonly Called the Black List!* (Philadelphia: 1802), 13.
160. The Malin trial is also noted in the September 1778 Chester sitting in a document preserved in Volume 16 of the Papers of the Shippen Family—Legal and Business, HSP.
161. Edward Burd to Jasper Yeates, Sept. 19, 1778, Jasper Yeates Papers, HSP.
162. On Wilson's political philosophy, see Jean-Marc Pascal, *The Political Ideas of James Wilson, 1742–1798* (New York: Garland Publications, 1991), and John Fabian Witt, *Patriots and Cosmopolitans* (Cambridge, MA: Harvard Univ, Press, 2007), ch. 1. On Wilson's Scottish background, see William Ewald, "James Wilson and the Scottish Enlightenment," *U. Pa. J. Const. L.* 12 (2010): 1053–1114; Martin Clagett, "James Wilson—His Scottish Background: Corrections and Additions," *Pa. Hist.* 79 (2012): 154–176. On Wilson's disappearance from historical memory, see Nicholas Pedersen, "The Lost Founder: James Wilson in Historical Memory," *Yale J. Law & Human.* 22 (2010): 257–337. In a modern popular account of the Benedict Arnold affair, Wilson is reduced to the ignominy of being described as "Pennsylvania lawyer Robert Wilson." Nathaniel Philbrick, *Valiant Ambition: George Washington, Benedict Arnold, and the Fate of the American Revolution* (New York: Penguin, 2016), 228.
163. Mark Bird, the brother of James Wilson's wife, Rachel, had married George Ross's sister Mary. George and Mary's nephew, John Ross, married Elizabeth Griscom, known to history as Betsy Ross. Marla R. Miller, *Betsy Ross and the Making of America* (New York: Henry Holt, 2010), 120. Marla Miller describes Ross and Wilson as brothers-in-law, ibid., 151, but that is not quite right. Mark Bird was a brother-in-law to both men.
164. A Philadelphia newspaper reported, for example, in April 1777 that England planned to prosecute the leaders of the American Revolution for high treason. *Pa. Evening Post,* April 8, 1777. It is an interesting question whether the mere signing of the Declaration of Independence constituted an act of treason under 25 Edward III. In itself, the Declaration did not fit easily within any of the categories identified in that statute. However, the members of the Continental Congress would almost certainly have been culpable for the actions they took to fund and support the Continental Army, actions they had taken long before the Declaration was signed. A similar analysis would apply under modern law. A handful of individuals who signed a "Declaration of Independence" from the United States of America would not be guilty of treason. But if they took steps to affect that alleged independence by force, they would be guilty of levying war against the United States.
165. *JCC,* 6:915 (Oct. 31, 1776).
166. *JCC,* 8:591, n.2 (July 31, 1777).

167. Craig W. Horle, "George Ross," in *Lawmaking and Legislators in Pennsylvania*, 3:1237–1255.
168. James Wilson et al. to Anthony Wayne, [1778], Wayne Papers, HSP.
169. Benjamin Chew to Edward Tilghman, July 15, 1778, in Konkle, *Benjamin Chew*, 161–163.
170. See generally Langbein, *Origins of Adversary Criminal Trial*.
171. Edward Burd to Jasper Yeates, Sept. 19, 1778, Jasper Yeates Papers, HSP. Alexander Dallas provides an account of this motion under the caption *Respublica v. Molder et al.* Edward Burd's contemporary letter, however, indicates that this motion was made as part of the Malin trial. Burd describes it as a "general motion," so it is possible that the motion was made on behalf of all treason defendants and was later attributed by Dallas to the Molder defendants. It is also possible that the same motion was later made on behalf of the Molder defendants and the court simply reiterated its previous ruling.
172. Foster, *Report*, 250.
173. Wilson and Ross unsuccessfully renewed this issue at the opening of the trial of Abraham Carlisle in Philadelphia, arguing for the full ten days required by the Statute of Anne on the theory that the 1778 Pennsylvania statute did not repeal the 1718 statute. The court reiterated its ruling from the Malin case. *Pa. Archives*, 7:51–52; *Pa. Eve. Post*, Sept. 23, 1778.
174. James Wilson, "A Charge Delivered to the Grand Jury in the Circuit Court of the United States, for the District of Virginia," *Works*, 2:803, 820.
175. Edward Burd to Jasper Yeates, Sept. 19, 1778, Jasper Yeates Papers, HSP.
176. I differ with G.S. Rowe's conclusion that through this "critical" ruling McKean "conceded a number of points" by the defense attorneys and "sought to mitigate many of the evils inherent in the current system." Rowe, *Thomas McKean*, 116.
177. *Pa. Packet*, Dec. 8, 1778.
178. Edward Burd to Jasper Yeates, Sept. 19, 1778, Jasper Yeates Papers, HSP.
179. Francis Bowes Sayre, "Criminal Attempts," *Harvard L. Rev.* 41 (1928): 821–859, 821. *Lord Preston's Case* (*Howell's State Trials*, 12:646), a prominent English decision from 1691, held that a person could be guilty of aiding the enemy by setting out for France, then at war with England, while carrying papers designed to further the French cause. Although the defendant was apprehended before reaching France, and thus no aid was actually given to the French, the court held that his actions nonetheless constituted treason. In some ways this holding can be seen as criminalizing attempted treason. It differs from the Malin case, however, in that Preston's actions, if completed, would have legally constituted treason, whereas Malin's did not.
180. John Temple had been imprisoned in Lancaster County in the fall of 1777 for attempting to pilot a party of the militia "who were pretending to be the British Light Horse," an offense similar to Malin's. John Temple to Timothy Matlack,

Nov. 3, 1777, Clemency File, RG-27, PSA. After taking the oath of allegiance, Temple was released on bond on condition of appearing at the Chester Court of Quarter Sessions. Minutes of the SEC, Nov. 14, 1777, *Col. Records*, 11:371. There is no record of his being tried.

181. Respublica v. Malin, 1 U.S. (1 Dallas) 33, 33–34 (Pa. Ct. Oyer & Terminer, 1778).
182. Ibid., 34. Wilson's biographer claims that "Wilson won his point that words were not treason," but that point was undisputed in the case. Smith, *James Wilson*, 121. Bradley Chapin contended that the "court refused to admit the evidence," but it did admit it, simply for a different purpose. Chapin, *American Law of Treason*, 68.
183. *Malin*, 1 U.S., at 34–35.
184. Edward Burd to Jasper Yeates, Sept. 19, 1778, Jasper Yeates Papers, HSP.
185. *Pa. Packet*, Sept. 22, 1778.
186. Rowe, *Thomas McKean*, 116.
187. Chapin, *American Law of Treason*, 68.
188. *Pa. Packet*, Sept. 22, 1778. This procedure is discussed in greater depth in Chapter 7.

CHAPTER 6

1. Martin Meyerson & Dilys Peglar Winegrad, *Gladly Learn and Gladly Teach: Franklin and His Heirs at the University of Pennsylvania, 1740–1976* (Philadelphia: Univ. of Penn. Press, 1978), 61.
2. See generally Mark David Hall, "James Wilson's Law Lectures," *PMHB* 128 (2004): 63–76.
3. James Wilson, "Lectures on Law," in *The Works of James Wilson*, ed. Robert Green McCloskey (Cambridge, MA: Harvard Univ. Press, 1967), 1:67, 74.
4. On Wilson's views on juries, see Aaron T. Knapp, "Law's Revolutionary: James Wilson and the Birth of American Jurisprudence," *J. of Law & Politics* 29 (2013): 189, 270–283; Shannon C. Stimson, *The American Revolution in the Law: Anglo-American Jurisprudence before John Marshall* (Princeton, NJ: Princeton Univ. Press, 1990), 127–136; Shannon C. Stimson, "'A Jury of the Country': Common Sense Philosophy and the Jurisprudence of James Wilson," in *Scotland and America in the Age of the Enlightenment*, ed. Richard B. Sher & Jeffrey R. Smitten (Edinburgh: Edinburgh Univ. Press, 1990), 193–208.
5. Wilson, "Lectures on Law," 2:332.
6. Ibid.
7. Historians Jack Marietta and G.S. Rowe have demonstrated that conviction rates at trial never dropped below 59.7% for any decade between 1680 and 1800 in Pennsylvania. Jack Marietta & G.S. Rowe, *Troubled Experiment: Crime and Justice in Pennsylvania, 1682–1800* (Philadelphia: Univ. of Penn. Press, 2006), 46. Similarly, in Frederick County, Maryland, between 1749 and 1779, 62% of all defendants in criminal jury trials were convicted. James D. Rice, "The Criminal Trial before and after the Lawyers: Authority, Law, and Culture in Maryland

Jury Trials, 1681–1837," *Am. J. Legal Hist.* 40 (1996): 455, 459; see also Douglas Greenberg, *Crime and Law Enforcement in the Colony of New York, 1691–1776* (Ithaca, NY: Cornell Univ. Press, 1976), 71 (finding that only 15% of criminal cases in eighteenth-century New York resulted in acquittal); P.J.R. King, "'Illiterate Plebeians, Easily Misled': Jury Composition, Experience, and Behavior in Essex, 1713–1815," in *Twelve Men Good and True: The Criminal Jury Trial in England, 1200–1800*, ed. J.S. Cockburn & Thomas A. Green (Princeton, NJ: Princeton Univ. Press, 1988), 254, 255 (finding acquittal rate of 34% in five English counties between 1782 and 1787).

8. Petition of Judges in Case of George Hardy, *Pa. Archives*, 7:326.
9. *Pa. Packet*, Aug. 25, 1778, 3.
10. Frank M. Etting, *An Historical Account of the Old State House of Pennsylvania* (Philadelphia: Porter & Coates, 1891), 24.
11. *Pa. Evening Post*, Oct. 7, 1778; *Pa. Evening Post*, Oct. 9, 1778; Minutes of the SEC, July 18, 1778, *Col. Records*, 11:534. The Supreme Court room underwent renovations in 1778–1779. Constance M. Greiff, *Independence: The Creation of a National Park* (Philadelphia: Univ. of Penn. Press, 1987), 156. By at least October 1779, the Supreme Court had returned to the State House and was hearing treason cases there. "Journal of Samuel Rowland Fisher, of Philadelphia, 1779–1781," *PMHB* 41 (1917): 145, 169.
12. George E. Thomas & David Brownlee, *Building America's First University: An Historical and Architectural Guide to the University of Pennsylvania* (Philadelphia: Univ. of Penn. Press, 2000), 31, 33–34.
13. Wilson, "Lectures on Law," 688.
14. The first indictment must have issued quickly. On Wednesday, September 23, Abraham Carlisle's attorneys renewed their motion with respect to the provision of the indictment, the panel list, and the witness lists. *Pa. Eve. Post*, Sept. 23, 1778. (This issue appears to have been published late, as the item is dated Thursday, Sept. 24 and refers to motions argued "yesterday.").
15. *Minutes of the Third General Assembly of the Commonwealth of Pennsylvania* (Philadelphia: John Dunlap 1778–1779), 11. The Assembly minutes indicate that a grand jury met again from November 9 to November 25, and again petitioned the Assembly for additional payments. Ibid., 21. The Assembly minutes refer to a "memorial from the (Second) Grand Jury for the Court of Oyer and Terminer for the County of Philadelphia," a reference that suggests that this grand jury was composed of different people. This possibility is supported by a record showing a Philadelphia Oyer and Terminer grand jury indicting two individuals for highway robbery on November 9, 1778. Record of Case of James O'Bryan and John Beard, Clemency File, RG-27, PSA. Only two of these grand jurors, James Young and John Dorsey, were on the first grand jury. This case is omitted from the cases listed in the Court's official docket book under the first grand jury, although it is mentioned in a newspaper account, along with an otherwise undocumented manslaughter case. *Pa. Packet*, Dec. 12, 1778. A record from April 1779 confirms that the first grand jury

indicted George Harding for treason, thus strongly suggesting that the first grand jury heard all of the treason cases, and that the second grand jury heard other cases. Record of Case of George Hardy, Clemency File, RG-27, PSA. A grand jury also met at some point in December. *Pa. Packet*, Dec. 12, 1778 (reporting grand jury's refusal to indict David Franks for treason); this may be a third grand jury, or it may reflect a continuation of either the first or second grand jury. Between March and August 1779, the state paid the members of the first grand jury approximately twenty-five pounds each for their service. *Report of the Committee of the Assembly on the State of Public Accounts, 1779* (Philadelphia: John Dunlap, 1779), 33.

16. Similar problems have been noted by other historians of early American law. E.g., Julius Goebel, Jr., & T. Raymond Naughton, *Law Enforcement in Colonial New York: A Study in Criminal Procedure* (New York: Commonwealth Fund, 1944), 347 ("We are badly informed as to how the work of the grand jury was managed when there were cases pending."). A 1781 treason indictment for Justin McCarty includes the names of seven witnesses at the bottom; these are likely the witnesses who testified before the grand jury. Indictment of Justin McCarty, April 1781, Oyer and Terminer Miscellaneous Papers, 1777–1781, RG-33, PSA.
17. This incident is described in more detail in Rowe, *Thomas McKean*, 183–188.
18. "The Memorial and Remonstrance of the Grand Jury for the City and County of Philadelphia," *Pa. Gazette*, Jan. 8, 1783. This view was also endorsed by James Wilson in his 1790 charge to the Philadelphia federal grand jury. James Wilson, Charge to the Grand Jury of the Circuit Court for the District of Pennsylvania, in *The Documentary History of the Supreme Court of the United States, 1789–1800*, ed. Maeva Marcus (New York: Columbia Univ. Press, 1988), 2:33, 37.
19. [Thomas McKean], "A true narrative of the conduct of the late Grand Jury of the city and county of Philadelphia, at a Session of Oyer and Terminer and General Goal Delivery, begun the 30th of December, 1782," *Pa. Gazette*, Jan. 29, 1783.
20. In a 1788 case, Chief Justice McKean formally ruled that the grand jury could not hear witnesses for the defense. Respublica v. Shaffer, 1 Dallas 236 (Philadelphia Co. Ct. Oyer & Terminer, 1788).
21. *Ind. Gazetteer*, Jan. 25, 1783.
22. Eighteenth-century grand juries meeting in taverns is well-documented in Massachusetts, but was apparently less common in Virginia. Martha J. McNamara, *From Tavern to Courthouse: Architecture and Ritual in American Law, 1658–1860* (Baltimore: Johns Hopkins Univ. Press, 2004), 41, 123 n.63.
23. Docket of the Court of Oyer and Terminer, RG-33, PSA, 1–11. Further precision is impossible, as the court's surviving docket book is incomplete. For example, the treason trial of James Stevens in April 1779 is amply documented in contemporary sources, but is omitted from the docket book. *Pa. Gazette*, April 14, 1779; *The Diary of Elizabeth Drinker*, ed. Elaine Forman Crane (Boston: Northeastern Univ. Press, 1991), 1:343. The docket book may have been compiled at a later time, with the result that these cases were inadvertently omitted. This practice is discussed in

Daniel D. Blinka, "Jury Trial on the Eve of the Revolution: The Virginia Experience," *UMKC Law Review* 71 (2003): 529, 543 n.76.

24. Marietta & Rowe, *Troubled Experiment*, 46.
25. Blackstone, *Commentaries on the Laws of England*, 4:299.
26. Wilson, Charge to the Grand Jury, 4:37.
27. These data derive from statistical analysis of the tax data printed as Effective Supply Tax of the City of Philadelphia, 1779, in *Pa. Archives* (3d Ser.), 14:469–838. I have checked the published version against the originals in the Pennsylvania State Archives. What appears in the published version as "amount of tax" appears to reflect a wealth assessment in the originals. Unfortunately, the published data for the county (as opposed to the city) of Philadelphia appear to be unreliable. Thus it is slightly misleading to compare the grand juror averages, which include several county grand jurors, against only city taxpayers. On the other hand, as a rough proxy for wealth, it is fully adequate. The tax data should also be read with the caveat that Philadelphia's wealth assessments were biased in favor of land and excluded "most forms of commercial wealth, including business inventories, vessels, notes and bonds, cash, and book debts." Thomas M. Doerflinger, *A Vigorous Spirit of Enterprise: Merchants and Economic Development in Revolutionary Philadelphia* (Chapel Hill: UNC Press, 1986), 64–65. Thus the tax assessments probably understate the overall wealth of many of Philadelphia's merchants.
28. Justices of the peace played a similar role in English grand juries. Norma Landau, *The Justices of the Peace, 1679–1760* (Berkeley: Univ. of Cal. Press, 1984), 57; J.M. Beattie, "London Juries in the 1690s," in *Twelve Men Good and True*, 214, 234.
29. Ralph B. Strassburger & William J. Hinke, *Pennsylvania German Pioneers: A Publication of the Original Lists of Arrivals in the Port of Philadelphia from 1727 to 1808* (Norristown, PA: Pa. German Society, 1934), 1:745.
30. Robert Gough, "Notes on the Pennsylvania Revolutionaries of 1776," *PMHB* 96 (1972): 89, 93.
31. Robert Gough found an average age of 44.7 for Pennsylvania's revolutionary leaders. Gough, "Notes on the Pennsylvania Revolutionaries," 91. Richard Alan Ryerson has aptly noted that it "is harder to determine the age of Philadelphia's resistance leaders than any other simple fact about them." Ryerson, *Revolution*, 71. Digitized sources have simplified research in many ways, particularly with respect to obtaining obituaries of individuals who later moved elsewhere, but the basic difficulty remains.
32. *Pa. Gazette*, Oct. 7, 1762.
33. *Pa. Gazette*, June 15, 1774 (Fleeson & Pryor).
34. *Pa. Gazette*, Nov. 16, 1774 (Cuthbert, Dean, Hasenclever, Loxley, Purviance); *Pa. Gazette*, Nov. 30, 1774 (Moore).
35. *Pa. Gazette*, Dec. 7, 1774 (Cuthbert, Dean, Hasenclever, Loxley, Pryor, Purviance).
36. *Pa. Gazette*, Feb. 1, 1775 (Cuthbert, Dean, Hasenclever, Laughlin, Loxley, Moore, Pryor, Purviance).

37. Ibid.
38. Rosswurm, *Arms, Country, and Class*, 272–274.
39. Ibid., 272 (Ball, Cuthbert, Loxley, Pryor, Purviance).
40. Ibid., 273 (Cuthbert, Dean, Hasenclever, Loxley, Pryor, Purviance).
41. Ibid., 274 (Dean, Cuthbert, Hasenclever, Pryor).
42. *Pa. Evening Post*, Aug. 17, 1775, at 363 (Ball, Cuthbert, Loxley, Pryor, Purviance).
43. *Pa. Gazette*, Feb. 21, 1776 (Ball, Cuthbert, Dean, Loxley, Pryor, Purviance).
44. Scharf & Westcott, *History of Philadelphia*, 1:312. At least three of the grand jurors provided military supplies to the revolutionary government between 1775 and 1776, and Thomas Pryor was paid for his expenses in examining letters on board a ship. *State of the Accounts of John Nixon, Esquire, From the 26th of October 1775, till the 7th of August, 1776* (Philadelphia: Robert Aitken, 1786), 14, 16–17, 31, 95–96 (Cuthbert, Ball, Potts).
45. A. Owen Aldridge, *Thomas Paine's American Ideology* (Newark: Univ. of Delaware Press, 1984), 32.
46. Marla R. Miller, *Betsy Ross and the Making of America* (New York: Henry Holt, 2010), 170. On Fleeson and the Philadelphia upholstery trade more generally, see ibid., 56–60. On Fleeson's political career, see Jeffrey L. Scheib, "Plunket Fleeson," in *Lawmaking and Legislators in Pennsylvania*, 3:501–506.
47. Benjamin Loxley, "Autobiography of Benjamin Loxley," HSP, 7–8.
48. *Pa. Gazette*, Sept. 4, 1776 (City: Ball, Cuthbert, Hasenclever, Quee, Young; County: Moore). Benjamin Franklin was also named.
49. Arrest Warrant for John Roberts, July 27, 1778, Elias Boudinot Papers, HSP, 2:41.
50. Minutes of the Council of Safety, Dec. 11, 1776, *Col. Records*, 11:45; Minutes of the SEC, March 13, 1777, *Col. Records*, 11:181.
51. *Pa. Gazette*, Aug. 7, 1776.
52. *JCC*, 6:968; Minutes of the SEC, Sept. 1, 1777, *Col. Records*, 11:286.
53. *Pa. Gazette*, Feb. 26, 1777.
54. Laurie M. Wolfe, "John Moor," in *Lawmaking and Legislators in Pennsylvania*, 3:917–922.
55. Minutes of the SEC, June 11, 1777, *Col. Records*, 11: 220.
56. *State of the Accounts of the Lieutenant & Sub Lieutenants of the City of Philadelphia, and Liberties* (Philadelphia: Francis Bailey, 1784), 27, 28, 36, 38, 48, 86, 149 (Ball, Cuthbert, Dean, Dorsey, Hasenclever, Pryor, Purviance). Ball at one point hired a substitute. A General Return of the Fourth Battalion, in *Pa. Archives* (6th Ser.), 1:280, 288; Ryerson, *Revolution*, 262–263; Francis S. Fox, "Pennsylvania's Revolutionary Militia Law: The Statute That Transformed the State," *Penn. Hist.* 80 (2013): 204–214.
57. *State of the Accounts of the Lieutenant*, 120 (Hasenclever [Captain]; Pryor [Captain]; Loxley [Artillery Officer]).
58. *Pa. Evening Post*, July 16, 1776 (Moore [Major]; Laughlin [Captain]; Neff [Captain]); Gregory T. Knouff, *The Soldier's Revolution: Pennsylvanians in Arms*

and the Forging of Early American Identity (University Park: Penn. State Univ. Press, 2004), xix–xx.

59. Philadelphia County Associators—1777, in *Pa. Archives* (2d Ser.), 13:588, 589–590.
60. Muster Rolls Relating to the Associators and Militia of the County of Philadelphia, in *Pa. Archives* (6th Ser.), 1:599, 601; Minutes of the SEC, July 23, 1778, *Col. Records*, 11:538.
61. Minutes of the SEC, Jan. 9, 1777, *Col. Records*, 11:398.
62. Light Dragoons, County of Philadelphia, in *Pa. Archives* (2d Ser.), 13:593; Captain Benjamin Loxley's Company—1776, in *Pa. Archives* (2d Ser.), 13:559. On Loxley's long career as an artillerist, see Joseph Seymour, *The Pennsylvania Associators, 1747–1777* (Yardley, PA: Westholme, 2012), 30–31, 120–128, 134–138, 153–155, 184. Alexander Graydon later recalled, "Here stood the artillery, under the command of captain Loxley, a very honest, though little, dingy-looking man, with regimentals, considerably war-worn or tarnished; a very salamander or *fire drake* in the public estimation, whose vital air was deemed the fume of sulphureous explosion, and who, by whatever means he had acquired his science, was always put foremost when great guns were in question." Graydon, *Memoirs*, 47.
63. James Young to George Bryan, June 24, 1778, James Young Folder, Society Collection, HSP; *Pa. Evening Post*, Nov. 6, 1777.
64. Whitfield Bell, Jr., *Patriot-Improvers: Biographical Sketches of Members of the American Philosophical Society* (Philadelphia: Am. Phil. Soc., 2010), 3:158.
65. *Diary of Elizabeth Drinker*, 1:247 ("Tom Prior").
66. Loxley, "Autobiography," 12.
67. Scharf & Westcott, *History of Philadelphia*, 1:386 n.2. Ball was later a victim of a burglary perpetrated by five men who had gone to New York with the enemy. Thomas McKean to John Dickinson, Feb. 10, 1783, Gratz Collection—Pennsylvania Provincial Conference, HSP.
68. *Pa. Evening Post*, July 25, 1778, at 256 (Dean, Hasenclever, Loxley, Pryor).
69. Record Book of Benjamin Paschall, Esq., HSP.
70. Young is identified as the foreman in Memorial of Grand Jurors in Favor of Roberts and Carlisle, *Pa. Archives*, 7:23.
71. Charles Penrose Keith, *The Provincial Councillors of Pennsylvania* (Philadelphia: W.S. Sharp, 1883), 164.
72. Anne M. Ousterhout, *The Most Learned Woman in America: A Life of Elizabeth Graeme Fergusson* (Univ. Park: Penn. State. Univ. Press, 2004), 179.
73. New York Committee of Safety to Philadelphia Committee of Safety, March 16, 1776, *Am. Archives*, 5:1377.
74. *JCC*, 4:227 (March 23, 1776).
75. Ousterhout, *Most Learned Woman*, 198.
76. *A List of the General and Staff Officers, and of the Officers in the Several Regiments Serving in North-America* (New York: James Rivington, 1778), 68.

77. John W. Jordan, *Colonial and Revolutionary Families of Pennsylvania* (New York: Lewis Historical Pub. Co., 1911), 2:1061. Stricker's career flourished after his acquittal of treason. In 1782 he was serving as a tax collector. Receipts signed by Adam Stricker, March 13, 1782 & May 9, 1782, Norris Manuscripts, Family Accounts, Vol. 3, Folder 2, HSP. By 1790, he was the Deputy Sheriff of Philadelphia County. *Pa. Gazette*, April 7, 1790; see also *United States Gazette*, Oct. 23, 1805 (Stricker obituary).
78. Minutes of the SEC, Oct. 26, 1779, *Col. Records*, 12:149.
79. Wilson, "Lectures on Law," 553.
80. Minutes of the SEC, Aug. 18, 1783, *Col. Records*, 13:651.
81. *Pa. Mercury & Universal Advertiser*, Sept. 24, 1784; *Pa. Gazette*, March 12, 1761; Charles Coleman Sellers, "James Claypoole—A Founder of the Art of Painting in Pennsylvania," *Penn. Hist.* 17 (1950): 106–109.
82. Effective Supply Tax of the City of Philadelphia, 1779, *Pa. Archives*, 14: 469, 476.
83. *Pa. Packet*, Sept. 20, 1773; *Journal and Proceedings of the General Assembly of the Commonwealth of Pennsylvania* (Philadelphia: John Dunlap, 1777), 31.
84. *Pa. Gazette*, Feb. 26, 1777.
85. Minutes of the SEC, June 9 & 14, 1777, *Col. Records*, 11:217, 222.
86. *Pa. Gazette*, Sept. 3, 1777; Sellers, "James Claypoole," 106; *Pa. Gazette*, Aug. 30, 1780.
87. *Pa. Packet*, Sept. 19, 1778; *Pa. Packet*, Sept. 26, 1778, 4.
88. *The Conductor Generalis* (Philadelphia: Robert Campbell, 1792), 211–212.
89. Minutes of the SEC, June 24, 1777, Nov. 3, 1778, *Col. Records*, 11: 231, 614.
90. Act of June 13, 1777, ch. 3, *Pa. Stat.*, 9: 110, 112.
91. Act of March 19, 1785, ch. 1138, *Pa. Stat.*, 11:486, 487.
92. Full panel lists survive for the Philadelphia Court of Oyer and Terminer from the early 1780s. One 1782 list shows a panel of 101 members; another shows 105 members. List of Grand Jury & Traverse Jury, April 2, 1782, Oyer & Terminer Papers, Roll 5, RG-33, PSA. A 1785 statute limited the panel in oyer and terminer cases to 80. Act of March 19, 1785, ch. 1138, *Pa. Stat.*, 11:486, 487–488.
93. Occasionally, jurors failed to appear. The most impressive failure occurred on April 6, 1779, at the trial of Samuel Garrigues, when forty jurors failed to appear and were fined ten pounds each. O&T Docket, 11. This was the first trial in over four months, so there may have been notification problems. Grand juror Seth Quee, in his capacity as a Philadelphia justice of the peace, wrote to the justices, to excuse a witness who had failed to attend the court in April. Quee noted that the man had attended the court in the fall, but did not attend in April, because he did not know "it was required of him." Seth Quee to Judges of the Supreme Court, n.d., Oyer & Terminer Miscellaneous Papers, 1778–1781, Records of the Supreme Court, RG-33, PSA.
94. The April 8, 1779 defendants appear to have been tried together, as the witness lists are identical; the November 11, 1778 trials, however, have different witnesses, so these were likely separate trials.

95. P.G. Lawson, "Lawless Juries? The Composition and Behavior of Hertfordshire Juries, 1573–1624," in *Twelve Men*, 117, 127.
96. J.S. Cockburn, "Twelve Silly Men? The Trial Jury at Assizes, 1560–1670," in *Twelve Men*, 158, 165–66.
97. Beattie, "London Juries," 214, 219, 236–237.
98. Douglas Hay, "The Class Composition of the Palladium of Liberty: Trial Jurors in the Eighteenth Century," in *Twelve Men*, 305, 345.
99. Blinka, "Jury Trial," 564; Rice, "Criminal Trial," 464; Robert L. Jones, "Finishing a Friendly Argument: The Jury and the Historical Origins of Diversity Jurisdiction," *NYU L. Rev.* 82 (2007): 997, 1064–1066.
100. Marietta & Rowe, *Troubled Experiment*, 57.
101. In its 1718 criminal justice statute, Pennsylvania limited the number of peremptory challenges in felony cases to twenty. Act of May 31, 1718, ch. 3, *Pa. Stat.*, 3:199, 201. After independence, some states experimented with a reduced number of peremptory challenges in treason cases. New Hampshire permitted only twenty-three, and Massachusetts only twenty. *N.H. Laws*, 1777:230; *Mass. Acts*, 1777:109.
102. Blackstone, *Commentaries*, 4:347.
103. Wilson, Charge to the Grand Jury, 4:38.
104. Wilson, "Lectures on Law," 548.
105. For James Wilson's defense of this distinction, see ibid., 701.
106. Blackstone, *Commentaries*, 3:358.
107. Act of March 19, 1785, ch. 1138, *Pa. Stat.*, 11:486, 489.
108. Mr. Townly's Case, 168 Eng. Rep. 4 (Fost. 7) (1746); Act of March 19, 1785, ch. 1138, *Pa. Stat.*, 11:486, 489. Challenges were not necessarily common. P.J.R. King, for example, studied trial records from eighteenth-century Essex and concluded that the "right of jury challenge was rarely used." King, "Illiterate Plebeians," 277. Similarly, James D. Rice found that in eighteenth-century Maryland "challenges were rather unusual . . . , and *voir dire* proceedings took up little or no time." Rice, "Criminal Trial," 464.
109. *Pa. Packet*, Nov. 7, 1778. McKean's handwritten notes of the Roberts trial show him marking down each challenge to the total of thirty-three. Notes of Chief Justice McKean in Respublica v. Roberts, LWS Collection, Morristown National Historic Park, Morristown, NJ. The notes include the scratched-out names of Cadwalader Dickinson and John Campbell as jurors. These jurors may have been challenged for cause, as there seems to be no reason that the notes would identify these two and not the other thirty-one challenged jurors.
110. David W. Maxey, "The Honorable Proprietaries v. Samuel Wallis: 'A Matter of Great Consequence' in the Province of Pennsylvania," *Penn. History* 70 (2003): 361, 375; David W. Maxey, *Treason on Trial in Revolutionary Pennsylvania: The Case of John Roberts, Miller* (Philadelphia: Am. Phil. Soc., 2011), 37.
111. Documents from later cases indicate defendants making extensive use of challenges. List of Jury & Challenges, Respublica v. Robinson, April 3, 1782, Oyer

and Terminer Papers, Roll 5, RG-33, PSA; Respublica v. McCullough, April 4, 1782, Oyer and Terminer Papers, Roll 5, RG-33, PSA.

112. Philadelphia County Tax Duplicate, 1775, RG-1, Philadelphia City Archives, Philadelphia, PA, 15, 69, 195.
113. *Conn. Gazette*, Dec. 13, 1782.
114. *Pa. Gazette*, Feb. 14, 1776.
115. Philadelphia Monthly Meeting Records, Jan. 28, 1779, MR-PH384, Friends Historical Library, Swarthmore College, Swarthmore, PA.
116. Tax and Exoneration Lists, 1779, Reel 225, RG-4, PSA, 17, 165.
117. Henry D. Biddle, *The Drinker Family in America* (Philadelphia: J.B. Lippincott, 1893), 9–10.
118. William Wade Hinshaw, *Encyclopedia of American Quaker Genealogy* (Ann Arbor: 1938), 2:508.
119. *Pa. Gazette*, March 6, 1776.
120. *Pa. Gazette*, Feb. 27, 1753; Charles E. Peterson, "Robert Smith, Philadelphia Builder-Architect," in *Scotland and America in the Age of the Enlightenment*, ed. Richard B. Sher & Jeffrey R. Smitten (Princeton, NJ: Princeton Univ. Press, 1990), 290.
121. Jackson, *With the British Army*, 22; *Pa. Gazette*, June 17, 1778; *Pa. Packet*, Dec. 12, 1778.
122. Philadelphia County Tax Duplicate, 1775, 164, 189; Tax and Exoneration Lists, 1779, 84, 194, 225.
123. *Pa. Packet*, July 25, 1778.
124. John M. Murrin, "Magistrates, Sinners, and a Precarious Liberty: Trial by Jury in Seventeenth-Century New England," in *Saints & Revolutionaries*, 152, 197.
125. For a map of Philadelphia's tax wards, see Doerflinger, *Vigorous Spirit*, 34–35.
126. English trial jurors also tended to be drawn from close proximity to where the court was sitting. J.M. Beattie, *Crime and the Courts in England, 1660–1800* (Princeton, NJ: Princeton Univ. Press, 1986), 382.
127. In many cases it has not been possible to determine precise birthdates, so the stated ages should be assumed to be accurate within plus or minus one year.
128. These ages are nearly identical to those found for Sangamon County, Illinois in 1850, where grand jurors had a median age of forty-nine and trial jurors a mean age of forty-four. Stacy Pratt McDermott, *The Jury in Lincoln's America* (Athens, OH: Ohio Univ. Press, 2012), 68–69. These ages are also similar to those of eighteenth-century Essex juries, in which "throughout the period 1734–1815, between half and two-thirds of the eligible jurors were in their forties or fifties." King, "Illiterate Plebeians," 261.
129. In my earlier work on this subject, I found little variance with age. Larson, "Revolutionary American Jury," 1470. The analysis presented here is based on additional research into juror ages.

130. Robert Francis Oaks, "Philadelphia Merchants and the American Revolution, 1765–1776," (Ph.D. diss., Univ. of Southern California, 1970), 206.
131. Jonathan Clark, "The Problem of Allegiance in Revolutionary Poughkeepsie," in *Saints & Revolutionaries*, 285, 303.
132. There were several family connections among the jurors. John Steinmetz's and Adam Zantzinger's wives were sisters, but the two men never served on the same jury. Laurie M. Wolfe, "Henry Keppele," in *Lawmaking and Legislators in Pennsylvania*, 3:783–793. By contrast, brothers John and Isaac Roush both served on Jacob Ming's jury. Julia Roush O'Melia, *History of the Roush Family in America* (Parkersburg, WV: Banner Printing, 1942), 2:45.
133. Billy G. Smith & Paul Sivitz, "Identifying and Mapping Ethnicity in Philadelphia in the Early Republic," *PMHB* 140 (2016): 395, 393, 398.
134. There are no precise data on the ethnic breakdown of Philadelphia as a whole, but estimates of the ethnic composition on the eve of the Revolution suggest that the ethnicity of the jury pool roughly tracked that of the population as a whole. Robert James Gough, "Towards a Theory of Class and Social Conflict: A Social History of Wealthy Philadelphians, 1775 and 1800," (Ph.D. diss., Univ. of Penn., 1977), 135–136.
135. In my earlier work on this subject, I found little variance with ethnicity. Larson, "Revolutionary American Jury," 1471. The analysis presented here is based on additional research into juror ethnicity.
136. Eric Foner, *Tom Paine and Revolutionary America* (New York: Oxford Univ. Press, 1976), 28–29, 38, 60–63. On artisans, see Charles S. Olton, *Artisans for Independence: Philadelphia Mechanics and the American Revolution* (Syracuse: Syracuse Univ. Press, 1975); Gary B. Nash, *The Urban Crucible: Social Change, Political Consciousness, and the Origins of the American Revolution* (Cambridge, MA: Harvard Univ. Press, 1979), 387–391.
137. Thomas Doerflinger emphasized that the terms merchant and shopkeeper had relatively precise meanings in the eighteenth century. "Merchants were wholesalers who—in America, at least—were typically active in foreign markets; shopkeepers were general retailers who obtained their goods from merchants." Doerflinger argued that most of Philadelphia's merchants were not wealthy aristocrats, but "part of the city's large middle stratum" and included many "upwardly mobile strivers." Doerflinger, *A Vigorous Spirit of Enterprise*, 16–17. Another scholar found that "many pretentious men who would ordinarily be termed shopkeepers often used the more prestigious term to describe themselves." Oaks, "Philadelphia Merchants," 11. Some of the jurors seem to fit this pattern. Adam Zantzinger, for example, described himself as a merchant in a context that seems much more typical of a shopkeeper. *Pa. Gazette*, Dec. 3, 1778.
138. On Philadelphia's laborers, see generally Billy G. Smith, *The "Lower Sort": Philadelphia's Laboring People, 1750–1800* (Ithaca, NY: Cornell Univ. Press, 1990).

139. In addition to the caveats about this data noted in n.27, at least one other anomaly should be noted. The 1779 returns indicated that steel manufacturer Whitehead Humphreys had no taxable wealth. In 1780, however, his taxable wealth was £28,000. Thus the 1779 returns almost certainly grossly underestimate his wealth.
140. Jack Marietta and G.S. Rowe found that eighteenth-century jurors in Chester County, Pennsylvania were generally in the seventieth and eightieth percentile of wealth distribution. This is roughly true for the Philadelphia jurors as well. Marietta & Rowe, *Troubled Experiment*, 54, 59, 104. Similar results have been found for Sangamon County, Illinois in 1850 where "grand jurors were nearly twice as wealthy as petit jurors, but petit jurors were wealthier than Sangamon County men who were qualified but did not serve on juries." McDermott, *Jury in Lincoln's America*, 71.
141. Oaks, "Philadelphia Merchants," 206. A study of Poughkeepsie, New York found that "Patriots as a group were, on the average, relatively wealthier than Loyalists." Clark, "Problem of Allegiance," 300.
142. This distinction between grand jurors and jurors did not last. In 1805, Pennsylvania began selecting its grand jurors and jurors at random from the same lists. John Reed, *Pennsylvania Blackstone* (Carlisle, PA: George Fleming, 1831), 3:326–327.
143. Blackstone, *Commentaries*, 3:380.
144. Thomas A. Green, "A Retrospective," in *Twelve Men*, 358, 397.
145. Hay, "Class Composition," 330.
146. King, "Illiterate Plebeians," 266.
147. Hay, "Class Composition," 343.
148. Excluding the improbable data for Whitehead Humphreys identified in n.139.
149. In his Law Lectures, James Wilson complained that capital juries were often composed of those "who have neither influence enough to avoid being returned, nor money enough to pay a fine for their non-attendance." Wilson, *Works*, 2:531.
150. On Quaker opposition to the Revolution, see Richard Bauman, *For the Reputation of Truth: Politics, Religion, and Conflict among the Pennsylvania Quakers, 1750–1800* (Baltimore: Johns Hopkins Univ. Press, 1971), 141–183; Jack D. Marietta, *The Reformation of American Quakerism, 1748–1783* (Philadelphia: Univ. of Penn. Press, 1984), 222–248.
151. Quoted in Owen S. Ireland, "The Ethnic-Religious Dimension of Pennsylvania Politics, 1778–1779," *William & Mary Q.* 30 (1973): 423, 424.
152. Fisher, "Journal," 333.
153. Charles Inglis to Joseph Galloway, Dec.12, 1778, in "Letters to Joseph Galloway," *Historical Magazine* (Oct. 1861): 297, 299.
154. O.S. Ireland, "The Crux of Politics: Religion and Party in Pennsylvania, 1778–1789," *William & Mary Q.* 42 (1985): 453, 455–456.
155. Foner, *Tom Paine*, 135.
156. J.P. Brissot de Warville, *New Travels in the United States of America, 1788*, trans. Mara Soceanu Vamos & Durand Echeverria (Cambridge, MA: Harvard Univ. Press, [1791] 1964), 331.

157. Oaks, "Philadelphia Merchants," 207.
158. One study found that wealthy Quakers and Anglicans were less likely to support the Revolution than wealthy Presbyterians. Gough, "Towards a Theory of Class and Social Conflict," 492–494. A study of colonial Anglican clergy found that of the sixteen Anglican clergy in Pennsylvania and Delaware, six supported the crown, nine remained neutral, and only one was an active patriot. Nancy L. Rhoden, *Revolutionary Anglicanism: The Colonial Church of England Clergy during the American Revolution* (London: Macmillan Press, 1999), 89.
159. Kevin Phillips, *1775: A Good Year for Revolution* (New York: Viking, 2012), 79–80.
160. Quakers who supported the Revolution tended to be ones not in good standing with the monthly meeting. Oaks, "Philadelphia Merchants," 210.
161. William C. Kashatus III, *Conflict of Conviction: A Reappraisal of Quaker Involvement in the American Revolution* (Lanham, MD: Univ. Press of Am., 1990), 164–165.
162. Susan E. Klepp, *Philadelphia in Transition: A Demographic History of the City and Its Occupational Groups, 1720–1830* (New York: Garland, 1989), 15.
163. Records of Christ Church, Philadelphia: Marriages, 1709–1800, HSP, 4382.
164. Records of the First Presbyterian Church: Baptisms, 1701–1853; Marriages, 1702–1855, HSP, 346, 427; *Pa. Gazette*, Nov. 1, 1780.
165. Edward L. Clark, *A Record of the Inscriptions on the Tablets and Gravestones in the Burial Grounds of Christ Church, Philadelphia* (Philadelphia: Collins, 1864), 102.
166. Hannah Benner Roach, "Genealogical Gleanings from Dr. Rush's Ledger A," in *Pennsylvania Vital Records* (Baltimore: Genealogical Publishing, 1983), 2:105, 107.
167. *Genealogies of Pennsylvania Families* (Baltimore: Genealogical Publishing, 1982), 2:668; Elfreth's Alley Association, *Inside These Doors: A Historic Guidebook of the Homes of Elfreth's Alley* (Philadelphia: Riegel, 2004), 18.
168. Minutes of the SEC, Oct. 26, 1778, *Col. Records*, 11:606.
169. Rush's relationship with Carlisle may lie behind an otherwise inexplicable statement in a 1782 petition to the General Assembly by several disowned Quakers. They stated, "Cadwallader Dickinson . . . was disowned, for sitting as a juryman on the trial of John Roberts and Abraham Carlisle, on a charge of high treason . . . although he was requested to serve on that duty, by a relation of one of those men." Memorial and Remonstrance of Isaac Howell and White Matlack, in *Minutes of the First Session of the Sixth General Assembly* (Philadelphia: John Dunlap, 1781–1782), 667, 669. The statement may simply reflect muddled information, as Dickinson did not serve on Roberts's jury. Yet the very oddity of the assertion suggests some kernel of truth. It is possible that Sheriff James Claypoole was a relation of Carlisle, or, more plausibly, a relation of Carlisle, such as William Rush, may have recommended Dickinson to Claypoole and encouraged him to fulfill his jury service.
170. Gough, "Class and Social Conflict," 138.
171. *Pa. Gazette*, Nov. 16, 1774; Feb. 1, 1775; Oct. 6, 1757; July 27, 1774.

172. *Pa. Gazette*, Nov. 15, 1775; *Pa. Gazette*, Feb. 7, 1776. On the Committee of Privates, see Rosswurm, *Arms, Country, and Class*, 66–72.
173. *Pa. Packet*, July 25, 1778.
174. *Pa. Gazette*, March 6, 1776.
175. Minutes of the Council of Safety, Nov. 26, 1776, *Col. Records*, 11:16–17; *Assembly Journal*, 30.
176. *Pa. Gazette*, Nov. 28, 1778.
177. *Pa. Evening Post*, Aug. 17, 1775; Ryerson, *Revolution*, 272–274; *Pa. Gazette*, Feb. 21, 1776; *List of the Sub-Committees, appointed by the Committee for the city and liberties of Philadelphia, to superintend the several districts of said city, &c.* (1776).
178. *Nixon Accounts*, 9, 16, 18, 19, 44, 45, 95 (Beach, Corgee, Eckhart, Forsberg, Goucher, Hood, Pringle, Rigden, Zantzinger).
179. Ibid., 44.
180. *Minutes of the First Session, of the Seventh General Assembly, of the Commonwealth of Pennsylvania* (1782), 931; Scharf & Westcott, *History of Philadelphia*, 1:301.
181. Minutes of the Council of Safety, Nov. 26, 1776, *Col. Records*, 11:16.
182. *JCC*, 6:888.
183. Minutes of the Council of Safety, Nov. 30, 1776, *Col. Records*, 11:24.
184. David Pancoast to Joseph Dean, n.d., Society Miscellaneous Collection, Box 15B, HSP; Minutes of the Council of Safety, Dec. 11, 1776, *Col. Records*, 11:44.
185. A. Virgil Barnhill, Jr., *Some Descendants of Robert Barnhill I* (Knoxville, TN: Arviba, 1994), 18, 20–21; *Pa. Gazette*, June 26, 1766.
186. Dock Ward Return of Arms in the Hands of Non-Associators, *Pa. Archives* (2d Ser.), 1:600.
187. Scharf & Westcott, *History of Philadelphia*, 1:301; *Report of the secretary of war on sixty petitions* (Philadelphia: Francis Childs & John Swaine, 1794), 11; John B.B. Trussell, Jr., *The Pennsylvania Line: Regimental Organization & Operations, 1775–1783*, 2d ed. (Harrisburg, PA: Pa. Historical & Museum Commission, 1993), 227–228.
188. Capt. Samuel Simpson's Company, *Pa. Archives* (2d Ser.), 13:579 (Simpson, Captain); Capt. George Honey's Company, *Pa. Archives* (6th Ser.), 1:591 (Forsberg, Corporal).
189. Minutes of the Committee of Safety, Dec. 19, 1776, *Col. Records*, 11:16 (Albertson, Lieutenant); Philadelphia City Return—1777, *Pa. Archives* (2d Ser.), 13:582 (Merriam, Ensign); Third Battalion, Col. Morgan, *Pa. Archives* (2d Ser.), 13:599, 600 (Merriam, First Lieutenant; Linnington, Captain; Burkhard, Second Lieutenant); Fourth Battalion, Col. Bayard, *Pa. Archives* (2d Ser.), 13:601, 602 (Wilkinson, Captain); Sixth Battalion, Col. Knox, *Pa. Archives* (2d Ser.), 13:602, 603 (Skinner, First Lieutenant; Beach, Ensign); Officers of Battalions, *Pa. Archives* (2d Ser.), 13:603, 605 (McLane, Captain); Captain James Hood's Company, *Pa. Archives* (2d Ser.), 13:690 (Hood, Captain); Minutes of the Convention of Delegates from the Associated Battalions, *Pa. Archives* (2d Ser.), 13:260, 261 (Bitting, Captain).

190. Absent Associators—1776, *Pa. Archives* (2d Ser.), 13:565, 569–570 (Clumberg, Forsyth, Gray, Linnington, Powell, Roush). Clumberg's absence may be explained by his service in the Continental Army.
191. Frederic Gregory Forsyth de Fronsac, *Memorial of the Family of Forsyth de Fronsac* (Boston: S.J. Parkhill, 1903), 30.
192. Captain Jacob Weidman's Company, *Pa. Archives* (2d Ser.),13:657, 659.
193. A General Return of the Second Battalion, *Pa. Archives* (6th Ser.), 1:121, 135.
194. Returns of Captn. John Linton's Compy., *Pa. Archives* (6th Ser.) 1:56 (Dickinson); A General Return of the Third Battalion, *Pa. Archives* (6th Ser), 1:194, 195 (Forsyth, I. Roush, J. Roush, Rush).
195. *Lieut. Accounts*, 24–25, 27–30, 33, 35–36, 38, 44, 56, 69, 74, 79, 83, 85, 122 (Adcock, Beach, Bitting, Corgee, Dickinson, Forsyth, Eckhart, Goucher, Gray, Grove, Humphreys, January, McLane, Merriam, Pancoast, Piles, Pringle, Rigden, Ritter, Rush, Shields, Steinmetz, Zantzinger). The lists of fines also include persons named John Drinker, Thomas Palmer, George Wilson, and John Wilson, any of whom might have been a juror. Ibid., 30, 40, 50, 117. George Dowig's failure to pay was excused. A General Return of the Fourth Battalion, *Pa. Archives* (6th Ser.), 1:280, 292. Wealthier individuals were more likely to pay the militia fine than poorer individuals. Rosswurm, *Arms, Country, Class*, 142.
196. In December, 1776, Cadwalader Dickinson and Samuel Simpson were appointed along with nineteen others, including future grand juror Thomas Cuthbert, to collect coats in Philadelphia to give to the soldiers. Council of Safety, *In Council of Safety* (Philadelphia: Dunlap, 1776). In September 1777, during the British invasion, Ricloff Albertson was appointed to a committee to collect boats on the Delaware River. Minutes of the SEC, Sept. 10, 1777, *Col. Records*, 11:297.
197. Minutes of a Meeting at the Indian Queen, 1776, *Pa. Archives*, 5:73.
198. *Pa. Gazette*, April 23, 1777.
199. *Pa. Gazette*, May 21, 1777.
200. *Pa. Evening Post*, Nov. 6, 1777 (Eckhart, Powell, Rigden, Utree); Letter from John Steinmetz and Henry Keppele to John Whitmore, Sen., April 9, 1778, Papers of John Steinmetz, Jasper Yeates Brinton Collection, Box 6, Folder 8, HSP.
201. Robert Eric Wright, *Origins of Commercial Banking in America, 1750–1800* (Lanham, MD: Rowman & Littlefield, 2001), 150.
202. *Diary of Elizabeth Drinker*, 1: 236. According to Steven Rosswurm, George Pickering was "taken off by the British when he left Philadelphia in 1778." Rosswurm, *Arms, Country, and Class*, 350 n.40.
203. *Pa. Evening Post*, July 6, 1778.
204. Smith, *The "Lower Sort,"* 138. In September 1777, Dickinson and Thomas Harrison were ordered by the county court to pay fifteen pounds to the overseers of the poor "for manumitting a Negro man named Harry." Docket Book of the Court of Quarter Sessions for Philadelphia County, Sept. 1777, Philadelphia City Archives, 119. On August 21, 1778, Dickinson appeared before Philadelphia magistrates to accuse Peter Holmes of treason and for doing "great evil in the

Jerseys." Recognizances Issued by Plunket Fleeson, Oyer and Terminer Papers, Roll 5, RG-33, PSA.

205. Scharf & Westcott, *History of Philadelphia*, 1:386 n.2.

206. Patriotic Association Book, HSP (Adcock, Albertson, Barnhill, Beach, Campbell, Dickinson, Falconer, Forsberg, Goucher, Gray, Hale, Humphreys, Linnington, McLane, Pancoast, I. Roush, Simpson, Skinner, G. Wilson, Zantzinger). The membership book also includes a John Palmer, a Thomas Palmer, and a John Wilson, who may well have been the jurors. I have identified George Wilson as the juror, based on the "Jr." designation used on his signature to a clemency petition and the "Jr." designation in the Patriotic Association records.

207. *Pa. Packet*, Aug. 15, 1778; Aug. 18, 1778; Sept. 2, 1778; Sept. 15, 1778; Sept. 19, 1778; Sept. 22, 1778; Sept. 26, 1778; Sept. 29, 1778; Oct. 6, 1778.

CHAPTER 7

1. James A. Jacobs, "William Hamilton and The Woodlands: A Construction of Refinement in Philadelphia," *PMHB* 130 (2006): 181, 184–185; Charlene Mires, *Independence Hall in American Memory* (Philadelphia: Univ. of Penn. Press, 2002), 4–8; *Pa. Gazette*, May 27, 1762.
2. Colonels Associated Battalions, 1775, *Pa. Archives*, 13:257; *Pa. Gazette*, March 27, 1776.
3. *Proceedings of the Provincial Conference of Committees* (Philadelphia: W. & T. Bradford, 1776), 4.
4. *Pa. Gazette*, July 9, 1788.
5. Catherine P. Fussell & Timothy Preston Long, "The Woodlands," available at http://www.lewis-clark.org/content/content-article.asp?ArticleID=266 6.
6. Peggy Cornett, "Inspirations from the Woodlands: Jefferson's Abiding Attachment to Philadelphia's Botanical Riches," http://twinleaf.org/articles/philadelphia/html.
7. *Votes of the House of Representatives* (Philadelphia: John Henry Miller, 1774–1776), 247. Jefferson took no umbrage at Hamilton's behavior during the Revolution, noting that "[d]uring the whole of the last war, which was trying enough, I never deserted a friend because he had taken an opposite side." Jefferson added, "[T]hose of my own state who joined the British government can attest my unremitting zeal in saving their property, & can point out the laws in our statute book which I drew, & carried through in their favor." Thomas Jefferson to William Hamilton, April 22, 1800, in *The Writings of Thomas Jefferson*, ed. Paul Leicester Ford (New York: G.P. Putnam, 1896), 7:440–441.
8. David Franks to Thomas Moore, n.d., *Pa. Packet*, April 29, 1779.
9. William Hamilton to William Tilghman, April 1779, William Hamilton Folder, Society Collection, HSP.
10. Maya Jasanoff, *Liberty's Exiles: American Loyalists in the Revolutionary World* (New York: Knopf, 2011), 8.

11. Ronald Hoffman, *A Spirit of Dissension: Economics, Politics, and the Revolution in Maryland* (Baltimore: Johns Hopkins Univ. Press, 1973), 225.
12. Maxey, *Treason on Trial*, 14; Memorial of George Harding, American Loyalist Claims, AO12.40.11, National Archives of the United Kingdom. The *Pennsylvania Gazette* would later describe Harding as a "poor man" with "few friends," *Pa. Gazette*, May 5, 1779, but he had significant real estate holdings.
13. Defendant Samuel Piles was described as "too old" in a militia return, suggesting that he was over sixty. A General Return of the Sixth Battalion, *Pa. Archives*, 1:404, 420.
14. Docket Book of the Court of Oyer and Terminer, RG-33, PSA, 8. Marietta and Rowe state that another woman, Mary Colley, was indicted for treason during the Revolution, Marietta & Rowe, *Troubled Experiment*, 197, but Colley was charged with poisoning her husband, a form of petty treason, Justice Fleeson's Recognizances, April 1781, Oyer and Terminer Papers, RG-33, PSA.
15. One of the Quakers, Joseph Bolton, had been disowned in 1773 for suing another Quaker in the courts of law. Philadelphia Monthly Meeting Minutes:1771–1777, April 1773, Friends Historical Library, Swarthmore College, Swarthmore, PA, 131.
16. Linda Przybyszewski, *The Republic According to John Marshall Harlan* (Chapel Hill: UNC Press, 1999), 53.
17. Jonathan Powell, "Presbyterian Loyalists: A 'Chain of Interest' in Philadelphia," *J. of Presbyterian History* 57 (1979): 135–160.
18. *Pa. Gazette*, June 22, 1774.
19. *Pa. Gazette*, July 27, 1774. Future juror William Rush was also a member, as was future assistant attorney general Joseph Reed. Ibid.
20. *Pa. Gazette*, Nov. 30, 1774.
21. *Pa. Gazette*, Dec. 21, 1774; Feb. 1, 1775.
22. Jeffery M. Dorwart, *Fort Mifflin of Philadelphia: An Illustrated History* (Philadelphia: Univ. of Penn. Press, 1998), 19–20; *State of the Accounts of John M. Nesbitt, Esq.* (Philadelphia: Robert Aitken, 1786), 55, 87 (Guion); *JCC*, 4:292 (Ming); Journal of Benjamin Loxley, 1771–1785, HSP, 231 (Deshong); Minutes of the Committee of Safety, Jan. 4, 1777, *Col. Records*, 11:75 (Woolfall); Minutes of the SEC, Aug. 7, 1777, *Col. Records*, 11:262 (Stricker).
23. *State of the Accounts of the Lieutenant & Sub Lieutenants of the City of Philadelphia, and Liberties* (Philadelphia: Francis Bailey, 1784), 33, 40, 42, 52, 62, 72, 126 (Bolton, Deshong, Garrigues, Hamilton, Huntsman, Ming, Stricker, Woolfall).
24. On the population of Philadelphia in the 1770s, see Sharon Salinger & Charles Wetherell, "A Note on the Population of Pre-revolutionary Philadelphia," *PMHB* 109 (1985): 369, 385.
25. Charles Peterson, "Benjamin Loxley and Carpenters' Hall," *J. Soc. Architectural Historians* 15 (1956): 23, 25. Juror Adam Zantzinger was also a member of the Company, although he did not serve at the trials of any of the members. http://www.ushistory.org/carpentershall/company/allmembers.htm.

26. Recognizance of Samuel Piles, Oct. 19, 1778, Recognizance File, RG-33, PSA.
27. Lenore Dickinson, *Dickinson Genealogy*, available at http://www.gwyneddfriends.org/dickinson.htm; Descendants of Edward Morgan, available at http://www.gwyneddfriends.org/morgan.htm; http://www.gwyneddfriends.org/jenkinschapter12.htm. Abijah and his sisters were first cousins to frontiersman Daniel Boone. Bradley Kerr generously provided me this information about his ancestors.
28. Letter from James Roberts to Robert Morris, Oct. 7, 1778, Robert Morris Papers, Levis Collection, HSP.
29. http://www.altlaw.com/edball/html/d0046/i00325.htm.
30. *Pa. Packet*, Aug. 27, 1778.
31. *JCC*: 13:453.
32. See generally Langbein, *Origins of Adversary Criminal Trial.*
33. Act of May 31, 1718, ch. 236, *Pa. Stat.*, 2:199, 201.
34. Wilson, "Law Lectures," 702.
35. *Pa. Packet*, Dec. 8, 1778.
36. Hugh Henry Brackenridge, *Incidents of the Insurrection in the Western Part of Pennsylvania, In the Year 1794* (Philadelphia: John M'Culloch, 1795), 42.
37. S.F.C. Milsom, introduction to Frederick Pollock and Frederic William Maitland, *The History of English Law*, 2d ed. (Cambridge: Cambridge Univ. Press, 1968), 1:xxv.
38. Letter from Jacob Rush to John Hancock, Oct. 10, 1778, Dreer Collection—American Lawyers, HSP.
39. Notes of C.J. McKean in case of Ab'm Carlisle, 1778, *Pa. Archives*, 7:44; Respublica v. Roberts, 1 U.S. (1 Dallas) 39, 40 (Pa. Oyer & Terminer 1778); Rosswurm, *Arms, Country, & Class*, 222 (quoting 1782 statement referring to "that damned Wilson that defended the Tory Hamilton"); "Addenda to Watson's Annals of Philadelphia: Notes by Jacob Mordecai, 1836," *PMHB* 98 (1974): 131, 151–152 (Wilson and Lewis defended Carlisle, Roberts, and Hamilton); Notes of Testimony in Respublica v. Deshong (photostat of unpublished manuscript, on file with Stephen Corson, Philadelphia, PA, and with author), 5. The provenance of the Deshong Notes cannot be established, but they bear all the indicia of authenticity.
40. Robert R. Bell, *The Philadelphia Lawyer: A History, 1735–1945*, (Selinsgrove, PA: Susquehanna Univ. Press, 1992), 83–87.
41. John Thomas Scharf & Thompson Westcott, *History of Philadelphia, 1680–1884* (Philadelphia: L.H. Everts, 1884), 2:1531. In 1780, North Carolina prohibited lawyers for both the state and the defense in treason cases. An Act for the speedy Trial of all persons accused of treason, *State Records of North Carolina*, 24:349.
42. Respublica v. Carlisle, 1 U.S. (1 Dallas) 35 (Pa. Oyer & Terminer 1778); *Pa. Eve. Post*, Oct. 7, 1778.
43. E.g., Indictment of Justin McCarty, Chester Co. Ct. of Oyer and Terminer (April 1779), Oyer and Terminer Miscellaneous Papers, 1777–1781, RG-33, PSA; Indictment of Justin McCarty, Philadelphia Co. Ct. of Oyer and Terminer

(April 1781), Oyer and Terminer Miscellaneous Papers, 1777–1781, RG-33, PSA; Indictment of George Clift, Bucks Co. Ct. of Oyer and Terminer (Dec. 1781), Autograph Collection, RG-33, PSA.

44. Notes of C.J. McKean in *Case of Ab'm Carlisle, Pa. Archives*, 7:44–49. A slightly different version of these notes is preserved in the records of the Quaker Meeting for Sufferings. These notes largely track the published version of McKean's notes, but they convert the fragments and abbreviations into full sentences. They also include certain details that are not included in the published version, but there are no significant material differences. Miscellaneous Papers, Meeting for Sufferings, MR-PH 507, Friends Historical Library, Swarthmore College, Swarthmore, PA. Carlisle's hostility to the Revolution was long standing. In April 1776, Carlisle had spoken of Christopher Marshall's participation in revolutionary activities with the most "opprobrious" words and "base calumny that language could form in a sober man." Christopher Marshall to Abraham Carlisle, April 30, 1776, Christopher Marshall Letterbook, Christopher Marshall Collection, HSP.

45. Minutes of the SEC, Oct. 23, 1778, *Col. Records*, 11:601–602. For a meticulous and legally informed analysis of the Roberts trial, see Maxey, *Treason on Trial*.

46. Notes of Chief Justice McKean in Respublica v. Roberts, LSW Collection, Morristown National Historic Park, Morristown, NJ. McKean's notes list twenty-nine witnesses for the defense; the court's docket book lists thirty-two. Notes of the trial from a Quaker observer also survive in the Miscellaneous Papers of the Meeting for Sufferings, MR-PH 507, Friends Historical Library, Swarthmore College, Swarthmore, PA. Another copy is at the Quaker Collection at Haverford College, Haverford, PA. A transcription of the McKean and Haverford notes is provided in Maxey, *Treason on Trial*, 137–157. On the hiding of the Journals of the Continental Congress, see James Lovell to George Washington, Jan. 31, 1778, *LDC*, 8:509–510.

47. Thomas Franklin to Elias Boudinot, Oct. 4, 1778, Elias Boudinot Papers, HSP, 2:50.

48. *Diary of Elizabeth Drinker*, 1:329.

49. Notes of Chief Justice McKean in Respublica v. Roberts, 11. The returning exiles from Virginia stayed at John Roberts's house in April 1778. They were told by his wife that Roberts was "under the necessity to reside in the city . . . in consequence of some exception the Americans had taken against him, and by whom he had suffered considerably in his property." "Journal of the Friends in Exile, Taken from the Diary of James Pemberton," in Thomas Gilpin, *Exiles in Virginia* (Philadelphia: 1848), 233.

50. John Roberts Oath of Allegiance, June 19, 1778, Zebulon Potts Folder, Society Collection, HSP.

51. *Pa. Evening Post*, Oct. 9, 1778.

52. Deshong Notes, 1–8.

53. *Pa. Evening Post*, Oct. 9, 1778. Five months later Deshong was convicted in the Court of Quarter Sessions for an assault on Caleb Armitage. Docket Book of the

Court of Quarter Sessions, Philadelphia County (March 1779), Philadelphia City Archives, 134.

54. Record Book of Benjamin Paschall, Esq., HSP.
55. Recognizance Papers, Court of Oyer and Terminer Records, Roll 5, PSA.
56. Fisher, "Journal," 152.
57. Notes, Respublica v. Joseph Bolton, Oyer & Terminer Miscellaneous Papers, RG-33, PSA.
58. Isaac Ogden to Joseph Galloway, Nov. 22, 1778, in "Letters to Joseph Galloway," *Historical Magazine* (Nov. 1861): 335, 336.
59. Blackstone, *Commentaries*, 4:30.
60. *Pa. Evening Post*, Oct. 9, 1778.
61. The humble Memorial and Petition of Elizabeth Ferguson, Feb. 7, 1779, in *Third Assembly Minutes*, 37, 38.
62. Fisher, "Journal," 152.
63. One of the acquitted defendants, Joseph Turner, Jr., was later arrested in Virginia for aiding the British. George Bryan to William Augustus Atlee, Aug. 8, 1780, William Augustus Atlee Papers, Library of Congress.
64. The witness lists are found in the Docket Book of the Court of Oyer and Terminer, RG-33, PSA.
65. Wilson, "Law Lectures," 332.
66. Wilson, Charge to the Grand Jury, 39.
67. It is possible that not all the witnesses identified in the docket book actually testified. Some may have been sworn but then proffered testimony that was disallowed by the court. The docket book lists several sworn witnesses in the Roberts and Carlisle trials who do not appear in Chief Justice McKean's notes.
68. *Pa. Packet*, July 25, 1778; Oyer & Terminer Papers, Roll 5, PSA. This Alexander Hamilton was not the more famous one, who seems to have been in New York at the time of the testimony. Alexander Hamilton to Major John Bigelow, Oct. 9, 1778, in *The Papers of Alexander Hamilton*, ed. Harold Syrett (New York: Columbia Univ. Press, 1961), 1:560.
69. *Pa. Evening Post*, Feb. 3, 1778.
70. Presiding justices and jurors in eighteenth-century Virginia county courts often appeared as witnesses. Blinka, "Jury Trial," 535, 569. Similarly, the *Pennsylvania Blackstone* treatise later noted that "being a witness in a cause . . . is no cause of challenge [to a juror]." Reed, *Pennsylvania Blackstone*, 3:340. The English practice of juror testimony is described in James Oldham, "Truth-Telling in the Eighteenth-Century English Courtroom," *Law & History Review* 12 (1994): 95, 106.
71. Reed, *Pennsylvania Blackstone*, 3:385.
72. Stephen G.C. Ensko, *American Silversmiths and Their Marks* (New York: privately printed, 1948), 127–128. This inkstand is now on display at Independence Hall.
73. David Hackett Fischer, *Washington's Crossing* (New York: Oxford Univ. Press, 2004), 27, 284–285.

74. *Carlisle*, 1 U.S. (1 Dallas), 36–38.
75. Notes of C.J. McKean in Case of Ab'm Carlisle, *Pa. Archives*, 7:47–48.
76. *Roberts*, 1 U.S. (1 Dallas), 39. The Dallas volume states, "In support of the prosecution, it was urged, that the attempt to prevail, constituted the crime; and that it was like a case of a man's sending intelligence to the enemy, which was an act equally criminal in the sender, whether the intelligence was received, or not." Chief Justice McKean's notes on the trial, however, do not include this argument on behalf of the prosecution. In fact, he notes that the state conceded that "persuading to enlist without actually enlisting may not be treason, but it may show *quo animo* that the prisoner joined the British army." These notes suggest that the prosecution arguments were not as strident as the Dallas reports, which were reconstructed at a much later date, made them out to be. Notes of Thomas McKean in the Roberts trial, Morristown National Historical Park, Morristown, NJ.
77. Notes of Thomas McKean in the Roberts trial, Morristown National Historical Park, Morristown, NJ. The Dallas volume describes the confession as an admission that Roberts "was going to the Head of Elk, in order to communicate some information to Mr. Galloway, who had at that time, gone over to the enemy." *Roberts*, 1 U.S. (1 Dall.), at 39. The actual "confession" was much less sinister. Maxey, *Treason on Trial*, 47.
78. Foster's treatise approved of the admission of confessions as corroboration. Foster, *Discourse*, 240–242.
79. *Roberts*, 1 U.S. (1 Dall.), at 39–40. This decision was cited approvingly by the United States Supreme Court in Haupt v. United States, 330 U.S. 631, 643 (1947).
80. Thomas Franklin to Elias Boudinot, Oct. 4, 1778, Elias Boudinot Papers, HSP, 2:50.
81. Joseph Reed to George Bryan, Oct. 23, 1778, Joseph Reed Papers, Reel 2, New-York Historical Society.
82. We do not know where the jury deliberated. It may have been in a separate room at the College of Philadelphia, or it may have been at a nearby house, as happened in an April 1779 misdemeanor trial. Timothy Matlack, "To the Free Independent Whigs of Pennsylvania," *Pa. Packet*, May 18, 1779.
83. Edward Burd to Jasper Yeates, Sept. 30, 1778, Yeates Family Collection, HSP.
84. *Diary of Elizabeth Drinker*, 1:329; Diary of John Pemberton, Oct. 6, 1778, Pemberton Papers, HSP.
85. Joseph Reed to George Bryan, Oct. 23, 1778, Joseph Reed Papers, Reel 2, New-York Historical Society.
86. *Pa. Packet*, April 29, 1779.
87. Memorandum of the Sufferings & Losses Sustained by George Harding/formerly of Philadelphia/in the late Rebellion, American Loyalist Claims, AO13.57.142, National Archives of the United Kingdom.
88. Wilson, "Law Lectures," 2:523.
89. *Pa. Packet*, May 1, 1779.
90. Wilson, "Law Lectures," 2:532.

91. William Bradford, *An Enquiry How Far the Punishment of Death is Necessary in Pennsylvania* (Philadelphia: T. Dobson, 1793), 8.
92. Recognizance Papers, Court of Oyer and Terminer Records, Roll 5, PSA; *Pa. Packet*, Dec. 8, 1778.
93. J.P. Brissot de Warville, *New Travels in the United States of America, 1788*, trans. Mara Soceanu Vamos & Durand Echeverria (Cambridge, MA: Harvard Univ. Press, [1791] 1964), 332.
94. Wilson, "Law Lectures," 2:528–531.
95. Cookie Stephan, "Selective Characteristics of Jurors and Litigants: Their Influences on Juries' Verdicts," in *The Jury System in America: A Critical Overview*, ed. Rita James Simon (Beverly Hills, CA: Sage Publications, 1975), 97, 113; Ronald C. Dillehay & Michael T. Nietzel, "Juror Experience and Jury Verdicts," *Law & Human Behavior* 9 (1985): 179, 185. This effect has also been demonstrated for eighteenth-century English jurors. Hay, "Class Composition," 348.
96. Norbert L. Kerr, "Effects of Prior Juror Experience on Juror Behavior," *Basic & Applied Soc. Psych.* 2 (1981): 175, 177.
97. Ibid., 180.
98. Carol M. Werner, Michael J. Strube, Allen M. Cole & Dorothy K. Kagehiro , "The Impact of Case Characteristics and Prior Jury Experience on Jury Verdicts," *J. Applied Soc. Pysch.* 15 (1985): 409, 421.
99. Kerr, "Effects of Prior Juror Experience," 187–190.
100. See generally Beattie, *Crime and the Courts in England.*
101. Smolenski, *Friends and Strangers*, 138–146; Paul Lermack, "Peace Bonds and Criminal Justice in Colonial Philadelphia," *PMHB* 100 (1976): 173-190. A massive study of criminal justice in colonial New York found only "occasional orders for recognizances after acquittal." Goebel & Naughton, *Law Enforcement in Colonial New York*, 517. On peace bonds and good behavior bonds in early modern England, see David Lemmings, *Law and Government in England during the Long Eighteenth Century* (New York: Palgrave Macmillan, 2011), 24–25.
102. O&T Docket, PSA, 1–11; *Pa. Gazette*, April 14, 1779 (bond for James Stevens).
103. On the distinction between good behavior bonds and peace bonds in English law, see Landau, *Justices of the Peace*, 24.
104. G.S. Rowe, "Judicial Tyrant and Vox Populi: Pennsylvanians View Their State Supreme Court, 1777–1779," *PMHB* 118 (1994): 33, 46.
105. O&T Docket, PSA, 7.
106. Pa. Const. of 1776, § 20. For a contemporary analysis of this provision, see *Pa. Packet*, Oct. 31, 1778. Abraham Carlisle "entreated [the justices] to have his punishment mitigated to banishment," but Pennsylvania law did not provide for such mitigation. *Pa. Eve. Post*, Oct. 7, 1778.
107. James Wilson, "A Charge Delivered to the Grand Jury in the Circuit Court of the United States, for the District of Virginia," in *The Works of James Wilson*, ed. Robert Green McCloskey (Cambridge, MA: Harvard Univ. Press, 1967),

2:803–804. One scholar has argued that by the time of the Civil War, mandatory capital punishment was widely regarded as a "dangerous failure" in America. The only deterrent effect was to deter "jurors from convicting palpably guilty men." Philip English Mackey, "The Inutility of Mandatory Capital Punishment: An Historical Note," *Boston Univ. Law. Rev.* 54 (1974): 32, 35.

108. Memorial of Jurors and Judges in Favor of Ar'm Carlisle, *Pa. Archives*, 7:52.
109. Ibid., 53.
110. Petition of the Jury in Case of John Roberts, *Pa. Archives*, 7:24–25. The only jurors who did not sign were James Hood and James Barns. These two jurors never served again.
111. *Pa. Gazette*, Nov. 7, 1778.
112. Petition of the Jury in Case of John Roberts, 25.
113. Memorial of Grand Jurors in Favor of Roberts and Carlisle, *Pa. Archives*, 7:23.
114. Joseph Reed to George Bryan, Oct. 23, 1778, Joseph Reed Papers, Reel 2, New-York Historical Society. Grand jurors Thomas Cuthbert and John Purviance and trial jurors Thomas Shields, William Rush, and Whitehead Humphreys had previously signed a petition urging clemency for four individuals sentenced to death under military authority for desertion. Petition re: Samuel Lyons et al., Clemency File, RG-27, PSA. On these military cases, see Scharf & Westcott, *History of Philadelphia*, 1:394.
115. *Pa. Packet*, Nov. 7, 1778. Presumably a similar sentence was delivered to Abraham Carlisle, but no record of it has survived.
116. Coleman, *Thomas McKean*, 231.
117. Quoted in Frank Moore, *Diary of the American Revolution* (New York: Charles Scribner, 1860), 122.
118. "The American Times: A Satire," in Winthrop Sergeant, *The Loyalist Poetry of the Revolution* (Philadelphia: n.p., 1857), 11.
119. Jasper Yeates to James Burd, Oct. 10, 1778, Burd-Shippen Family Collection, MG-30, PSA.
120. Memorial of Phil. & Chester Co's in behalf of Jno. Roberts, *Pa. Archives*, 7:29–36.
121. To the Honourable, the Supreme Executive Council of Pennsylvania, *Pa. Archives*, 7:25–27.
122. Memorial of the Beneficiaries of John Roberts, *Pa. Archives*, 7:36–37.
123. Petition of Wm. Young &c., in favor of John Roberts, 1778, *Pa. Archives*, 7:38–39.
124. Ibid., 39.
125. Memorial of Ministers of the Gospel in Favor of Roberts and Carlisle, 1778, *Pa. Archives*, 7:24.
126. Memorial in favor of Abr'm Carlisle, 1778, *Pa. Archives*, 7:56–57.
127. An anonymous broadside later praised the Council for its "great wisdom" in allowing the executions to go forward and claimed that the "whigs in the city and the country approved the conduct of Council." A Whig Citizen, "To the Freemen of Pennsylvania," Broadside, Evans 43709, Broadsides Collection, HSP.

128. An anonymous 1784 newspaper statement claimed that over seven thousand individuals signed petitions on behalf of the two men, but I have found no independent verification of this claim. "Anecdotes of George Bryan," *Ind. Gazetteer*, Sept. 4, 1784. For an analysis of the controversy over the decision to execute Carlisle and Roberts, see Peter C. Messer, "'A Species of Treason & Not the Least Dangerous Kind': The Treason Trials of Abraham Carlisle and John Roberts," *PMHB* 123(1999): 303-332. The article's title is slightly misleading, as it focuses almost entirely on the post-conviction controversy rather than on the trials themselves.
129. Memorials in Favor of John Roberts and Ab'm Carlisle, *Pa. Archives*, 7:21–22.
130. To the Honourable, the Supreme Executive Council of Pennsylvania, *Pa. Archives*, 7:27.
131. To the Honourable, the Supreme Executive Council of Pennsylvania, *Pa. Archives*, 7:28–29.
132. Memorial of Phil. & Chester Co's in behalf of Jno. Roberts, *Pa. Archives*, 7:29–36.
133. Memorial in Favor of Abr'm Carlisle, *Pa. Archives*, 7:55–56 (Barnhill, Campbell, Forsyth, Pickering, Rush, Wilkinson, Zantzinger); Memorial in Favor of Abr'm Carlisle, *Pa. Archives*, 7:56–57 (Bitting, Burkhart, Humphreys, Steinmetz); Memorial in Favor of Abr'm Carlisle, *Pa. Archives*, 7:57–58 (Adcock, McClenachan, Pancoast, Pringle, Pryor, Uttree).
134. Joseph Reed to George Bryan, Oct. 23, 1778, Joseph Reed Papers, Reel 2, New-York Historical Society.
135. Ibid.
136. Joseph Reed to Nathaniel Greene, Nov. 5, 1778, *Collections of the New-York Historical Society for the Year 1873* (New York: 1874), 248, 250.
137. Benjamin Rush to William Gordon, Dec. 10, 1778, in *Letters of Benjamin Rush*, ed. L.H. Butterfield (Princeton, NJ: Princeton Univ. Press, 1951), 1:221.
138. Joseph Reed to Nathaniel Greene, Nov. 5, 1778, in *Collections of the New-York Historical Society for the Year 1873* (New York: 1874), 248, 250.
139. Minutes of the SEC, Oct. 12, 1778; Oct. 17, 1778, *Col. Records*, 11:594, 595.
140. Minutes of the SEC, Dec. 1, 1778, *Col. Records*, 11:632–633.
141. Joseph Reed to George Bryan, Oct. 23, 1778, Joseph Reed Papers, Reel 2, New-York Historical Society. It was later claimed that Reed had stated that nothing "would induce George Bryan to pardon them, and that rather than pardon them he believed George Bryan would stand hangman himself." Bryan was also claimed to have said that "if a majority of the Council had agreed to pardon them after he had signed the death warrant, he would have set them at defiance, and ordered them out for execution." "Anecdotes of George Bryan," *Independent Gazetteer*, Sept. 4, 1784.
142. Joseph Reed to Nathaniel Greene, Nov. 5, 1778, *Collections*, 250.
143. Joseph Reed to George Bryan, Oct. 23, 1778, Joseph Reed Papers, Reel 2, New-York Historical Society.

144. Joseph Reed to Nathaniel Greene, Nov. 5, 1778, *Collections*, 250.
145. Brackenridge, *Incidents of the Insurrection*, 65.
146. Reed, *Joseph Reed*, 34.
147. Chapin, *American Law of Treason*, 58.
148. Maxey, *Treason on Trial*, 2.
149. Raymond Werner, ed., "Diary of Grace Growden Galloway," *PMHB* 55 (1931): 48, n.29.
150. Steven R. Boyd, "Political Choice—Political Justice: The Case of the Pennsylvania Loyalists," in *American Political Trials*, ed. Michal R. Belknap (Westport, CT: Greenwood Press, 1994), 43, 54.
151. Geoffrey Seed, *James Wilson* (Milwood, NY: KTO Press, 1978), 186.
152. Scharf & Westcott, *History of Philadelphia*, 1:394.
153. Richard Alan Ryerson, "Republican Theory and Partisan Reality in Revolutionary Pennsylvania: Toward a New View of the Constitutionalist Party," in *Sovereign States in an Age of Uncertainty*, ed. Ronald Hoffman & Peter J. Albert (Charlottesville: UVA Press, 1981), 95, 121.
154. Thomas P. Slaughter, "'The King of Crimes': Early American Treason Law, 1787–1860," in *Launching the "Extended Republic": The Federalist Era*, ed. Ronald Hoffman & Peter J. Albert (Charlottesville: UVA Press, 1996), 54, 75.
155. *The Examination of Joseph Galloway, Esq.; Late Speaker of the House of Assembly of Pennsylvania, Before the House of Commons, in a Committee on the American Papers, with Explanatory Notes* (London: J. Wilkie, 1779), 76–77.
156. Thomas Franklin to Elias Boudinot, Oct. 4, 1778, Elias Boudinot Papers, HSP, 2:50.
157. Minutes of the SEC, Oct. 23, 1778, *Col. Records*, 11:606; *Diary of Elizabeth Drinker*, 1:333.
158. Minutes of the SEC, Nov. 2, 1778, *Col. Records*, 11:613.
159. Deposition of Samuel Wallis in Favor of John Roberts, *Pa. Archives*, 7:41.
160. Carl Van Doren, *The Secret History of the American Revolution* (New York: Viking Press, 1941), 218. See also Maxey, *Treason on Trial*, 81–84; David W. Maxey, "A Cunning Man's Legacy: The Papers of Samuel Wallis (1736–1798)," *PMHB* 136 (2012): 435–456; Nagy, *Spies in the Continental Capital*, 118–121, 137. James Wilson had represented Wallis in earlier civil litigation and later became partners with him in unsuccessful land speculation. Maxey, *Treason on Trial*, 131; Maxey, "The Honorable Proprietaries," 386.
161. Minutes of the SEC, Nov. 3, 1778, *Col. Records*, 7:614.
162. *Diary of Elizabeth Drinker*, 1:333.
163. James Humphreys to Joseph Galloway, Nov. 22, 1778, in Catherine S. Crary, *The Price of Loyalty: Tory Writings from the Revolutionary Era* (New York: McGraw Hill, 1973), 237.
164. Isaac Ogden to Joseph Galloway, Nov. 22, 1778, in Crary, *Price of Loyalty*, 237. David Maxey doubts that Roberts uttered these words. Maxey, *Treason on Trial*, 91.

165. Humphreys to Galloway, Nov. 22, 1778; Diary of John Pemberton, Nov. 4, 1778, Pemberton Papers, HSP. Elizabeth Drinker similarly described the Carlisle burial as "remarkable large." *Diary of Elizabeth Drinker*, 1:334. The four-thousand-person claim originates in a letter from James Humphreys to Joseph Galloway, Nov. 23, 17[7?]8, printed in "Letters to Joseph Galloway," *Historical Magazine* (Sept. 1861): 272.
166. "Diary of Grace Growden Galloway," *PMHB* 55 (1931): 32, 56, 72.
167. Sergeant, *Loyalist Poetry of the Revolution*, 164.
168. Diary of John Pemberton, Sept. 26, 1778; Nov. 4, 1778, Pemberton Papers, HSP.
169. Report of the Committee of the Meeting for Sufferings on the case of John Roberts & Abraham Carlisle, 1779, Philadelphia Yearly Meeting, Meeting for Sufferings, Miscellaneous Papers, Quaker Collection, Haverford College Library, Haverford, PA, printed in Maxey, *Treason on Trial*, 163, 166–167.
170. Joseph Reed to John Armstrong, *LDC*, 11:25–26.
171. Report of the Committee of the Meeting for Sufferings, 166.
172. Charles Stewart to Joseph Galloway, Dec. 1, 1778, in "Letters to Joseph Galloway," *Historical Magazine* (Oct. 1861): 296.
173. Memorandum of the Sufferings & Losses Sustained by George Harding/formerly of Philadelphia/in the late Rebellion, American Loyalist Claims, AO13.57.142, National Archives of the United Kingdom.
174. Petition of Judges in Case of George Hardy, *Pa. Archives*, 7:326. The *Pennsylvania Gazette* claimed, "It is remarkable that much less interest has been made to save him than any other person under sentence of death since the establishment of the present government." *Pa. Gazette*, May 6, 1779. This claim should not be taken too seriously. Although Harding received far less public support than John Roberts or Abraham Carlisle, he still received significantly more than Abijah Wright.
175. Petition of Jurors re: George Hardy, Clemency File, RG-27, PSA.
176. Petition of Judges, 326–327.
177. Memorandum of the Sufferings & Losses Sustained by George Harding/formerly of Philadelphia/in the late Rebellion, American Loyalist Claims, AO13.57.142, National Archives of the United Kingdom.
178. *Pa. Gazette*, May 5, 1779.
179. Fisher, "Journal," 152.
180. Minutes of the SEC, Oct. 18, 1779, *Col. Records*, 12:136; Memorandum of the Sufferings & Losses Sustained by George Harding/formerly of Philadelphia/in the late Rebellion, American Loyalist Claims, AO13.57.142, National Archives of the United Kingdom; Fisher, "Journal," 176.
181. Rowe, *Embattled Bench*, 162.
182. Marietta & Rowe, *Troubled Experiment*, 76–77.
183. Petition re: Abijah Wright, Clemency Papers, RG-27, PSA.
184. *Pa. Packet*, Dec. 8, 1778.

185. Louis P. Masur, *Rites of Execution: Capital Punishment and the Transformation of American Culture, 1776–1865* (New York: Oxford Univ. Press, 1989), 39.
186. Juror William Adcock's shop, for example, was once next door to that of Joseph Stansbury, who was detained in 1776 for expressing loyalist sentiments and was later attainted of treason. *Pa. Gazette*, Jan. 14, 1768. Grand juror William Ball owned land adjacent to that of Samuel Shoemaker, one of the most prominent defectors to the British cause. Return of John Moore, Agent for Philadelphia County, June 24, 1779, Stauffer Collection, HSP, 8:555. As Jonathan Clark has pointed out with respect to revolutionary Poughkeepsie, New York, "A large proportion of Poughkeepsie residents would have known someone, related to them by blood or marriage, who chose an allegiance other than their own." Clark, "The Problem of Allegiance in Revolutionary Poughkeepsie," 285, 296.
187. *Pa. Gazette*, June 17, 1778.
188. Thomas W. Yardley, *Genealogy of the Yardley Family, 1402–1881* (Philadelphia: William S. Schofield, 1881), 25; *Pa. Gazette*, Oct. 6, 1768 (election as Bucks County Commissioner). Yardley appears to have later been reinstated with the Quaker meeting.
189. List of Grand Inquest for Court of Oyer and Terminer to be held at Newtown the 5th day of April 1774, Court of Oyer and Terminer Papers, RG-33, PSA.
190. Joseph Reed to George Bryan, October 23, 1778, Joseph Reed Papers, Reel 2, New-York Historical Society. A witness charged Yardley with aiding the British by serving as a pilot and guarding their provisions. Testimony of Ambrose Smith, Aug. 19, 1778, Oyer and Terminer Miscellaneous Papers, RG-33, PSA.
191. *Pennsylvania Packet*, Nov. 3, 1778. One of the acquitted defendants, Richard Tomlinson, who may have spied for the British, later fled to the British in New York. Ruma Chopra, *Unnatural Rebellion: Loyalists in New York City during the Revolution* (Charlottesville: UVA. Press, 2011), 155. Another, John Tomlinson, who almost certainly spied for the British, was executed a few years later for felony for his role in a robbery planned by the infamous Doan gang. Minutes of the SEC, Oct. 14, 1782, *Col. Records*, 13:394; *The New Doane Book: Bucks County's Bandittories of the Revolution* (Doylestown, PA: Bucks Co. Hist. Soc., 1952), 73, 422.
192. *Pa. Packet*, Oct. 29, 1778.
193. Edward Burd, Transcript of the Record of the Trial of John Elwood, *Pa. Archives*, 7:59, 61.
194. Minutes of the SEC, Nov. 30, 1778, *Col. Records*, 11:631.
195. Minutes of the SEC, July 15, 1779, *Col. Records*, 12:48.
196. *Pa. Packet*, Oct. 15, 1778.
197. Minutes of the SEC, Jan. 2, 1779, *Col. Records*, 11:656.
198. Minutes of the SEC, May 7, 1779, *Col. Records*, 11:770.
199. Act of March 16, 1779, ch. 4, *Pa. Stat.*, 9:320, 322.

200. Philadelphia Monthly Meeting Records, Feb. 26, 1779, MR-PH384, Friends Historical Library, Swarthmore College, Swarthmore, PA.
201. *Pa. Gazette*, March 31, 1779.
202. *Extracts from the Diary of Christopher Marshall*, ed. William Duane (Albany: Joel Munsell, 1877), 215.
203. Joseph Reed to Thomas McKean, April 20, 1779, *Pa. Archives*, 7:328.

CHAPTER 8

1. Mark Abbott Stern, *David Franks: Colonial Merchant* (Univ. Park: Penn. State Univ. Press, 2010), 116–135.
2. *Pa. Packet*, April 29, 1779. The letter is reprinted in Stern, *David Franks*, 180–181.
3. *JCC*, 12:1032.
4. *JCC*, 12:1110. The order came three days after the executions of Carlisle and Roberts; the Congress may have concluded that Pennsylvania was adequately dealing with cases of treasonous behavior.
5. *Pa. Packet*, Dec. 12, 1778.
6. *Pa. Packet*, May 13, 1779.
7. *Pa. Packet*, April 29, 1779. The *Packet* describes the trial as "before the Supreme Court," and it had previously referred to Franks's bail hearing "before the Supreme Court." *Pa. Packet*, Nov. 17, 1778. This could well refer to the Supreme Court justices sitting as a court of oyer and terminer, but the case may also have been brought directly under the jurisdiction of the Supreme Court.
8. "Addenda to Watson's Annals," 152.
9. Jonathan Dickinson Sergeant to George Bryan, May 12, 1779, *Pa. Archives*, 7:395–396.
10. *Pa. Packet*, April 29, 1779.
11. Ibid.
12. John Hill Martin, *Chester (and its Vicinity,) Delaware County, in Pennsylvania; with Genealogical Sketches of Some Old Families* (Philadelphia: Wm. H. Pile & Sons, 1877), 42.
13. *Pa. Packet*, May 1, 1779.
14. *Pa. Packet*, May 4, 1779.
15. *Pa. Packet*, May 6, 1779. Humphreys' authorship is revealed in *Pa. Packet*, May 18, 1779. Humphreys may have had personal reasons for resentment of the attorney general; in April 1779, Humphreys paid a bond for a writ of certiorari on behalf of his uncle Charles Humphreys, who had been indicted for misprision of treason in the Philadelphia Quarter Sessions Court. Recognizance sur Certiorari, Respublica v. Charles Humphreys, April 21, 1779, High Court of Error and Appeal Papers, RG-33, PSA. Timothy Matlack claimed that Humphreys had vowed to "cut off Mr. Sergeant's ears and drive him out of the state." Timothy Matlack, "To the Free Independent Whigs of Pennsylvania," *Pa. Packet*, May 18, 1779.

16. *Pa. Packet*, May 6, 1779.
17. *Pa. Packet*, May 13, 1779.
18. *Pa. Packet*, May 13, 1779.
19. Timothy Matlack, "To the Free Independent Whigs of Pennsylvania," *Pa. Packet*, May 18, 1779. Matlack did not identify the other author, describing him only as a "gentleman as well acquainted with the laws and customs in such cases, and as much a friend to liberty and the rights of Jurors, as any man in Pennsylvania." Joseph Reed is a likely candidate.
20. Ibid.
21. *Pa. Packet*, May 13, 1779.
22. *Pa. Packet*, May 18, 1779. Several months later, the combative Humphreys, under the pseudonym "Cato," published a blistering attack on Thomas Paine in the *Pennsylvania Evening Post*, insinuating that Paine amounted to a British agent. *Pa. Evening Post*, July 9, 1779. A large group of men subsequently seized the newspaper's printer and demanded the anonymous author's name. Dwight L. Teeter, Jr., "From Revision to Orthodoxy," *Reviews in Am. Hist.* 13 (1985): 518, 521. They then marched on Humphreys's home, attacked his sister, and repeatedly threatened him with violence. Humphreys responded by threatening to shoot anyone who crossed the threshold of his door, and eventually the men dispersed. Whitehead Humphreys, "To the citizens of America," *Pa. Evening Post*, Aug. 2, 1779. Several years later, Humphreys and Timothy Matlack engaged in a public fistfight. Foner, *Tom Paine*, 110.
23. *Pa. Packet*, May 20, 1779.
24. Foner, *Tom Paine*, 161.
25. John K. Alexander, "The Fort Wilson Incident of 1779: A Case Study of the Revolutionary Crowd," *William & Mary Q.* 31 (1974): 589, 593–597. On the turmoil of 1779 generally, see Ousterhout, *State Divided*, 194–207; Olton, *Artisans for Independence*, 82–89.
26. Foner, *Tom Paine*, 166. On this meeting, see Rosswurm, *Arms, Country, and Class*, 179–184.
27. *Pa. Gazette*, June 2, 1779. Grace Growden Galloway, wife of noted Loyalist Joseph Galloway, noted in her diary that "a Mob is raised in the Town & they are taking Up Tories we were much alarmed." "Diary of Grace Growden Galloway," *PMHB* 55 (1931): 32, 82.
28. Minutes of the SEC, May 28, 1779, *Col. Records*, 12:8–9.
29. "The Address of the Committee of the City and Liberties of Philadelphia," *Pa. Gazette*, July 7, 1779.
30. James Read to George Read, Aug. 7, 1779, in William Thompson Read, *Life and Correspondence of George Read* (Philadelphia: J.B. Lippincott, 1870), 350–351.
31. "An Historical Ballad of the Proceedings at Philadelphia May 24th–25th 1779 by a Loyalist," Gratz Collection—Winthrop Sergeant Items, HSP.
32. *Pa. Gazette*, Feb. 14, 1776; Council to Thomas McKean, March 5, 1779, *Pa. Archives*, 7:225; Thomas McKean to Joseph Reed, March 31, 1779, *Pa. Archives*,

7:279; "Journal of Samuel Rowland Fisher," 145–152; Timothy Matlack to James Claypoole, April 4, 1779, *Pa. Archives*, 7:291.

33. Fisher, "Journal," 153–158.
34. Ibid., 159–164.
35. Ibid., 164–165.
36. William Hawkins, *A Treatise on Pleas of the Crown*, 2d ed. (E. & R. Nutt: London, 1726), 2:442. On this practice at the Old Bailey, see John H. Langbein, "The Criminal Trial before the Lawyers," *U. Chicago. L. Rev.* 45 (1978): 263, 291–296, and in Connecticut, see Cornelia Hughes Dayton, *Women before the Bar: Gender, Law & Society in Connecticut, 1639–1789* (Chapel Hill: UNC Press, 1995), 51.
37. John Hawles, *The Englishman's Right: A Dialogue between a Barrister at Law, and a Juryman* (1680; reprint London: Tho. Wotton, 1732), 13.
38. Fisher, "Journal," 164–165.
39. Ibid., 165–166.
40. Fisher, "Journal," 438, describes the death of "___ Burns, the barber, who threatened those so called Magistrates." Philadelphia tax records confirm that this can only be the barber Archibald Byrnes. E.g., Provincial Tax, City of Philadelphia—1774, *Pa. Archives* (3d Ser.), 14:223, 235.
41. Fisher, "Journal," 196. Fisher made the same claim in a letter to Joseph Reed. Samuel Rowland Fisher to Joseph Reed, Feb. 6, 1780, Joseph Wharton Family Papers, RG5/162, Series 1-B, Box 10, Friends Historical Library, Swarthmore College, Swarthmore, PA.
42. The extant docket starts in October 1779. The jury in a misprision case from April 1780 included none of the jurors who served at the court of oyer and terminer. Commonwealth v. Stevens, Mayor's Court Docket Book, 1779–1783, Philadelphia City Archives, 20. In 1781, a carpenter named James Guy visited Fisher in prison and claimed that he "was the sole means of [Fisher's] being brought in guilty." Fisher suspected that Guy was mentally unbalanced. Fisher, "Journal," 429–430.
43. *Diary of Elizabeth Drinker*, 1:356.
44. Benjamin Mason to Joseph West, April 4, 1781, Joseph Wharton Family Papers, RG5/162, Series 1-B, Box 10, Friends Historical Library, Swarthmore College, Swarthmore, PA.
45. McKean described the outcome of Fisher's case in a letter to his wife without mentioning the irregular proceedings. Thomas McKean to Sally McKean, July 26, 1779, Thomas McKean Papers, HSP, 6:26. Fisher later learned that McKean had supposedly said that he had not proceeded against Fisher "on his own accord, as he was not so clear therein, but that some others thought different," a statement that angered Joseph Reed. Fisher, "Journal," 186. In July 1781, Fisher, now in poor health after two years of imprisonment, was pardoned. Minutes of the SEC, July 23, 1781, *Col. Records*, 13:13; Fisher, "Journal," 443–448.
46. Fisher, "Journal," 166–167. Isaac Howell, one of the presiding justices of the peace, later visited Fisher in jail, with an offer to parole to him his father's house if Fisher

would post security. Fisher refused and told Howell that "you should never make use of the word ['justice'], you have not even the shadow of it" and claimed that his trial was a "persecution in a great degree." Ibid., 188–189.

47. *Pa. Gazette*, Aug. 4, 1779.
48. *Pa. Packet*, Aug. 5, 1779.
49. Fisher, "Journal," 167–168.
50. Alexander, "Fort Wilson Incident," 601–604; *Diary of Elizabeth Drinker*, 1:361.
51. Journal of Captain M'Lane, in Reed, *Joseph Reed*, 2:150, 152.
52. Fisher, "Journal," 171.
53. Benjamin Rush to John Adams, Oct.12, 1779, *Letters of Benjamin Rush*, 1:240–241; Alexander, "Fort Wilson Incident," 605–606; "Philip Hagner's Narrative," in Reed, *Joseph Reed*, 426–428. One account, recorded nearly fifty years later, claims that "the door was not forced, but opened by the besieged." "Addenda to Watson's Annals," 151.
54. Fisher, "Journal," 171.
55. Pay Roll of the Troop of Philadelphia Light Horse, *Pa. Archives* (6th Ser.), 1:981.
56. Alexander, "Fort Wilson Incident," 589.
57. Minutes of the SEC, Oct. 6, 1779, *Col. Records*, 12:121, 122.
58. Minutes of the SEC, Oct. 19, 1779, *Col. Records*, 12:137.
59. *Diary of Elizabeth Drinker*, 1:362.
60. Act of March 13, 1780, ch. 894, *Pa. Stat.*, 10:117–119.
61. Minutes of the SEC, Nov. 13, 1779, *Col. Records*, 12:167, 168.
62. Statement of Charles Wilson Peale, in *Life and Correspondence of Joseph Reed*, ed. William B. Reed (Philadelphia: Lindsay & Blakiston, 1847), 2:424.
63. Fisher, "Journal," 170.
64. Quoted in Rosswurm, *Arms, Country, and Class*, 222.
65. Minutes of the SEC, Oct. 6, 1779, *Col. Records*, 12:121, 122.
66. The Memorial and Representation of a Deputation from the Several Battalions of Militia of the City and Liberties of Philadelphia, Oct. 8, 1779, Stauffer Collection, HSP, 9:633. This document is transcribed in Steve Rosswurm, "Equality and Justice: Philadelphia's Popular Revolution 1775–1780," in *Life in Early Philadelphia: Documents from the Revolutionary and Early National Periods*, ed. Billy G. Smith (University Park: Penn. State Univ. Press, 1995). Alexander Graydon later recalled the incident as a "well-known outrage on Mr. Wilson, who, for the exercise of his professional duty as a lawyer, in behalf of certain persons who had been proscribed for treason, had been proscribed by the mobility." Graydon, *Memoirs of His Own Time*, 333.
67. William Augustus Atlee to Esther Atlee, Sept. 27, 1779, Peter Force Collection, Manuscripts Division, Library of Congress; *Pa. Gazette*, Oct. 6, 1779. Justice Atlee found the treason cases "disagreeable" and was more than happy to postpone Peter Miller's trial "to a future day." Shortly after Fort Wilson, the Council ordered Miller confined until his trial. Minutes of the SEC, Oct. 16, 1779, *Col. Records*, 12:133.

68. John F. Watson, *Annals of Philadelphia* (Philadelphia: E.L Carey & A. Hart, 1830), 551; Notes of Recognizances, Aug. 8, 1778, Oyer and Terminer Miscellaneous Papers, RG-33, PSA. Cutbush's son Edward, a surgeon, later became known as the father of American naval medicine. Jack E. McCallum, *Military Medicine from Ancient Times to the 21st Century* (Santa Barbara, CA: ABC Clio, 2008), 96–97.
69. Ryerson, *Revolution*, 113, 157.
70. *Pa. Gazette*, Jan. 11, 1775; *Pa. Gazette*, May 3, 1775.
71. Robert Strettel Jones, "A Narrative of the Difference between Doctor Alison Vice Provost of the College of Philadelphia & Robert Strettel Jones late Student in the Senior Class of the Said College," 1762, Robert Strettel Jones Papers, APS; Bell, *Patriot-Improvers*, 3:381.
72. Trial Notes, Respublica v. Robert Jones, Sept. 28, 1779, Robert Strettel Jones Papers, APS. The item is labeled "Depositions in re indictment for high treason" in the American Philosophical Society archives, but the document consists of trial notes, not depositions.
73. *Scots Magazine*, Jan. 1780, 24–25.
74. Arthur St. Clair to Joseph Reed, Oct. 1779, in Reed, *Joseph Reed*, 2:153.
75. Foner, *Tom Paine*, 176; Alexander, "Fort Wilson Incident," 601.
76. *Pa. Gazette*, June 30, 1779; *Pa. Packet*, Oct. 16, 1779. On the fisheries issue, see Gouvernor Morris to Benajamin Towne, July 9?, 1779, and annotations, *LDC*, 13:176–182.
77. Foner, *Tom Paine*, 178.
78. Rosswurm, *Arms, Country, and Class*, 223.
79. Act of Oct. 10, 1779, ch. 865, *Pa. Stat.*, 9:440–441. The act was extended for an additional six months in March 1780. Act of March 24, 1780, ch. 906, *Pa. Stat.*, 10:182–183.
80. Act of March 8, 1780, ch. 889, *Pa. Stat.*, 10:110–112.
81. Anne Ousterhout identified eighty-two cases of treasonable misdemeanor in Pennsylvania. Her data are not divided by year, and it is not clear that these cases all involved offenses directly cognizable as treason or misprision of treason. Ousterhout, *State Divided*, 320. Christopher Marshall described the indictment of three people in Lancaster County in 1781 for "aiding, abetting and encouraging the enemies of this state" as a charge of "high misdemeanor," a telling fusion of high treason and misdemeanor. *Diary of Christopher Marshall*, 275.
82. E.g., Indictment of William Mackey and Jacob Miller, Philadelphia Co. Ct. of Oyer and Terminer (Sept. 1781) (providing provisions to the British army) (true bill); Draft Indictment of Peter Kerr, Chester Co. Ct. of Oyer and Terminer (Nov. 1781) (joining the king's armies); Indictment of John Lewis, Bucks Co. Ct. of Oyer and Terminer (Dec. 1781) (joining the king's armies) (ignoramus); Indictment of David Reader, Bucks Co. Ct. of Oyer and Terminer (Dec. 1781) (joining the king's armies) (true bill); Indictment of Samuel Scott, Bucks Co. Ct. of Oyer and Terminer (Dec. 1781) (joining the kings' armies) (true bill), all in the Autograph

Collection, RG-33, PSA; Indictment of Abraham Beam, Lancaster Co. Ct. of Oyer and Terminer (May 1781), Oyer and Terminer Miscellaneous Papers, Records of the Supreme Court, RG-33, PSA (providing provisions to the British army) (true bill).

Cases of misprision being charged as misdemeanor include Indictment of John Thompson, Lancaster Co. Ct. of Oyer and Terminer (May 1781), Autograph Collection, RG-33, PSA (speaking against the public defense and urging people to join the British army) (true bill); Indictment of Abraham Beam, Lancaster Co. Ct. of Oyer and Terminer (May 1781), Oyer and Terminer Papers, Records of the Supreme Court, RG-33, PSA (urging people to join the British army) (true bill); Indictment of Jacob Berkman, Lancaster Co. Ct. Oyer and Terminer (May 1781), Oyer and Terminer Papers, Records of the Supreme Court, RG-33, PSA (urging a return to dependence on Great Britain and speaking against the public defence); and Indictment of Daniel Kraus, York Co. Ct. of Oyer and Terminer (May 1781), Oyer and Terminer Miscellaneous Papers, 1778–1781, Records of the Supreme Court, RG-33, PSA (urging someone to join the British army). In a petition, Daniel Kraus described himself as "indicted for treason." Daniel Kraus to Chief Justice McKean, May 1781, Oyer and Terminer Miscellaneous Papers, 1778–1781, Records of the Supreme Court, RG-33, PSA. Jasper Yeates's notes of the case describe the offenses as persuading someone to join the enemy, conveying intelligence to the enemy, and opposing measures for the common defense. Notes of Evidence, Respublica v. Crauss, York Co. Ct. Oyer & Terminer, May 25, 1781, Miscellaneous Legal Papers, Jasper Yeates Papers, HSP.

The state may have previously attempted to prosecute more serious offenses under the heading of misprision. In an undated Northampton County case, Attorney General Sergeant prepared a misprision indictment that charged the defendant with attempting to enlist men in the British army, with sending intelligence to the enemy, with publicly speaking against the public defense of the commonwealth, and with stirring up tumults and disorders. Although the last two offenses fit squarely under the misprision statute, sending intelligence to the enemy was high treason under Pennsylvania law. Indictment of Adam Rosnick, Miscellaneous Box, Northampton County Papers, HSP.

Other misdemeanor cases involved conduct not directly cognizable under either the treason or misprision statutes, such as the four men indicted in Philadelphia in October 1781 for "misdemeanor in taking an oath to the king of Great Britain." Docket Book of the Court of Oyer and Terminer (Philadelphia, Oct. 1781), RG-33, PSA.

83. E.g., Indictments of David Reader and Samuel Scott, Bucks Co. Ct. Oyer & Terminer (Sept. 1781) (true bills), Miscellaneous Papers, Records of the Supreme Court, RG-33, PSA.

84. Similar problems occurred during the Civil War. The Union abandoned the mandatory death penalty for treason, permitting sentences of at least five years in prison and at least $10,000 in fines. Leonard L. Richards, *Who Freed the Slaves? The Fight over the Thirteenth Amendment* (Chicago: Univ. of Chicago Press, 2015), 69–70.

85. Minutes of the SEC, May 27, 1778, *Col. Records*, 11:501.
86. Minutes of the SEC, Jan. 6, 1780, *Col. Records*, 12:222.
87. Act of March 8, 1780, ch. 889, *Pa. Stat.*, 10:110–112.
88. Minutes of the SEC, April 7, 1780, *Col. Records*, 12:309. Cassedy's clemency petition stressed that he was young and of good character, and had been misled by the British. Petition of William Cassedy, Clemency File, RG-27, PSA. It took over half a year for Cassedy to finally leave jail and board the *Confederacy* frigate. Fisher, "Journal," 319.
89. Docket Book of the Cumberland County Court of Quarter Sessions, Cumberland County Courthouse, Carlisle, PA (July 1779); Notes of testimony in Respublica v. Thomas Kerr, Pennsylvania Manuscripts, Peter Force Collection, Manuscripts Division, Library of Congress.
90. Respublica v. Thomas Kerr, Notes on Motion for a New Trial, April 20, 1780, Miscellaneous Legal Papers, Jasper Yeates Papers, HSP; Docket Book of the Cumberland County Court of Quarter Sessions, Cumberland County Courthouse, Carlisle, PA. The Kerr case appears to be the only misprision case for which detailed notes of both evidence and legal arguments have survived. A petition for a pardon from Kerr's wife was rejected by the Council, because it lacked an attested copy of the trial record and a recommendation from the presiding magistrates. Minutes of the SEC, July 7, 1780, *Col. Records*, 12:412. Robert Whitehill reported to the Council that it was "the general opinion of the Whigs of Carlisle" that Kerr should be pardoned. Robert Whitehill to Joseph Reed and Council, July 3, 1780, Pennsylvania Committee and Council of Safety Items, Simon Gratz Collection, HSP.
91. Respublica v. Weidle, 2 U.S. (2 Dallas) 88, 88–90 (Pa. Oyer & Terminer, 1781).
92. Ibid., 90–91.
93. Minutes of the SEC, Oct. 2, 1782, *Col. Records*, 13:383.
94. Minutes of the SEC, Feb. 4, 1780, *Col. Records*, 12:243.
95. Minutes of the SEC, March 6, 1780, *Col. Records*, 12:270.
96. Minutes of the SEC, April 6, 1780, *Col. Records*, 12:307–308. The Cooglers were later released on a £30,000 bond. Minutes of the SEC, June 12, 1780, *Col. Records*, 12:384–385. The prime witness against John Coogler appears to have recanted her testimony, stating that she had acted "merely from spite and malice." Fisher, "Journal," 290.
97. Minutes of the SEC, May 10, 1780, *Col. Records*, 12:342.
98. Minutes of the SEC, June 27, 1780, *Col. Records*, 12:401.
99. Minutes of the SEC, June 7 & 8, 1780, *Col. Records*, 12:378–379.
100. Fisher, "Journal," 282.
101. Diary of John Pemberton, June 9, 1780, Pemberton Papers, HSP.
102. Minutes of the SEC, June 6, 1780, *Col Records*, 12:377.
103. Fisher, "Journal," 293.
104. Minutes of the SEC, July 16, 1780, *Col. Records*, 12:425.

105. *Pa. Gazette*, Nov. 29, 1780; Arrest Warrant for Joseph Griswold, Nov. 27, 1780, Records of the Court of Oyer and Terminer, Eastern District, RG-33, PSA.
106. Fisher, "Journal," 326.
107. Thomas McKean to Joseph Reed, Dec. 12, 1780, *Pa. Archives*, 8:650–652.
108. Minutes of the SEC, Dec. 11, 1780, *Col. Records*, 12: 564–565.
109. Thomas McKean to Joseph Reed, Dec. 12, 1780, *Pa. Archives*, 8:649–650.
110. Thomas McKean to Joseph Reed, Dec. 12, 1780, *Pa. Archives*, 8:650–652.
111. Minutes of the SEC, Dec. 11, 1780; Dec. 13, 1780, *Col. Records*, 12:566–567. Samuel Rowland Fisher noted that "it seems as if the Council were displeased with T. McKean letting him out & are determined that no person shall undo what they undertake." Fisher, "Journal," 330.
112. Joseph Reed to Thomas McKean, Dec. 15, 1780, *Pa. Archives*, 8:657–658.
113. Fisher, "Journal," 332.
114. Minutes of the SEC, March 19, 1781, *Col. Records*, 12:663.
115. See Chapter 4.
116. Blackstone, *Commentaries*, 4:315.
117. Edward Burd to Jonathan Dickinson Sergeant, July 21, 1779, Recognizance File, RG-33, PSA.
118. Joseph S. Foster, "Charles Humphreys," in *Lawmaking and Legislators in Pennsylvania*, 3:717–724.
119. *Pa. Gazette*, Dec. 22, 1779; Supreme Court Appearance and Continuance Dockets, RG-33, PSA.
120. Respublica v. Weidle, 2 U.S. (2 Dallas) 88 (Pa. Oyer & Terminer, 1781).
121. Respublica v. Gilmore, Respublica v. Wood; Respublica v. Stephens, Docket Book of the Court of Quarter Sessions for Westmoreland County, Westmoreland County Courthouse, Greensburg, PA (Oct. 1781).
122. Record of Commonwealth v. Gottschalk, Clemency File, RG-33, PSA.
123. Petition of Peter Gottschalk, Clemency File, RG-33, PSA.
124. Minutes of the SEC, Oct. 2, 1782, *Col. Records*, 13:383.
125. Supreme Court Appearance and Continuance Docket, RG-33, PSA; Fisher, "Journal," 180, 415.
126. Fisher, "Journal," 180–181.
127. *Pa. Gazette*, Dec. 22, 1779; Minutes of the SEC, Oct. 24, 1781, *Col. Records*, 13:94.
128. Docket Book of the Court of Oyer and Terminer (March 1780), RG-33, PSA, 51.
129. *Pa. Gazette*, March 22, 1775; *Pa. Gazette*, Jan. 10, 1776.
130. Fisher, "Journal," 324.
131. *Pa. Eve. Post*, March 30, 1778.
132. Record of Commonwealth v. Haughton, Clemency File, RG-27, PSA; Docket Book of the Court of Oyer and Terminer (March 1780), RG-33, PSA, 55.
133. Minutes of the SEC, Aug. 9, 1780, *Col. Records*, 12:447. According to Samuel Rowland Fisher, the "very worst men" from the prison were placed on the *Confederacy*. He described Haughton as "intemperate in drinking," lacking "a

principle of integrity," and "tossed about with every wind." According to Fisher, Haughton planned to escape from the ship and proceed to New York. Fisher, "Journal," 320, 324. Haughton died in Philadelphia in 1783. *Independent Gazetteer*, Sept. 27, 1783.

134. Another Philadelphia case, that of Thomas Livezey, removed by certiorari from the Philadelphia County Court of Quarter Sessions, ended when the defendant skipped bail. Docket Book of the Philadelphia County Court of Quarter Sessions, 1780–1785 (March 1781), Court Records, HSP; Supreme Court Appearance and Continuance Docket (Sept. 1780), RG-33, PSA. Livezey had served from 1765 to 1771 as a member of the Pennsylvania Assembly. Jeffrey L. Scheib, "Thomas Livezey," in *Lawmaking and Legislators in Pennsylvania*, 3:838–843.
135. Docket Book of the Court of Oyer and Terminer (Lancaster Co., June 1782), RG-33, PSA, 134; Recognizance of Jacob Haufmann in Respublica v. Graybill, March, 16, 1781, Oyer and Terminer Papers, RG-33, PSA; *Pa. Evening Post*, June 21, 1782.
136. Mayor's Court Docket Book, 1779–1783, Philadelphia City Archives, Philadelphia, PA, 2, 19, 46, 76, 104, 130, 145, 182, 199; *Pa. Eve. Post*, June 21, 1782.
137. Philbrick, *Valiant Ambition*, 228, 231.
138. *Diary of Christopher Marshall*, 211.
139. *Pa. Gazette*, Oct. 4, 1780.
140. *Pa. Gazette*, Oct. 4, 1780; "A Representation of the Figures exhibited and paraded through the streets of Philadelphia, on Saturday, the 30th of September, 1780," Broadside, Stauffer Collection, HSP; Diary of John Pemberton, Pemberton Papers, HSP, 174.
141. Fisher, "Journal," 314.
142. Diary of Grace Growden Galloway, September 28, 30, 1780, Grace Growden Galloway Papers, HSP. Galloway deeply resented the Shippen family and was "glad that it happened" to Peggy Shippen, "the one most deserving." Ibid.
143. Charles Royster, "'The Nature of Treason': Revolutionary Virtue and American Reactions to Benedict Arnold," *William & Mary Q.* 36 (1979): 163, 186–187. See also Robert A. Ferguson, *Reading the Early Republic* (Cambridge, MA: Harvard Univ. Press, 2004), 138, 146–147; Robert A. Ferguson, "Becoming American: High Treason and Low Invective in the Republic of Laws," in *The Rhetoric of Law*, ed. Austin Sarat & Thomas R. Kearns (Ann Arbor: U. of Mich. Press, 1994), 103–133.
144. "A Representation of the Figures exhibited and paraded through the streets of Philadelphia, on Saturday, the 30th of September, 1780," Broadside, Stauffer Collection, HSP.
145. Benjamin Rush to John Adams, Oct. 23, 1780, *Letters of Benjamin Rush*, 1:255–256.
146. Tench Coxe to William Tilghman, Sept. 28, 1780, Tench Coxe Collection, HSP.
147. *Pa. Gazette*, Oct. 4, 1780. Jared Ingersoll noted that "Wilkinson is ready to burst with indignation—is drawing up Associations against any Intercourse with Tory & Suspicious Characters. He will find enough to Subscribe, but I am afraid few,

or at least not all, will observe the Engagements they enter into." Jared Ingersoll to Joseph Reed, Oct. 4, 1780, *LDC*, 16:147–148.

148. Minutes of the SEC, Oct. 2–3, 1780, *Col. Records*, 12:495–496.
149. Minutes of the SEC, Oct. 6, *Col. Records*, 12:499.
150. Minutes of the SEC, Oct. 27, *Col. Records*, 12:520.
151. *Pa. Gazette*, Oct. 18, 1780.
152. George Lux to Owen Biddle, Oct. 17, 1780, Biddle Family Papers, RG5/177, Series One, Folder 20, Friends Historical Library, Swarthmore College, Swarthmore, PA.
153. *Pa. Gazette*, Oct. 18, 1780.
154. John Cadwalader to William Hamilton, Oct. 16, 1780, Cadwalader Collection, HSP.
155. Isaac Gray to Joseph Reed and the SEC, Oct. 23, 1780, Joseph Reed Papers, Reel 2, New-York Historical Society.
156. Remonstrance of divers of the Freemen of this Commonwealth, n.d., Clemency File, RG-27, PSA.
157. Tench Coxe to William Tilghman, Oct. 16, 1780, Tench Coxe Correspondence, Coxe Family Collection, HSP.
158. Stern, *David Franks*, 154–157.
159. Minutes of the SEC, Oct 11, 1780, Nov. 21, 1780, *Col. Records*, 12:503, 549.
160. William Tilghman to Tench Coxe, Jan. 2, 1781, Tench Coxe Correspondence, Coxe Family Collection, HSP; Minutes of the SEC, April 2, 1781, *Col. Records*, 12:681.
161. Minutes of the SEC, May 8, 1778, *Col. Records*, 11:484.
162. *Pa. Gazette*, Nov. 29, 1780; Fisher, "Journal," 298; William Clinger to Constable of Chester County, May 16, 1780, Records of the Court of Oyer and Terminer, RG-33, PSA.
163. Docket Book of the Court of Oyer and Terminer (Sept. 1780), RG-33, PSA, 74.
164. Fisher, "Journal," 287; Minutes of the Court of Oyer and Terminer (Chester, April 24, 1780), Records of the Court of Oyer Terminer, RG-33, PSA.
165. Minutes of the SEC, July 10, 1780, *Col. Records*, 12:419; Petition on behalf of Edward Grissell and John Wilson, n.d., Clemency File, RG-27, PSA.
166. Fisher, "Journal," 327.
167. Petition of David Dawson, Oct. 13, 1780, Clemency File, RG-27, PSA.
168. Petition of Margret Dawson, Sept. 1780, Clemency File, RG-27, PSA.
169. Petition of the Sisters & Relations of David Dawson, n.d., Clemency File, RG-27, PSA.
170. Minutes of the SEC, Nov. 10, 1780, *Col. Records*, 12:536.
171. Diary of Grace Growden Galloway, Nov. 25, 1780, Grace Growden Galloway Papers, HSP; Fisher, "Journal," 326–327.
172. Fisher, "Journal," 327. Dawson's case can be contrasted with that of Isaac Green, five months later. On April 8, 1781, the justices of the Supreme Court sentenced Green to death for failure to appear by the required date. Transcript of Record

re: Isaac Green, Clemency File, RG-27, PSA. In his petition to the Council, Green noted that, although he had joined the British army during the occupation of Philadelphia, he abandoned the British and returned to the American side in July 1778 and took the oath of allegiance. Petition of Isaac Green, May 21, 1781, Clemency File, RG-27, PSA. Chief Justice McKean recommended mercy for Green, noting "it appears to be politic to encourage such desertions in the privates by extending mercy to them." Thomas McKean to Joseph Reed, [May 1781], *Pa. Archives*, 9:125–126. On July 6, 1781, Green received a pardon, conditional upon his service on the Continental Frigate *Trumbull.* Minutes of the SEC, July 6, 1781, *Col. Records*, 12:778. Green sought to have the condition removed, arguing that if the ship was captured by the British, he would be hanged as a deserter to their cause. Petition of Isaac Green, July 7, 1781, Clemency File, RG-27, PSA. The Council rejected this request. Minutes of the SEC, July 15, 1781, *Col Records*, 13:4.

173. Edward Hand to George Washington, March 20, 1779, *The Papers of George Washington, Revolutionary War Series*, ed. Philander D. Chase & William Ferraro (Charlottesville: UVA Press, 2009), 19:537–540.
174. George Washington to Oliver Spencer, April 9, 1779, *The Papers of George Washington, Revolutionary War Series*, ed. Edward G. Lengel (Charlottesville: UVA Press, 2010), 20:24.
175. Ibid.
176. John M. Coleman, "The Treason of Ralph Morden and Robert Land," *PMHB* 79 (Oct. 1955): 439–451, 445. The judge allegedly had not found Land's name on the attainder proclamation. Samuel Rea to Joseph Reed, May 20, 1780, in T. Roy Woodhouse, *The History of the Town of Dundas* (Dundas, Canada: Dundas Hist. Soc., 1965), 9.
177. Coleman, "Treason of Ralph Morden," 447–448. Land founded Hamilton, Ontario, where he remains a revered figure, commemorated most prominently by the Robert Land Academy, a military institute for boys. Land's great-great-great grandson was the noted American aviator, Charles Lindbergh.
178. John Coleman asserted that Morden's wife and children were Quakers, and that he may have converted himself. Coleman, "Treason of Ralph Morden," 441. More recent genealogical research, however, casts significant doubt on this conclusion. See, e.g., Charles Field, "Ralph Morden-Quaker???," http://www.genealogy.com, July 7, 2007. Morden is a direct ancestor of the famous American actress Sally Field. Henry Louis Gates, Jr., *Finding Your Roots, Season 2: The Official Companion to the PBS Series* (Chapel Hill: UNC Press, 2016), 329–330.
179. Docket of the Court of Oyer and Terminer (Northampton Co., Oct. 1780), RG-33, PSA, 80.
180. Coleman's stated trial date of October 30 confuses the trial date with the opening of the court. Coleman, "Treason of Ralph Morden," 449. Justice John Evans was not present, so three justices, McKean, Atlee, and Bryan, presided. Docket of the Court of Oyer and Terminer (Northampton Co., Oct. 1780), RG-33, PSA, 78.

181. Docket of the Court of Oyer and Terminer (Northampton Co., Oct. 1780), RG-33, PSA, 80; William J. Heller, *History of Northampton County and the Grand Valley of the Lehigh* (New York: Am. Hist. Soc., 1920), 1:134.
182. Edward Burd to Jasper Yeates, Sept. 30, 1778, Yeates Family Collection, HSP.
183. Edward Burd to Jasper Yeates, Oct. 5, 1780, Jasper Yeates Papers, HSP.
184. *A Journal by Thos. Hughes*, ed. E.A. Benians (Cambridge: Cambridge Univ. Press, 1947), 101, quoted in Coleman, "Treason of Ralph Morden," 439.
185. Thomas McKean to Sally McKean, Nov. 2, 1780, Thomas McKean Papers, HSP.
186. George Bryan to Joseph Reed, Nov. 7, 1780, Joseph Reed Papers, Reel 2, New-York Historical Society.
187. Francis Bowes Sayre, "Criminal Attempts," *Harv. L. Rev.* 41 (1928), 821–859, 821.
188. According to the deposition of a magistrate, Isaiah McCarty, one of the men who escaped, "had furnished a certain Robert Land who with others intended to join the savages with a gun and otherwise aided them." Deposition of Robert Hoops, May 14, 1780, Miscellaneous Manuscripts, Northampton County Papers, HSP.
189. Minutes of the SEC, April 3, 1780, *Col. Records*, 12:303.
190. Foster, "Pursuit of Equal Liberty," 12, 61.
191. George Bryan to Thomas Evans, Aug. 18, 1778, *Pa. Archives*, 6:709.
192. "Anecdotes of George Bryan," *Independent Gazetteer*, Sept. 4, 1784.
193. Rowe, "Judical Tyrant and Vox Populi," 41. The animosity was mutual.
194. George Bryan to Joseph Reed, Nov. 7, 1780, Joseph Reed Papers, Reel 2, New-York Historical Society.
195. King v. Cowper, Skinner 637, 90 Eng. Rep. 286 (K.B. 1696).
196. Foster, *Report*, 196–197. A similar point had been made by Hale: "If the king of England and the king of France be in amity, yet if a subject of the king of England solicits by letters the king of France to invade this realm this is high treason: it was the case of cardinal Poole, who wrote a book to that purpose to Charles the emperor. It is certainly an overt-act to prove treason in compassing the king's death, but it seems not an overt-act to convict him of adhering to the king's enemies, for at the time of this act done the emperor was not an enemy." Hale, *Historia Placitorum Coronae*, 1:167.
197. Thomas McKean to Joseph Reed, Nov. 3, 1780, *Pa. Archives*, 8:597–598.
198. Minutes of the SEC, Nov. 9, 1780, *Col. Records*, 12:535.
199. Minutes of the SEC, Nov. 21, 1780, *Col. Records*, 12:549. John Coleman's assertion that no petition was filed may be explained by the spelling of Morden's name as "Merden" in the published version of the Council's minutes. Coleman, "Treason of Ralph Morden," 439.
200. Indictment of John Hock, et al., Berks Co. Ct. of Oyer & Terminer, Nov. Sessions, 1780, Records of the Court of Oyer and Terminer, RG-33, PSA.
201. Joseph Reed to George Bryan, Nov. 4, 1780, Joseph Reed Papers, Reel 2, New-York Historical Society.

202. George Bryan to Joseph Reed, Nov. 7, 1780, Joseph Reed Papers, Reel 2, New-York Historical Society.
203. Recognizance of Jacob Read, Oct. 20, 1780 ("Misprision of Treason, for signing a Written Paper, tending to raise Insurrection in the State"); Recognizance of Thomas Kurr, Oct. 20, 1780 ("Misprision of Treason, for aiding and abetting in writing and signing a certain paper tending to raise insurrection in the State"); Recognizance of Andreas Winder, Oct. 20, 1780 ("Charge of having entered into a treasonable association to oppose the laws"); Recognizance of Gottfried Rehrer, Oct. 23, 1780 ("Misprision of Treason, to be an Instigator in a certain Association, who signed a Written Paper tending to raise Insurrection in the State"), all in Berks County Court of Oyer and Terminer, Records of the Court of Oyer and Terminer, RG-33, PSA.
204. Bryan to Reed, Nov. 7, 1780.
205. Ibid.
206. Ibid.
207. Joseph Reed to William Henry, Nov. 10, 1780, Joseph Reed Papers, Reel 2, New-York Historical Society.
208. Minutes of the SEC, Dec. 13, 1780, *Col. Records*, 12:568.
209. Minutes of the SEC, Nov. 20, 1780, Nov. 23, 1780, *Col. Records*, 12:548, 550.
210. William Bradford to Joshua Wallace, April 25, 1781, Wallace Papers, HSP.
211. Docket Book of the Court of Oyer and Terminer (Chester Co., April 1780), RG-33, PSA, 59.
212. Persons in the Gaol of the City and County of Philadelphia to be tried at the Court of Oyer and Terminer and General Gaol Delivery the 9th of April 1781, Oyer and Terminer Papers, RG-33, PSA.
213. Respublica v. McCarty, 2 Dallas 86, 86 (Philadelphia Co. Ct. Oyer & Terminer, 1781).
214. Ibid., 86–88; Oyer & Terminer Docket, 95.
215. Joseph Reed to Jeremiah Powell, May 19, 1780, *Pa. Archives*, 8:254; *Pa. Gazette*, March 8, 1780.
216. Fisher, "Journal," 325.
217. Ibid., 419–420, 424.
218. Respublica v. Chapman, 1 Dallas 53 (Pa. 1781); Fisher, "Journal," 424.
219. *Chapman*, 1 Dallas, 53–54.
220. Ibid., 54–55.
221. Wilson, "Lectures on Law," 2:666.
222. George Washington to William Livingston, Dec. 11, 1777, in *The Papers of George Washington, Revolutionary War Series*, ed. Frank E. Grizzard & David R. Hoth (Charlottesville: UVA Press, 2002), 12:596.
223. Elizabeth Ferguson to SEC, July 10, 1778, *Pa. Archives*, 6:617–619. On Ferguson's efforts on behalf of her husband, see Ousterhout, *Most Learned Woman*, 219–258.
224. Minutes of the SEC, Aug. 11, 1779, *Col. Records*, 12:71.
225. Thomas McKean to Joseph Reed, Aug. 13, 1779, *Pa. Archives*, 7:644–646.

226. Thomas McKean to Joseph Reed, Sept. 20, 1779, *Pa. Archives*, 7:703. The Council resolved to postpone consideration of the issue, but directed that William Bradford not exchange any of the named prisoners. Minutes of the SEC, Sept. 23, 1779, *Col. Records*, 12:112. A few months later, however, it rescinded this direction, and most of the prisoners, including those subject to Pennsylvania's treason law, were exchanged as prisoners of war. Minutes of the SEC, Jan. 31, 1780, *Col. Records*, 12:241. Joseph Paxton was later named in an attainder proclamation. Minutes of the SEC, March 20, 1781, *Col. Records*, 12:665.
227. *Chapman*, 1 Dallas, at 56–57.
228. Ibid. at 58–60; Fisher, "Journal," 424. Chapman's jury, like McCarty's, included previous Philadelphia jurors Andrew Burkhard and David Reese. Supreme Court Appearance and Continuance Docket, RG-33, PSA.
229. James H. Kettner, *The Development of American Citizenship, 1608–1870* (Chapel Hill: UNC Press, 1978), 195–196.
230. G.S. Rowe's assertion that "thousands of Pennsylvanians were saved by the ruling of the McKean bench in the Chapman case" seems significantly overstated. Rowe, *Embattled Bench*, 151. Issues similar to those in *Chapman* were raised in McIlwain v. Coxe's Lessee, 8 U.S. (4 Cranch) 209 (1808), in which the United States Supreme Court held that a man who left New Jersey in 1777 remained a citizen of New Jersey and owed allegiance to it. The court based its decision largely on contemporary New Jersey legislative pronouncements to that effect. Arguments of counsel in *McIlwain* are reported at 6 U.S. (2 Cranch) 280 (1804). For an analysis of *McIlwain*, see Kettner, *American Citizenship*, 199–202.
231. Thomas Fisher to Samuel Rowland Fisher, Oct. 24, 1781, J.F. Fisher Items, Cadwalader Collection, HSP; *Diary of Elizabeth Drinker*, 1:393; Representation of the Quakers, Nov. 22, 1781, *Pa. Archives*, 9:450; Marietta, *Reformation of American Quakerism*, 245.
232. Diary of Anna Rawle, Oct. 25, 1781, Rebecca Shoemaker Papers, HSP.
233. Marietta, *Reformation of American Quakerism*, 245.
234. Diary of Anna Rawle, Oct. 26, 1781, Rebecca Shoemaker Papers, HSP.
235. Joseph Reed to Nathaniel Greene, June 16, 1781, in *The Papers of Nathanael Greene*, ed. Dennis M. Conrad (Chapel Hill: UNC Press, 1995), 8:395, 399.

CHAPTER 9

1. See generally Daniel J. Hulsebosch, "Exile, Choice, and Loyalism: Taking and Restoring Dignity in the American Revolution," *Law & Social Inquiry* 41 (2016): 841–865. Rawle's law firm, Rawle & Henderson, is still in existence and is the oldest continuously operating law firm in the United States. Rawle was also the first president of the Historical Society of Pennsylvania. Historical Society of Pennsylvania, "Rawle Family Papers," http://www2.hsp.org/collections/manuscripts/r/rawle536.htm.

2. Supreme Court Appearance and Continuance Dockets, RG-33, PSA, 194.
3. Claim Against Christopher Wilson Estate, Claims Papers Relating Primarily to Forfeited Estates, 1778–1791, RG-33, PSA.
4. Supreme Court Appearance and Continuance Dockets, RG-33, PSA, 194.
5. Petition of Christopher Wilson, Nov. 20, 1782, Clemency File, RG-27, PSA.
6. Supreme Court Appearance and Continuance Dockets, RG-33, PSA, 239. The Council also pardoned John Jeremiah Rice, an attainted traitor who had been captured while serving on a British vessel. Rice was recommended for a pardon by the President of the Continental Congress for revealing "the designs of the enemy at New York." Minutes of the SEC, Oct. 31, 1781, *Col. Records*, 13:100. John Taylor, another attainted traitor, was pardoned on condition of taking the oath of allegiance and entering into a good-behavior bond. Minutes of the SEC, May 30, 1782, *Col. Records*, 13:294. For debate over the propriety of the Assembly rescinding an attainder, see *Minutes of the First Session, of the Seventh General Assembly of the Commonwealth of Pennsylvania* (Philadelphia: John Dunlap, n.d.), 760–769.
7. Notes of George Bryan in Commonwealth v. John Bulla, Chester Co. Ct. Oyer & Terminer, May 7, 1783, George Bryan Papers, HSP. Bulla was convicted, fined fifty pounds, and ordered imprisoned until the next July 4. The Council promptly remitted the sentence of the imprisonment, and several months later remitted the fine as well. Minutes of the SEC, May 16, 1783, July 5, 1783, *Col. Records*, 13:578, 619.
8. Notes of George Bryan in Commonwealth v. Jacob Myers, George Bough, and Nicholas Cline, Oct. 20, 1782, George Bryan Papers, HSP.
9. Notes on Motion for a New Trial, Respublica v. John Brooks, Aug. 1, 1782, Miscellaneous Legal Papers, Jasper Yeates Papers, HSP.
10. Minutes of the SEC, Dec. 31, 1781, *Col. Records*, 13:163.
11. Indictment of Peter Kerr, Chester Co. Ct. of Oyer and Terminer (Nov. 1781), Oyer and Terminer Papers—Chester County, RG-33, PSA; *Pa. Eve. Post*, June 21, 1782.
12. The affidavits are in the Papers of the Court of Oyer and Terminer, RG-33, PSA.
13. Respublica v. Buffington, 1 Dallas 60, 61 (Pa. 1781).
14. *Buffington*, 1 Dallas, at 61. A similar idea had been expressed even in the tumultuous atmosphere of 1778. A broadside, largely vituperative against Tories, nonetheless noted that a "misnomer in the Christian name of Mr. Walton, is alleged, sufficient perhaps to vacate all the proceedings against him. The spelling not only varies, but the words differ in sound. On being demanded to answer in the Court, why execution should not be awarded against him, he might have answered, that he was not the same person named in the proclamation. The plea would have merited attention; more attention, perhaps, from a Court of Law, than from the wisdom of the legislature." A Whig Citizen, "To the Freemen of Pennsylvania," Broadside, Evans 43709, Broadsides Collection, HSP.
15. Indictment of Joshua Buffington, Ct. of Oyer and Terminer, Philadelphia, Co, Sept, 1782, Autograph Collection, RG-33, PSA.

16. Notes of George Bryan in Commonwealth v. Buffington, Sept. 30, 1782, George Bryan Papers, HSP.
17. The case of Abijah Wright complicates this data slightly. Wright was indicted for treason and burglary, and convicted on the burglary charge. There is no indication whether Wright's jury considered the treason charge. He is thus included in the indictment data previously discussed, but not in the trial data, although I have included his trial in Appendix 2.
18. The most likely additional trial is the possible case of James Hartnett, who is listed in several later compiled records as tried and acquitted of treason, although with no reference to the county where the trial took place. List of Persons who were ordered . . . to surrender themselves for trial. Papers in Attainder, Roll 836, RG-3, PSA. Such a trial is certainly possible. The context suggests Chester County in 1778, a sitting for which the court's docket book does not survive. I have found no other direct evidence, however, for this trial, and a separate record indicates that a grand jury declined to indict Harnett. List of Persons against whom no Indictments were preferred. Oyer and Terminer Papers-Chester County, roll 5, RG-33, PSA. In April 1779, Thomas McKean wrote to his wife that we have "five persons to try for treason" in Chester county. Thomas McKean to Sally McKean, April 28, 1779, Thomas McKean Papers, HSP, 6:20. However, only one person, Justin McCarty, appears to have been tried. McKean may be referring to cases in which the grand jury refused to indict, or perhaps Hartnett was one of the additional cases.

   Additional indictments may also have been possible. Later compiled records state that Elisha Malin and George Davis were indicted for treason (also likely in Chester County in 1778) and that Malin was pardoned and that Davis escaped. I have found no further confirmation of these indictments or any subsequent pardon, and have not included them in the preceding data. List of Persons ordered . . . to surrender themselves, Papers in Attainder, Roll 836, RG-33, PSA; List of Persons Against Whom Proclamations Were Issued . . . , *Pa. Archives* (6th Ser.), 13:475.

   I have been especially cautious with indictment papers. Unless the document explicitly states "true bill," I have treated it as a draft. As a cautionary tale, full indictments for high treason, with notations of witnesses being sworn, survive for James Meese and William West for the Philadelphia Court of Oyer and Terminer in April 1781. Indictments of James Meese & William West, Philadelphia Co. Ct. of Oyer and Terminer (April 1781), Oyer and Terminer Miscellaneous Papers, 1777–1781, RG-33, PSA. William West had been named in an attainder proclamation in Oct. 1780. *Pa. Gazette*, Oct. 4, 1780. But no grand jury approved these indictments and the men were instead prosecuted for abuse of office at the recommendation of the Continental Congress. Minutes of the SEC, Jan. 15, 1781, *Col. Records*, 12:599; Minutes of the SEC, Jan. 22, 1781, *Col. Records*, 12:604; Paul A.W. Wallace, "Historic Hope Lodge," *PMHB* 86 (1962): 115, 136–138.

   In April 1779, Thomond Ball, deputy prothonotary of Northumberland County, informed the Council that there were six men in jail charged with either treason or misprision of treason. Ball sought the appointment of justices to try the cases. I have found no record of any response to this letter, or any record of trials that may have ensued. But the possibility cannot be ruled out. Thomond Ball to SEC, April 27, 1779, *Pa. Archives* (2d Ser.), 3:291–292.

19. These statistics differ from some previous statements on the subject. Henry J. Young did not report total indictment numbers, although he found 118 prosecutions "begun," a rather ambiguous description. Young found forty-three trials, with thirty-six acquittals and seven convictions. These data are close to my finding of forty-five trials and thirty-eight acquittals. Henry J. Young, "Treason and Its Punishment in Revolutionary Pennsylvania," *PMHB* 90 (1966): 287, 295. Because Young's article reported cases of persons named in the attainder prosecutions separately from persons not named, his numbers have confused subsequent scholars. For example, in his 1994 book *Embattled Bench: The Pennsylvania Supreme Court and the Forging of a Democratic Society, 1684–1809*, G.S. Rowe, relying on Young, wrote, "Of the one hundred and eighteen persons indicted for treason under the Pennsylvania law of treason, only four were convicted. Of those, three were pardoned and one, Ralph Morden, was executed." Rowe, *Embattled Bench*, 162. Rowe converts Young's ambiguous description of prosecutions "begun" into 118 indictments, a figure significantly inflated from the actual total of 54. Moreover, by missing the attainder prosecutions, Rowe understated the convictions and executions. Marietta and Rowe repeat Young's 118 "indictment" figure in their 2006 book *Troubled Experiment: Crime and Justice in Pennsylvania, 1682–1800*. Marietta & Rowe, *Troubled Experiment*, 189. Anne Ousterhout found 53 indictments, 33 refusals to indict, 37 acquittals, and 8 convictions. Our numbers agree on refusals to indict and on number of convictions (she included Abijah Wright as a conviction). I find one more indictment and one more acquittal. Ousterhout, *State Divided*, 288, 319–320.
20. The data in the table are drawn from the following: Court of Oyer and Terminer Docket Book, Supreme Court Appearance and Continuance Dockets, Papers in Attainder, Records of the Supreme Court of Oyer and Terminer, RG-33, PSA; Papers of the Shippen Family, Legal and Business, Vol. 16, HSP; Summary Extracts of the Proceedings of the Special Court of Oyer and Terminer held at Bedford 28th Sept. 1778 by Archibald McLean Esq., Executive Correspondence and Petitions, 1777–1790, Records of Pennsylvania's Revolutionary Governments, RG-27, PSA; *Pa. Gazette*, Nov. 3, 1778, Oct. 6, 1779 & Dec. 22, 1779; *Col. Records*, Vols. 11–13.
21. One source indicates over 4300 persons who took the oath of allegiance to the king in British-occupied Philadelphia; another shows 1488 American soldiers who deserted to the British cause during the first six months of the occupation. Ousterhout, *State Divided*, 306–307. Some of these individuals most likely came from other states.
22. Robert Morris et al. to William Livingston, Nov. 12, 1777; William Livingston to George Washington, Nov. 5, 1777, in *The Papers of William Livingston*, ed. Carl

E. Prince & Dennis P. Ryan (Trenton: New Jersey Hist. Comm., 1980), 2:111–118; 102. The 35 convictions were bloated to 105 in James Kirby Martin & Mark Edward Lender, *A Respectable Army: The Military Origins of the Republic 1763–1789* (Wheeling, IL: Harlan Davidson, 1982), 93, a number repeated in Ray Raphael, *A People's History of the American Revolution: How Common People Shaped the Fight for Independence* (New York: New Press, 2001), 169.

23. Livingston to Washington, Nov. 5, 1777.
24. William Livingston to George Washington, Dec. 1, 1777, *Papers of William Livingston*, 2:128–129.
25. *Pa. Packet*, Dec. 10, 1778; David J. Fowler, "'Loyalty Is Now Bleeding in New Jersey': Motivations and Mentalities of the Disaffected," in *The Other Loyalists*, 45, 56. Fowler found that seventeen of the eighteen men convicted of high treason in Gloucester county during the war were pardoned.
26. Harold B. Hancock, *The Loyalists of Revolutionary Delaware* (Newark: Univ. of Del. Press, 1977), 6, 92. At a court of oyer and terminer in New Castle, Delaware, in April 1779, one man was convicted and one man was acquitted of high treason. *Pa. Gazette*, April 21, 1779.
27. Sentence of Death for High Treason, Evans 43990, Broadsides Collection, HSP; *Pa. Gazette*, Aug. 15, 1781.
28. Dorothy Mackay Quynn, "The Loyalist Plot in Frederick," *Maryland Historical Magazine* 40 (1945): 201–210.
29. Kettner, *Development of American Citizenship*, 182 n.22; Commonwealth v. Caton, 8 Va. (4 Call) 5 (1782); Harry M. Ward, *The War for Independence and the Transformation of American Society* (London: UCL Press, 1999), 57.
30. A similar pattern prevailed after Shays's Rebellion in Massachusetts. Most participants received pardons, and only the ringleaders were tried. Most of these men were convicted, and fourteen were sentenced to death, but all were eventually pardoned. Sean Condon, *Shays's Rebellion: Authority and Distress in Post-Revolutionary America* (Baltimore: Johns Hopkins Univ. Press, 2015), 108–118.
31. Sufferings of Moses Roberts and Job Hughes, Prisoners in Lancaster Goal, 1780, Society of Friends items, Parrish Collection, HSP.
32. Questions proposed to Moses Roberts, Job Hughes, John Webb & Joseph Rossbury Prisoners in Lancaster Goal when separately examined at Sunbury, Meeting for Suffering—Miscellaneous Papers, Friends Historical Library, Swarthmore College, Swarthmore, PA.
33. Sufferings of Moses Roberts and Job Hughes, Prisoners in Lancaster Goal, 1780, Society of Friends Items, Parrish Collection, HSP.
34. Joseph Reed to George Bryan, May 18, 1780, in Reed, *Life and Correspondence of Joseph Reed*, 2:199.
35. Sufferings of Moses Roberts and Job Hughes, Prisoners in Lancaster Goal, 1780, Society of Friends items, Parrish Collection, HSP; Job Hughes to General Assembly of Pennsylvania, Nov. 8, 1780, Meeting for Sufferings—Miscellaneous

Papers, Friends Historical Library, Swarthmore College, Swarthmore, PA; Fisher, "Journal," 428.

36. *Freeman's Journal*, Dec. 12, 1781.
37. Prominent Philadelphia Quaker John Pemberton regularly visited the men in the Lancaster jail. Diary of John Pemberton, July 29, 1780; Oct. 29, 1780; Oct. 31, 1780; Nov. 1, 1780; March 16, 1781, Pemberton Papers, HSP.
38. Pemberton Diary, June 16, 1780, Pemberton Papers, HSP, 166.
39. Record of the Meeting for Sufferings, Sept. 21, 1780, Meeting for Sufferings—Miscellaneous Papers, Friends Historical Library, Swarthmore College, Swarthmore, PA. In some states, such as North Carolina, extrajudicial killings of Loyalists were not uncommon. Robert O. DeMond, *The Loyalists in North Carolina during the Revolution* (Durham, NC: Duke Univ. Press, 1940), 120–123. Such attacks were rare in Pennsylvania.
40. On Pennsylvania's British prisoners generally, see Ken Miller, *Dangerous Guests: Enemy Captives and Revolutionary Communities during the War for Independence* (Ithaca, NY: Cornell Univ. Press, 2014).
41. Miller, *Dangerous Guests*, 157.
42. Adam Hubley to Joseph Reed, May 21, 1781, *Pa. Archives*, 9:156.
43. William Atlee to Joseph Reed, June 13, 1781, *Pa. Archives*, 9:203–205.
44. Notes of George Bryan in Commonwealth v. Martin Usner, et al., Chester Co. Ct. Oyer & Terminer, Oct. 22, 1782, George Bryan Papers, HSP.
45. Act of April 13, 1782, ch. 932, *Pa. Stat.*, 10:464, 467.
46. *Pa. Eve. Post*, June 21, 1782; Transcript of Conviction of Nathaniel Forsyth, Clemency File, RG-33, PSA.
47. Petition of Nathaniel Forsyth, Jan. 13, 1783, Clemency File, RG-27, PSA.
48. Minutes of the SEC, Jan.13, 1783, *Col. Records*, 13:480.
49. Notes of George Bryan in Commonwealth v. Myers et al., Lancaster Co. Ct. Oyer & Terminer, Oct. 20, 1782, George Bryan Papers, HSP.
50. Respublica v. Shirk & Myers, Docket Book of the Court of Oyer & Terminer, Lancaster Co., Oct. 20, 1782, RG-33, PSA; Respublica v. Usner et al., Docket Book of the Court of Oyer & Terminer, Chester Co., Oct. 23, 1782, RG-33, PSA; Respublica v. Hammer & Tyson, Docket Book of the Court of Oyer & Terminer, Philadelphia Co., Jan. 11, 1783, RG-33, PSA; Indictment of Rachel Hammer et al., Philadelphia Co. Ct. of Oyer & Terminer, Dec. 1782, Oyer and Terminer Papers, Records of the Supreme Court, RG-33, PSA.
51. Notes of George Bryan in Commonwealth v. Martin Usner, et al., Chester Co. Ct. Oyer & Terminer, Oct. 22, 1782, George Bryan Papers, HSP (Lewis & Wilcocks); Notes of George Bryan in Commonwealth v. Myers et al., Lancaster Co. Ct. Oyer & Terminer, Oct. 20, 1782, George Bryan Papers, HSP (Yeates & Chambers); Notes of George Bryan in Commonwealth v. Snyder, Lancaster Co. Ct. Oyer & Terminer, Oct. 18, 1782, George Bryan Papers, HSP (Yeates & Chambers); Notes of George Bryan in Commonwealth v. Prince, Chester Co. Ct. Oyer & Terminer,

Oct. 24, 1782, George Bryan Papers, HSP (Wilson). In the case of Nathaniel Forsyth, Justice Bryan's notes disclose no defense counsel, but state cryptically, "Mr. Yeates declines to speak." Notes of George Bryan in Commonwealth v. Forsyth, York Co. Ct. Oyer & Terminer, May 31, 1782, George Bryan Papers, HSP.

52. Notes of George Bryan in Commonwealth v. Snyder, Lancaster Co. Ct. Oyer & Terminer, Oct. 18, 1782, George Bryan Papers, HSP.
53. Respublica v. Prichardson et al., Docket Book of the Court of Oyer & Terminer, Philadelphia Co., Jan. 4, 1783, RG-33, PSA.
54. Notes of George Bryan in Commonwealth v. Snyder, Lancaster Co. Ct. Oyer & Terminer, Oct. 18, 1782, George Bryan Papers, HSP.
55. Notes of George Bryan in Commonwealth v. Myers et al., Lancaster Co. Ct. Oyer & Terminer, Oct. 20, 1782, George Bryan Papers, HSP; Docket Book of the Court of Oyer & Terminer, Lancaster Co, Oct. 1782, RG-33, PSA.
56. Rebecca Roiphe, "The Serpent Beguiled Me: A History of the Entrapment Defense," *Seton Hall L. Rev.* 33 (2003): 257–302; Paul Marcus, "The Development of Entrapment Law," *Wayne L. Rev.* 33 (1986): 5–37.
57. Notes of George Bryan in Commonwealth v. Martin Usner, et al., Chester Co. Ct. Oyer & Terminer, Oct. 22, 1782, George Bryan Papers, HSP.
58. Ibid. Usner was convicted, and the Council initially rejected his petition for clemency. Minutes of the SEC, Feb. 10, 1783, *Col. Records*, 13:502. Several months later, the Council relented and reduced his fine by one-half. Minutes of the SEC, April 1, 1783, *Col. Records*, 13:546.
59. A note from Attorney General Bradford indicates that the fines imposed under the common law did not have to be shared with the prosecutor, but would go entirely to the state. Note of William Bradford re: Rowland Evans, n.d., Clemency File, RG-27, PSA.
60. Peter Miler to John Dickinson, Nov. 23, 1782, Dickinson Folder, R.R. Logan Collection, Box One, HSP.
61. Minutes of the SEC, Dec. 24, 1782; Jan. 30, 1783; Feb. 20, 1783; March 2, 1783; March 17, 1783; March 18, 1783; March 28, 1783; April 8, 1783; May 18, 1783, *Col. Records*, 13:457, 495, 511–512, 520, 534, 535, 544, 550–551, 576–577.
62. Petition of Christian Carpenter, n.d., Clemency File, RG-27, PSA. Carpenter also made the underwhelming argument that he "had at all times paid his taxes without giving unnecessary trouble to the collector."
63. Minutes of the SEC, Feb. 20, 1783, *Col. Records*, 13:512.
64. Petition of Jacob Grove, n.d. Clemency File, RG-27, PSA; Minutes of the SEC, Dec. 2, 1782, *Col. Records*, 13:442. Chief Justice McKean and Justice Bryan noted their support for this petition.
65. Petition of Frederick Buzzard, Feb. 14, 1783, Clemency File, RG-27, PSA; Minutes of the SEC, March 1, 1783, *Col. Records*, 13:520.
66. Petition of John Evans, March 6, 1783, Clemency File, RG-27, PSA. This petition was supported by Chief Justice McKean and grand juror Seth Quee, among others. Minutes of the SEC, March 7, 1783, *Col. Records*, 13:526.

67. *Freeman's Journal*, Aug. 28, 1782.
68. Anthony Sharp, *The Continental Almanac* (Philadelphia: Francis Bailey, 1782). On almanacs, see Patrick Spero, "The Americanization of the Pennsylvania Alamanac," in *Pennsylvania's Revolution*, ed. William Pencak (Univ. Park: Penn. State. Univ. Press, 2010), 36–55.
69. *Pa. Gazette*, June 18, 1783.
70. *Pa. Gazette*, Aug. 6, 1783.
71. *Pa. Gazette*, Aug. 6, 1783.
72. Instructions to the Representatives of Northampton County, Aug. 20, 1783, Northampton County items, Society Collection, HSP.
73. William Adcock, "Philadelphia, August 1783," Broadside, Evans 18136, Broadsides Collection, HSP.
74. Treaty of Paris, Sept. 3, 1783, arts. 5 & 6. See generally Roberta Tansman Jacobs, "The Treaty and the Tories: The Ideological Reaction to the Return of the Loyalists, 1783–1787" (Ph.D. diss., Cornell Univ., 1974); Hoock, *Scars of Independence*, 361–387.
75. Judith L. Van Buskirk, *Generous Enemies: Patriots and Loyalists in Revolutionary New York* (Philadelphia: Univ. of Penn. Press, 2002), 188.
76. Kevin J. Dellape, *America's First Chaplain: The Life and Times of the Reverend Jacob Duché* (Bethlehem, PA: Lehigh Univ. Press, 2013), 137–149, 171–176.
77. Minutes of the SEC, June 9, 1790, *Col. Records*, 16:378.
78. Minutes of the SEC, March 30, 1789; May 14, 1789; July 1, 1789; July 22, 1789; Aug. 21, 1789; Feb. 6, 1790; March 9, 1790; *Col. Records*, 16:43, 76, 107, 115, 179, 273, 297.
79. Thomas Jefferson to George Hammond, May 29, 1792, *The Papers of Thomas Jefferson*, ed. Charles T. Cullen (Princeton, NJ: Princeton Univ. Press, 1990), 23:551–613.
80. Act of March 8, 1792, ch. 88, *Pa. Stat.*, 14:204.
81. *Pa. Gazette*, Feb. 8, 1792.
82. "To the Freemen of Philadelphia . . . ," Broadside, Evans 43709, Broadsides Collection, HSP.
83. Memorial of Samuel Shoemaker, American Loyalist Claims, AO12.038.168, National Archives of the United Kingdom; "A Pennsylvania Loyalist's Interview with George III," *PMHB* 2 (1878): 35–39.
84. Clement Biddle, *The Philadelphia Directory* (Philadelphia: James & Johnson, 1791), 118.
85. Executive Minutes of Governor Thomas Mifflin, Dec. 27, 1793, *Pa. Archives* (9th Ser.), 1:699. For an overview of Shoemaker's life, see David Haugaard, "Samuel Shoemaker," in *Lawmaking and Legislators in Pennsylvania*, 3:1284–1300.
86. Executive Minutes of Governor Thomas Mifflin, Sept. 12, 1792, *Pa. Archives* (9th Ser.), 1:444; David Haugaard, "Andrew Allen," in *Lawmaking and Legislators in Pennsylvania*, 3:199–219.

87. See generally John M. Coleman, "Joseph Galloway and the British Occupation of Philadelphia," *Penn. Hist.* 30 (1963): 272–300.
88. *Pa. Journal and Weekly Advertiser*, n.d., quoted in Oliver C. Kuntzleman, *Joseph Galloway: Loyalist* (Philadelphia: Temple Univ. Press, 1941), 135.
89. Joseph Galloway to Thomas McKean, March 7, 1793, Thomas McKean Papers, HSP.
90. Executive Minutes of Governor Thomas Mifflin, Feb. 28, 1795, *Pa. Archives* (9th Ser.), 2:937; John E. Ferling, *The Loyalist Mind: Joseph Galloway and the American Revolution* (University Park: Penn. State Univ. Press, 1977), 64.
91. Samuel Wharton to George Read, Nov. 17, 1782, *LDC*, 19:394. On the Virginia dispute more generally, see Ousterhout, *State Divided*, 247–271.
92. Act of Dec. 3, 1782, ch. 1000, *Pa. Stat.*, 11:14.
93. *A Report of the Committee of the Council of Censors* (Philadelphia: Francis Bailey, 1784), 23.
94. Moyer, *Wild Yankees*, 33, 42.
95. Thomas Grant to Benjamin Franklin, May 20, 1786, *SCP*, 8:334–335; William Montgomery to Thomas McKean, May 20, 1786, *SCP*, 8:337.
96. Warrant for the Arrest of John Franklin, Aug. 31, 1787, *SCP*, 9:174–175; Votes Cast in Luzerne County Election, *SCP*, 9:18.
97. Franklin Arrest Warrant, *SCP*, 9:175.
98. Samuel Hodgdon to Timothy Pickering, Oct. 5, 1787, *SCP*, 9:222–223; Minutes of the SEC, Oct. 8, 1787, *Col. Records*, 15:291.
99. *Pa. Gazette*, Oct. 10, 1787.
100. *Conn. Courant*, Oct. 22, 1787, *SCP*, 9:249–250; see also John Franklin to SEC, Jan. 31, 1788, *SCP*, 9:321–323.
101. John Franklin to SEC, April 28, 1788, *SCP*, 9:370–371.
102. Timothy Pickering to Rebecca Pickering, July 3, 1788, *SCP*, 9:391–393; John Hyde et al. to SEC, July 15, 1788, *SCP*, 9:410–412; Moyer, *Wild Yankees*, 68–75. Pickering later served as United States Secretary of War and Secretary of State.
103. Thomas McKean & George Bryan to SEC, Aug. 7, 1788, *SCP*, 9:455–456; William Bradford, Jr., to Timothy Pickering, Aug. 23, 1788, *SCP*, 9:476.
104. Timothy Pickering to John S. Whitcomb & David Woodward, Sept. 5, 1788, *SCP*, 9:485–486.
105. Timothy Pickering to Samuel Hodgdon, Nov. 9, 1788, *SCP*, 9:516–517.
106. Indictment of John Franklin et al, *SCP*, 9:513–514. Franklin was also indicted on a separate misdemeanor charge. Docket Book of the Court of Oyer and Terminer, Luzerne Co., Nov. 1788, RG-33, PSA, 75.
107. Docket Book of the Court of Oyer and Terminer, Luzerne Co., Nov. 1788, RG-33, PSA, 75; *Pa. Gazette*, Nov. 26, 1788.
108. John Franklin to Thomas Mifflin, Feb. 17, 1789, *SCP*, 10:8.
109. Thomas McKean to Timothy Pickering, March 13, 1789, *SCP*, 10:9–10.
110. Timothy Pickering to Simon Spaulding, Sept. 26, 1789, *SCP*, 10:17–18.

111. Docket Book of the Court of Oyer and Terminer, Luzerne Co., May 1792, RG-33, PSA, 192.
112. Samuel Wallis to Samuel Meredith, Oct. 11, 1792, *SCP*, 10:161.
113. *Journal of the First Session of the Sixth House of Representatives of the Commonwealth of Pennsylvania* (Philadelphia: Francis & Robert Bailey, 1795), 39.
114. Although several indictments were issued for treason against Pennsylvania after the Homestead Strike in 1892, the cases did not go to trial, and the indictments were widely condemned for prosecutorial excess. Hurst, *Law of Treason*, 199–200.
115. David Ramsay to Nathanael Greene, June 9, 1782, *LDC*, 18:566.
116. *Pa. Gazette*, July 10, 1782.
117. Thomas Paine to Robert Morris, Nov. 28, 1782, Thomas Paine Papers, APS.
118. Paine, *Complete Writings*, 1:234.
119. Minutes of the SEC, Aug. 18, 1783, *Col. Records*, 13:648–649.
120. See, e.g., *Francia's Case* (1717), *Reports of Sir Peter King, Chief Justice of Common Pleas, 1714–1722*, ed. Lloyd Bonfield & L.R. Poos (London: Selden Society, 2017), 82–84.
121. William Ewald, "James Wilson and the Drafting of the Constitution," *U. Pa. J. Const. Law* 10 (2008): 901–1009, 992.
122. Hurst, *Law of Treason*, 136.
123. Draft of the Committee of Detail, Aug. 6, 1787, in Max Farrand, *The Records of the Federal Convention of 1787*, rev. ed. (New Haven, CT: Yale Univ. Press, 1966), 182.
124. Edmund Randolph to James Madison, Oct. 5, 1782, in *Papers of James Madison*, ed. William T. Hutchinson & William M.E. Rachal (Chicago: U. of Chicago Press, 1967), 5:183.
125. Farrand, *Records*, 348.
126. Ibid., 349, 346.
127. On the convention, see Pauline Maier, *Ratification: The People Debate the Constitution, 1787–1788* (New York: Simon & Schuster, 2010), 97–124.
128. *Pennsylvania and the Federal Constitution 1787–1788*, ed. John Bach McMaster & Frederick D. Stone (Philadelphia: HSP, 1888), 2:723–724; Minutes of the SEC, Oct. 19, 1779, *Col. Records*, 12:137. A year-and-a-half after the ratifying convention, Chambers was killed in a duel.
129. Juror John Steinmetz unsuccessfully ran for the ratifying convention. A newspaper observed that "Mr. Steinmetz, who is a federalist, was low in votes, only from being in antifederal company." *Pa. Gazette*, Nov. 14, 1787. Andrew Burkhard, who was a juror in the John Roberts case, was the messenger for the Pennsylvania ratifying convention. *The Documentary History of the Ratification of the Constitution*, ed. Merrill Jensen (Madison: State Hist. Soc. of Wisconsin, 1976), 2:614.
130. *Documentary History of the Ratification*, 2:483.
131. Ibid., 2:493.
132. Ibid., 2:515–516.

133. Cramer v. United States, 325 U.S. 1, 46–47 (1945).
134. Farrand, *Records*, 347–349.
135. William Cushing to John Adams, Aug. 22, 1789, *Documentary History of the Supreme Court of the United States, 1789–1800*, ed. Maeva Marcus (New York: Columbia Univ. Press, 1992), 4:501.
136. John Adams to William Cushing, Sept. 14, 1789, available at https://founders.archives.gov/documents/Adams/06-04-02-0109.
137. Thomas Jefferson to James Madison, Oct. 1, 1792, *The Papers of Thomas Jefferson*, ed. John Catanzariti (Princeton, NJ: Princeton Univ. Press, 1990), 24:432–433.
138. The best modern analysis of state treason laws is J. Taylor McConkie, "State Treason: The History and Validity of Treason against Individual States," *Kentucky L.J.* 101 (2012–2013): 281–336.
139. On the Dorr Rebellion, see generally Marvin E. Gettleman, *The Dorr Rebellion: A Study in American Radicalism* (New York: Random House, 1973; reprint, New York: Robert E. Krieger, 1980); on John Brown, see Brian McGinty, *John Brown's Trial* (Cambridge, MA: Harvard Univ. Press, 2009); and on the Mine Wars, see James Green, *The Devil Is Here in These Hills: West Virginia's Coal Miners and Their Battle for Freedom* (New York: Atlantic Monthly Press, 2015).
140. William Bradford, *An Enquiry How Far the Punishment of Death is Necessary in Pennsylvania* (Philadelphia: T. Dobson, 1793), 12.
141. An Act for the Better Preventing of Crimes, and for Abolishing the Punishment of Death in Certain Cases (1794), ch. 1777, *Pa. Stat.*, 15:174. See generally Bradley Chapin, "Felony Law Reform in the Early Republic," *PMHB* 113 (1989): 163–183.
142. Thomas McKean to Paul Hamilton, Sept. 1, 1806, Society Collection, HSP.
143. Edward Shippen, Undated Charge Number 2, Written ca. 1794, in *Gentlemen of the Grand Jury*, 2:1092, 1093.
144. As James Willard Hurst has pointed out, "The evidence . . . poses a most difficult problem, which it does not resolve." Hurst, *Law of Treason*, 140.
145. Thomas McKean's Charge, City & County of Philadelphia, Nov. 17, 1797, in *Gentlemen of the Grand Jury*, 1: 966, 968.
146. Wilson, *Works*, 2:668.
147. Foster, *Report*, 211.
148. Bradford, *Enquiry*, 43.
149. Conference Concerning the Insurrection in Western Pennsylvania, Aug. 2, 1794, *The Papers of Alexander Hamilton*, ed. Harold C. Syrett (New York: Columbia Univ. Press, 1972), 17:9–14.
150. James Wilson to George Washington, Aug. 4, 1794, *Documentary History of the Supreme Court of the United States*, 2:438–439.
151. For the basic facts of the Whiskey Rebellion, see Thomas P. Slaughter, *The Whiskey Rebellion: Frontier Epilogue to the American Revolution* (New York: Oxford Univ. Press, 1986).
152. Ibid., 218–219.

153. *Documentary History of the Supreme Court of the United States*, 6:514–518; United States v. Hamilton, 3 U.S. (3 Dall.) 17 (1795).
154. These data are drawn from the Criminal Case Files of the U.S. Circuit Court for the Eastern District of Pennsylvania, 1791–1840 (National Archives Microfilm Publication M986), and the Minutes of the U.S. Circuit Court for the Eastern District of Pennsylvania, 1790–1844 (National Archives Microfilm Publication M932).
155. United States v. The Insurgents of Pennsylvania, 2 U.S. (2 Dall.) 335, 342 (C.C. Pa. 1795).
156. United States v. Porter, 2 U.S. (2. Dall.) 345 (C.C. Pa. 1795).
157. These data are drawn from the Minutes of the U.S. Circuit Court for the Eastern District of Pennsylvania, 1790–1844 (National Archives Microfilm Publication M932).
158. Albert Gallatin to Hannah Gallatin, June 1, 1795, *Documentary History of the United States Supreme Court*, 3:52, 53.
159. Minutes of the U.S. Circuit Court for the Eastern District of Pennsylvania, 1790–1844 (National Archives Microfilm Publication M932).
160. Albert Gallatin to Hannah Gallatin, June 1, 1795, *Documentary History of the United States Supreme Court*, 3:52, 53.
161. United States v. Stewart; United States v. Wright, 2 U.S. (2 Dall.) 343 (C.C. Pa. 1795).
162. United States v. Mitchell, 2 U.S. (2 Dall.) 357 (C.C. Pa. 1795).
163. United States v. Vigol, 2 U.S. (2 Dall.) 346, 347 n.* (C.C. Pa. 1795).
164. William Findley, *History of the Insurrection, in the Four Western Counties of Pennsylvania* (Philadelphia: Samuel Harrison Smith, 1796), 210.
165. United States v. Porter, 2 U.S. (2 Dall.) 345 (C.C. Pa. 1795).
166. William Rawle to Alexander Addison, Aug. 15, 1795, *Pa. Archives* (2d Ser.), 4:535, 536.
167. Hugh Henry Brackenridge, *Incidents of the Insurrection in the Western Part of Pennsylvania, In the Year 1794* (Philadelphia: John M'Culloch, 1795), 66.
168. Findley, *History of the Insurrection*, 211.
169. Memorial of the Jurors, United States v. Mitchell, n.d., Pennsylvania Whiskey Rebellion Collection, Manuscript Division, Library of Congress.
170. Edward Tilghman and Joseph Thomas to George Washington, June 13, 1795, Pennsylvania Whiskey Rebellion Collection, Manuscript Division, Library of Congress.
171. Albert Gallatin to Hannah Gallatin, May 25, 1795, Albert Gallatin Papers, New-York Historical Society, quoted in Richard A. Ifft, "Treason in the Early Republic: The Federal Courts, Popular Protest, and Federalism during the Whiskey Insurrection," in *The Whiskey Rebellion: Past and Present Perspectives*, ed. Steven R. Boyd (Westport, CT: Greenwood Press, 1985), 165, 175.
172. Findley, *History of the Insurrection*, 211.
173. Memorial of the Jurors, United States v. Vigol, n.d., Pennsylvania Whiskey Rebellion Collection, Manuscript Division, Library of Congress.

174. Jurors to George Washington, n.d., Pennsylvania Whiskey Rebellion Collection, Manuscript Division, Library of Congress.
175. William Lewis to Edmund Randolph, June 12, 1795, Pennsylvania Whiskey Rebellion Collection, Manuscript Division, Library of Congress.
176. Alexander Hamilton, *Letter from Alexander Hamilton, concerning the public conduct and character of John Adams, Esq. president of the United States* (New York: John Lang, 1800), 42.
177. Citizens of Philadelphia to George Washington, June 13, 1795, Pennsylvania Whiskey Rebellion Collection, Manuscript Division, Library of Congress.
178. Grand Inquest for the City of Philadelphia to George Washington, June 15, 1795, Pennsylvania Whiskey Rebellion Collection, Manuscript Division, Library of Congress.
179. William Rawle to Alexander Addison, Aug. 15, 1795, *Pa. Archives* (2d Ser.), 4:535.
180. William Bradford to George Washington, Aug. 1794, *The Papers of George Washington: Presidential Series*, ed. David R. Hoth & Carol S. Ebel (Charlottesville: UVA Press, 2011), 472–478.
181. [Alexander Hamilton], "To the People of the United States," Aug. 28, 1794, *The Papers of Alexander Hamilton*, 17:159–161.
182. William Cushing, Charge to the Grand Jury of the Circuit Court for the District of Rhode Island, Nov. 7, 1794, *Documentary History of the Supreme Court*, 2:491, 493.
183. William Paterson, Charge to the Grand Jury of the Circuit Court for the District of Pennsylvania, May 4, 1795, *Documentary History of the Supreme Court*, 3:40–42. On Paterson's role in the Whiskey Rebellion cases, see Linda Myrsiades, "A Tale of a Whiskey Rebellion Judge: William Paterson, Grand Jury Charges, and the Trials of the Whiskey Rebels," *PMHB* 140 (2016): 129–165.
184. United States v. Mitchell, 2 U.S. (2 Dall.) 348, 348–349 (C.C. Pa. 1795).
185. United States v. Vigol, 2 U.S. (2 Dall.) 346 (C.C. Pa. 1795).
186. Alexander Dallas stated that these attorneys were Edward Tilghman, the Middle Temple–trained son-in-law of Benjamin Chew, and Joseph Thomas. *Mitchell*, 2 U.S. (2 Dall.) at 350. Albert Gallatin, however, noted only Thomas as representing as Mitchell. Albert Gallatin to Hannah Gallatin, June 1, 1795, *Documentary History of the Supreme Court*, 3:52, 53.
187. United States v. Mitchell, 2 U.S. (2 Dall.) 348, 350–351 (C.C. Pa. 1795). The defense also raised challenges to the applicability of the two witness requirement to the overt acts alleged in the indictment and argued that certain allegations amounted only to conspiracy to levy war, which was not in itself treason.
188. United States v. Mitchell, 2 U.S. (2 Dall.) 348, 354 (C.C. Pa. 1795).
189. *Mitchell*, 2 U.S. (2. Dall), at 355–356.
190. Brackenridge, *Incidents of the Insurrection*, 59–60.
191. The leading modern account is Paul Douglas Newman, *Fries's Rebellion: The Enduring Struggle for the American Revolution* (Philadelphia: Univ. of Penn. Press, 2004). See also Terry Bouton, "'No Wonder the Times Were Troublesome';

The Origins of Fries Rebellion, 1783–1799," *Penn. Hist.* 67 (Winter 2000): 21–42; Whitman H. Ridgway, "Fries in the Republican Imagination: A Crisis of Republican Society, *Penn. Hist.* 67 (Winter 2000): 141–160.

192. Newman, *Fries's Rebellion*, 56.
193. Ibid., 140–141.
194. Ibid., 142–164.
195. *Case of Fries*, 9 F. Cas. 826, 840 (C.C.D. Pa. 1799) (No. 5126).
196. Minutes of the U.S. Circuit Court for the Eastern District of Pennsylvania, 1790–1844 (National Archives Microfilm Publication M932). A number of other defendants were charged with lesser offenses. On the defendants charged under the Sedition Act, see Wendell Bird, *Press and Speech under Assault: The Early Supreme Court Justices, the Sedition Act of 1798, and the Campaign against Dissent* (New York: Oxford Univ. Press, 2016), 356–367.
197. The selection of counsel was controversial, and at one point Dallas challenged Lewis to a duel over his role in the case. Newman, *Fries's Rebellion*, 166.
198. United States v. Insurgents of Pennsylvania, 3 U.S. (3 Dall.) 513 (C.C.D. Pa. 1799).
199. *Case of Fries*, 842.
200. Ibid., 847.
201. Ibid., 848. Rawle made similar points later in the trial. Ibid., 875–877.
202. Ibid., 887.
203. Ibid., 897–898.
204. Ibid., 899.
205. Ibid., 908.
206. Ibid., 912–913.
207. United States v. Fries, 3 U.S. (3 Dall.) 515 (C.C.D. Pa. 1799); *Case of Fries*, 916.
208. *Case of Fries*, 916.
209. James Iredell to Hannah Iredell, May 11, 1799, *Documentary History of the Supreme Court*, 3:361.
210. *Case of Fries*, 916–917.
211. Declaration of John Rhoad, May 15, 1799, Criminal Case Files of the U.S. Circuit Court for the Eastern District of Pennsylvania, 1791–1840 (National Archives Microfilm Publication M986).
212. *Case of Fries*, 922.
213. Ibid., 923; United States v. Fries, 3 U.S. (3 Dall.) 515 (C.C.D. Pa. 1799).
214. Case of Fries, 9 F. Cas. 924, 943–944 (C.C.D. Pa. 1800) (No. 5127).
215. See generally William H. Rehnquist, *Grand Inquests: The Historic Impeachments of Justices Samuel Chase and President Andrew Johnson* (1992). Chase was defended by Joseph Hopkinson, who had defended several of the defendants in the Fries's Rebellion cases.
216. Stephen B. Presser, "A Tale of Two Judges: Richard Peters, Samuel Chase, and the Broken Promise of Federalist Jurisprudence," *Northwestern Law Review* 73 (1978): 26–111, 92.

217. *Case of Fries*, 941.
218. Ibid., 939.
219. Ibid., 926; Presser, "A Tale of Two Judges," 91.
220. *Case of Fries*, 930–932.
221. Minutes of the U.S. Circuit Court for the Eastern District of Pennsylvania, 1790–1844 (National Archives Microfilm Publication M932); Criminal Case Files of the U.S. Circuit Court for the Eastern District of Pennsylvania, 1791–1840 (National Archives Microfilm Publication M986). John Fries used thirty-four challenges, Conrad Marks used thirty-one, Gettman and Heaney used thirty-five, and Stähler used twenty-eight.
222. Depositions of Charles Deshler & Isaac Roush, Minutes of the U.S. Circuit Court for the Eastern District of Pennsylvania, 1790–1844 (National Archives Microfilm Publication M932).
223. *Case of Fries*, 946.
224. William Lewis & Alexander Dallas to John Adams, *Case of Fries*, 947–948.
225. John Adams to the Heads of Department, May 20, 1800, *The Works of John Adams*, ed. Charles Francis Adams (Boston: Little Brown, 1854), 9:57–59.
226. Charles Lee, Oliver Wolcott & Benjamin Stoddert to John Adams, May 20, 1800, *Works of John Adams*, 9:59–60.
227. John Adams to Charles Lee, May 21, 1800, *Works of John Adams*, 9:60.
228. John Adams to James Lloyd, March 31, 1815, *Works of John Adams*, 10:152–155.
229. Newman, *Fries's Rebellion*, 180–188.
230. Alexander Hamilton, *Letter from Alexander Hamilton, concerning the public conduct and character of John Adams, Esq. president of the United States* (New York: John Lang, 1800), 43.
231. Ibid., 43.
232. Ibid., 44.
233. Ibid., 44. During Shays's Rebellion, Samuel Adams similarly argued for executions, claiming that republics should punish treason more harshly than monarchies. As Adams put it, "In monarchies, the crime of treason and rebellion may admit of being pardoned or lightly punished; but the man who dares to rebel against the laws of a republic ought to suffer death." Quoted in Condon, *Shays's Rebellion*, 97.
234. Chapin, *American Law of Treason*, 97.
235. Hurst, *Law of Treason*, ix.
236. Ibid., 260–265.

CONCLUSION

1. *Mass. Spy*, Feb. 16, 1775.
2. Chapin, *American Law of Treason*, 71.
3. Similar attitudes prevailed during the American Civil War. There were approximately one hundred treason prosecutions of questionable legal validity

under military authority, as well as numerous indictments in federal courts. No Confederate, however, was ever executed for treason. Even Jefferson Davis, the most plausible defendant, escaped trial when federal officials concluded that no southern jury could be trusted to convict him. William A. Blair, *With Malice toward Some: Treason and Loyalty in the Civil War Era* (Chapel Hill: UNC Press, 2014), 52–58, 234–236, 244–251, 311–315. On the Davis case, see Cynthia Nicoletti, *Secession on Trial: The Treason Prosecution of Jefferson Davis* (New York: Cambridge Univ. Press, 2017).

4. The failure of American courts to adhere to this rule in cases arising from World War II and the War on Terror is fundamentally inconsistent with the treatment of this issue during the Revolution. See generally Carlton F.W. Larson, "The Forgotten Constitutional Law of Treason and the Enemy Combatant Problem," *Univ. of Penn. Law Review*, 154, no. 4 (2006): 863–926.
5. Steven R. Boyd, "Political Choice—Political Justice: The Case of the Pennsylvania Loyalists," in *American Political Trials*, ed. Michal R. Belknap (Westport, CT: Greenwood Press, 1994), 43, 48.

Index

For the benefit of digital users, indexed terms that span two pages (e.g., 52–53) may, on occasion, appear on only one of those pages.

Note: page numbers followed by f and t refer to figures and tables respectively. Those followed by n refer to notes, with note number.